For Eleanor.

ECDL

COMPLETE GUIDE

For Microsoft Office 2003

The complete IT training provider

For bulk orders of this book, and educational licenses of our Multimedia ECDL guide please contact IACT directly:

UK: 0800-587 0003
ROI: 1850 924 023
INT: +353 1 434 7600

VISIT OUR WEB SITE AT HTTP://WWW.IACTONLINE.COM

CONTENTS

INTRODUCTION

On behalf of IACT - *International Academy of Computer Training* we would like to welcome you to the world of computing and your ECDL studies. This book has been designed to teach you practical IT skills. We have included many real-world examples that will help you learn new topics as you meet them as well as helping prepare you for your ECDL certification. At the end of each section there are exercises and you should complete these exercises to become familiar with each lesson.

The book is broken into seven modules covering the complete ICDL/ECDL syllabus and more. These modules build on each other to provide a solid framework for working with and using modern computer systems.

Here is an overview of what we'll meet in each module:

Module 1: IT Concepts

This module explains the fundamentals of *Information Technology*. We'll look at the common terminology associated with computers and the rules for working with them. This is a very interesting module and one that will explain many important concepts about computers.

Module 2: File Management

This module introduces you to working with a computer and its file system. You'll learn about the common programs running under Windows and in particular about organising information stored on the PC into folders or directories.

Module 3: Word Processing

This is a detailed module explaining how to use Microsoft Word. You'll learn everything from basic typing and formatting to advanced editing with features like tables and headers and footers. You'll even learn how to produce a mail merge letter. We'll use the skills learned here extensively throughout the course.

Module 4: Spreadsheets

This module introduces you to the world of Microsoft Excel and spreadsheet programs. You'll learn to build spreadsheets, enter formulae, learn about absolute and relative cell referencing and how to build and edit charts and graphs.

Module 5: Databases

This module works with Microsoft Access to teach you the skills needed to build simple databases. You'll learn about tables, fields, indexes and how to query the data held in a database. You'll also learn to build forms and reports to make data entry and retrieval easier.

Module 6: Presentation Graphics

If you've ever had to present to a group of people or prepare a presentation this will be your favourite module. PowerPoint is a terrific tool for building presentations quickly and professionally. This module starts from the beginning building on your Word skills but by the end you'll be able to include organisational charts, clipart graphics and apply transitions and slide animation to your presentation.

Module 7: Information and Communication

This module is all about the information age and using the Internet and E-Mail. You'll learn to search the web, book mark favourite sites, and how to send and retrieve e-mail messages with attachments and copy colleagues and friends at the same time.

Getting the most from this book

To get the most from this book we suggest you follow the course in the order it appears taking notes as you do so and testing yourself along the way.

- ❑ Start at the beginning and read the section you are about to study taking notes as you do so. This will keep you focused on the material you are about to learn. Don't worry if it doesn't all make sense the first time.
- ❑ Repeat this for each of the lessons in a given section.
- ❑ Complete the exercises at the end of each section to gain practice using the computer and its software
- ❑ Repeat these steps for each module in the course.

Practice each section until you have it perfected.

Notes about files and practice examinations

Any files needed for exercises in this book are available on the CD-ROM or are created from previous exercises. All clipart graphics and other images are available in the standard installation of *Microsoft Office* or are downloaded automatically by Office when connected to the Internet.

Sample examination papers can be found on our website at <u>http://www.iactonline.com/ecdl/</u>

For more information about our other courses or to provide feedback about this book write to:

INFO@IACTONLINE.COM

or write to:

INTERNATIONAL ACADEMY OF COMPUTER TRAINING,
98 ST. STEPHEN'S GREEN,
DUBLIN 2,
IRELAND.

HAPPY COMPUTING AND GOOD LUCK WITH YOUR EXAMS.

THE IACT TEAM.

INSTALLING THE DEMO CD-ROM

This book includes a demonstration CD-ROM attached to the inside back cover. It includes exercise files and a demonstration of our Multimedia companion CD-ROM for this book.

Place the CD into your CD-ROM drive. The demonstration software will usually run automatically. If it does not you may need to start the software manually (instructions below).

Follow these instructions to start the software manually:

❑ Your CD-ROM drive will be probably be drive **D:** or drive **E:** on your computer. The icons will look something like this if you double-click on the **My Computer** icon on your Desktop. Take a note of the letter in brackets (in this case **D:** or **E:**)

Compact Disc   Compact Disc
(D:)   (E:)

❑ From the  menu choose **Run**

The following window will appear:

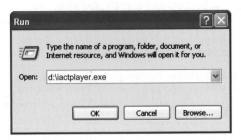

❑ Type **D:\iactplayer.exe** (where **D:** is the letter of your DVD or CD-ROM drive) and follow
the on-screen instructions.

USING THE DEMO MULTIMEDIA PLAYER

The demo multimedia guide has been designed to be easy to use. Once the guide is running you can navigate through the lessons and modules by clicking on the topic headings with your mouse.

Once a lesson has started you will see a screen something like this:

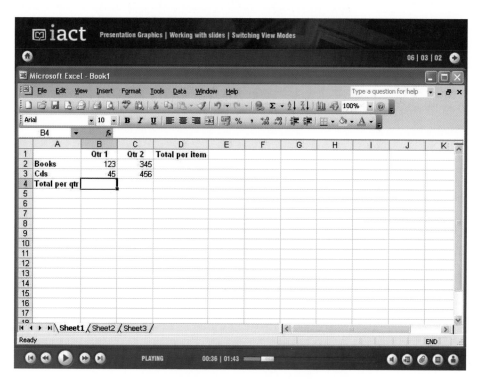

We use the *navigation* buttons at the bottom of the screen to **Play** and **Pause** a lesson. We can also **Rewind** and **Advance** the current lesson and move to the **Next** or **Previous** lesson in a section.

We can also *pause, rewind* and *fast-forward* the lessons as often as needed. As the lesson progresses a timeline advances to show how far the lesson has left to complete. We can also click and drag on the timeline to jump a particular part of the lesson.

From within the player window we can adjust the sound settings and view other options available in the player.

To return to the main page press the **Home** button ![home] in the top left corner of the screen.

Please note that the free version accompanying this book only contains a selection of lessons.

For the full version of this product or information about network and site licences please visit our website at www.iactonline.com or call us on free-phone 0800 587 0003

EXERCISE AND TRIAL EXAMINATION FILES

On our web site **http://www.iactonline.com/ecdl** you will find sample ECDL examinations and test files.

These trial examinations are also located on the CD drive in the "Trial Exam Files" folder for your convenience.

Copy these files to your local Hard disk to try the examinations.

Exercise files that are used in some of the exercises are also contained on the CD-ROM.

Module 1
IT CONCEPTS

iact

The complete IT training provider

MODULE 1: IT CONCEPTS

Computers are amazing devices - they can perform trillions of calculations per second helping us with everything from cooking to flying to the moon. Computing technology is evolving at an extraordinary rate, doubling in speed and capacity sometimes in less than a year. For this we must pay tribute to *Charles Babbage* widely recognised as the *father* of the computer. Although his computer was very different to what we know today, he laid the groundwork for those who followed in his footsteps.

Everyone will agree that computers are full of technical terminology and jargon. Sometimes it feels like we need a special dictionary just to talk about them! It is important to learn to understand and correctly use the terminology in order to successfully work with computers.

Charles Babbage 1791-1871
"Father of the Computer"

The ICDL/ECDL starts with *IT Concepts* – the principles behind computers and the most important terminology associated with them. In this module we'll learn some of the history of PCs and the systems they work with. We'll learn about *floppy disks* and *hard disks* and the way we measure the information stored on them.

We'll also learn about the different uses we can put computers to and the different types of application software we can run on them. Later we'll use these applications and put the theory into practice.

We'll also learn about the *Information Society* and some of its implications in using computers day to day. So let's get started.

SECTION 1.1:   INTRODUCTION TO COMPUTERS

In this section we will learn about:

❑ The different types of computer systems available

❑ The visible components of a Desktop PC

❑ Information flow in a PC

LESSON 1.1.1:   TYPES OF COMPUTERS

There are several different categories of computer ranging from pocket-sized PCs to liquid cooled super computers. The following section outlines the types and general applications of these different computer systems.

Microcomputers (Personal Computers) and PDAs

Microcomputers *or personal computers* are intended generally for just one user at a time. The regular PC running Windows is a *Microcomputer*. Microcomputers are very versatile and can be used for many different applications - everything from word-processing to factory automation. Microcomputers are the cheapest computers to buy with prices usually under $1000.

| The Compaq/HP Ipaq Pocket PC | A Handspring Treo PDA and phone | Nokia 7600 PDA, camera and video phone |

| A Dell Desktop Computer with flat screen and DVD | A Sony laptop computer with digital video camera | An Acer tablet PC – with twisting screen |

Within the *microcomputer* category we also have **Palmtops and PDAs** (*Personal Digital Assistants*) and **Laptops** – smaller versions again of their bigger brothers. PDAs are more portable and tend to be used on the road for data collection, quick reference and delivering presentations. Mobile phones now integrate many of the features of the traditional PDA and include features to allow remote access to the Internet and company services.

Wireless Technology similar to that found in mobile phones now allows portable computers to access data held on servers and mainframes back at base via the Internet or the company's network. This is an area of technology which is moving very fast and will radically change the way information is gathered and distributed to mobile workers.

Mobile *hot spots* are now appearing in hotels and coffee shops to allow users of laptops and PDAs to gain Internet access without the need for cables.

Minicomputers

Minicomputers are computers smaller than mainframes but much more powerful than PCs or Microcomputers. These refrigerator sized machines would typically provide similar functionality to a mainframe but require less maintenance. Digital's VAX minicomputer was one of the most widely used minicomputers and it allowed hundreds of users to work simultaneously on different applications.

IBM AS/400 series of minicomputers

The use of minicomputers is declining as PCs become more powerful. Minicomputers range in price from about $3000 to $250,000.

Mainframe Computers

Until the 60s nearly all computers used in businesses were Mainframe computers. Computers such as the IBM 360s were monstrous machines which took up whole rooms and required their own air-conditioning and full time support personnel. They were also extremely expensive – companies spent millions on machines which were less powerful than some of today's PCs.

A modern IBM e-Server mainframe computer

Mainframes were traditionally accessed via *dumb terminals*. These terminals such as the Digital VT100 were small PC-like boxes that had no intelligence and relayed all of the instructions back to the mainframe computer. Today PCs can act as terminals running software like *telnet* and *Reflections* to communicate with mainframes. Mainframes were multi-user systems – many users would simultaneously work on the same computer sharing the systems resources. Mainframe computers are still used today – even some of the early mainframes can be found working for business and governments around the world.

Supercomputers

During the 70s a new breed of computer emerged which was tuned to perform with blinding speed. Many engineering and scientific applications of computers require many *trillions* of calculations a second. Even the most advanced mainframe computers would be far too slow to complete these types of operations in a reasonable amount of time. Applications like weather forecasting, image manipulation, film studio work (like *Bugs Life* and *Jurassic Park*), airflow simulation and car crash simulations require huge numbers of parameters to be processed very quickly.

Supercomputers are designed to process this type of data very quickly. Generally they wouldn't be suited to applications like payroll processing, or word processing because of their design. The most powerful supercomputers are the CRAY family of supercomputers. *Seymour Cray* and his company are devoted to developing the worlds most powerful supercomputers.

A specification sheet from *Cray Incorporated* web site of a *Cray Super Computer.*

No. of CPUs	32
Peak Performance	56 GFLOPS
Memory Size	416GB
Peak Memory Bandwidth	900GB/sec
Peak I/O Bandwidth	32GB/sec
Cooling Technology	Liquid

The Peak performance of this Cray Supercomputer is **56GFLOPs** – that is 56,000,000,000 Floating point operations per second on a machine with 416Gbof memory and 32 separate processors! In time our Desktop PCs might have this type of power! Supercomputers tend to cost millions of dollars and need a very specialised team to operate them.

Network Computers

The advent of the Internet has spawned a new category of computer called the *Network Computer.* This type of computer is a cross between a dumb terminal and a Microcomputer. Network Computers provide the same graphic functionality as a traditional PC but perform most of their processing centrally (rather like the traditional mainframe). This has many advantages as it may lead to lower maintenance costs and easier and less expensive upgrades than the current trend.

The basis of the Network Computer would be a browser such as *Internet Explorer* or *Netscape Navigator* (or a system developed by the manufacturer of the Network Computer). Only time will tell how big the shift will be away from Microcomputers to Network Computers.

LESSON 1.1.2: THE VISIBLE PC

A PC splits into two main elements: the *hardware* and the *software*. The hardware elements are the bits of our PC that we hold, touch and see. The computer itself, the monitor, the printer, the mouse, the modem, the add-on boards that plug into the PC, even the cables that connect it all together are all examples of *hardware*.

Monitor

Keyboard

Mouse

Modern IBM PC System

To a large extent the **CPU** and the amount of available **RAM** determines how fast a PC will run and how much it will cost. Intel® are the leading chip makers for PCs having made the processors for PCs since their inception.

The main factors that impact the computer's performance are:

- ❑ CPU speed (modern PC today over 3000MHz or 3GHz or faster!)
- ❑ RAM size (256MB up to 8GB!!)
- ❑ Number of applications running at once

PCs today usually have some form of *Pentium* processor. The speed of the processor is measured in megahertz and now gigahertz – millions or billions of cycles per second. Here are some examples going from the slowest to the fastest processors.

Name	Speed
Pentium I	200 MHz
Pentium II	400 MHz
Pentium III	1000 MHz or 1 GHz
Pentium IV	3000 MHz or 3 GHz

Hardware
The term hardware refers to the physical components of our computer such as the system unit, mouse, keyboard, monitor and so on. Hardware also refers to the add-ons or *peripheral devices* that we plug into the computer, such as printers, modems and so on.

Software
Software consists of programming instructions that make the computer work. Programs like *Microsoft Word* and *Excel* are examples of *software*. Software is held either on our computer's hard disk or on a diskette and is loaded from the disk into the computer's memory, as and when required.

Information Technology (IT)
Information Technology encompasses all forms of technology used to create, store, exchange and use information (in all its different forms – text, images, video, sound, etc.). It is a term that includes both computer technology *and* communications technology. It is driving what has often been called the "information revolution".

Information Flow

All computers work in pretty much the same way. Information or data are *input* into the computer. The computer analyses or *processes* the data and when the work is complete it *outputs* the results. This cycle continues thousands and millions of times a second.

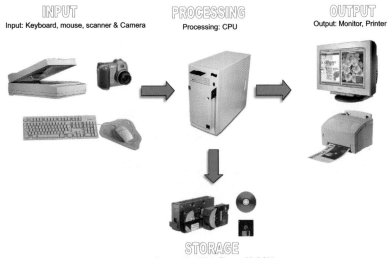

INPUT
Input: Keyboard, mouse, scanner & Camera

PROCESSING
Processing: CPU

OUTPUT
Output: Monitor, Printer

STORAGE
Storage: Hard Disk, Floppy, CD-ROM

❑ Information or data is *input* using devices like keyboards, scanners, networks and modems.

❑ Software programs and data are *processed* by the CPU

❑ Software and data are *stored* on hard disks, floppy disks and CD-ROMs

❑ Results of processing are *output* using devices like printers, monitors and sound cards.

EXERCISES TO PROVE YOU KNOW

1. Who is credited with inventing the first computer?
2. How does a PDA differ from a Laptop computer?
3. What are the main differences between *microcomputers* and *mainframe* computers?
4. What is a supercomputer?
5. What are the main components of a PC?
6. What are the main factors that influence the 'speed' of a computer?
7. What is the difference between *hardware* and *software*?
8. Draw a diagram showing information flow in a computer.
9. What is *Information Technology* or IT?

SECTION 1.2:   INPUT AND OUTPUT DEVICES

The computing process breaks down into three areas: *input, processing* and *output*. Without a way of receiving or inputting information the computer is useless. Similarly if it cannot display the results of its calculations or *output* those results so we can see them it is equally useless. To a large extent the number of input and output devices (also known as *peripherals*) connected to a computer determines its usefulness. As a minimum modern computer systems have a keyboard, mouse, disk drive and CD-ROM as *input* devices and have a printer and monitor as their main *output* devices. Most have many more.

In this section we will learn about:

- ❑   Input devices for reading information into the PC
- ❑   Output devices for displaying the results of calculations and other work.
- ❑   Devices that are used for both Input and Output

A *peripheral* is a device that we can plug into a computer. These usually sit beside the computer and are not inside the main computer box. Most input and output devices are peripherals.

LESSON 1.2.1:   INPUT DEVICES

The easiest way to learn about input devices is to look at hardware that provides input. Here are some examples of *input devices*

Keyboard and Mouse

The one input device everyone recognises is the keyboard and mouse. The PCs keyboard is essential for typing in text and numbers. The mouse is used for navigating and moving around the screen and is good for things like drawing and painting.

Music Keyboard

Soundcards turn sound into digital information that a computer can handle. They take the sound from a CD, hi-fi or microphone and convert it into digital audio. The soundcard can take in real sound and the special MIDI information used by music synthesisers and electronic keyboards. So a PC can be used as the heart of a music studio.

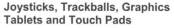

Scanners

This is a flat-bed scanner. It converts images from magazines or photographs into a digital format that can be used in programs like Word, Corel DRAW and PhotoShop. Scanners can also work with FAX software to allow printed and hand-written documents to be faxed by the computer.

Digital Cameras

Digital cameras do away with the film we would normally use in a camera. They turn the image directly into a digital picture for our computer to use. We can take a picture with one, and then connect it up to our PC to download the image so we can see it on our computer screen and then edit or print it at a later stage.

Joysticks, Trackballs, Graphics Tablets and Touch Pads

As well as general input devices like keyboards and mice, there are those designed for particular applications. There are *joysticks* and pilot controls for games and flight simulators. *Touch Pads* are pressure sensitive areas often used on portable computers and palmtops instead of mice to write or control the cursor.

Trackballs are used in CAD applications and smaller versions on laptop computers. *Graphics Tablets* and *Light pens* allow us to use a pen-like device to draw on the screen and control the mouse.

Joystick, graphics tablet and trackball

LESSON 1.2.2:   OUTPUT DEVICES

Being able to *input* information and process it would be a pointless if we couldn't get it back out of our PCs. As with input systems, there are some very common output devices. Here are some common *output* devices

LCD flat screen monitor – now almost standard

Monitors

PCs now mainly use colour monitors – rather like TVs. Monitors display the information sent from the *video card* inside a PC. The video card turns data into a video signal, which the monitor can display as a picture. Over the years the quality of monitors has continued to improve. In the future flat-screen LCD panels are likely to completely replace today's bulky cathode ray tube (CRT) monitors. Standard monitors are now 15" or 17" in diameter but monitors as big as 42" and larger are available.

TV and VIDEO

There are video and TV input cards so we can use our PC to watch or even record and edit video on our computer.

TV Tuner card, headphones and speech synthesiser

Speech Synthesizers

Speech synthesisers convert typed text into spoken language – although clearly recognisable as "robotic" such systems have helped deaf people communicate over telephones and continue to improve. Talking computers may not be too far away.

Soundcards, speakers and headphones

With a soundcard connected to a computer the computer can output sound to speakers or headphones.

Printers and Plotters

Printers come in many shapes and sizes. Laser printers use a laser, toner and drum to produce high quality page output. Most laser printers are currently black white.

Plotters are usually used for large drawings (such as those used in CAD) or posters.

Inkjet printers spray ink onto the page and provide a very cheap way of getting high quality colour print output.

Laser Printer   Plotter

Virtual Reality

New input devices on the horizon include various types of virtual-reality sensors like gloves, headsets and body sensors. These pick up our body movements and send them directly to the PC. So we could feel something in our hand, which isn't physically there, but the computer simulates the sensation.

Sony® Corporation's Glasstron Virtual reality glasses

LESSON 1.2.3: INPUT AND OUTPUT DEVICES

Some devices are capable of both input *and* output. These devices are often hybrids that combine the functions of two devices in one.

LCD touch-screen monitor – a transparent layer on the surface of the screen makes it touch-sensitive

Combined Printer, Scanner and FAX

There are now a number of devices that incorporate the features of a scanner, fax and a printer in one device. These devices allow us to scan information **(input)** and print or fax **(output)** the results.

Touch-screen Monitors

Touch-screen monitors allow a user to move the mouse around the screen by touching the screen **(input)** and view the results at the same time on the monitor **(output)**.

These devices are regularly used in restaurants and banks to simplify the operation of tills and cash machines.

Touch-screens are also widely used in kiosks and Internet access points.

A combined scanner, printer and fax machine

Network cards

Network cards allow information to be sent and received on a computer across a network. As such they are both **(input)** and **(output)** devices.

A modern laptop network card

Modems

Modems, like network cards, receive information sent to them and send information. They can be classed as **(input)** and **(output)** devices.

An external modem

Sound Cards

Sound cards allow us to hear the sounds played on the computer **(output)** but they also allow us to record sounds played into the computer **(input)**.

An internal sound card for input and output

LESSON 1.2.4:   CONNECTING YOUR PC TO ITS DEVICES OR PERIPHERALS

Let's have a look at what's involved in connecting up our PC. A large number of support calls can be quickly resolved by checking the cabling of a PC. Cables can easily be knocked out from the back of a PC or occasionally placed into the wrong socket or port. Checking the power connection and cabling is one of the steps to resolving PC peripheral problems including problems with printers, modems, sound cards, monitors and networks.

The back of a typical PC will look something like this:

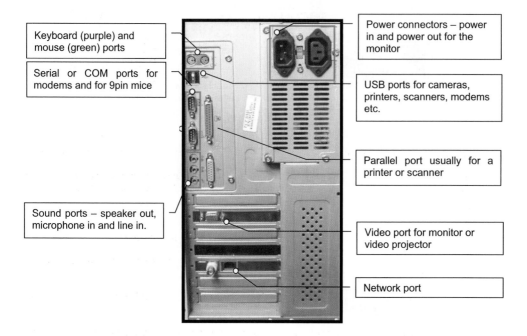

Keyboard (purple) and mouse (green) ports

Serial or COM ports for modems and for 9pin mice

Sound ports – speaker out, microphone in and line in.

Power connectors – power in and power out for the monitor

USB ports for cameras, printers, scanners, modems etc.

Parallel port usually for a printer or scanner

Video port for monitor or video projector

Network port

Remember: when plugging in cables check that the cable is the right way up. Plugging in the cable should NOT require excessive force. If it does you may find you are plugging it in upside down or into the wrong socket. Be careful with the connectors if they are damaged it can be expensive.

Keyboard and Mouse connectors

The keyboard and mouse are connected by similar cables which makes it very easy to plug the keyboard and mouse connectors into the wrong sockets by mistake. If you do this Windows will usually fail to start!

Helpfully the *mouse* connector is usually (!) coloured **GREEN** to match the **GREEN** connector on the PC. However, believe it or not, this is not always the case.

Typical connectors on the back of a PC

The *keyboard* connector is usually (!) coloured PURPLE to match the PURPLE connector on the PC.

These connectors only plug in one way but be gentle with them as the pins can bend easily. There is a small notch at the top of the connector and this should be lined up to slide in to the connector on the back of the PC.

Video or Monitor connections

If you can't see anything on your PC's screen and the computer is turned on check:

1. The monitor has power and is switched on. A red, yellow or green light on the front of the monitor will usually indicate that it is powered on.

2. The power save mode has not been activated – usually pressing a key or moving the mouse will wake up the PC and activate the monitor.

3. Check the cable to the back of the computer is properly connected and hasn't become loose. The video connector (usually called a SVGA connector) is a 15 pin connector that can only plug in one way. When connecting the cable ensure it is the right way up and DO NOT force the pins. Bent or damaged pins are very hard or impossible to repair. When the cable is in properly use the screws on the left and right of the cable to firmly secure the cable in place.

Typical SVGA video connector on back of a PC

Game port, microphone, lineout and line-in ports

Most PCs now also have a built in game port and sound capability for playing music or recording sound. The game port is a 15 pin connector that will connect a joystick or similar device to the PC. It is usually YELLOW. Sound is enabled with 3 separate cables. The **GREEN** connector is *usually* the speaker out or headphone socket. The **BLUE** connector is *usually* the *line-in* socket for connection to a CD-Player or other audio equipment. The PINK connector is *usually* the Microphone socket.

The game port, microphone, line in and speaker out connectors

Connecting scanners and printers

Most scanners or printers are now connected using the **USB** or **Parallel** port interfaces. Before scanning or printing the computer and scanner or printer must be connected and switched on.

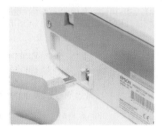 

Ensure the cable is connected to the scanner and PC and that the Scanner is switched on

Make sure the power is also connected to the scanner or printer and that it is switched on.

Network cabling

If you can't access your network drives the first thing to check is the flashing light (or LED) usually located on your network card at the back of the PC.

Typical RJ45 network connector and cable

If there is a flashing LED this is usually a good sign. If the LED light is off check that the cable is fully plugged in (it should click into place). Also check the connection of the cable at the other end to check it is plugged into a live network point in the wall or hub. Be careful as telephone socket connectors can look exactly the same as network connectors – so don't swap around the connections without checking first.

Occasionally network cables will get stuck under tables or get stretched or damaged in some other way. Try using another cable as a final check.

LESSON 1.2.5:   CARING FOR A COMPUTER SYSTEM

A computer represents a sizeable investment. Maintaining a system properly on an on-going basis is easy and will pay for itself many times over by reducing the hardware failures and support calls required to maintain the machine.

Here are some things to consider when working with computers.

Temperature

Computers should be kept at a constant temperature to avoid a build up of moisture on the circuits and possible damage to the electronics in the computer and monitor. Where a computer is moved between environments it should be allowed to stabilise in that environment for at least half an hour before being switched on.

The ideal temperatures for a computer are between 60-90° F but a constant temperature is more important than a fixed temperature.

Temperature changes cause expansion and contraction, this can cause chips to loosen in their sockets inside the computer and hard disks to have read/write failures. Avoid placing computers in air vents or in direct sunlight.

Shutting down a computer

When we are using any computer system it is important to remember that just switching off the computer or losing power due to a power cut (or power outage) can damage the computer and cause loss of data. To protect against this we should save our work regularly and follow the procedure for shutting down the PC. If we are on a network make sure that other users are not connected to our machine before we try to shut it down.

Some operating systems, such as the later versions of Windows and also Windows NT have a facility that will automatically detect that the computer was not shut down correctly the last time it was used. If this situation is detected, then a special recovery program will be run that will attempt to fix any damage caused by the power cut. There are NO guarantees however that it will succeed.

When using all versions of Windows and most other operating systems we *must* always use the *Shut down* or *Turn Off* options (located on the **Start** menu) to safely close down the operating system prior to switching off the power.

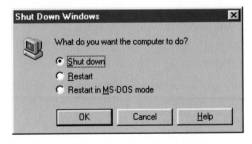

Shutdown options with earlier versions of Windows   Shutdown options displayed on Windows XP

Power Cuts and Spikes

If the power suddenly dies on our PC due to a storm, power failure or something similar all the work we were currently working on (and possibly much more) is probably lost. To protect against power loss make sure of the following:

- ❏ Use the power cables that came with the PC or of a similar grade
- ❏ Don't overload sockets
- ❏ Avoid long trailing cables

UPSs or Uninterruptible Power Supplies

Where our computer simply cannot die due to a power cut or spike a UPS must be used. These are devices which can be connected to the power supply of the computer that will guard against power cuts (or indeed someone tripping over the power cable). They contain batteries that will keep our computer alive long enough for us to use the shutdown command and turn off the computer in the proper way. This is especially important for PCs on a network that might provide data for many users on the network such as a file server.

A range of external UPSs
Larger units supply power for longer or for bigger computers

Computer failures and break downs

If we are working within a large organisation, we should be aware of the company's policy if the computer suddenly breaks down. Many large companies have a special computer support department and we should make sure that we know how to contact them in case of emergency.

In many smaller organisations the situation is much less formalised. If we are not qualified to make repairs on the computer, do NOT attempt to open the computer case and investigate. This is especially true of the computer monitor, inside which, are many components operating at VERY HIGH VOLTAGES, which can kill!

If in doubt get a qualified technician to fix the problem.

Prior to contacting our computer support staff we may check that the various external components, such as the mouse, keyboard, monitor and network connections are in fact properly connected to the back of the computer.

EXERCISES TO PROVE YOU KNOW

1. Name four *input* devices and describe their uses.
2. Name four *output* devices and describe their uses.
3. Name four devices that can be used for both input *and* output and describe their uses.
4. What colour are the keyboard and mouse connectors on your PC? What are the normal colours for these connectors?
5. Where would you expect to plug in a scanner on your PC?
6. What is the difference (if any) between switching off your PC and shutting it down?
7. Outline some ways you can help protect your PC from power cuts

SECTION 1.3:   PC COMPONENTS AND DATA STORAGE

In this section we will learn:

- ❑   The main components inside a PC
- ❑   PC Storage devices

Look inside any PC and we will see similar items of hardware. They all have *motherboards, processors, disk drives, power supplies* and *memory chips.* Many of these items are built to a fixed set of standards. This means many of the parts are interchangeable and computers can be fairly easily upgraded with additional items of hardware which just plug into the main system.

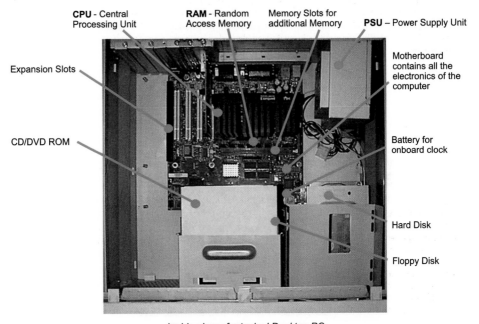

Inside view of a typical Desktop PC

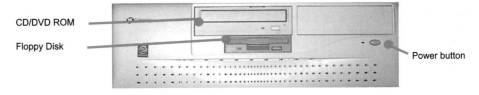

Front view of same Desktop PC

It is worth getting to know our way around the inside of a PC. There may be a time when we want to add more memory or an expansion card for a special purpose, such as a fax/modem. **Remember though – NEVER open a PC when it is turned on!** PCs will look different depending on their design but we should be able to identify the most common components easily enough.

LESSON 1.3.1:   CPU - CENTRAL PROCESSING UNIT

The **CPU** or *Central Processing Unit* is the main chip inside a computer. This is the computer's *brain*. Modern CPUs perform billions of calculations a second and aren't much bigger than a postage stamp.

Intel® is the world's leading manufacturer of CPUs. They make the Pentium® family of processor chips which we find in most of our PCs.

To a large extent the CPU and the amount of available RAM determines how fast a PC will run and how much it will cost. Intel® are the leading chip makers for PCs having made the processors for them since they were invented.

PCs today usually have some form of *Intel Pentium* processor. The speed of the processor is measured in megahertz (MHz) and now gigahertz (GHz) – millions or billions of cycles per second. Here are some examples going from the slowest to the fastest processors.

Name	Speed
Pentium I	200MHz
Pentium II	400MHz
Pentium III	1000 MHz or 1 GHz
Pentium IV	2000 MHz or 2 GHz

The CPU repeatedly carries out millions of simple calculations per second. The calculations combine to run the programs we use on our PCs. These calculations usually involve reading or writing information to memory or testing for different conditions (or logical states – TRUE or FALSE values). A typical CPU has several distinct areas within it carrying out different functions – the ALU and the CU are two important parts of the CPU carrying out the arithmetic and control functions of the processor.

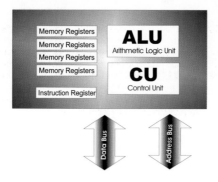

A high level view of the insides of a basic CPU

The tremendous power of our CPUs is made possible because of precise microscopic etchings on the surface of a silicon wafer and tiny amounts of electric current.

LESSON 1.3.2:   RAM - RANDOM ACCESS MEMORY

How much storage a PC has in terms of its *memory* or *RAM* and its hard disk capacity effect greatly its usefulness for a particular task. Memory is the working area the computer has for performing calculations and other tasks.

RAM – Random Access Memory

The PC uses its own internal memory to work with programs and files that are currently being processed.

RAM Memory DIMMS

A wafer used to manufacture RAM chips. The wafer will hold hundreds of individual chips which are diced into packets.

The working memory of a PC is known as its RAM (Random Access Memory).

RAM chips are placed onto SIMMS or DIMMS, which are placed into slots inside the PC. This allows the memory of the PC to be expanded by adding extra DIMMS or replacing existing ones with larger capacity versions.

Although programs usually run if there isn't enough RAM, they will run much more slowly.

There is a big difference in the speed of a computer system if we increase the amount of RAM (up to a point). Today new computers come with about 256Mb of RAM. In the early 1990s computers were shipped with about 4Mb of RAM. In 1970 0.25Mb of RAM would have cost over $1,000,000!

RAM is volatile. This means that when the computer is switched off the contents of RAM is lost. We use hard disks to hold the data permanently available on the PC.

Other Types of Memory

RAM is the most common type of memory in a computer but there are other types. Here are some other common types of memory found in a computer and their uses.

	Description	Mode
ROM Memory	Read Only Memory (ROM) is a special type of memory chip that holds software that can be read but not written to. A good example is the ROM-BIOS chip, which contains read-only software. Often network cards and video cards also contain ROM chips.	*Read only*
Video Memory	The picture that we see on our screen is a form of data and this data has to be stored somewhere. The on-screen pictures are held in special memory chips called video memory chips; these chips are usually located on the video card. A modern computer will be supplied with several Megabytes of video memory.	*Read and write* *Volatile*
Memory sticks	Portable storage devices like the Disgo memory stick let us carry around large amounts of information on a small portable memory stick. The information can be retrieved by plugging it into a USB port on our computer. The memory then appears as an extra "memory drive" on our computer.	*Read and write and non-volatile*
SD Memory	Secure Digital (SD) Card memory is a stamp-sized memory card. The SD Card can be used in devices such as digital cameras, printers, mobile phones and PDAs. We can read the contents of an SD card on our PC if we have an SD card reader. Capacities of 1Gb and higher are possible with these tiny memory cards and as costs decrease we can expect to see them in wide circulation.	*Read and write and non-volatile*

Make sure you understand that there is a difference between RAM and ROM. RAM is the working memory inside your PC and it is **volatile**, whereas ROM is *read only memory* which is a memory that we can read from but not save to (**non-volatile**).

LESSON 1.3.3:   PERMANENT STORAGE

Since RAM is volatile we need some way of holding onto the information permanently – hard disks, CD-ROMs and floppy disks are the main devices we use for this purpose.

Hard Disk Drives

Nearly all PCs have a hard disk installed. This is used as the PCs permanent store for programs and data. It contains our PCs own library of programs and files.

A 100Gb Hard Disk Drive with its innards exposed

All of the programs that have already been loaded onto the PC are stored on the hard disk so that they are always available at the click of a mouse button. When we buy any new programs, the first thing that we have to do is install it. This copies any necessary files onto the hard disk.

Modern hard disks have a very high capacity. Currently it is not unusual to have a home computer with an 80Gb hard disk (five years ago this would have a run a large business). The reason for the ever-increasing size of hard disks is the increase in the size and complexities of programs and the increased use of *multimedia*. Programs that include lots of multimedia files (sound, graphics, animation and video clips) take up a lot of room, as do application programs like *Microsoft Office* and *Corel DRAW*.

Within a couple of years it won't be unusual to have a PC with a 1000Gb hard disk which currently seems unthinkable.

Hard disks are normally internal, however there are also external hard disks available. These would be disks that we can plug into the computer when needed (usually via a USB port).

Floppy Disks

All the information that a PC uses is stored on its internal *hard disk* or on a *floppy disk*. A computer file is just like a real file. We give it a name and file it away. When we want to get the file back, we just look for the file name on the disk and get the PC to open it up. By using the **My Computer** icon in Windows we can see all the files on any of the disks in the PC.

The most common way of saving files for transfer to another PC is to use a floppy disk.
The floppy disk can also be used as a backup but its capacity is quite small. `

Floppy disks are cheap and reliable but have limited capacity.

- ❏ High Density Disks (HDD) hold up to 1.44Mb
- ❏ Standard Density Disks (SDD) hold up to 720Kb

The new *Super Density* disks can hold 120Mb and *Zip Disks* have a similar capacity. These look set to become the standards over the next couple of years.

Formatting Floppy Disks

Before we can use a disk it must be formatted. Most disks can be bought pre-formatted to work on PCs or Macintoshes. The reason we format a disk is because formatting helps the disk drive know where on the disk particular bits of information have been stored. Formatting magnetically marks *tracks* onto the surface of the disk. Therefore this helps when it comes to recording and reading data on the disk.

To format a floppy disk in Windows

- ❏ Place a blank disk into the disk drive
- ❏ Go to the *My Computer* icon
- ❏ Select the 3½ Floppy (A:)
- ❏ From the **File** menu choose **Format**
- ❏ Give the disk a label or name
- ❏ Click **Start** to format the disk

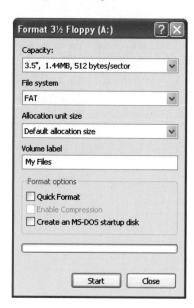

Zip Disks

A relatively new addition to the external storage formats are *Zip disks*. These proprietary disks store large amounts of data on removable disks (similar to floppies). These devices are relatively inexpensive but allow for large amounts of portable storage. They have become very popular in the world of Desktop Publishing or DTP where transferring large graphics files has always been a problem.

ZIP Disk Drive
This model has a capacity of 250Mb of storage

CD-ROM and DVD-ROM Drives

The CD-ROM is the latest way of distributing software. For most people the CD-ROM is a read-only system, which is what its name stands for: CD-Read Only Memory. There are CD writers which are becoming more popular and these allow us to record our own CDs. One CD can hold a vast amount of information (approximately 650Mb or about 450 floppy disks).

A relatively new development is the DVD drive (Digital Versatile Disk), which is the same size and shape as a CD-ROM but holds vastly more information. Most new computers will now ship with DVD drives instead of CD drives which allows the PC to be used to view full feature length movies on their PC or to play advanced video games.

PCs can now play feature length movies direct from DVD

LESSON 1.3.4:   MEASURING STORAGE CAPACITY

Computer storage is now usually measured in Megabytes and Gigabytes. These measurements are based on the computer's fundamental unit of measurement - the *bit*.

Bits and Bytes

Computers store everything in streams of binary numbers. Binary numbers are simply a string of ones and zeros put together in groups to make up useful numbers. Our normal number system works in the same way, but where we work on the basis of multiples of tens, binary works on multiples of twos.

For example, the number **174** is made up of one set of 100, seven sets of 10 and four sets of 1:

100s		10s		1s		
1		7		4		
100	+	70	+	4	=	174

The same number in binary is **10101110** made up of one set of 2, one set of 4 one set of 8, one set of 32 and one set of 128.

128s		64s		32s		16s		8s		4s		2s		1s		
1		0		1		0		1		1		1		0		
128	+	0	+	32	+	0	+	8	+	4	+	2	+	0	=	174

Each group of ones and zeros is called a *bit*

A group of 8 bits make up *1 byte.*

1 or 0	=	1 bit
8 bits	=	1 byte

e.g.   10101110 is 8 bits or 1 byte

Once mastered we can use the binary system just as we would any other number system. Below is a watch that shows the time using binary numbers. The top row of lights represent the hours and the bottom row represents the minutes. There are 4 lights on the top row representing 8, 4, 2 and 1 for the hours and the bottom row lights represent 32,16, 8, 4, 2, 1. Binary watches are a novelty and good practice in counting binary numbers – but they have yet to reach wide appeal![1]

a) Time: 8:08	b) Time: 12:08	c) Time: 10:09
Top row has 8 bit lit	**Top row has 8 and 4 bit lit**	**Top row has 8 and 2 bit lit**
Bottom row has 8 bit lit	**Bottom row has 8 bit lit**	**Bottom row has 8 and 1 bit lit**
Time is 8:08	**Time is 12:08**	**Time is 10:09**

Often computers are specified as a 32bit computer or 64bit computers and so on and this means that the hardware can process 32 or 64 bits at a time. Obviously the more bits that can be processed at a time the faster the computer will be.

1 *Byte* is equivalent to storing 1 character (e.g. 'A')

---

[1] Binary watches can be bought on the web at http://www.binarywatch.net/

Database *fields* consist of many individual characters. A *name field* for example might hold 10 characters and therefore take up 10 Bytes of information. We will see more about fields in *Module 5 – Databases.*

Kilobytes, Megabytes and Gigabytes

RAM is always measured by the number of bits its can store. For Windows to work we need at least 8 *Megabytes* of memory. Because a byte is such a small unit of storage, hard disks and floppy disks are measured in terms of thousands of bytes (Kilobytes or Kb) or millions of bytes (Megabytes or Mb) and the largest hard drives can store thousands of millions of bytes (Gigabytes or Gb). There are even Terabytes (Tb) which refer to 1000 Gigabytes (1024 Gb).

1 or 0	=	1 bit
8 bits	=	1 Byte
1024 bytes	=	1 Kilobyte (Kb)
1024 Kb	=	1 Megabyte (Mb)
1024 Mb	=	1 Gigabyte (Gb)
1024 Gb	=	1 Terabyte (Tb)

Files and *Folders* display the storage they occupy when we view them in Explorer for example this list shows that the *readme* file takes 78Kb (kilobytes) of storage:

Workspace		File Folder	24/08/2001 09:22
newdaisy	4 KB	GIF Image	24/03/1998 07:25
readme	78 KB	Internet E-Mail Mes...	09/10/2001 04:06
readme	90 KB	HTML Document	04/10/2001 20:04

We will see more about this later in *Module 2 – File Management.*

What does this mean in real terms?

A Word document containing about 1000 words will take up about 15Kb. A half screen full colour picture will take up about 150Kb. So the average floppy disk could hold around 100 short letters or 10 images. The hard disk needs to be much larger because it permanently stores all the programs that are going to be used. A program like Microsoft Word could take up 100Mb or more on a hard disk between graphics and other files that it installs.

	Capacity	Number of bytes	Number of Megabytes
Standard density floppy	720kb	737,280	.72Mb
High Density Floppy	1.44Mb	1,444,000	1.44Mb
CD-ROM	650Mb	681,574,400	650Mb
ZIP Disks	100Mb+	104,857,600	100Mb+
Hard Disk	10Gb	10,737,418,240	10240Mb+

Although the individual media can become more expensive as we move from *floppy disks* to *hard disks* the actual "cost per byte" decreases enormously. Here we compare the cost of using different media to store 100Mb of information.

	Capacity	Approximate Cost	Cost/100Mb
Floppy Disk (re-writeable)	1.44Mb	$0.50	$34.73
ZIP DISKS (re-writeable)	100Mb	$10.00	$10
CD-ROM (write once)	650Mb	$1.00	15cent
Hard Disks (re-writeable)	100Gb	$100.00	10cent

For example although CD-ROMs at least twice the price of floppy disks they hold over 450 times the amount of information – considerably better value.

Storage Device Speed

As well as the cost - the speed of our media greatly increases as we move to higher capacity devices like hard disks. Floppy disks are the slowest form of media to access from a computer. Followed by CD/DVD-ROMS and then Zip Disks. The fastest storage devices with moving parts are Hard Disks. The most expensive and fastest storage is RAM but since it is volatile (looses information when turned off) it is not considered permanent storage.

EXERCISES TO PROVE YOU KNOW

1. What is a CPU? What are the main components of a CPU?

2. How is the speed of a CPU measured?

3. Which is faster a 200MHz CPU or a 2GHz CPU?

4. Draw the inside of a PC and show the motherboard, RAM, CPU, Hard disk units

5. What is RAM?

6. Name four common types of memory and their uses.

7. What is the difference between RAM and ROM?

8. Rearrange the following devices in order of increasing storage capacity (typical values):

   a) Hard disk

   b) Zip disk

   c) DVD Rom

   d) USB memory stick

   e) Floppy disk

   Recreate the same table and rearrange the devices in terms of cost/byte of storage.

9. Assuming a floppy disk can hold 1.44Mb of information and a CD-ROM can hold 720Mb how many floppy disks will fit on one CD-ROM?

10. Which of these devices is removable?

    a) Floppy disk

    b) CD-ROM

    c) Hard disk

    d) RAM

11. How many bits in one byte?

12. What time are the binary watches showing in the images below?

13. How many bytes in one Megabyte?

SECTION 1.4:   COMPUTER SOFTWARE

Computer Software is the name given for all types of computer programs. Programs are simply long lists of instructions that make the computer do something useful. They tell the computer what to do with the information we are feeding into it, what to show on the screen, and what to print.

Software is usually supplied on CD-ROMS, which is ultimately transferred to the computers hard disk. When we buy a PC, we should find the important software like *Windows* already loaded on the hard disk.

Computer software breaks into two main categories:

- **Systems Software** – which directly controls the hardware of the PC
- **Applications Software** – which runs on the PC

The next section looks at some of these software types and their uses.

LESSON 1.4.1:   SYSTEMS SOFTWARE

The most important type of *systems software* are Operating Systems software.

Operating Systems Software

The computer's *operating system* consists of a set of programs that load automatically when we start our computer. The *operating system* allows us to use the features of the computer without having to learn all the details of how the hardware works.

There are a number of different types of operating system in common use. The original IBM PC was introduced back in 1981 and was originally supplied with an operating system called **DOS** (Disk Operating System). This operating system was very basic, and we had to be a bit of a computer expert just to understand how to use it. It was not very user friendly. The system required us to type commands to run programs or control the computer.

So for example to run a program like *Word* for example we might type at the prompt:

```
DOS>    WORD    <return>
```

Today when we want to *run* or start a particular program, like a word-processor or spreadsheet we click on a visual icon on the screen.

Most PCs today use software that runs under *Microsoft*® *Windows*®. There are however other operating systems developed by different companies.

Graphical User Interfaces

A GUI or *Graphical User Interface* is simply an additional part of the operating system that displays Windows and drop down menus, and also enables us use our computer using a mouse. Most modern operating systems have a GUI.

What are the advantages?

All programs running under the same GUI look similar. So when we switch from a program supplied by one manufacturer to one from another the programs are faster and easier to learn.

Apple® Computer have developed their own very popular *operating system* called MAC OS. **IBM®** have an operating system called OS/2 WARP and a new popular alternative to Windows called **LINUX** (which is free – or cheap) and is making good headway.

Screenshot from the Mac OSX

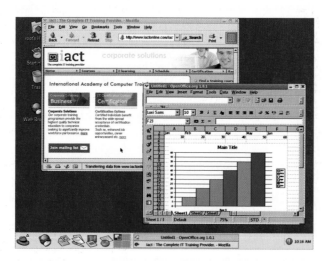

Screenshot from RedHat Linux with the free Open Office applications

To complicate matters further there are a number of different versions of Windows. The first widely used version of Windows was called *Windows 3.1*. This was more powerful than DOS and easier to use. It also had a *Graphical User Interface* (GUI) like the popular and easier to use Macintosh computer. This meant for the first time we could 'drive' our PC using a mouse and drop down menus. This type of interface is often described as a WIMP interface (*Windows, Icons, Mouse* and *Pull-down Menus*).

There are lots of images of the Windows interface throughout this book.

LESSON 1.4.2:   APPLICATIONS SOFTWARE

There are literally thousands if not millions of different software applications for the PC. The amount and quality of the software for a computer determines its success and usefulness.

There are sometimes different versions of the same software application. This is because software is updated to work better with the new operating systems as they develop and also to add more options and uses to the package. Microsoft® Word is a good example of a software package that regularly updates – Word 97, Word 2000, Word XP, Word 2003. These are all different versions of the one software application with new and better features in each edition.

Corel PhotoPaint

Corel are a Canadian company that write the leading graphics software for PCs. PhotoPaint allows users to scan images and create brochures, newsletters, and surreal graphic art pictures using its paint features. Packages like this make it possible to create effects and work with images in ways that were impossible 10 or 15 years ago.

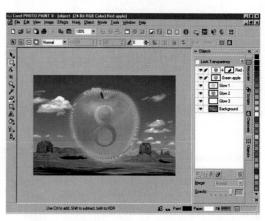

Browser Software

The battle of the browsers is big news in America where both Microsoft and Netscape fight in court over the right to ship browsers with MS-Windows.

A browser allows users to view web pages, send e-mail and navigate to particular web sites. Browsers are very powerful software packages incorporating many of the features of an operating system.

Microsoft and Netscape believe the browser is the future of computing with the world replacing its OS with browsers.

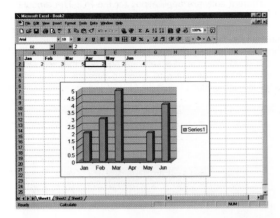

Spreadsheets

Microsoft Excel is now probably the most popular spreadsheet program for PCs.

Spreadsheets allow us to work with numbers to perform calculations and create graphs and worksheets based on live business data.

Spreadsheets have probably contributed the most to the adoption of computers by modern businesses (far more than the word processor) or other software.

Word Processors

Corel WordPerfect and *Microsoft Word* are the most popular word processors at the moment. A word processor enables a user to create letters; mail-shots and new sophisticated features of the packages allow us to create newsletters and other complex designs.

Corel's latest version of WordPerfect even allows a user to *talk* or dictate to the PC using powerful speech recognition software.

Entertainment Software

Games like *Solitaire* and *Minesweeper* come free with Windows. But there is big business in writing games for PCs and 'games consoles' now often associated with big screen movies. For some people, the best reason to buy a computer is for the games!

Modern computer games are tremendously powerful and often push computers to their limit using all the *multimedia* features of the computer (sound, graphics and animation). The trend is towards even more powerful software that lets users play together interacting in games that run across networks and the Internet.

Although games get a lot of bad press new users often learn a lot about the general use of computers by installing and playing video games.

Educational Software

This type of software teaches users how to perform a particular skill such as typing or using a machine. As the computer has the ability to display video, text and animation on demand it provides an ideal medium for many forms of education. The computer is *interactive* which means the student can stop it and focus on areas on which they have difficulty or need expansion. This is much more flexible than books or videos.

In the future the Internet will play an important part in teaching allowing schools, colleges and individuals to work together. WBT (*Web Based Training*) is becoming popular where users can learn at their own pace and the computer provides testing and feedback.

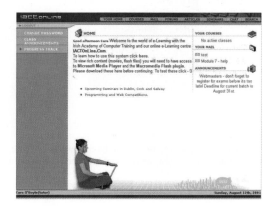

Online learning at
www.iactonline.com

LESSON 1.4.3: CREATING SOFTWARE SYSTEMS

Unfortunately software does not yet write itself. Software systems are created through the process of *Systems Analysis and Design*. The final result will be implemented in a programming language such as C/C++, *Visual BASIC*, *JAVA* or a similar language.

Systems Analysis and Design (carried out by *Systems Analysts*) is the process by which organisations build their computer based information systems. It seeks to analyse systematically the information processing requirements (input, manipulation and output) within the context of a particular business.

The systems analysis life cycle looks like this:

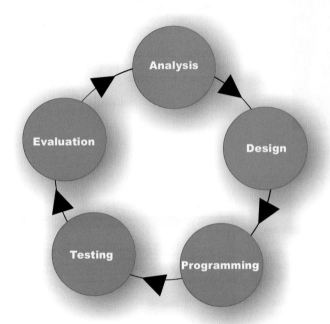

Analysis Phase
Gathering requirements for the project from the customer. Who will use it? What will it do etc.

Design Phase
Design of the system and the architecture used to build the system.

Programming Phase
Implementation of the system by programmers using a programming language (C, Visual BASIC etc.)

Testing Phase
Design of test criteria and then testing the system in isolation and as part of the live environment

Evaluation
Review and evaluation of the system for continued improvement and refinement. Results feed back to the analysis phase.

This life-cycle model is the basic model on which computer systems are developed. This model continues to evolve as our systems and requirements continue to change.

Although it takes a lot of training to become a systems analyst, the system user is always involved in defining the needs of a system as he/she will ultimately use the system.

As a user we may:

❏ Have to explain how the current system works in our department. For example what manual procedures we use or what we do to support an existing computer based system.

❏ We might be asked to describe departmental requirements to the analysts and designers. For instance, if we expect that the new system will produce useful reports, then we should plan to assist the computer specialists in designing them.

❏ As the development of a new system nears completion, we may help in testing it to ensure that it meets our requirements and works as expected.

Information Systems are tools to facilitate people in accomplishing their work more efficiently. In the past, many systems have failed because the components and the functions of the system were not clearly defined in terms of specific objectives. Many of these problems can be avoided through user participation in the systems development process. Indeed it is now very common to have a user representative elected as project "champion" for a systems development project, with the overall responsibility of ensuring a tight fit between the delivered system and the original requirements.

EXERCISES TO PROVE YOU KNOW

1. What is the difference between *systems software* and *applications software*?

2. Name three different Operating Systems in use today.

3. What is a GUI?

4. Name four different pieces of application software and describe what they do.

5. What is the *Systems Analysis and Design* life cycle?

6. What are languages such as Visual BASIC and C used for?

SECTION 1.5: COMPUTERS IN DAILY LIFE

Computers are everywhere. Even when we are crossing the road at a traffic light a computer is involved. In this section we will look at computers in our everyday lives. We will look at the instances where a computer might be more appropriate than a person for carrying out certain tasks. We'll look at:

- ❑ Computers in Banking and on the Internet
- ❑ Computers used in Business and Government
- ❑ Computers in Shops and in Manufacturing
- ❑ Computers in Education

LESSON 1.5.1: COMPUTERS IN BANKING

Retail Banking

Most banks offer 'hole in the wall' cash machine facilities. These machines are known as ATMs (*Automatic Teller Machines*). Using ATMs with our bank card we can withdraw cash, check our balance, transfer money between accounts and pay bills.

ATMs are much more convenient for most common bank transactions and help customers avoid queues in busy banks. They also offer a 24-hour service.

From the bank's point of view they can offer a more flexible service to their customers while reducing their overheads. Most banks have streamlined their services by implementing new technologies such as these.

Internet Banking

Many banks now provide *on-line banking*. Using our computer we can connect to the bank's computer system via the Internet and control our day-to-day finances from home – or anywhere else. The concept of on-line banking has enormous benefits to the banks and their customers; the Internet lets the banks increase the service and support they provide their customers while reducing their costs.

Many customers find the advantage of paying bills, dealing in shares, moving money between accounts from the comfort of their own home (or anywhere in the world) very convenient. Online banking with most banks allows us to pay bills, deal in shares and transfer funds.

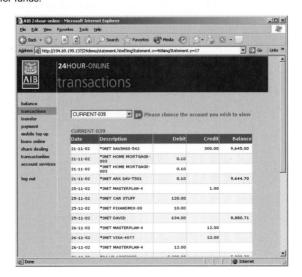

Screenshot from Allied Irish Banks (AIB) online banking system

---

www.iactonline.com

Smart Cards

'Smart cards' are now used in many countries for many different applications. Smart cards are usually the same size as a credit card but they contain a small memory chip embedded onto the card. Card phones like those used in mobile phones are examples of smart cards. Certain types of bus and train tickets use smart card technology as do lift passes in ski resorts. Smart cards need special hardware to read and write the information stored on them – sometimes this works wirelessly so we don't even have to hand in our card for the information to be accessed.

Sample smart cards

| Personal health card | Phone card | Visa smart card |

Experiments with 'virtual money' have used smart card technology. The money is carried on the card and can then be spent by altering the balance held on it. Smart cards can be used to hold medical records, travel arrangements and other important information and make it instantly available. We will find that governments and companies will use smart cards more as the technology becomes more widespread.

LESSON 1.5.2:   COMPUTERS IN RETAIL BUSINESS

For many years the food we buy in a supermarket has been scanned at the checkout. The information gathered about what we buy, how often we buy it and where we buy helps the supermarkets analyse their sales and the type of goods they are selling. Most supermarkets now provide "loyalty cards" so they can record who we are as well as what we buy in return for discounts and special offers.

Modern cash registers are connected to servers and scanner systems

Shops and retail outlets make extensive use of computers – although at first glance they may not look like traditional PCs. Most 'cash registers' are complex computer systems connected to servers which control stock levels and provide detailed sales analysis for buyers.

LESSON 1.5.3:   COMPUTERS IN MANUFACTURING

Computers assist greatly in manufacturing. They control everything from the heat in a chemical reaction to the amount of chocolate on a biscuit.

Computer Aided Manufacturing

Many car factories are almost completely automated and computer-controlled robots assemble the cars. This type of automation is becoming increasingly common throughout industry and is known as **CAM**

CAM (*Computer Aided Manufacturing)* employs the use of robotics to assist in assembling everything from sky-scrapers to mobile phones

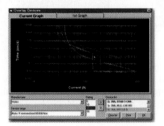 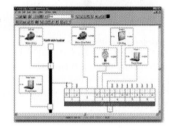

Monitoring software used to control factory automation

LESSON 1.5.4:   COMPUTERS IN ARCHITECTURE AND DESIGN

Computer Aided Design

Many products are designed using **CAD** (*Computer Aided Design*) programs to produce exact specifications and detailed drawings on the computer before producing models of new products.

CAD Drawings of modern buildings

Database Applications

Database applications allow us to compile information and then to search this information to extract just the data we require. For instance, if we have a database of all the equipment housed within an office we can very simply produce a report listing only the equipment above a certain value.

Presentation Software

Presentation software such as *PowerPoint* greatly improves the quality and speed with which presentations can be put together.

Other business uses

Other uses in business might be airline booking (check out www.aerlingus.com, www.ebookers.com), insurance claims processing, booking hotels and concert tickets etc.

LESSON 1.5.5: COMPUTERS IN EDUCATION AND SCHOOLS

Computers are used extensively for educating adults and children in schools and colleges. Interactive tutorials in Geography, Maths and Science and other subjects help master important concepts. Programs like *Microsoft's Encarta* and the Internet provide fantastic learning resources. Many student projects and homework assignments can use the Internet for research and collaboration with foreign schools. Photographs, maps and simulations can all be found on the Internet as valuable student resources. The Internet and specialist educational sites are set to revolutionise the way we all learn – supplementing and improving our education systems.

Presentation software is used in delivering training courses

Computer Based Training (CBT) is becoming more and more popular with courses available through the Internet and on a CD for people to learn at a time and place that suits them (check out www.iactonline.com). Interactive learning and web-based learning allows students to supplement what they learn on their own with expert tuition available through the computer. Simulations, videos, and interactive classes are changing the way we can learn.

The school's administration also relies heavily on computers to handle class scheduling, student registration, exam results, accounts, staff rosters as well as general office administration.

LESSON 1.5.6:   COMPUTERS IN THE HOME

Computers for Homework

Computers are used extensively in homes – homework projects can be completed with the help of computers (projects, essays and so on). In the future copy books and fountain pens might be completely replaced by wireless computer tablets connected to the Internet.

Prototype POGO tablet

Computers for Household Accounts

Household accounts can be managed using computers and spreadsheet programs helping control budgets.

Computers as a Hobby

Hobbyists use computers for programming, games and research. Some of the most innovative and exciting programs developed have started as the brainchild of a computer enthusiast based in their garage or bedroom.

LESSON 1.5.7:   COMPUTERS IN THE GOVERNMENT

Every Government department uses computers to store information. For example it uses databases to hold information collected from the census which can be processed easily and efficiently. Vehicle registration offices and the Revenue Commissioners rely on computers to hold our car and employment details.

Only recently, electronic voting has become an option that different countries are considering. In Ireland, some elections held in 2004 used electronic voting which allowed the votes to be counted instantly. There are substantial *e-Government* initiatives in place in most countries to improve services provided by Governments and make them available online. The *Revenue Commissioners* in Ireland now allow tax returns to be completed online. The *Department of Education* allows final exam results to be retrieved online and there are many other initiatives underway.

LESSON 1.5.8:   COMPUTERS IN HOSPITALS AND HEALTHCARE

In hospitals, computers play an important role. There are computer systems that have been built for holding information on patient records and treatments. They are also used in ambulance control systems, diagnostic tools and instruments as well as specialist surgical equipment.

Computerised devices such as this ventilator are widely used in hospitals

EXERCISES TO PROVE YOU KNOW

1.   Describe how computers are used in banking to automate transactions.

2.   How can computers be used in schools and businesses for education?

3.   What are *smart-cards?* Outline some uses you have seen for smart-card technology.

SECTION 1.6: INFORMATION NETWORKS

In this section we will learn about:

- LANs and WANs
- The Telephone Network (PSTN and ISDN)
- Electronic Mail
- The Internet, Intranets and Extranets

LESSON 1.6.1: INTRODUCTION TO NETWORKS

Networks consist of computer hardware as well as the programs used to link the hardware. Network configurations depend on an organisations needs and application areas. Full connectivity of office equipment – telephones, fax machines, and printers as well as computers – can be achieved through a network configuration. There are two basic categories of networks: Local Area Network (LAN) and Wide Area Network (WAN)

Local Area Network – a network of personal computers in a small area (like an office) that are linked by cable and can communicate directly with other devices in the network and can share resources.

Wide Area Network – a network that provides links to a larger number of independent users than are usually served by a LAN. This is usually spread over a larger geographic are than that of a LAN.

Client/Server

A Client is an application that allows the user to access a service from the server computer. A Server is a network device that provides service to the users by managing the shared resources. The combination of these two terms is referred to a client/server.

Network configurations

The type of network configuration is called the network *topology*. The topology differs depending on how the network will be used. The topology used will depend on the type of equipment in use and the layout of the building. Different topology have different implications for the network designer.

The main three topologies are:

- Ring Network
- Bus
- Star

The three basic types of network topologies – *ring*, *bus* and *star*.

Ring Network

This topology is common in workgroup environments and small peer-to-peer networks.

1. It can also be used to connect a series of devices where there is no central computer.

2. Nodes are linked to each other as well as to the file server.

3. A message transmitted from one node to another must pass through the ring from node to node until it reaches its destination.

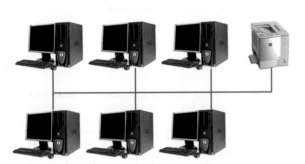

Bus Topology

1. Nodes share the same bus, or channel, for transmitting to other nodes or hosts.

2. Ethernet, a popular type of LAN that interconnects PCs via coaxial cable has a bus topology.

3. Nodes can access a host as well as each other.

4. For communication with a main office.

Star Topology

1. All devices can access a host but not necessarily each other.

2. Typically there are no difficulties if one node is down – it is simply bypassed.

3. The central computer or host monitors all processing.

This topology is ideal for networks where branch offices need to communicate with a main office.

Why use a Network?

There are many advantages to using a network within a company. Some of the main advantages are:

- ❏ Central management – networked computers can be centrally administered and managed
- ❏ Sharing files – if we save a file (like a Word document) onto a network drive, that file can now be opened and edited by other users
- ❏ Sharing Printers – all computers in a network can be linked to the one printer
- ❏ Workgroup applications can take advantage of a network to help teams communicate and manage data
- ❏ We can grant access to all users on a network to the Internet
- ❏ We can forward e-mails directly to an individual through a network
- ❏ Remote access to resources – e.g. Teleworking

LESSON 1.6.2: THE TELEPHONE NETWORK AND COMPUTERS

Computers make extensive use of the traditional phone network for communication. In fact more digital information now travels through the old phone networks than voice traffic.

In this section we'll look at some communication technology and how computers take advantage of these technologies.

Electronic Communication

Telex Machines

One of the earliest tools for the transmissions of information was the *telex* machine. Telex machines provided much hi-tech high-drama in many black and white movies.

It consisted of a ticker-tape style readout and eventually a type-writer style read-out. Its early adopters were the newspapers, police, stockbrokers and betting shops –companies that relied on accurate data fast and needed the information sent when nobody was there to receive it. Telex machines existed up until the 1980s but were more or less completely replaced by fax machines and electronic mail. Some banks still use telexes in international money transfers as the telex network has much more secure PSTN lines. If we instruct our bank to transfer money overseas, the bank may make the arrangements by telex.

Curiously the telex network still exists and some of its connections allow for fast inter-continental communication using these old wires and new techniques.

Facsimile or Fax machines

FAX machines are now ubiquitous in every office. They allow for pages of text or graphics to be transmitted anywhere in the world over a standard telephone line. Fax are clever and easy to use and were adopted quickly by businesses.

PSTN, PSDN and ISDN

The traditional phone network was known as the PSTN – *public switched telephone network* –was responsible for making the connections involved in a telephone call. The PSTN consists of millions of electronic and digital switches, underground and overground wiring through exchanges and countries and continents are linked with sub-aqua cables and satellite links. Satellites now play a vital part in helping the world communicate and also play important roles in weather forecasting, TV broadcasts and surveillance.

Satellite dish

As more data was transmitted across the network a need arose for PSDNs – *public switched data networks* which allowed companies to transmit data digitally between computers.

Further development of digital services such as that required by telesales centres and the need for direct dial numbers with a huge capacity for digital data lead to the development of ISDN – *Integrated*

Services Digital Network. These networks could handle huge volumes of digital data all on a single connection. Standards such as these will help bring the digital world closer together.

Voice over IP

Voice over IP is a term used to describe the transmission of telephone style conversations on computer networks. With companies increasing their data bandwidth we are starting to use computer networks for our phone calls and somehow turning our use of these systems on their head. We can now make long-distance phone calls using an Internet connection for the same price as a local call.

Computer Communications

The Traditional phone network or PSTN consists of millions of cables and switching circuits used to transmit *analogue* information (traditionally human voices). Computers now extensively use this network to access digital data. In order for computers to send and receive information across this analogue system we need to employ a device called a *Modem*. A modem is a device for converting digital signals that come from the computer into *analogue signals* that be sent across an analogue network and then back again.

Modems convert *analogue* signals into *digital* signals (discrete 1s and 0s) and then back again.

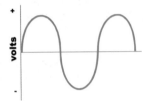

An *analogue* signal is a range of voltages which is transmitted over the PSTN (*Public Switched Telephone Network*). If we lift the handset of a telephone while a modem is communicating – we'll hear the analogue signal as a noisy squeaky sound.	A representation of a *digital* signal used by computers. Modems convert the digital signal into an analogue signal for transmission across the PSTN phone network and then back again at the other end – hence their name *Modulator – Demodulator*

Conceptual view of a modem converting an analogue signal into a digital signal.

Analogue signal enters modem – digital signal comes out and vice versa

A modern external *multi-modem*

Connection Speeds

The connection speed of a modem determines how fast information can be sent and received. Modems connect at different speeds depending on the quality of the phone line and the maximum speed both modems can talk at. Most modems have a maximum speed of 56KBPS – Kilo Bits Per Second. This measurement replaces an early measurement system called the *baud rate*. Information is usually compressed at one end and decompressed at the other end in order to maximise the connection throughput – this is called *data compression*.

ADSL

ADSL - Asymmetric Digital Subscriber Line is a new technology which provides very high speed data connections over standard telephone lines. ADSL is likely to replace the traditional modem for connection to the Internet over the next couple of years. Its download speed is usually 512Kbps – about 10 times faster than the currently fastest modems.

Eventually when speeds reach 2Mbps (Megabytes per second) and higher – we'll be able to watch movies in real time over our telephone network!

The Internet and E-mail

The Internet is a worldwide system of computer networks – a network of networks in which users at any one computer can, if they have permission, get information from any other computer. The most widely used applications of the Internet are the *World Wide Web* and *e-mail*.

Information Superhighway

The information superhighway is another word to describe the *Internet* and *World Wide Web*. It refers to the communications network that allows information to flow around the world through the complex connection of different computer systems.

Electronic Commerce or e-Commerce

With the advancement of the Internet electronic commerce has become the buzzword of the 21st Century. E-commerce refers to business carried out over the Internet – collaborating with colleagues, making online purchases, receiving support or services from companies (such as training or education) all comes under the banner of e-commerce.

Most major companies now have an Internet strategy which includes e-commerce and experts predict more and more transactions will take place over the Internet during the coming years. The web will replace many traditional distribution channels and give more power and choice to the purchaser. Although some early adopters in the .COM revolution have fallen, e-commerce and its implications will have very far-reaching implications for everyone in society.

The Internet has revolutionised the way we communicate and gather information. Please read through the introductory section of *Module 7 – Information and Communication on page 534* where will look at the Internet and e-mail in detail.

Intranets

An *Intranet* is a private network that is contained within a company. Often we will want to share information with our colleagues in the work place. This information might be sensitive or confidential information only accessible to staff or particular groups within the company. It might contain sales results, job procedures, strategies and so on. This type of information is often shared on a company *intranet*. An intranet is accessed through a browser just like the web. Intranets can be shared between offices in different locations or even in different countries. The tools used to build web sites are also used to build intranets.

Extranets

An Extranet can be viewed as part of a company's Intranet that is extended to users outside the company. Sometimes we will want to share some of the information on our Intranet with partners, customers or other businesses. An Extranet requires security and privacy. These require *firewalls,* the use of *digital certificates* or similar means of user authentication, *encryption* of messages and the use of virtual private networks that tunnel information through the public network.

Companies can use an Extranet to:

❏ Exchange large amounts of data with suppliers and customers using technology such as EDI (Electronic Data Interchange)

❏ Share product catalogues and pricing with wholesalers and trade customers

❏ Collaborate with other companies in development efforts

❏ Share news of common interest exclusively with partner companies.

EXERCISES TO PROVE YOU KNOW

1. Draw the three common network topologies described in this section.

2. Building a network is not worth the disruption it causes. Would you agree? Why?

3. What is a MODEM?

4. What is the *information superhighway*?

5. What is e-commerce?

6. What is the difference between the Internet and an Intranet?

7. What is an Extranet?

8. Rearrange in order of increasing Internet connection speed:

    a)   56Kbps Modem

    b)   ADSL

    c)   28Kbps Modem

SECTION 1.7:   IT AND SOCIETY

Analysts tell us that our society has developed through different eras starting with *agriculture* and then to *heavy industry* and *services* societies into an *Information Society*. A large proportion of the working population are in so called *Information Professions* – most of their work involves the processing of information. Computers have greatly speeded up this process and helped in the management and collection of this data.

This section looks at some of the ways in which the Information Society can help us and how we can avoid some of its pitfalls.

LESSON 1.7.1:   THE INFORMATION SOCIETY

The development of the information society has led to problems including:

- Higher stress levels
- Lack of physical development due to nature of work leading to illness
- Sickness due to poor ergonomics
- Lack of social contact
- Privacy and data protection issues
- Information overload

We can all think of situations where these have affected us.

LESSON 1.7.2:   TELEWORKING

Traditionally people travelled into a large town or city and worked in a centralised office where they had access to their computer equipment as well as meeting with their other workers in order to determine what work had to be processed that day. With the advent of modern telecommunications networks and the right software it is now possible for many people to work at home on a computer that is connected to the office.

Teleworker is term used to describe a person that is working from home. The person that works from home will be transmitting data and documents to and from a nominal workplace over telephone lines using a telephone, fax machine and modem-equipped computer.

Some advantages of teleworking:

- Reduced or no commuting time (some teleworkers might commute to a tele-centre rather than working from home)
- Greater ability to focus on one task
- Flexible schedules
- Reduced company space requirements

Some disadvantages of teleworking:

- Lack of human contact
- Less emphasis on teamwork

We are seeing a growth in the number of companies supporting teleworking and it is a trend that is likely to grow as the Information Society evolves.

LESSON 1.7.3: OFFICE AUTOMATION

The computer has totally revolutionised the modern office. This goes far beyond simply replacing the typewriter with a computer. A computer can be linked to other computers. The computer can be linked to the telephone system. The fax machine is fast being replaced in many companies where faxes are sent and received directly via the computer, or replaced entirely by email!

Many repetitive jobs have been almost eliminated. One person using a computer with the right software can send letters to thousands of people in a day. Word-processing software incorporates a mail-merge facility (which allows a single letter to merge with a large list of names, and addresses to produce "personalised" letters). The weekly or monthly payroll has been completely automated, so that a relatively small department can keep track of payments to the entire company.

LESSON 1.7.4: ROBOTICS

Although at the moment we don't tend to see Robots in the office or at home, science fiction has always predicted they would arrive to finish the vacuum cleaning and make breakfast in bed. The Robot on the right is an experimental unit which can play symphonies on an electronic organ by reading sheet music directly into a camera (its *eye*)

Although no generally recognised criteria exists that distinguishes them from other automated systems, robots tend to be more versatile and adaptable (or reprogrammable) than less sophisticated devices. They offer the advantages of being able to perform more quickly, cheaply, and accurately than humans in conducting set routines. They are capable of operating in locations or under conditions hazardous to human health, ranging from areas of the factory floor to the ocean depths and outer space.

The concept of robots dates back to ancient times, when some myths told of mechanical beings brought to life. Such so-called automata also appeared in the clockwork figures of medieval churches, and in the 18th century some clockmakers gained fame for the intricately clever mechanical figures that they constructed. Today the term automaton is usually applied to these handcrafted, mechanical (rather than electromechanical) devices that are restricted merely to imitating the motions of living creatures. Some of the "robots" used in advertising and entertainment are actually mere automata, even with the addition of remote radio control.

The term *robot* itself is derived from the Czech word *robota*, meaning "compulsory labour". It was first used in the 1921 play R.U.R. (which stands for "Rossum's Universal Robots") by the Czech novelist and playwright *Karel Capek*, to describe a mechanical device that looks like a human but, lacking human sensibility, can perform only automatic, mechanical operations. In the play, however, the robots proved much more capable than that, eventually conquering and destroying their makers—a recurrent theme in science fiction since that time. The term androids is now generally reserved for humanlike figures of this sort, ranging from electromechanical robots in human form to humanlike creatures made entirely of biological materials.

Robots as they are known today are not really imitative of human or other living forms except in the limited aspect of digital dexterity. The roots of their development lie in the effort to automate some or all of the operations required on the factory floor. This effort began in the 18th century in the textile industry, when some looms were designed to perform under the control of punched paper tapes. With the burgeoning of the Industrial Revolution, more factories sought to bring a greater degree of automation to the repeated processes of the assembly line. True robots did not become possible, however, until the invention of the computer in the 1940s and the progressive miniaturization of computer parts.

One of the first true robots was an experimental model called SHAKEY, designed by researchers at the Stanford Research Institute in the late 1960s. It was capable of arranging blocks into stacks through the use of a television camera as a visual sensor, processing this information in a small computer.

Sony's new AIBO robot and walk, respond to voice commands, play with a ball and interact with its environment. It has a digital camera in its nose and can be controlled wirelessly

Thereafter engineers tried to adapt robot like devices to useful tasks. In the mid-1970s, General Motors financed a development program in which Massachusetts Institute of Technology researcher Victor Scheinman expanded upon a motor-driven "arm" he had invented to produce a so-called "programmable universal manipulator for assembly," or PUMA. The PUMAs that resulted mark the beginning of the age of robots.

Unmanned space exploration provides plenty of challenges for Robot innovation. Some of the most successful missions in space have been manned by Robots including the recent Mars landings

LESSON 1.7.5:   COMPUTERS VS. HUMANS

There are many jobs where computers are better suited to do the job than we are, and in turn, many more to which humans are better adapted.

Here are some situations where *computers* are more suitable.

Repetitive tasks	In the past, people carried out many repetitive jobs. Now it is more often more competitive and preferable to use computers instead.
Easily automated tasks	Phone systems are now largely automatic, in a former time all calls were made through an operator.
Mathematical calculations	A computer is ideally suited to performing mathematical calculations. Before computers were widely available accountants used to work on manual, paper based spreadsheets. With a spreadsheet a common task would be adding up a column of figures and then taking the total, which is added to other columns of figures. If we change one number within a column that is being totalled there can be a knock-on effect on many other calculations within the spreadsheet. Recalculating a spreadsheet could take hours (or days). On a computer this re-calculation can take seconds!
Dangerous Situations	Monitoring polluted or radioactive environments is suited to robots, where the use of a human would expose that person to unacceptable risks.
Space Exploration	Unmanned, computer-controlled machines almost exclusively carry out serious space exploration. The recent exploration of Mars involved a computerised 'buggy', which had to make decisions for itself. It could not be fully remotely controlled from earth, as the time taken for the signal to reach Mars is too long.

Where are humans superior to computers?

In fact most jobs - thankfully - people are far better at than computers – often these are the tasks that we take for granted.

Intelligent tasks	Where a judgment or choice must be made on the value of something based on complex criteria computers aren't suitable here. They provide a cold and inflexible judgment.
Interaction with people	Where interaction with people and entertainment is concerned people are much more suitable.
Innovation and new situations	People are inventive and creative. Although computers can draw on vast databanks of knowledge they currently can't draw useful conclusions from the data or propose an alternative new way of doing things.
Creativity	Computers are not creative - humans excel in this area over computers.
Awkward terrain	Although robots can navigate certain terrain, stairs, mountains, traffic on the road can confuse them.

EXERCISES TO PROVE YOU KNOW

1. What is the information society?

2. What is *teleworking*? Outline some advantages and disadvantages of teleworking.

3. "Computers will replace humans in all non-creative jobs within 20 years". Discuss outlining the advantages and disadvantages of computers and robotics in the workforce.

SECTION 1.8: HEALTH, SAFETY AND THE ENVIRONMENT

LESSON 1.8.1: HEALTH PROBLEMS AND OUR COMPUTER

Computers and our health and safety in the work environment

Working with computers has its problems. There are several common problems that arise from using computers everyday and some precautions we can take to avoid them.

Repetitive Strain Injury - RSI

This is caused by constant use of the keyboard or mouse. We should take regular breaks to help avoid this type of injury. We may want to consider the use of a pad that we can rest our arms on which will help to some extent.

Alternative keyboard layouts like Microsoft's (shown above) can make typing more comfortable.

Eye strain

Good lighting is crucial to avoid damaging our eyes. The monitor should be placed away from direct sunlight and no shadows or glare should be seen onscreen.

We should take regular breaks to avoid constantly staring at the screen and straining our eyes. We should consider using the best (i.e. most expensive) monitor that we can afford. The better the monitor the better the screen resolution and the higher the refresh rate. For detailed work we should also consider using a large screen rather than the 'standard' 14" or 15" screens that are in common use.

Back, arm and neck strain

Bad posture when working with a computer can lead to back, neck, arm, wrist and muscle pain and can lead to permanent injury. Sitting correctly at our computer, taking regular breaks and using ergonomic seating and peripherals can help reduce the risk of developing these problems.

Contamination from dust and toner

Ventilation is important to ensure proper air flow around your computer and printer. Both you and the computer will benefit. Be particularly careful of ventilation around laser printers to ensure the toner is not directed towards you.

LESSON 1.8.2:   ERGONOMICS

Ergonomics is the relationship between our computers and our environment. Good ergonomics means a better work environment and healthier computing.

Below you will find suggestions for improving the ergonomics of your work environment.

- ❑ Use a chair that supports the lower back and that is height adjustable.
- ❑ Clear the area under your desk or use a foot rest
- ❑ Place monitor in centre of desk with top of monitor at eye level about arms length away.

- ❑ Clean the monitor screen regularly to avoid eye strain and use an anti-glare screen if appropriate
- ❑ Keep keyboard and mouse at same level as elbows
- ❑ When typing centre your keyboard in front of you
- ❑ Keep wrists straight while typing

LESSON 1.8.3:   SAFETY

Powering our PC

Without power our PC definitely won't work. Modern PCs all take the same type of power cable affectionately known as a "kettle lead".

Occasionally the fuse will blow in the plug of this lead or the power outlet to which it is connected will blow a main fuse. If you find that your PC is loosing power continuously you should definitely consider investing in a **UPS** (see *Protecting computer systems* on page 52) which will keep your computer on long enough to shut it down safely. Continuous power cuts will cause your computer and its hard disk to fail.

We should always exercise caution when connecting a PC to a power outlet to avoid risk of electric shock. Check that power sockets are not overloaded by use of too many extension leads or badly fitted plugs.

LESSON 1.8.4: THE ENVIRONMENT

As computer users we need to be aware of how our computers effect the environment. There are recycling schemes for printed paper that we should use and also special recycling for our printer toner and inkjet cartridges (you should ask your supplier about these). Also to try to work with the electronic versions of files rather than printing versions to reduce the amount of paper being wasted in the office or at home.

We should also be aware of the different devices available that will help save power when using our computer, for example, flat screen monitors use less power than traditional monitors.

Buy equipment where possible with energy saving features. This equipment often has the *Energy Star* logo printed on it.

There are several ways to conserve power while using your computer:

1. Turn off your computer at night and when you are not using it for several hours – monitors can use a lot of power.

2. Enable the Power Management features for your monitor and PC – the available options will be found in your PC manual.

3. If you buy a new computer, consider a laptop. Laptops use about ¼ the energy of a Desktop computer.

4. If you are buying a monitor, consider a flat screen. They use about 1/3 the energy.

Recycling

Paper – we waste massive amounts of paper unnecessarily. Quite often e-mails, documents, spreadsheets are printed and viewed just once. Recycle paper that is no longer of use and try to work with documents on-screen – it will help reduce our paper consumption.

Printers – both laser and inkjet use 'consumable' items. Toner cartridges and inkjet cartridges contain many valuable resources. Refilling our inkjet cartridges and recycling our toner cartridges will help reduce the waste mountain and improve our environment. Most computer stores now have kits to help refill your inkjet cartridges and accept toner cartridges for recycling.

EXERCISES TO PROVE YOU KNOW

1. What is RSI and what can be done to help prevent it?

2. Outline four ways in which we can improve the ergonomics of our work environment.

3. How can we help conserve power while using our PCs?

SECTION 1.9: SECURITY, COPYRIGHT AND THE LAW

Since our computer systems contain sensitive data perhaps client details, account records and so on it is important that the data is appropriately protected against unwanted intrusion. The Internet has made everyone aware of the dangers of unprotected systems – where VISA card numbers, access codes and another sensitive information can be stolen by a computer criminal.

It is extremely important that every organisation is proactive in dealing with security risks, this includes:

❏ Adopting an information security policy with respect to handling sensitive data

❏ Having procedures for reporting security incidents

❏ Making staff members aware of their responsibilities with respect to information security

Let's take a look at some of the ways in which we can help protect our computer systems

LESSON 1.9.1: PROTECTING COMPUTER SYSTEMS

User IDs and Passwords

The most basic of *information security* policy, which is quite effective, are the use of *user IDs* and *passwords*. Without the correct user ID and password it will be very difficult to access the information on our computers. If our computer has a password that prevents other users from accessing it then do NOT give this password to anybody else. Programs like *Word* and *Excel also* provide a password protection mechanism for each file if required. This allows personal information to be protected from anyone in an organisation.

A user ID is a system name used by the computer to identify you when you log onto a computer. It is used by the system to uniquely identify you as a user. This is one half of the credentials to logon, the other, is the password. The password is a sequence of characters required for access to the computer system. With a valid user ID and password you gain access rights to a computer and its network.

Typical login screen to Windows

Access rights can be defined as the extent to which a user may operate a system resource on a network. In many cases, permission to access a server, view its contents and modify or create files is limited by the network's administrator. These access rights are important in order to maintain security. Security is vitally important in order to adhere to laws on privacy issues (see data legislation act later in this module).

Physical Security

Traditional security protects equipment by isolating it and guarding it in a safe place. Locks, bolts, alarms and security guards make up the arsenal of protection to secure the machinery and data on the computer.

Biometrics

Technology can help us secure our systems by validating users. *Biometrics* is an emerging field of technology devoted to identifying individuals using biological traits, such as those based on retinal or iris scanning, fingerprints and handprints, or face recognition.

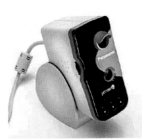

Panasonic Iris Scanner authenticates a user by scanning their retina

Omron face recognition device can authenticate by scanning faces

AcroPrint Handprint technology recognises individuals from their handprint

We can restrict access to systems and buildings using biometric technology. Over the next few years we will see this type of technology used much more extensively as security continues to become a more important issue.

Encryption

Encryption is an encoding mechanism which scrambles data usually for transmission across a network. When encrypted the data is useless without the decryption key which must be protected.

LESSON 1.9.2: PROTECTING DATA

Performing Backups

The most important thing that we store on our computer is information. Often the contents of a hard disk can represent years of work. If the hard disk stops working one day we could lose all those years of work. For this reason it is **vital** that we take regular backups of the information that is stored on the computer. In large organisations this backup procedure is normally performed on the file servers by the IT Department - but this backup process will normally *not include* data stored on our own local machines. In smaller organisations it is often up to the individual to organise some sort of data backup. If nothing else is available, copy files onto a floppy disk and make sure that these backup disks are stored away from the computer, ideally off site. If there is a fire and our office burns down, if our backup disks are stored next to the computer they too will be incinerated!

Organising our computer for more efficient backups

Our computer's Hard Disk contains many programs as well as the data we wish to backup. If we create a sensible folder structure for our data only these directories need to be backed up.

Complete vs. Incremental backups

A complete backup means that we backup all the programs and data on our computer. This has the advantage that the entire hard disk is backed up, but suffers from the disadvantage that the process can take a long time if our computer contains a lot of files. An incremental backup means that we only backup files that have been newly created or modified since the last backup so saving much time. With the right backup software, this process is automatic, and normally we only have to select full or incremental.

'Off-site' storage

It is no good backing up our data, only to leave the backup next to the computer. If someone steals our computer it is likely that they will also steal our backups if they are there to steal! If we have a fire then again we will lose our backups if the backups are stored next to the computer. Ideally, backups should be stored off-site at a safe location. At the very least, consider storing our backups in a fire-proof safe, which will give some protection against fire damage.

Implications of Theft

If you own a laptop, PDA or a mobile phone on which you store your data, you should be aware of what might happen if it were stolen:

- Possible misuse of confidential files
- Loss of files
- Loss of important contact details if they are not available from a separate source
- Possible misuse of telephone numbers

LESSON 1.9.3: COMPUTER VIRUSES

Viruses are small programs that hide themselves on our disks (both diskettes and our hard disk) in our e-mail or on web pages. Unless we use Virus detection software the first time that we know that we have a Virus is when it activates. Different Viruses are activated in different ways. For instance, the famous Friday the 13th Virus will activate only when it is both a Friday and the 13th of the month.

BEWARE: Viruses *can and do* destroy all our work and data.

There are 1000s of different Viruses which fall into several categories

- ❏ *Computer Virus* – this term was first used by Fred Cohen in 1984. A computer Virus is a small program that attaches itself to another program and attacks other software by making copies of itself.

- ❏ *Worm* - A worm is a program (usually stand-alone) that "worms" its way through either the computer's memory or a disk and alters data that it accesses. It is different from a computer Virus since it does not require a host.

- ❏ *Trojan horse* - A program which attaches itself to a seemingly innocent program. Trojan horses do not necessarily replicate.

- ❏ *Logic or time bomb* - A program that is activated or triggered after or during a certain event. This may be after several executions or on a certain day like Friday the 13th.

How do Viruses infect PCs?

Viruses hide on a disk and when we access the disk (either a diskette or another hard disk over a network) the Virus program will start and infect our computer. The worst thing about computer Viruses is that they can spread from one computer to another, either via use of infected floppy disks, or over a computer network.

The *Internet* allows us to access files from all over the world and we should never connect to the Internet unless we have a Virus checking program installed on our computers. E-mail messages are now one of the most common ways we are infected with Viruses. Viruses arrive as attachments to an e-mail message or embedded in some way in the message itself. We'll learn some more about this when we look at *Module 7 – Information and Communication* and look at e-mail messages.

Preventing Virus damage

There are a number of third party anti-Virus products available. Most of these are better than the rather rudimentary products available within DOS and Windows, but of course we do have to pay for them! The main thing about our Virus checker is that it should be <u>kept up to date</u>. Most anti-Virus software companies supply updated disks or automatic web downloads on a regular basis to keep our software up to date and aware of the latest Virus threats.

In *Module 2 – Viruses* on page 142 we will learn how to use Virus software to protect and repair our PC if it becomes infected with a Virus. You should also look at *E-mail attachments* on page 598 and note the issues regarding opening e-mail attachments and security and Virus risks.

Making a diskette read-only

If we are using 3.5" diskette, there is a notch that can be opened or closed and used to protect the disk.

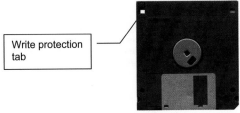

Write protection tab

Password protecting our computer

We can set a power-on password on our computer. The mechanism for setting this will vary from one computer to another, and is determined by the makers of the computer, rather than by Windows. The advantage of a power-on password is that the computer will not boot to DOS until we supply the correct password. This means that no one else can play around with our computer, and in the process accidentally infect it with a Virus.

LESSON 1.9.4:   SOFTWARE COPYRIGHT

Most programs that we purchase are copyrighted and we must not copy them. If we do so we may be breaking the law, and if caught we could find ourselves being prosecuted! Many people will buy a copy of a game and make a copy for their friends or other family member. This is also normally unlawful. Even lending our program disks or CD-ROM to other people may be breaking the law in most cases. There are numerous organisations, such as *FAST* (the *Federation Against Software Theft*), which are dedicated to preventing the illegal copying of software. In a business situation, if our manager tells us to copy software, ALWAYS first make sure that we have a Licence that entitles us to copy the software, because in many countries, we will be personally liable for damages!

In order to check the *Product ID* of a program that you are using, you can usually go to the **Help | About** menu. Here you will able to view the Product ID.

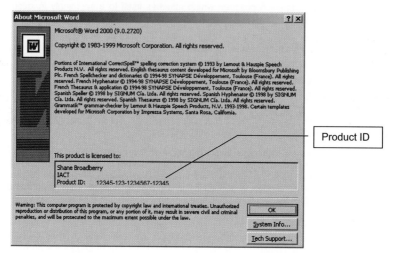

It's not just software that is covered by copyright laws. Graphic images, text, audio and video files are also usually copyrighted.

When downloading information from the Internet we need to be aware of these copyright issues.

Freeware

Some software is made freely available. Demonstration disks often come under this category. Also a lot of software is produced by the educational community and is made freely available. Always read any Licences supplied with such software very carefully before use. If the software falls into this category it is known as *Freeware* and it will normally indicate so in the documentation.

Shareware

Shareware is software that is freely available and is designed to let us use the product for free, for a limited period while we decide if we like it or not. After this period we must legally either remove it, or pay an amount to the producers of the product. Some shareware does not include this extra restriction and sending a donation or comments about the program are all that are required.

Software downloaded from the Internet

Many companies now sell their software directly over the Internet. By entering in our Visa card or similar we can download the complete product and start using it immediately. Many hundreds of millions of euros and dollars are spent online in this way each year.

Be aware however that there are many illegal sites on the Internet run by dubious organization's that make pirate copies of commercial software freely available. If we download any software from the Internet, we must make sure that it is legal or face the consequences.

Quite often we can download "trial" versions of commercial products for free which we are authorised to use to test the software for a limited period – very rarely however will a commercial organization give away their software for free. We will occasionally find utility software (such Adobe's *Acrobat Reader* program) available free for download. If in doubt – check it out.

Free software on Zip disks, CD-ROMs and DVD-ROMs

If you are offered commercial software on unmarked CD-ROMs, floppy disks, Zip disks or some other form – be aware of copyright restrictions regarding the use of this software. It is illegal to load software onto your computer that is not Licensed (see below) and there are severe penalties for breaking these rules.

EULA and Site Licences

Usually we don't in fact 'buy' a piece of software – we *licence it*. The licence includes certain restrictions – such as prohibiting copying and lending of the software. The licence shipped with commercial software is known as an EULA – *End User Licence Agreement.* The EULA may be included in printed format with the software or it will appear on screen as we start to install the product. We must agree with the terms of the licence to use the software.

Most large companies do not go out and buy thousands of 'shrink-wrapped' copies of each software product that they need, instead they will buy a *site Licence*. A site Licence allows a company use a fixed number of copies of a product throughout an organisation. The IT manager is responsible for safeguarding the site licences and ensuring all other licences are up to date.

LESSON 1.9.5:   DATA PROTECTION LEGISLATION

Data is by far the most important commodity we store on our computers. 'Data' refers to any of the information saved on the computer – this includes everything from a letter typed in Word to a database of ten thousand names and addresses. It is the data that we value on our PCs.

The *Data Protection Legislation* was brought about to protect personal data stored on computers. This is data about individuals (such as their name and address) that we may have collected or stored on our computer systems. This data might be stored and then used as part of a marketing campaign or in a mail-shot. This lesson outlines some of your responsibilities with this data.

Important: Please refer to the official *Data Protection Guide* for your country to fully ensure that you carry out your obligations under the act. The authors do not accept responsibility for mis-interpretation of the act or the text included here.

http://www.hmso.gov.uk/acts/acts1998/19980029.htm

Below is an outline of the **Irish Data Protection Act 1988**. It will give you an idea of your responsibilities when you keep personal information on a computer. This Act shows the guidelines for Data Controllers issued by the data Protection Commissioner. The Act was passed to deal with privacy issues arising from the increasing amount of information kept on computer about individuals. In giving new rights to individuals, the Act also puts new responsibilities on those who keep personal information on computers.

The following terms are important for us to understand the Act correctly:

A *Data Controller* is a person who, either alone or with others, controls the contents and use of personal data.

A *Data Processor* is a person who processes personal data on behalf of a data controller, but does not include an employee of a data controller who processes such data in the course of his/her employment.

The act outlines the key responsibilities for a Data Controller, in relation to the information, which he/she keeps on a computer. These may be summarised in terms of eight rules which he/she must follow:

1. Obtain and process the information fairly

2. Keep it only for one or more specified and lawful purposes

3. Use and disclose it only in ways compatible with these purposes

4. Keep it safe and secure

5. Keep it accurate and up to date

6. Ensure that it is adequate, relevant and not excessive

7. Retain it no longer than is necessary for the purpose or purposes

8. Give a copy of his/her personal data to any individual, on request

These provisions are binding on every data controller. Any failure to observe them would be in breach of the Act.

There are **practical steps** to follow to ensure that the above rules are followed:

1. Where we use application forms or standard documentation in signing up new customers or clients, we should explain our purposes/uses etc on such forms or documentation.

2. Prepare a statement of the purpose or purposes for which we hold computerised information about others. Any individual has the right to ask us to state the purposes for which we keep such information.

3. Carry out an inventory of all current and proposed uses and disclosures and check each one against the stated purposes.

4. Compile a check-list of security measures for our own systems.

5. Assign specific responsibilities for data accuracy under the Data Protection Act and arrange periodic review and audit.

6. Decide on specific criteria by which to decide what is adequate, relevant, and not excessive. Apply those criteria to each information item and the purposes for which it is held.

7. Assign specific responsibility to someone for ensuring that files are regularly purged and that personal information is not retained on computer any longer than necessary.

EXERCISES TO PROVE YOU KNOW

1. What are *biometrics*? Describe some technology that use biometrics and what it is used for.

2. What is the difference between a complete and an incremental backup?

3. Why is the security of passwords on laptops, PDAs and PCs so important?

4. Viruses destroy the data and programs on our PCs and cost billions of dollars each year. Why is finding the author of a Virus so difficult? Discuss.

5. How can we check if our software is correctly Licensed?

6. What is the difference between *shareware* and illegal pirated software downloaded from the Internet?

7. What is a *data controller?*

SECTION 1.10: EXAM OVERVIEW AND TIPS

In the exam for *Module One, IT Concepts*, you will be given a test paper. This test paper will have 36 multiple choice questions.

Each question is worth 1 mark and you must answer all 36 questions.

This pass mark in Module 1 is 75% (that is 27/36).

Answers to the questions should be marked on the exam paper and then handed to the supervisor when finished. Make sure that you have written your candidate id number on the paper.

The duration of this test is 45 minutes.

All of the topics covered in this Module could be asked in the exam.

For further tips on examinations visit http://www.iactonline.com/ecdl

Module 2
FILE MANAGEMENT

iact

The complete IT training provider

MODULE 2: FILE MANAGEMENT

File Management is one of the most important modules of the ECDL. In this module we will learn how to use the standard *Windows* interface and some of the most common Windows applications (like *Calculator*, *Notepad* and *Paint*). We'll also learn about the *Start* menu and the common components of a window including how to switch between them and what to do with them.

The other crucial topic covered in this module is *File Management* and how to work with *Windows Explorer* to create folders or directories. This is a skill that will be useful with every application we meet and save us many hours of searching and frustration!

The Windows filing system is like any other – but it has its own rules and mechanisms for working. Mastering it is just a matter of practice.

So let's get started.

SECTION 2.1:   INTRODUCTION TO WINDOWS

In this section we will learn:

- ❏ A brief history of how Windows evolved
- ❏ How to start and logon to Windows
- ❏ How to work with folders or directories
- ❏ How to start or run applications
- ❏ How to correctly restart and shutdown Windows

LESSON 2.1.1:   BRIEF HISTORY OF WINDOWS

The earliest PCs ran an operating system known as DOS – of which there were two main favourites – IBM DOS and MS-DOS (MS for Microsoft). **DOS** is short for **D**isk **O**perating **S**ystem. Early DOS machines worked just with Floppy disks and had a maximum of 640Kb of memory – tiny by today's standards.

DOS was a *command line* operating system which meant we had to type in commands in order to run programs or perform file management or other house-keeping tasks.

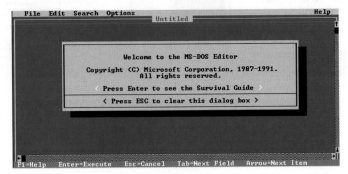

Original DOS command prompt
DOS commands like DIR and MD were used for common tasks

We can still bring up the old "DOS" interface even with the latest versions of Windows but it is only die-hard computer enthusiasts that tend to use it extensively!

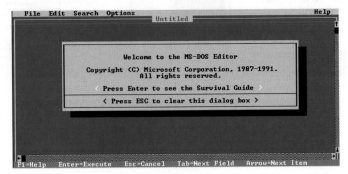

DOS Editor

DOS was not originally designed to allow the user to work with a mouse but with the advent of the Macintosh and the huge popularity of its graphical interface, later versions were written to allow mouse usage.

At the start of 1983 *Apple*® developed the first personal computer with a *Graphical User Interface* (or GUI) called the *Apple*® *Lisa*® · This was the forerunner to the hugely successful *Apple Macintosh* computer and spurred the development of GUIs for the PC and other computers. The writing was on the wall for DOS.

Apple's Lisa – Jan 1983   Apple's Mac - 1984

GUI (pronounced 'gooey') *interfaces* brought many advantages.

- ❑ To start with the interface was much more intuitive to learn and use.
- ❑ The first WYSIWYG (*What You See is What You Get*) editors like Word and Write appeared
- ❑ It was easier for us to work with and install printers
- ❑ We could "multi-task" for example we could print and edit our document at the same time
- ❑ We had access to more memory
- ❑ Above all we had a *standard* way of doing things. Keyboard shortcuts and the "look and feel" of programs became standardised.

Windows has undergone many re-incarnations and interface changes. An earlier version of the Windows interface (shown below) now looks very old fashioned. Compared to DOS however it was revolutionary and brought the PC into the WIMP age (**W**indows **I**cons **M**ice and **P**ull down menus).

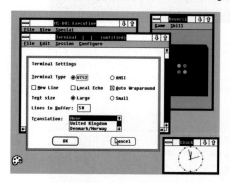

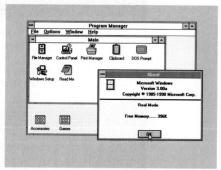

*The original Windows **2.0** and Windows **3.0** interfaces shown above*

The 'new' Interface for Windows

Windows underwent a massive overhaul and interface re-design and was launched spectacularly and with much anticipation with the release of Windows '95. Since then Microsoft have made additional releases including:

- ❑ Windows 95
- ❑ Windows 98
- ❑ Windows Me (Millennium Edition)
- ❑ Windows XP Home

Simultaneously a new operating system built from scratch called Windows NT was also developed by Microsoft. This has also gone through several incarnations.

- ❑ Windows NT 4.0 Workstation
- ❑ Windows 2000 Professional
- ❑ Windows XP Professional

Using any of the above systems is much the same since the interface that we see and use is practically identical. The differences lie in the environments these operating systems work in. For example home PCs tend to run Windows XP *Home Edition* and they are used for a wide mixture of uses (games, word processing, programming etc.).

Office PC's generally use Windows 2000 or Windows XP *Professional* for their extensive networking and security capabilities. These *Operating Systems* focus on ensuring the computers efficiency, security, reliability and stability.

The original Windows 95 Interface

LESSON 2.1.2: STARTING WINDOWS AND LOGGING ON

To start Windows we must first start-up our computer. Ensure the power leads, keyboard and mouse are connected and press the POWER button. We will also need to power up the monitor and any other peripherals attached to the PC.

Power button

Front view of a Desktop PC

As Windows prepares to start a loading screen like the one below will appear. During this stage Windows is loading up the software and device drivers needed to control the PC.

When Windows first starts we will usually see a login screen something like this:

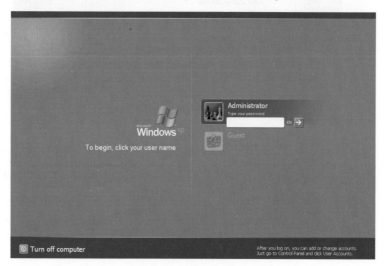

We may need to enter a user ID and password to logon and start using Windows. This username and password will be provided by whoever setup the computer.

LESSON 2.1.3: THE WINDOWS DESKTOP

Depending on how our computer is set up we'll see different things on our *Desktop* when we start Windows. Everything we use in Windows however can be found from the **Start** menu.

The most important components found in the Start menu or on the Windows Desktop are:

Start Button

We can click the start button to start or run a program, open a document, change system settings, get help, find items on our computer, and much more. Press this to start exploring Windows.

My Network Places

My Network Places

This tool lets us see all the available computers and resources on the network, including printers, shared network drives, scanners and other peripherals.

Control Panel

Control Panel

The Control Panel allows us to adjust the settings for Windows – including the login names, display and Desktop settings.

Internet

Internet Explorer Icon

This tool lets us browse and search the Internet. It also includes access to an e-mail program called *Outlook Express*. We'll look in detail at this tool in *Module 7 – Information and Network Services.*

Recycle Bin

Recycle Bin Icon

The Recycle Bin is a temporary storage place for deleted files. We will see how to empty the bin and recover files from here later on in this module.

LESSON 2.1.4:   THE START MENU

The *Start* menu button looks like this:

When we click the Start button (usually located at the bottom of our screen), we will see a menu that contains almost everything we need when using Windows. The **All Programs** sub-menu will contain all the programs that are installed on the computer.

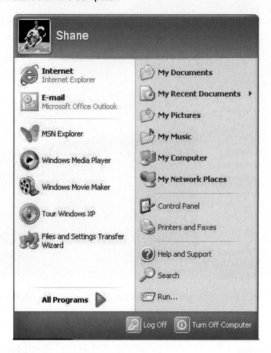

Clicking on one of the icons in the *Start* menu will:

❏   Display the contents of a menu or sub-menu

❏   Start up a program or shortcut.

We will use the Start menu all the time when using Windows. Becoming familiar with the location of icons and programs within the Start menu will greatly help our understanding of Windows.

LESSON 2.1.5: STARTING A PROGRAM AND USING WINDOWS

Let's start up the Window's *Paint* program. The Paint program comes with Windows and is found in the *Accessories* sub-folder of the Start menu. We will go into more detail about the Accessories sub-folder in *Section 2*.

To open and start Paint:

- ❏ Go to **Start** and choose **All Programs** and then
- ❏ Go to **Accessories** and choose **Paint**

Using our alternative notation we could also write this as **Start | All Programs | Accessories | Paint**

In a couple of seconds *Paint* will start and its window will appear on screen. The icon will also appear on the Taskbar.

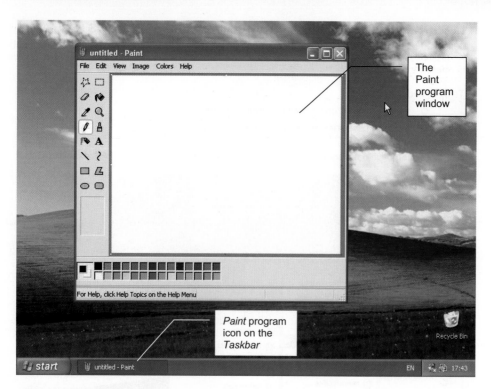

The Paint program window

Paint program icon on the *Taskbar*

All windows have the same basic components:

❑ The *menu bar* is usually located below the *Title bar*. In the above window there are 6 menu options. Pressing the **Alt** + **F** key, or clicking with the left mouse button on the word **File** will bring up the **File** menu option

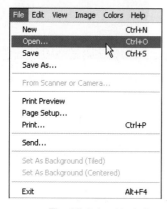

Note: Throughout this book when we refer to a menu option we will use the following notation:

❑ **Menu name | Item name**

For example to indicate the **Open** option in the **File** menu we will write:

❑ **File | Open**

To indicate the **Close** option in the **File** menu we will write:

❑ **File | Close**

❑ The *Minimise*, *Maximise* and *Close* buttons are located in the top right hand corner of most windows.

Minimise the current window

Maximise the current window

Close the current window

Lets experiment with a window and see what we can do with it. Using any application try the following:

Minimising windows

When we work with a number of programs together – or when we need to return to the Windows Desktop – it's useful to be able to *Minimise* it.

Every window should have a *Minimise* button like this:

When we press *Minimise* the window returns to the Taskbar and appears as an icon.

Restoring a window

To bring the window back to life press on icon on the Taskbar.

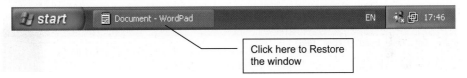

Once restored the program should continue exactly as before.

Maximising and Restoring a window

To enlarge an applications window to the full size of our screen, click on the *Maximise* button or double-click on the window's *Title bar*.

The Maximise button looks like this:

When a window is Maximised, the Maximise button is replaced by a ***Restore*** button

Restore Button

This button allows us to revert back to the pre-Maximised state.

Resizing and scrolling a window

A windows *resize* handle allows a window to be resized.

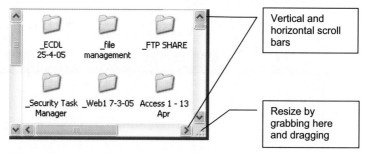

Click on the resize handle and drag with the mouse in order to manually resize a window.

If the contents of a window are not fully displayed we can usually *scroll* or pan the window using vertical and horizontal scroll bars located on the right and bottom of a window area.

Moving a window

To move a window click on the window's *Title bar* and drag with the mouse.

Release the mouse when the window is positioned in the right location.

Closing a window

To close a window click on the *close* icon or choose **Close** from the **File** menu or click on the ☒ icon in the top right hand corner of the window.

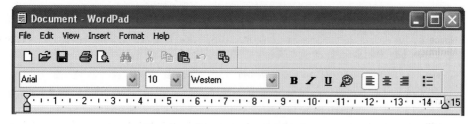

The program will ask us if we want to save our changes before we quit:

□   Choose **Yes** to save changes, **No** to quit without saving and **Cancel** to return to the program.

LESSON 2.1.6:   THE WINDOWS TASKBAR

The Windows *Taskbar* shows a list of programs (also known as *tasks)* that are currently open in Windows. Windows can run many different programs at the same time – because of this it is known as a *multitasking operating system*.

As we saw earlier - every time we start a program or open a new window, an icon representing that program usually appears along the Taskbar. We can easily switch between programs just by clicking the icon on the Taskbar.

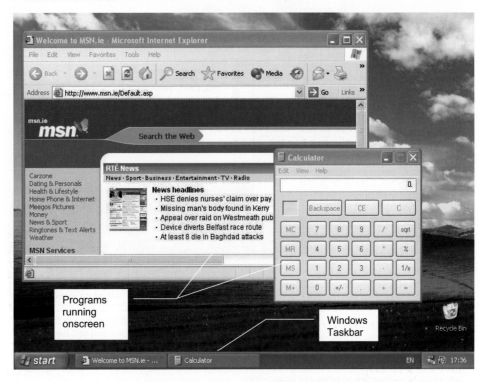

A typical Windows Desktop showing a number of running programs
and the Taskbar icons all the Taskbar.

Notice that when we close a window, the button disappears from the Taskbar. Experiment with the **Minimise, Maximise** and **Close** buttons to be clear about what they do.

Switching between Applications
When we have more than one application open at the same time, we may want to switch between them quickly and easily.

Any program that is currently open, will usually appear as an icon on the Taskbar. The button that is brighter and indented is the button that represents the program currently active on screen.

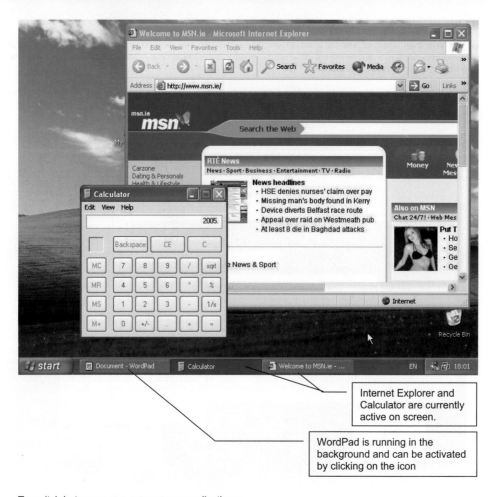

Internet Explorer and Calculator are currently active on screen.

WordPad is running in the background and can be activated by clicking on the icon

To switch between open programs or applications:

❑   Click on the icon representing the program on the Taskbar

or

❑   Press the **Alt+Tab** key combination.

LESSON 2.1.7:   PROPERLY SHUTTING DOWN A COMPUTER

We can't just switch off our computer when we've finished with it – or we risk losing our work. To shut down the computer we must save any open files, properly close all the open applications, and then follow the correct shutdown procedure.

    ❏   To shut down Windows – choose **Turn Off Computer** from the **Start** menu

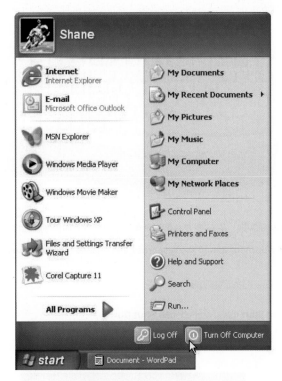

Windows will ask us to confirm if we want to *Stand By*, *Turn Off* or *Restart* the computer. **Stand By** requests that the computer save power but store the status of all running programs. **Restart** requests a reboot of the computer and will close all running programs. **Turn Off** will shut down the computer and close all running programs.

If we choose to **Turn Off** or **Restart** the computer it will close all running programs and possibly loose any unsaved work.

Note: Shutting Down or Restarting a computer will cause any unsaved work to be lost!

LESSON 2.1.8: RESTARTING A COMPUTER

Occasionally we will need to restart our computer in order to clean out its memory and start afresh. Rather than turning off the computer we can simply *reset* or *restart* it.

To restart the computer we press three keys on the keyboard together (don't do it yet!) the **Ctrl+Alt+DEL** keys. This special combination is programmed to confirm we want to restart the computer and re-login:

Ctrl

Alt

Delete

Keyboards can differ slightly – but this is a typical arrangement and positioning for these keys

Hold down the ***Ctrl*** *Key* press the *Alt key* and press and release the *Delete* key with the index finger of the right hand.

Alternatively, as we saw earlier we can

- ❑ Go to the **Start** menu and choose **Shut Down**
- ❑ Choose **Restart**
- ❑ Click **Yes**

Note: Before shutting down, we should ensure that all programs are closed, as unsaved work may be lost at shutdown.

LESSON 2.1.9:   SHUTTING DOWN A NON-RESPONDING APPLICATION

Sometimes when we have an application up and running, like Microsoft Word®, the application will "hang". 'Hanging' means that the program will not respond to any mouse clicks and the mouse pointer usually changes into the egg-timer icon. If this happens, we need to be able to close down the program that is causing the problems. To close a non-responding application:

❑   Press the **Ctrl + Alt + Delete** keys together – just like restarting the PC – and choose the **Task Manager** option.

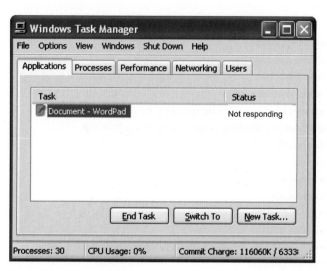

The Windows Task Manager will appear.

❑   Click on the application that has the status of **Not responding** and then click on **End Task** button.

❑   Now close the **Task Manager** window

Note: Shutting Down a program in this way will normally mean that we will loose any unsaved work. Sometimes programs can take a long time to respond – particularly when working with large documents or graphics files. If in doubt give the computer some more time before ending the task.

EXERCISES TO PROVE YOU KNOW

1. Which of the following Desktop icons is most likely to contain deleted files?

    My Computer   My Network   Recycle Bin   Internet
                     Places

    a)   b)   c)   d)

2. What does the **X** in the top right-hand corner of a window normally do?

    a) Minimise a window
    b) Restore a window
    c) Close a window
    d) Enlarge a window

3. What three keys must be held down in order to reset / restart a computer?

4. Re-arrange these PC operating systems according to their age:

    a) Windows 95
    b) Windows 98
    c) Windows NT
    d) Windows XP
    e) DOS
    f) Windows 2000

5. Which of these programs is used to shut-down a non-responding application:

    a) Program Manager
    b) Task Manager
    c) Windows Explorer
    d) Application Manager

6. Which of the following statements are TRUE?

    a) We can switch between an application using the **Alt+Tab** keys
    b) Open applications show icons along the Taskbar
    c) Windows can run a maximum of 5 applications at any one time
    d) We should never just switch off our PC.

SECTION 2.2:   THE ACCESSORIES MENU

There are many useful applications built into Windows. Most of these applications live in the *Accessories* folder within the **Start** menu. In this section we will look at some of these programs and what they do.

We will look at the following programs:

- ❑ Calculator
- ❑ Character Map
- ❑ Backup utility
- ❑ Paint

To start any of these programs go to the **Start** menu, choose **Programs | Accessories**.

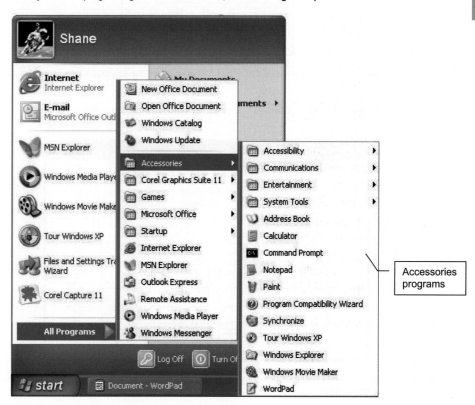

Accessories programs

Now that we are in the **Accessories** menu we will start looking at the first application, the *Calculator*.

LESSON 2.2.1:   THE CALCULATOR

The Calculator allows us perform simple calculations. Start the Calculator:

❑   Choose **Start | All Programs | Accessories | Calculator**

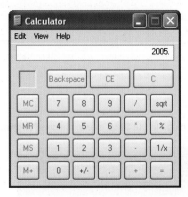

We can use the keyboard or the mouse to select the options on the keypad – this works the same as any regular Calculator.

The Calculator also includes a *scientific* mode for advanced functions. Choose **Scientific** from the **View** menu.

From the
View menu
choose
Scientific

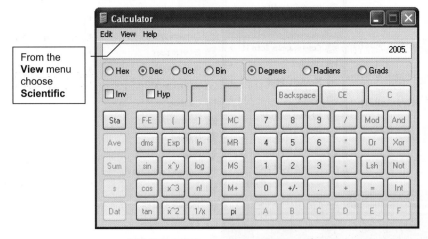

The Calculator is a handy tool for quickly performing calculations and can be Minimised and left on the Desktop until needed later.

LESSON 2.2.2:   CHARACTER MAP

The Character Map application lets us view all the characters in a particular font set. This is useful if we are trying to find a symbol or character to use as a bullet or icon. The Character Map program lives inside the **System Tools** subfolder inside the **Accessories** folder.

❑   Choose **Start | All Programs | Accessories | System Tools | Character Map**

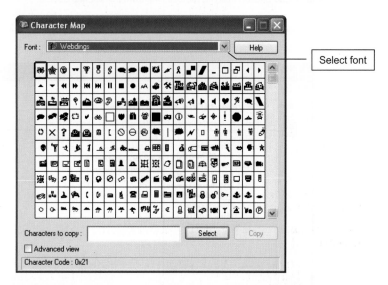

Select font

Selecting from the drop down arrow allows us to view lots of different fonts from different font sets. We can then choose any character in the font.

Clicking on a character magnifies it enabling us to pick the character we need. Pressing the *Select* button and then the *Copy* button will copy the character onto the clipboard. We can then 'paste' it into the program of our choice, Word or Excel or PowerPoint.

LESSON 2.2.3:   BACKUP

The *Microsoft Backup* utility allows us to backup our data onto floppy disk, Zip disk, another hard disk or to a backup tape or any other storage medium.

The utility works like **Windows Explorer** (which we meet later) allowing us to select folders and files to backup. The backup program also *compresses* the data to save space. If we later need to recover a file we can use the same backup utility to restore files from the backup device.

❑   Choose **Start | All Programs | Accessories | System Tools | Backup**

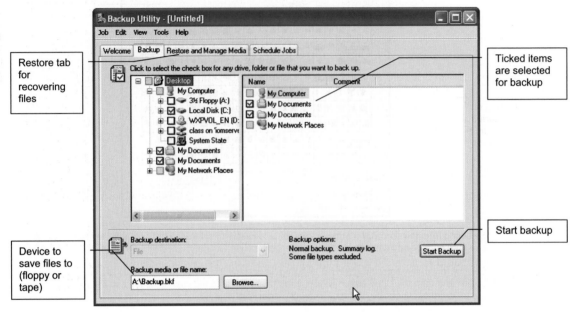

Restore tab for recovering files

Ticked items are selected for backup

Start backup

Device to save files to (floppy or tape)

Generally we will only backup our data (*documents*, *spreadsheets* etc.) onto our backup media – as we will usually find it easier to re-install software applications from their original media.

Note: Backing up our data onto removable media (such disk, tape, CD or DVD) helps to protect us from device failures, Viruses and accidental deletion which can erase or destroy all of our work and data. We should make regular backups of all our personal and work files.

LESSON 2.2.4:   PAINT

Paint allows us to crudely edit photos and touch up images using a set of tools.

❑   Choose **Start | All Programs | Accessories | Paint** to start up Paint.

Experiment with the toolbar buttons to see how to paint with a *pencil*, *paint-brush* and an *eraser*.

Use the toolbox to draw in different modes

Paint in different colours by choosing from the palette

We can use Paint to make simple edits to images that we download from the web or take with a digital camera or scanner. For professional image and digital photograph manipulation we will usually use a program such as *Adobe*® *PhotoShop* (www.adobe.com) or *Corel*® *PhotoPaint* (www.corel.com) as these are much more sophisticated programs.

Grabbing the current screen

Windows has special button that when pressed "grabs" the current screen. This "print screen" feature allows us to capture the items on screen just like taking a photograph. Once grabbed we can paste the image into any program that can display "bitmap" graphics. Many of the screen images taken for this book were taken using the *Print Screen* feature.

On the keyboard, near the top right hand side, there is a key marked **PSc, PrtSc** or **Print Screen**

Print Screen key

To grab the current screen:

❑   Press the **PrtSc** key (pressing **Alt+PrtSc** we capture just the current window)

Windows puts the current screen image onto the clipboard – and from here we can paste it into a program – like Paint or Word. To paste the screen shot into Paint – open up the Paint program:

❑   Go to **Edit | Paste** or press **Ctrl+V**

A picture of the current screen will then appear inside Paint.

EXERCISES TO PROVE YOU KNOW

1. Using the Calculator program work out the following:

    (720 / 1.44) = number of floppy disks that fit onto one CD-ROM

    (12 / 2.54) = number of centimetres in one foot

    (365.25 * 24 * 60) = number of minutes in a year

2. Open the character map program and insert the following characters from the symbols font:

3. Create a backup of the **My Documents** folder onto floppy disk.

4. Take a screen grab of the **Backup** program and paste it into the **Paint** program.

SECTION 2.3:   FILE MANAGEMENT

Computers hold vast amounts of information – far more information than we would normally work with at any one time. One of the most important lessons to learn when using a computer is how to save and retrieve a document or file.

In this section we will learn how to:

- ❑ Understand how computers organise their storage and how to
- ❑ Create and edit folders or directories

LESSON 2.3.1:   COMPUTER STORAGE

A new computer today could have over 100Gb of storage and probably even more by the time you read this. This is a truly enormous amount of storage by any standards. To put this in perspective this is equivalent to storing about 100,000 text books in your home!

If we had 100,000 text books and we were looking for one particular book – or even a page in one particular book how on earth would we find it? It could be like looking for a needle in a haystack…

Libraries have had this problem for centuries. Some libraries store millions of books – yet most of the time they have no difficulty finding any book they are looking for. That's because they have a structured system that tells them where a book must go when its returned to the library and therefore where it should be when they are looking for it.

Let's look at how a computer helps us to organise the files it stores for us and we can use this information to help us retrieve and store files in an organised way.

Understanding storage devices

Our computer will probably have at least 3 different types of storage devices connected to it which can be identified by different drive *letters*:

A

Floppy Disks
The Floppy disk drive **A:** must be inserted into the computer for use and can be removed to transfer information to another computer. This is the most common use for floppy disks. Floppy disks have a small capacity (equivalent to about 1.44Mb of storage – about enough to store the text of a 500 page book) or 20/30 small photographs. Floppy disks are also useful for backing up very important data, like for example a sales spreadsheet for the week etc. The days of the floppy are numbered mainly due to their small capacity and lack of durability. *Memory sticks* and *SD cards* (see page 19 for more information) are widely replacing their use.

C

Hard Disks
The computers main hard disk drive **C:** has enormous capacity. The hard disk contains the *Operating System* (probably Windows) and all the application programs that we use (programs like *Word, Excel* and so on). It has a huge capacity and is very fast. The hard disk drive is usually inside the computer and can't be readily removed. Larger computers may have more than one hard disk or the hard disk could be split into different drive letters **E: F:** etc.

D

CD-Rom and DVD-Rom Disks
Modern computers all contain a CD-Rom drive or a DVD-Rom drive to allow it to access programs and other information held on CDs and DVDs. CDs have a huge capacity (about 650Mb of storage) and are ideal for distributing programs like *Microsoft Office* or *Corel DRAW!* Most CD drives are *read only* – that is we can not save on to them, unless we have a drive that allows us to save. In the future all machines will have these "recordable" drives, so that we will be able to use CD's/DVD's instead of floppies. DVD-ROMs have a truly remarkable capacity holding close to 18,000Mb of storage! These are now widely used to hold high-quality movies.

Computer Storage

Our computer stores information on different storage devices – like hard-drive, memory sticks and floppy disks. The different devices on our computer need to be broken into separate sections – like the drawers of a filing cabinet.

In the real world if we were looking at the filing cabinets below we might say:

- ❑ Go to the **A:** filing cabinet
- ❑ Find the drawer called **Marketing**
- ❑ Retrieve the file called **January**

Floppy Disk **A:**   Hard Disk **C:** drive   CD/DVD-Rom **D:**

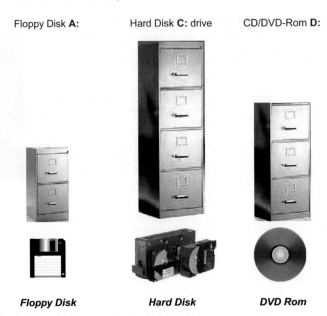

Floppy Disk   *Hard Disk*   *DVD Rom*

This seems straightforward, as we know which filing cabinet we are talking about. We know the drawer to look for – its called **Marketing** and we know we are looking for a folder called **January**

If we organise the information we store on our computers in much the same way – we'll find things just as easily. The computer is even more flexible however – as there is really no limit on the number of drawers we can have and we can even create sub-drawers to help organise the information further.

LESSON 2.3.2:   WINDOWS EXPLORER

In order to save and retrieve information successfully on our PCs we have got to understand it's filing system and use it properly.

The program used to create and manage the Windows filing system is called **Windows Explorer**.

- ❑ We can start *Windows Explorer* by going to the **Start | All Programs | Accessories** menu and clicking on **Windows Explorer** icon

or

- ❑ By pressing the Windows **Start** key (next to **Ctrl** and **Alt** on the keyboard) + **e**

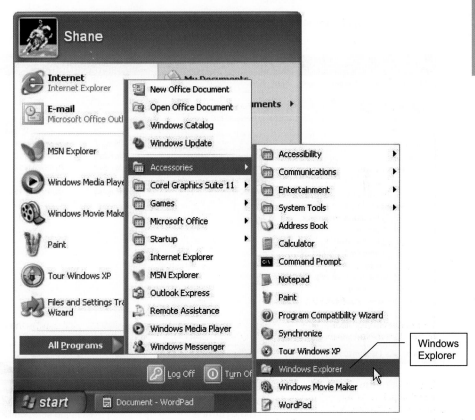

Touring Windows Explorer

We use Windows Explorer to:

- ❏ Create folders or directories on our different storage devices
- ❏ Move or copy files
- ❏ Delete files
- ❏ Format Disks
- ❏ Search for Files or Folders

Let's take a tour of the Explorer screen.

When we open Explorer we will see a screen something like this:

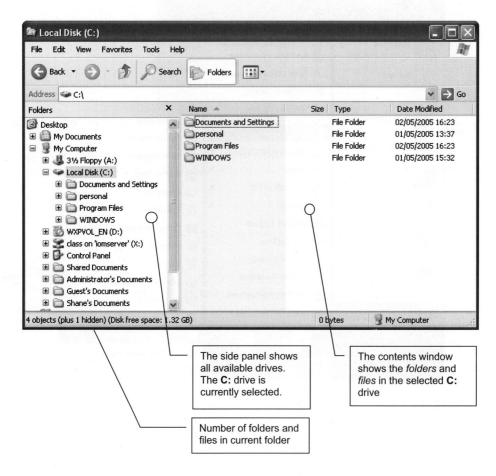

The side panel shows all available drives. The **C:** drive is currently selected.

The contents window shows the *folders* and *files* in the selected **C:** drive

Number of folders and files in current folder

Notice the left hand side panel shows the different drives and shortcuts on our Windows system. This is like a list of *filing cabinets*.

The right hand panel shows the *folders* and *files* on the selected drive. These are like the *drawers* and *files* in our filing cabinet.

Our side panel in Explorer looks like this:

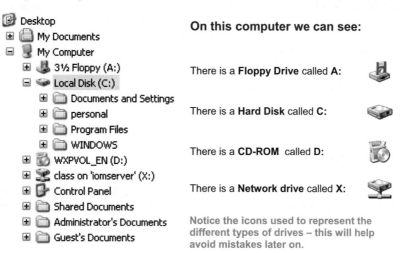

On this computer we can see:

There is a **Floppy Drive** called **A:**

There is a **Hard Disk** called **C:**

There is a **CD-ROM** called **D:**

There is a **Network drive** called **X:**

Notice the icons used to represent the different types of drives – this will help avoid mistakes later on.

When we select one of the drives *Windows Explorer* will show the contents of the drive in the main Window.

With the **C:** drive selected we can see the following information for our PC. (See *Lesson 2.3.14:Viewing and Sorting files* on page 100 if you screen does not look like this).

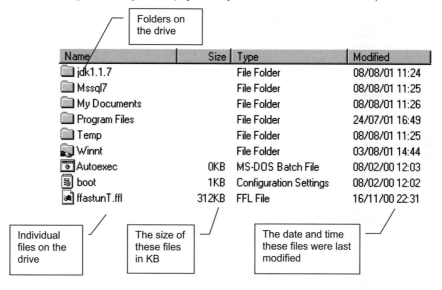

Counting the files and folders in a folder or directory
It is useful to note the number of files and folders in a given directory. In the above window our **C:** drive has 6 folders and 3 files immediately visible. To determine the number of files and folders in any folder or sub-folder – firstly open the folder and view the status bar at the bottom of the Explorer window:

| 5 objects (plus 3 hidden) (Disk free space: 1.32 GB) | 257 KB | My Computer |

Identifying folders and files

What we can see is the contents of the **C:** drive. It consists of folders (the yellow icons) and files. We can tell the type of file, when it was last modified and its size from this window.

❑ Files and programs are represented by different icons depending on their type. Here are a few of the most common types of files that we are likely to come across:

Icon	File Type	File Extension
	Folder	
word.doc	Word documents	***.doc**
excel.xls	Excel Workbooks	***.xls**
powerpoint.ppt	PowerPoint Presentation	***.ppt**
access.mdb	Access Database	***.mdb**
text.txt	Text File	***.txt**
Bitmap.bmp	Image Files	***.bmp, (*.gif, *.jpg)**
CorelDraw.cdr	Corel Draw File	***.cdr**
webpage.html	Web Page	***.html, *.htm**
acrobat.pdf	Adobe Acrobat	***.pdf**
zip_file.zip	WinZip File	***.Zip**

LESSON 2.3.3: CREATING A FOLDER OR A "DIRECTORY"

When we save a file we will decide where we are going to save it and also what we are going to name it. Before we can do this however we need to create a structure into which we can save our files.

Step 1: Choosing the Drive

The first step in creating this structure is determining the **Disk** that we want to save the file onto.

Usually we will save our files onto our **Hard Disk**. Occasionally we will want to save our files onto a **Floppy** disk in order to send it to someone, move it to another computer or to back it up.

Let's suppose we plan to save our documents onto our hard disk. We must first open Windows Explorer:

- ❑ Click on **Start | All Programs | Accessories**
- ❑ Click on **Windows Explorer**

Our hard disk is represented by the letter **C:** so we must first select this drive.

- ❑ Select the **C:** drive from the list of drives in the drive window.

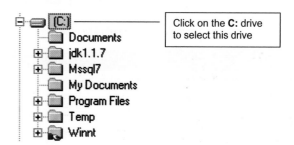

(If we had wished to create a folder on the *floppy disk* we would have inserted the disk and chosen the **A:** drive.)

We are now going to create a filing system on the **C:** to help us retrieve and save our files in a consistent manner. This is just like creating and labelling the drawers of our filing cabinet.

Step 2: Creating a Folder

Let's create a new folder (also called a directory) on our **C:** drive called "Documents" which will hold document files – probably files we create in Word.

From Windows Explorer:

- ❑ Ensure that the **C** drive is still selected
- ❑ Go to the **File** menu and choose **New | Folder**

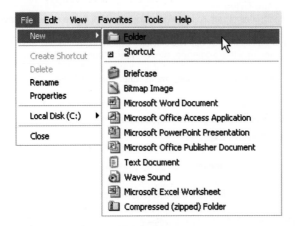

A new folder will appear in the contents window requesting that we type a name for the folder:

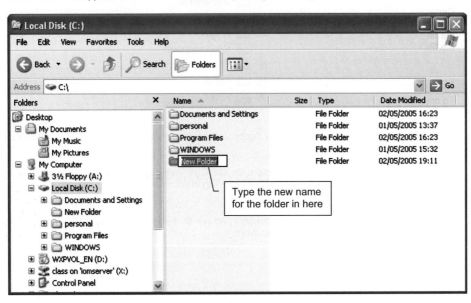

Type the new name for the folder in here

We are calling this folder *Documents* so type "Documents" as the name and press **Enter**

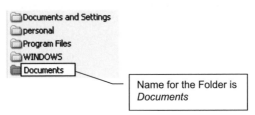

Name for the Folder is *Documents*

LESSON 2.3.4:   RENAMING A FOLDER OR A FILE

Sometimes we will want to rename a folder or a file. Renaming a folder or a file is easy.

- ❑ Select the folder or file by clicking on it once with the mouse.

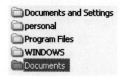

- ❑ Single-Click again with the mouse on the folder name and the name becomes highlighted. Type the new name; it will automatically replace the old name.

- ❑ Press **Enter** to finalise the changes.

Renaming an individual file is done in exactly the same way, however, it is important that when we type in the new name for the file that the original file extension (e.g. **.doc** or **.xls**) stays the same. Changing the file's extension will change program associated with the file and Windows may not be able to open the file.

LESSON 2.3.5:   CREATING SUB-FOLDERS

To create a folder inside another folder:

- ❑ Open Windows Explorer
- ❑ Select the **Documents** folder.

We can see that we have the folder open as the side pane will show an open-folder icon for the folder:

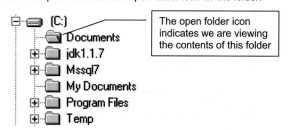

The open folder icon indicates we are viewing the contents of this folder

Now we repeat the steps we used to create our first folder.

❏   Choose **File | New | Folder**.

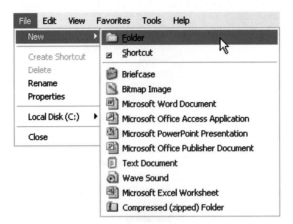

A new folder will appear in the contents window. We must type a name for the folder:

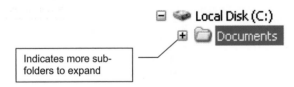

❏   We are calling this folder *Personal* so type "Personal" as the name and press **Enter**

LESSON 2.3.6:   EXPANDING FOLDERS AND SUB-FOLDERS

When there is a folder inside another folder, Windows shows a **+** symbol next to the parent folders icon. This means that we can expand the folder to show its contents.

Indicates more sub-folders to expand

When we click on the **+** we can see the sub-folders

As we add more folders and sub-folders Windows builds a "tree-like" structure which we can expand, using the **+** to open the folders as we need them.

This is like opening the drawers of our filing cabinet.

Exercise
Create subfolders inside our *Documents* folder for:

Marketing, **Administration**, **Accounts**, **Sales,** and **Travel**

The results should look like this:

LESSON 2.3.7:   NAVIGATING DRIVES, FOLDERS AND SUB-FOLDERS

We can open and close folders easily either by expanding them by clicking on the **+** symbol or by double clicking on the folder to open it up. Both achieve the same results.

We can choose the drive or the folder to move to immediately by selecting the drive from the drop-down menu at the top of the Explorer window.

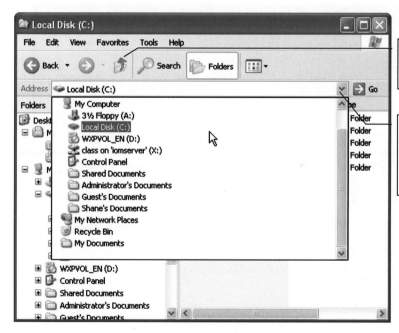

Use the "Up" tool to move to the next level in the folder tree

Clicking here quickly reveals the drives and folders available. Selecting the drive immediately moves us to that location.

If we want to move back from the **Documents** folder into the **C** drive – we can simply use the "up" tool on the toolbar.

This is a very useful button for navigating through our files and folders.

Note: Creating and naming folders is a very important part of file management. All applications will use this filing system. When we study *Module 3 - Word, Module 4 - Excel, Module 5 -Access and Module 6 – PowerPoint,* we will be constantly referring to saving files in particular drives and folders.

Take note of this section, as we may need to refer back to it during our study.

LESSON 2.3.8:   MOVING OR COPYING FOLDERS AND FILES

Sometimes we will need to move folders and files to another folder or to another drive. Windows Explorer makes this easy by allowing us to *Cut and Paste* files and folders between drives and other folders.

Let's move the *Travel.txt* document from the *Travel* folder into the *Accounts* folder.

❑   Open Windows Explorer

❑   Select the file or folder to move. In this case it is just one file – so click on the file called ***Travel***

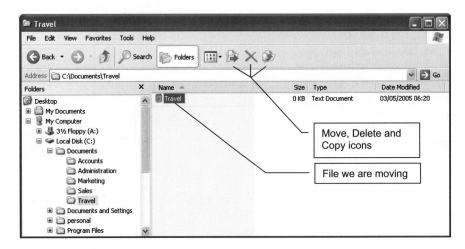

❑   Now press **Ctrl+X** or choose **Edit | Cut** if we are *moving the file*

❑   Click press **Ctrl+C** or press **Edit | Copy** if we are *copying the file*.

Next we select the folder we wish to move/copy the file or folder to. In this case it's the *Accounts* folder.

❏ Click on the *Accounts* folder in the drive list window (it is inside the *Documents* folder)

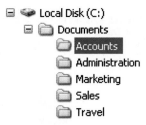

❏ Now click **Ctrl + V** or choose **Edit | Paste** to complete the process.

The file now appears in the *Accounts* folder and it will have been deleted from the *Travel* folder if we chose 'cut' or we will have created a copy if we chose 'copy'.

LESSON 2.3.9:   BACKING UP FILES ONTO A FLOPPY DISK OR OTHER DRIVE

To backup or copy files onto a floppy disk or another drive we follow the same steps as we did for moving or copying a file into a different folder - but we choose the *Floppy* disk or other drive as the destination.

❏ Open Windows Explorer

❏ Select the file(s) or folders to back up and press **Ctrl+C** or choose **Edit | Copy**.

❏ Next select the ![floppy icon] **A:** drive and press **Ctrl+V** or choose **Edit | Paste**.

Providing the files will fit on the floppy disk, and the floppy disk is formatted, the files will be copied onto a floppy disk.

LESSON 2.3.10: DELETING A FOLDER OR FILE

Deleting a folder or file removes it from the drive.

Let's delete the *Travel* folder:

❏ Open Windows Explorer and select the file or folder to delete. If we select a folder, the folder **and its contents** will be deleted. We'll select the *Travel* folder.

❏ Press the **Delete** key on the keyboard or press the ✕ icon if it is visible on the toolbar.

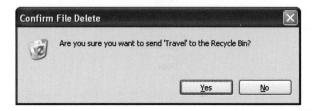

Deleted files usually go to the *Recycle Bin* prior to being completely deleted, but don't count on this as some machines are configured to completely delete the file (particularly if it is a large file).

❏ Click **Yes** to confirm the deletion

The folder and its contents have now moved to the Recycle Bin and deleted.

LESSON 2.3.11: RECOVERING FILES FROM THE RECYCLE BIN

Occasionally, we will delete something in haste only to discover we need it back. The following technique may be able to help in these situations – but don't rely on it. Always create backups of your work in order to avoid disappointment later on!

If a file was recently deleted, it may still exist in the Recycle Bin. If it does we can recover it to its original location. Let's try that with our *Travel* folder.

   ❏   Select or open the *Recycle Bin* – it can be found in the Explorer side panel and on the Desktop

Recycle Bin

   ❏   If there is something contained in the bin the icon changes to show "paper" inside the bin.

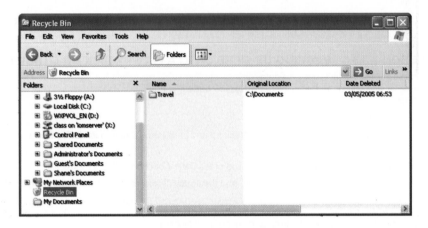

The contents of the *Recycle Bin* is like any other folder or directory. To recover a file from the Recycle Bin:

   ❏   Select the *Travel* folder from the Recycle Bin and choose **Restore** from the **File** menu.

The folder and its contents should now be restored to their original locations (in our case inside the *Documents* folder).

LESSON 2.3.12: EMPTYING THE RECYCLE BIN

To delete files permanently from the Recycle Bin:

   ❏   Open the *Recycle Bin* and choose the **File | Recycle Bin | Empty Recycle Bin**.

Note: Files deleted from the Recycle Bin can no longer be restored.

LESSON 2.3.13: WORKING WITH MULTIPLE FILES

When we need to select more than one file or folder at a time in order to **move**, **copy** or **delete** it, Windows gives us a handy shortcut to achieve this.

Let's suppose we want to **Delete** the following files:

> *Adobe Pagemaker*
> *Confirmation*
> *Dicey Rylies*
> *Timetable*

These appear here inside our *Administration* folder:

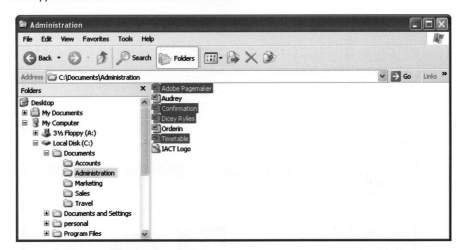

We need to *select* these files if we plan to move them, delete them or copy them to another location at the same time. Selecting one is easy – we simply click on it with the mouse. But to select more than one item we've got to use a different technique.

Selecting consecutive items from a list
If we are selecting consecutive items (items next to each other), we select the first file, hold down the **Shift** key and then select the last file. The selection increases to include all the items up to and including the last item selected.

Selecting non-consecutive items from a list
If we are selecting non-consecutive files from a list, we hold down the Ctrl key and select the items by clicking with the mouse.

We can use these two techniques in combination to great effect.

This technique should work with all list boxes that we meet in Windows.

Once the files are selected we can do what we want with them by following the techniques we met earlier.

> ❑ For example to **Delete** them simply press **Delete** on the keyboard or choose **File | Delete**.

LESSON 2.3.14:   VIEWING AND SORTING FILES

In *Windows Explorer*, when we have selected a folder, we will see the files in that folder listed. This list can be viewed and sorted in many different ways.

Viewing a file list:
Open Windows Explorer and choose a folder. On the right hand side of the Explorer window we will see the list of files and folders it contains.

The default view for any folder is the *List* view. To change the view used:

❑   Click on the **View** menu or click on the **Views** icon

There are **5** views to choose from:

Thumbnails View

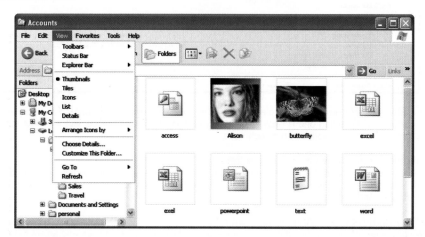

The *Thumbnails View* of a folder shows us a large icon (or thumbnail) representing the type of file displayed or if possible it will show a preview of the document or image. Notice here the file called *Alison* and *butterfly* show a preview of the content of the file. This view is particularly useful if previewing a folder full of images.

Tiles View

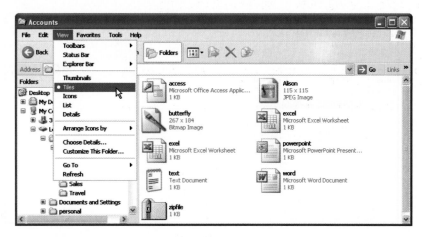

The *Tiles View* shows an icon for each file type along with a description of the type of file represented and the size or dimensions of the file. This view is useful for looking at a summary of the information for all files in a particular directory.

Icons View

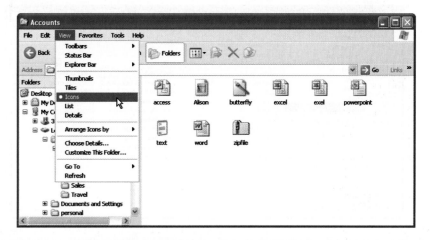

The *Icons View* shows an icon for each file type arranged side by side in a window. This view is useful for selecting or moving files between folders.

List View

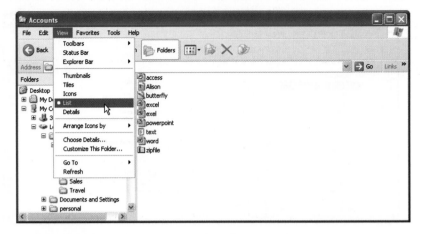

The *List View* provides us with a very similar view to the icons view but is more suitable if there are a large number of files or folders to view as the icons are smaller.

Details View

The *Details View* provides us with additional information about the files and folders we are viewing.

By default the details view shows us the:

- ❑ File Name, Size and Type
- ❑ The Date and time the file was last modified

LESSON 2.3.15: SORTING A FILE LIST IN THE EXPLORER WINDOW

We can *sort* the contents of the file list by clicking on the column headings at the top of the window. Clicking on a column rearranges the contents of the file list to be sorted by that column. Clicking on the column again sorts by the same column – but this time in reverse order.

An upward and downward arrow indicates that the column is being sorted in *Ascending* or *Descending* order respectively.

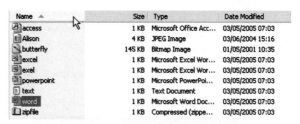

*File list sorted in **Ascending** order by file **name***

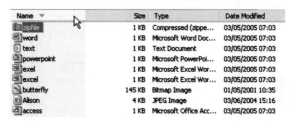

*File list sorted in **Descending** order by file **name***

Notice the upward and downward pointing arrows in the above images indicate *Ascending* or *Descending* order.

We can sort by any of the column headings in the file viewer. Below we can see the same list of files this time sorted by **file type** – this has the effect of *grouping* the same types of files together.

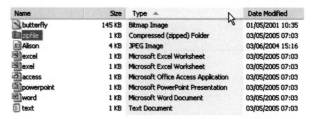

*File list sorted in **Ascending** order by file **type***

LESSON 2.3.16: FILE ATTRIBUTES

All files have an associated set of attributes that determine some of the things we can do with the file. These attributes are set by programs or they can be changed manually from within Windows Explorer.

- ❑ All files have the following attributes:
    - ○ A – Archive
    - ○ R – Read Only
    - ○ H – Hidden
    - ○ C – Compressed

It is sometimes useful to be able to change the attributes of a file.

Let's make a file **Read Only** so that it cannot be accidentally overwritten.

- ❑ Open Windows Explorer and select the file and choose **File | Properties**.

From Properties window we can make the file Read-only to prevent accidental modification of the file.

- ❑ Click the **Read-only** check box and press **OK**.

Now if we try to overwrite or edit the file Windows will tell us that the file is **Read only** and won't allow us to change it.

Note: The *Read-only* attribute does not prevent us from Deleting a file – only from overwriting it.

LESSON 2.3.17: FORMATTING A DRIVE

Before we can use a floppy disk or other drive it must first be formatted. When we buy floppies they are mostly pre-formatted to use on a PC however there are occasions when we will want to reformat a drive to completely erase it and prepare it for use.

To format a floppy disk (or other drive):

❑ Place the floppy disk into the disk drive ensuring the right-protection tab is turned off (*see page 55 for the location of the right-protection tab on a floppy disk*)

❑ Select the drive letter (**A:** in the case of floppy disks) from Windows Explorer

 3½ Floppy (A:)

❑ If the device is already formatted right click on the disk icon and choose **Format**

or

❑ If the disk has never been formatted Windows will prompt us to format the disk.

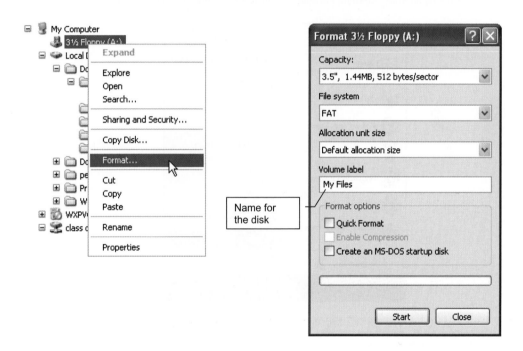

Give the disk a name or *label* – this will help identify it whenever it is placed into the computer.

❑ Click **Start** to format the disk.

If the disk is not damaged it will take about one minute to format. We can tick **Quick Format** to quickly erase and format a disk that has been previously formatted.

NOTE: Formatting a drive completely erases everything on it! Do NOT format a drive that we need to use again as this cannot be undone! Our hard-disks will usually already be correctly formatted.

LESSON 2.3.18:   SEARCHING FOR FILES OR FOLDERS

Although it shouldn't happen too often – occasionally we'll misplace a file or need to find an old version of a document that's been misplaced or wrongly named.

Windows provides a powerful (but processing intensive) tool to help us locate missing files based on:

❑   The date the file was created or last changed

❑   The type, name or size of the file

It also searches any other file attributes we wish to search with and any combination of these options.

Let's suppose we are searching for a file called *Audrey* and we don't know where we put it.

Start the *Search* program by:

❑   Clicking on **Start | Search | For Files or Folders…** or choose **Start | Search**

Note: Finding files is convenient but very processing intensive – and usually takes longer than expected. It is far better to have the files correctly saved into their right folders than to use this technique all the time.

The search assistant will appear by default:

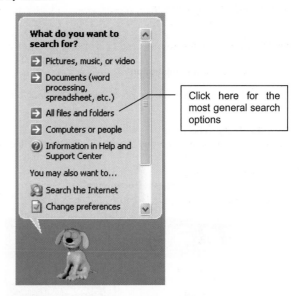

Click here for the most general search options

The search assistant allows us to search for specific items – such as pictures or videos, Spreadsheets or Word documents. If we know the type of file we are looking for this can be very helpful. If however we are looking for files just based on the file *name* or the *date* it was created – we need to choose the **All files and folders** option. This is the most flexible search option available.

To start the search:

❑ Click on **All files and folders** and the following window will appear:

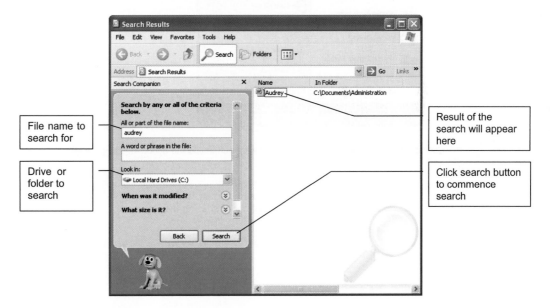

File name to search for

Drive or folder to search

Result of the search will appear here

Click search button to commence search

❑ Type the name of the file to search for into the *name* box. If we only know part of the name we type as much of the name as we are sure of and end with an asterix *

For example to search for all files that begin with **AUD** use **AUD*** as the search criteria (this is known as a *wildcard* search)

❑ Help Windows by choosing the drive that contains the file. Choose *Local Hard Drives* to search all local drives.

If Windows can find a file matching our search criteria it will appear in a list below. Our file was found in:

C:\Documents\Administration

This is a Word document and we can open it directly by *Double-Clicking* on the file name with the left mouse button.

Finding Recently used files

Windows keeps a list of *recently used files* that we can call up to quickly access a file we were working on recently. To view this list:

❑ Go to **Start | My Recent Documents**.

A flyout list will appear.

❑ Click on the file name to be opened and it will open inside the associated application.

Note: Once the recently used file list becomes full the oldest item in the list will be replaced with the second oldest and so on. The recently used file list is also specific to the currently logged on user and won't appear the same for other users sharing the computer.

LESSON 2.3.19: CREATING A SHORTCUT TO A FILE

In this lesson we will learn how to create *shortcuts* to particular programs or files. Shortcuts provide a fast way to open programs and files that we use frequently. Shortcuts are often placed on our Desktop for easy access, but can be placed elsewhere.

Let's create a shortcut on our Desktop for an image file.

❑   Press the **Right** mouse button whilst on the Desktop or right mouse click on a drive or folder name.

❑   Choose **New**, then click on **Shortcut**

❑   This will start up the shortcut wizard. Click on the **Browse** button to find the files or program file that we need to build a shortcut to.

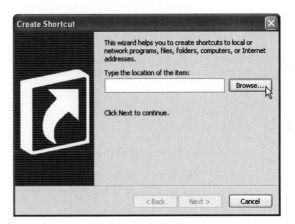

❑   Navigate to the file or program file. For this example, we are going to navigate to **"C:\Documents\IACT Logo.bmp"** which is a graphic image.

Path for file for which we are creating a shortcut

❑   Click **Next** and type in a name for the shortcut so that we will recognize it as a link to the logo.

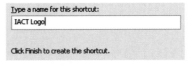

❑   Click **Finish**.

The *IACT Logo* will now appear on our Desktop.

IACT Logo

Notice the right-pointing arrow – this indicates that the icon is *shortcut*.

Note: Shortcuts are "links" to files or folders – deleting a shortcut does not delete the file or folder – similarly copying a shortcut is not the same as copying the file or folder!

LESSON 2.3.20:   SELECTING AND MOVING ICONS AROUND THE DESKTOP

To move items around the Desktop, we can simply click on the icon, hold down the mouse and drag the icon from one place and drop it in another.

For example to move the **Internet Explorer** icon click and hold the left mouse button on the *Internet Explorer* icon and drag it to its new location.

When we release the mouse button the icon will move to its new location. We can use this technique to drag and drop icons from the Start menu onto the Desktop and vice versa.

Another way of moving all the icons on the Desktop is to right mouse click on the Desktop and choose **Arrange Icons By**. This allows us to arrange all the icons on the Desktop by *size*, *name* and *type*.

EXERCISES TO PROVE YOU KNOW

1. What are each of the following storage devices called, what is their *typical* storage capacity and what are they usually used for?

Name:			
Capacity:			
Use:			

2. Create the following folder structure on the **C:** drive:

```
□ 💿 Local Disk (C:)
  □ 📁 content
    □ 📁 2003
      □ 📁 Admin
            📁 Holidays
            📁 Policies
            📁 Recruit
            📁 Staff
      □ 📁 Databases
            📁 IT Companies
            📁 Recruit
            📁 Top Companies
      □ 📁 Marketing
            📁 Press
            📁 Radio
            📁 TV
      □ 📁 Sales
            📁 Targets
            📁 Teams
      📁 2004
```

3. Rename the **Press** folder created above to **Magazines**

4. Move the **Policies** folder inside the **Staff** folder. Move the **Teams** folder inside the **Targets** folder

5. Delete the **Recruit** folder.

6. Create two new folders inside **Radio** called **98FM** and **Radio 1**

7. Why might we format a floppy disk?

    a. To erase everything that is on it.

    b. To prepare it for saving information.

    c. To protect it from erasure.

    d. To speed up access to information stored on it

8. What is the difference between a *file shortcut* and the file itself?

9. Fill in the *File type* and usual *extension* represented by each of the following icons:

Icon	File Type	Extension	Icon	File Type	Extension

5. How many folders are showing in this image of the **C:** drive?

6. Locate all files on the PC:

a) Created in the last week.

b) Starting with the letter **Y**

7. Create a shortcut to the Calculator on your Desktop.

SECTION 2.4:   WINDOWS CONTROL PANEL

Windows is a powerful *Operating System* with many settings and options that can be changed. Windows allow us to change the configuration and setup of our PC through the **Control Panel**. In this section we will learn how to:

❑   Determine the hardware configuration of our PC

❑   Change the look of our Desktop and Windows environment

❑   Install and remove software from our PC

❑   Work with printers

❑   Get help when using Windows

LESSON 2.4.1:   OPENING THE CONTROL PANEL

The Control Panel can be accessed from the **Start** menu.

❑   Choose **Start | Control Panel**

The Windows XP Control Panel looks like this:

The Control Panel is split into different categories that help us determine what we wish to do. Clicking on the category name expands those settings.

LESSON 2.4.2: GETTING BASIC INFORMATION ABOUT OUR PC

We can check the configuration of our PC and perform other maintenance tasks from the *Performance and Maintenance* options in the Control Panel.

❑ Click on the **Performance and Maintenance** settings in the Control Panel

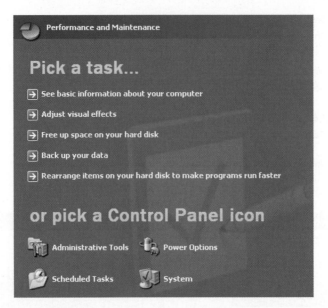

Once selected we can see a task list that gives us shortcuts to common tasks we might perform with tools in the performance and maintenance category. These are like "wizards" and assist us in getting the information we want or in carrying out the tasks we need.

Clicking on the first option **"See basic information about your computer"** or clicking on the **System** icon displays the system properties of our computer. From here we can tell the version of the operating system that we are using, our computers processor and the amount of RAM we have available to us:

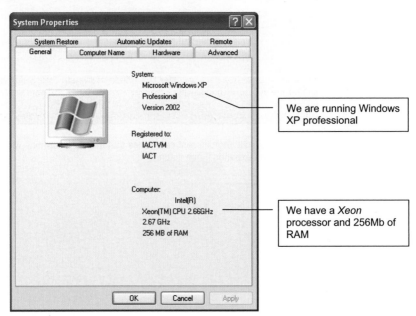

From this screen we can determine how much memory (RAM) we have, what processor we have, what Operating System we are using (Windows XP). This can be helpful for diagnostic purposes. The other tabs in this window give us additional information and settings about our computer.

Experiment with the other tasks in this category to see what jobs they perform.

LESSON 2.4.3: CHANGING THE SYSTEM DATE AND TIME

All computers have a built-in clock. This clock should be set to the correct date and time as it is used by the system when writing files and for other purposes. Once set the computer's clock should keep track of the time very accurately unless the computer is turned off for a prolonged period.

To change the system date and time click on the **"Date, Time, Language and Regional Settings"** option in the Control Panel or double-click on the clock in the system tray.

System time

The system calendar and clock will then appear:

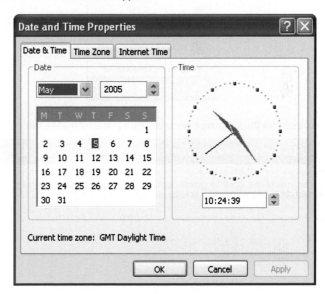

Changing the time and date here will alter the Windows system time which is used when saving files and whenever the system needs to check the date or time for a particular task.

We can also change our *time zone* which will affect how Windows updates the clock in the spring and autumn months.

Setting the input language used by Windows

Windows runs in practically every language in nearly every country throughout the World. Different countries – even those speaking the same languages often have 'regional' differences – for example in the UK we are usually using the £ symbol, in the US we'll use the $ symbol in Ireland we'll use the € symbol. In the UK we'll spell colour – 'colour' in the US the spelling is 'color'. These differences often change the way our keyboards, dates and other settings are interpreted by programs running in Windows.

We may need to alter the regional settings used by Windows – and helpfully there is a quick and easy way to this using the Language bar.

The Language Bar can be accessed from the bottom right-hand corner of the Windows Taskbar.

Click here to
change the input
language settings

To change the input language for Windows click on the Language Bar icon and choose from the list of available languages.

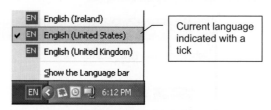

Current language
indicated with a
tick

❑   Choose **Show the Language bar** to display a pop up menu like this

From here we can adjust the input language for our keyboard, control the speech input options (that allow us to actually *talk* to our PC!) and get help.

LESSON 2.4.4:   CHANGING THE MOUSE 'ORIENTATION' AND SPEED

Left handed computer users often reverse the behaviour of the left and right mouse buttons.

❑   Choose "**Printers and Other Hardware**" from the Control Panel and **double-click** on the **Mouse** icon

To switch the left and right button behaviour click here

Test double-click folder

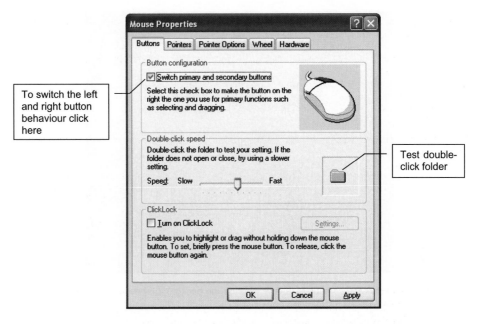

We can also adjust the **double-click** speed from the Mouse Properties window and we can test the double-click speed by double-clicking on the sample folder within the mouse window.

❑   To adjust the mouse speed click on the **Pointer Options** tab and drag the mouse speed slider.

LESSON 2.4.5:   MODIFYING THE APPEARANCE OF OUR DESKTOP

We can easily change the "look and feel" of Windows by altering its colours, fonts and background images. To change the settings of Windows we need to open the Control Panel.

    ❑   Choose **Start | Control Panel** and click on **Appearances and Themes**

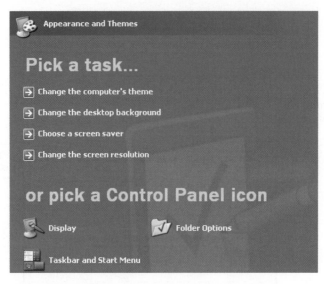

From here we can alter the computer's theme, change the background image of our Desktop, change our screen saver and modify the screen's *resolution*.

    ❑   Click the **Display** icon to bring up the **Display Properties** window or click on the **Change the computer's theme** task.

The Display Properties window will appear:

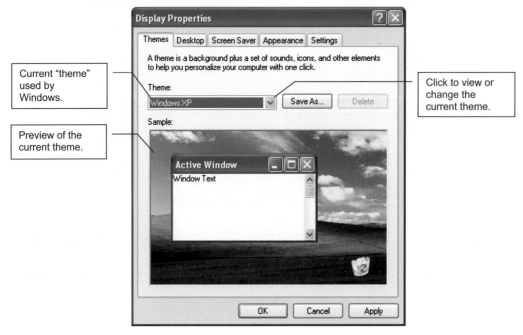

Microsoft have created a number of built in **Themes** for Windows that can completely change the look and feel of our Desktop – and we can also create and modify our own themes. The built in themes alter the Desktop image as well as the colours and the style of icons that Windows uses. Compare these two Desktops that use two different themes on the same computer – they look completely different but the computer works the same way as before:

The default Windows XP Theme

Modified Windows XP Theme (different wallpaper)

Modifying the appearance of our computer's Desktop and interface can be fun – and we can always return to the original "theme" by choosing **Windows XP** from the list of themes if we don't like the changes that we have made.

❑ To change the theme, open the **Display** option from the **Control Panel** and click on the **Theme** drop-down list.

❑ Click **Apply** to activate the theme.

Windows Classic - a special theme

Windows XP has a special built-in theme called **Windows Classic**. This is an important theme because it not only changes the Desktop image – it changes the way common features of Windows can appear when we use them. Switching the theme to **Windows Classic** forces Windows XP to look more like the earlier versions of Windows. This book is based on Windows XP and uses the default Windows XP theme. If your computer has the **Classic** theme the screen images will look different. Compare the two images below – the windows, Start menu and menu bars look quite different.

The default Windows XP Theme

*Windows **Classic** Theme*

We can quickly switch between these two themes using the **Display** options in the **Control Panel** as we saw earlier.

Changing the Desktop wallpaper

From within the **Display Properties** panel we can also change the Desktop wallpaper on our computer to any image we like - this includes changing to a photograph or a scanned image.

To change the Desktop wallpaper:

❑ Click on the **Desktop** tab and click on the different built in backgrounds

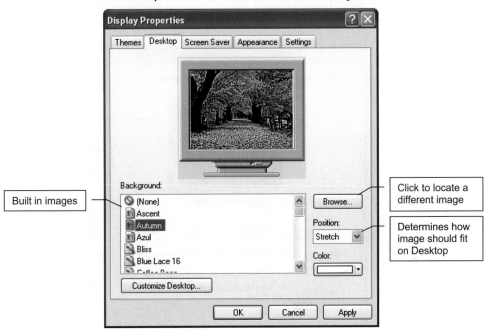

Built in images

Click to locate a different image

Determines how image should fit on Desktop

To choose a different image from another folder or directory we can click on the **Browse** button. Choosing the **Stretch** or **Tile** options we determine how the image will appear on our Desktop.

Stretching makes the image fit to the screen if it is too small for the Desktop and **Tiling** repeats the image.

Screen savers

The Windows screen saver appears when our computer has been out of use for a specified period of time. The idea of a "screen saver" is to protect our monitor from screen "burn" (which can occur if the same un-moving image remains on the screen for a prolonged period of time) and also to save energy or power when the computer is not being used.

❑ We can set or change the screen saver by selecting the *Screen Saver* tab in the Display Properties panel.

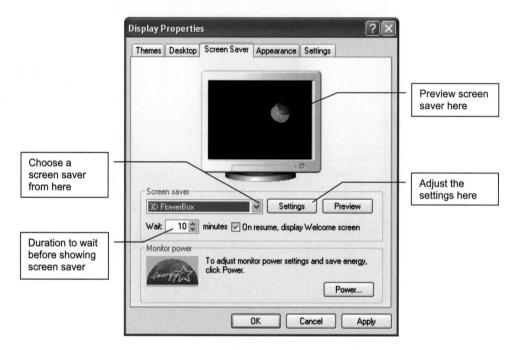

❑ Click on the **Screen saver** drop down arrow to change the choice of Screen Saver.

We can see a preview of the screen saver in the miniature monitor in the centre of the Display Properties window.

To alter the duration the computer waits before displaying the screen saver:

❑ Click on the *Wait* period text box and change the value (this is set to 10 minutes by default).

Changing the Appearance of Windows

The *Appearance* tab allows us to alter the style of Windows and buttons and the colour scheme used by the current theme. We can also adjust the **font size** of text used on our Desktop.

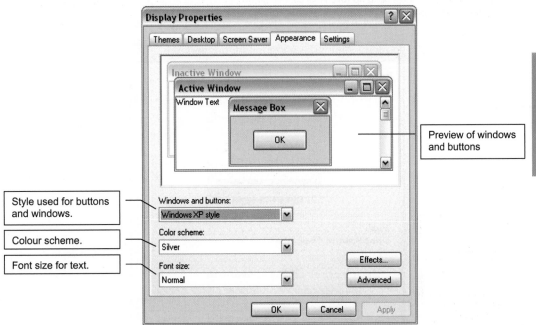

Style used for buttons and windows.

Colour scheme.

Font size for text.

Preview of windows and buttons

Experiment with the different styles for buttons and windows to determine the style that you prefer.

Changing the screen Resolution

The screen resolution is the number of "dots" used to make up our Windows Desktop. Most computers have a screen resolution of 1024 x 768 pixels – but this resolution is dependent on the computer's graphics card and the monitor to which it is connected.

We can alter the "resolution" that we display our Desktop in from the **Settings** menu.

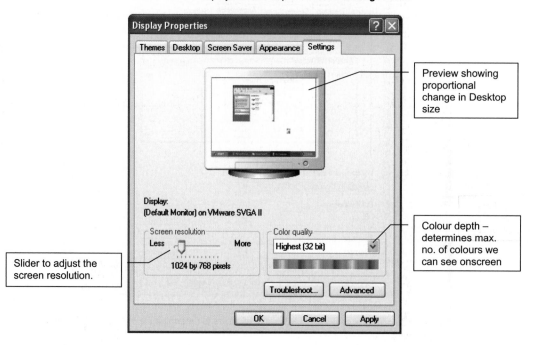

Preview showing proportional change in Desktop size

Slider to adjust the screen resolution.

Colour depth – determines max. no. of colours we can see onscreen

When we press **Apply** Windows will make the necessary changes to the Desktop resolution. Sometimes when we adjust the screen resolution the picture can become fuzzy or disappear. To prevent this becoming a problem Windows always displays the following window just after the changes are made:

Note: If we don't press the **Yes** button within 15 seconds Windows will put the screen settings back to the way they were. So if a problem arises – remain calm – the screen should be restored to normal after a few seconds.

This concludes our overview of the Windows Desktop settings – there are many different settings that we can change – and they can make a big difference to how our computer looks and feels.

LESSON 2.4.6: INSTALLING / UNINSTALLING SOFTWARE

When we buy or download software onto our computer it has to be *installed* before we can use it. Similarly we no longer want to use software installed on our PCs we have to be able to remove or un-install it.

To install or uninstall a program we follow these steps:

- ❑ Firstly close down all open files and applications – leaving programs running can affect the success of the installation
- ❑ Go to **Start | Control Panel**
- ❑ Click on **Add or Remove Programs**

We should now see a screen something like this:

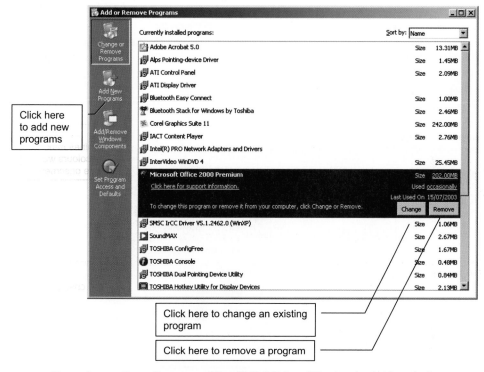

New software will usually come on CD or DVD-ROM or will be downloaded from the Internet.

To **Add or Install** software:

- ❑ Insert the CD/DVD-ROM into the drive
- ❑ Press the **Add New Programs** button and follow the on-screen instructions.

To **Remove or Uninstall** software:

- ❑ Click **Change or Remove programs**
- ❑ Locate the program from the list of installed software and click **Remove**. Windows will uninstall the software after asking for confirmation.

LESSON 2.4.7:   PRINTERS

Most computers have a printer attached to them directly or available to them through a network. There is nothing quite as satisfying as seeing work that we have created on the computer finally in a printed format - it just does not seem the same on screen. In this lesson we will learn how to work with printers in Windows.

Adding a new printer

If we have a new printer to install it won't work until we properly install the *drivers* for it. A printer's *driver* tells Windows how to prepare output for the printer correctly and what features the printer supports (*colour, envelopes, duplexing* etc.).

To install a printer directly connected to our computer:

❑   Check the printer is properly connected and switched on (review *Lesson 1.2.4:Connecting your PC to its devices or peripherals* on *page* 12)

❑   Insert the Floppy disk or CD/DVD ROM that came with the printer

The installation software should autorun. If it does not – run the program called **SETUP** located on the disk or CD/DVD-ROM

❑   Follow the on-screen instructions.

When setup has completed it will ask us if would like to print a test page.

❑   Click **YES** to test the printer.

Viewing available printers

Windows works with all types of printers ranging from *Laser Printers* right up to full scale *Plotters*.

Printer settings can be viewed by choose **Start | Printers and Faxes**

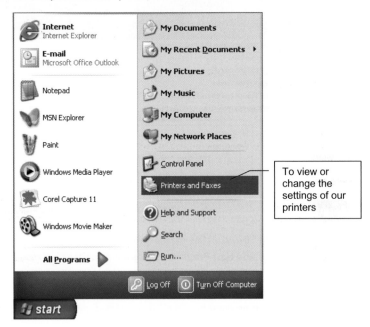

Once the **Printers and Faxes** window opens, we have access to all the printers available from this computer.

The computer above has three printers connected:

> HP Color LaserJet 5m (default printer)
> HP LaserJet 4050

And a
> HP ColorLaserjet 4650

Viewing the status of a print job
Once we have sent a document to print we can view its progress by double clicking on the printer in this window. From here we can see our print jobs status.

Here are the settings for a printer called **HP Color LaserJet 5m:**

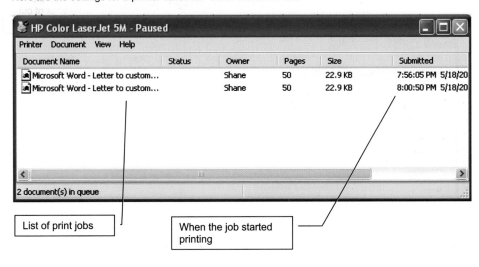

List of print jobs

When the job started printing

Viewing the status of a print job

When we are printing a large print job – it is useful to be able to see how far our print job has progressed.

Document Name	Status	Owner	Pages	Size
Microsoft Word - Letter to custom...		Shane	50	150KB / 450KB
Microsoft Word - Letter to custom...		Shane	50	22.9 KB

150KB of 450KB has printed about 33% of the print job has finished.

From the above view we can see the progress made in printing the documents from the *size* field. The first document is approximately 1/3 printed.

Pausing, Deleting and Restarting a print job

From this Printer menu we can *pause* the print job. We might pause a print job if we were printing on the wrong paper for example and wanted to stop the printer to reload the print tray. We can later *resume* printing to carry on printing from that point onwards.

We can also *delete* a print job to stop it printing.

    ❑   To delete the print job choose **Document | Delete**

To *restart* a print job:

    ❑   Choose **Document | Restart**.

Setting the default printer

Where there are several printers installed on the computer we can set the **Default** printer to be the printer that is used normally for print jobs, so for example, if we click on the *Print* icon on the standard toolbar in Word, the document gets sent to the default printer. We will see this later in *Module 3 – Word Processing*.

To set a printer to be the default:

    ❑   Open the Printer settings window, by going to the **Start | Printers and Faxes**

    ❑   Double click on the printer that we wish to be the default printer

    ❑   Click on the **Printer** menu and choose **Set As Default Printer**

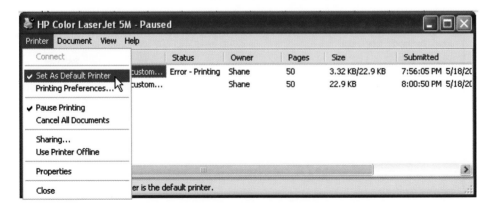

LESSON 2.4.8: GETTING HELP

Throughout this book we will be learning about different applications or programs that we can use on a daily basis. These programs – like *Word* and *Excel* usually have built in *help* that we can reference. The idea of these help files is that if, while using a program, we get stuck and need help, we can access the help files and follow the instructions. Windows XP has made the built in help system much easier to use and can be quite useful in many situations.

Help files can be displayed in two ways – we can press function key **F1** or we can use the **Help** option in the menu. Press **Start | Help** to display Windows help.

A window like the one below will appear. We can click on any of the text links or icons to display more information about a particular topic. Windows help is like browsing a web page.

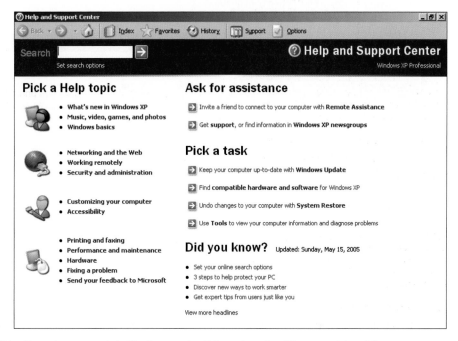

We will see how to use help files in more detail throughout the different modules of the course.

EXERCISES TO PROVE YOU KNOW

1. Determine the amount of *RAM* and the CPU (processor) used in your PC

2. What version of Windows is the PC running?

3. Change the Desktop image on your PC to another image or photo you may have

4. Adjust the timing interval for the screen-saver so that it appears every 30 minutes.

5. Using the Windows clock tool what is the earliest date we can set the Windows date to? What is the latest year?

6. How do you think Windows keeps an accurate measure of time even when the PC is powered off? Search the web for the answer or ask at your computer store.

7. Below is a snap shot from a print queue.

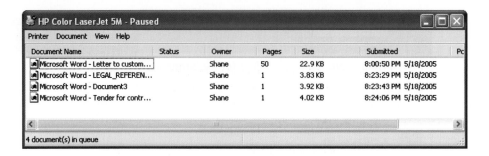

   a) How many documents are currently printing?

   b) What is the size of the largest print job?

SECTION 2.5: NOTEPAD

Notepad is a useful tool for creating text files. For the ICDL/ECDL exam we will occasionally need to create a text file - and Notepad is the ideal tool to use.

In this section, we will learn how to:

- ❑ Start Notepad
- ❑ Save a Notepad file
- ❑ Re-open that file
- ❑ Configure page setup for printing the file

LESSON 2.5.1: STARTING NOTEPAD

To start Notepad:

- ❑ Click on the **Start** button and choose **All Programs | Accessories**
- ❑ Of the list available in accessories, click on **Notepad**

or

- ❑ Click on **Start** Button choose **Run** and type **Notepad** and press **OK**

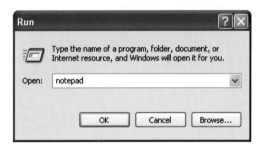

Notepad is a basic text editor. Let's create a text file:

- ❑ Type some text into the window.

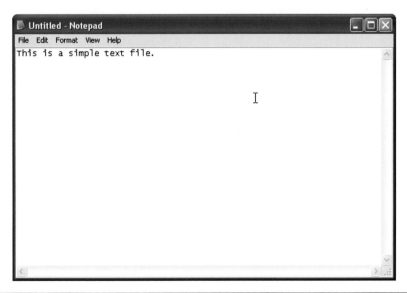

LESSON 2.5.2: SAVING A FILE FROM NOTEPAD

We are going to save this file onto our **C:** drive into the **My Documents** folder:

❑ Go to the **File** menu and Choose **Save As**

The following dialog will appear showing the list of files and folders on the current drive. Here we can see the **My Documents** folder:

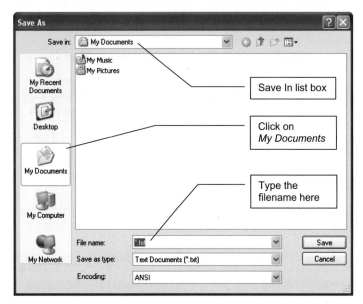

If we want to save our work on a different drive click on the drop down arrow in the **Save in:** list box. To save the file onto a *Floppy* disk choose the **A:** drive from the list of available drives.

❑ Locate the **My Documents** folder from the **Save in** drop down list.

Next we must give the file a name:

❑ Click into the *File name* text box and type "**test**"
❑ Press the **Save** button.

The file is now saved and we could view it from Windows Explorer:

❑   We have now saved the file.

If we close *Notepad* we'll be able to recover the file whenever we need it by re-opening it.

Closing the Notepad Application
To close the Notepad application:

❑   Choose **File | Exit**

Getting Help
To get help at any time from within an application press the **F1** key or choose **Help Topics** from the **Help** menu. Using one applications help feature is very similar to using another's. *See page 257* for details on using Word's help feature.

LESSON 2.5.3:   OPENING A NOTEPAD FILE

Let's restart *Notepad* and retrieve the file we just saved.

❑   Open **Notepad**

After a few seconds Notepad will appear:

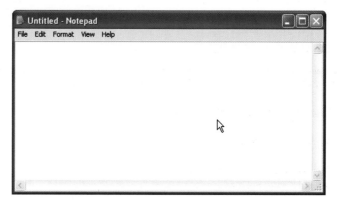

❑ From the **File** menu choose **Open**

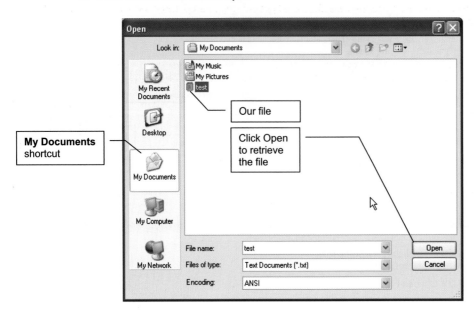

My Documents
shortcut

Our file

Click Open
to retrieve
the file

Our file lives in the *My Documents* folder.

❑ Locate the **My Documents** folder by clicking on the **Save in: List box** drop down list or by choosing **My Documents** from the list of shortcuts.

Our file will appear in the list of files:

❑ Click on the file **test.txt** and choose **Open**

The file will now appear in the Notepad window.

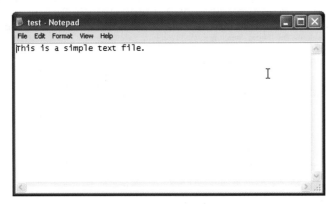

As an exercise: re-save the file back onto a floppy disk.

LESSON 2.5.4: PAGE SETUP AND PRINTING

Before printing our document we should adjust our page setup and orientation. To change the page print options from within Notepad:

❑ Choose **File | Page Setup**

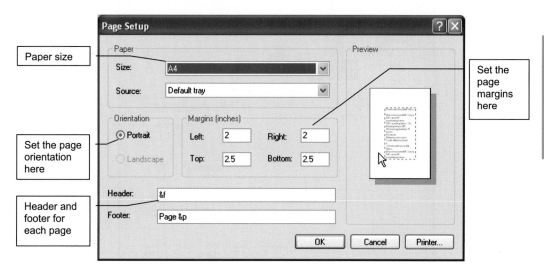

Page setup options:

❑ We can adjust the paper *size* from the size drop-down list. Our normal paper size is **A4** but other sizes such as **A3** and **DL** are common. **A3** is *twice* **A4** in size, **A2** is *twice* **A3** in size. Similarly **A5** is *half* **A4** in size and **A6** is half **A5** in size. **DL** is standard envelope size.

❑ We can adjust the *margins* around each page by setting the *top, bottom, left* and *right* margin values. The values shown in the above window are measured in inches. These settings will leave a blank border of 2" on the left and right of the page and a 2.5" border at the top and bottom of the page.

❑ We can also add a *header* and *footer* to each page that will appear on every page in the document. The default footer is shown as **&f** – representing the *filename* and the default footer is **Page &p** representing the current *page number*. We can change the header and footer here if required perhaps adding a reference number or the date.

❑ We can also adjust the page *orientation* from this window. Choose a landscape page if the page width or image will fit better with this orientation.

Portrait layout of page   Landscape layout of page

❑ Choose **OK** to confirm the changes to the page setup.

Once we have adjusted the page setup we can *print* our document.

❑ To print the document we choose **File | Print**

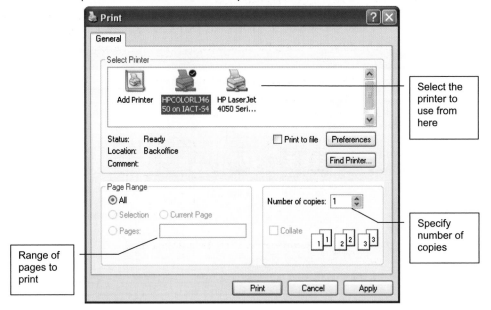

Select the printer to use from here

Range of pages to print

Specify number of copies

❑ Select the printer to print to from the *select printer* region.

The default printer is indicated with a ● tick symbol.

❑ Specify the number of copies to print by adjusting the number of copies:

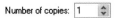

❑ Specify the range of pages to print by entering a starting and ending page into the *Pages* text box. To print just the current page tick **Current Page**. To print the selected text in the document click on **Pages** and enter the range of pages to print into the text box.

When all the settings are correct:

❑ To print the page click **Print**.

To print from any application in Windows - including *Word, Excel, PowerPoint and Access* we follow much the same procedures.

EXERCISES TO PROVE YOU KNOW

1. Open Notepad and type the following text:

   The third tab in the setup dialog box is headers and footers. Headers and footers are important as they allow us to number and identify pages when they are printed.

2. Save the file into the **C:\My Documents** folders and name it **Headers.txt**

3. Close Notepad

4. Re-open Notepad and open the file **Headers.txt** saved earlier

5. Print the file to any available printer.

6. What is the orientation of the following pages?

7. Rearrange the following paper sizes in order of physical SIZE:

   a) **A4**   b) **A5**   c) **A3**   d) **DL**

8. Which of these printers is the default printer?

| Acrobat Distiller | Acrobat PDFWriter | HP LaserJet 5/5M Pos... | Microsoft Office Doc... |

SECTION 2.6:   COMPRESSED FILES

A compressed file is a file that is considerably smaller than the original file (sometimes by as much as 10 times or more). We compress files to save space. By fitting more data into the same space we can send files faster or using fewer floppy disks (for example). Most of the files and programs that we download from the Internet are compressed. We can compress a number of separate files into one folder – which is useful if we want to keep these files together. This is extremely useful when it comes to sending multiple files by email – instead of having to attach each file separately, we could put all files into the one folder and then compress the folder which we could then attach and send by email.

The most popular file compression program for Windows is called *WinZip*. WinZip is freely available to download from www.winZip.com - a small registration fee is required but it is very valuable and useful 'utility' well worth having.

LESSON 2.6.1:   WINZIP

WinZip is a very useful utility and is regularly used on the Internet and when sending files using e-mail.

WinZip allows us to compress or squash many files (or even entire folders) into a single file called a ZIP file. As a result these files are much faster to send by e-mail or download from the Internet. As a ZIP file can contain whole folders of information it also means that only a single file needs to be sent when we want to send lots of files to someone by e-mail or using a floppy disk and this is much more convenient.

We can download a trial version of WinZip from www.winZip.com. Follow the links to download WinZip and then run the install program (to learn how to do this see *Section 7.4:Downloading files* on page *572*).

LESSON 2.6.2:   COMPRESSING FILES IN A FOLDER

Start WinZip –and the following window will appear:

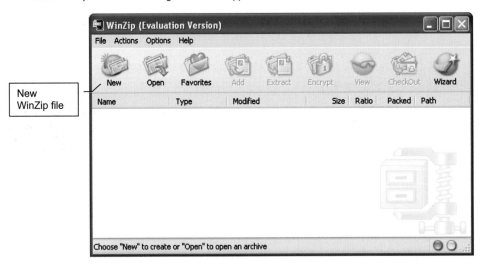

We are going to create a new ZIP file that contains a number of documents.

    ❑   Click on the **New** button.

WinZip asks us for a location to store the Zip file. We're going to save it to a folder called **c:\book_files** and call the Zip file **version1.Zip**

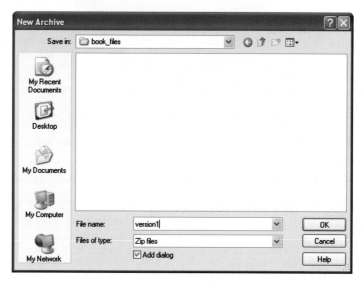

❑ Type the name for the Zip file into the *File name* box and click **OK**.

WinZip will now ask us for the files that we want to compress into the Zip file. We're going to include a number of Word documents.

❑ Select the files to include in the Zip file. We can add multiple files as well as files from more than one folder. Click **Add** to add the files to the Zip file.

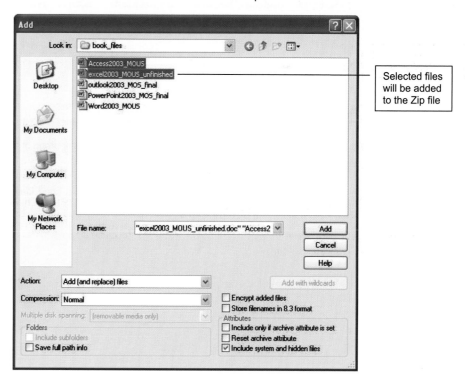

Selected files will be added to the Zip file

WinZip will now compress these files and add them to our Zip file.

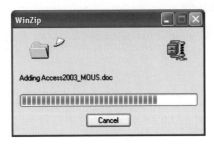

We can add as many files as we want to the Zip file. Once we have finished adding files we can close WinZip (choose **File | Exit**) and use it as we please

To learn how to e-mail the Zip file as an attachment see *Section 7.7:Attachments on page 598*

LESSON 2.6.3: OPENING A ZIP FILE (EXTRACTING FILES)

If we receive a Zip file by e-mail or in some other way we need to be able to extract the contents of the Zip file.

❑ Open the Zip file (by double-clicking it if it is an attachment) or from within WinZip by pressing **Open**. WinZip will then show us a list of files the Zip file contains:

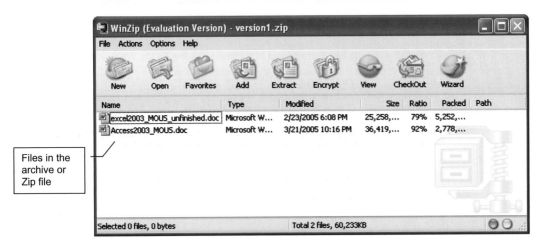

Files in the archive or Zip file

Extracting a file allows us to take out a file to save elsewhere. To *extract* a file or group of files:

❑ Select the file from the list and click on the **Extract** button.

WinZip will then ask where we want the extracted files to be placed. It is a good idea to create a **download** folder on your **C:** drive where you can place extracted files if there is nowhere obvious to place the extracted files - that way we can find them again.

❑ Choose the folder to extract the files into and press **Extract**

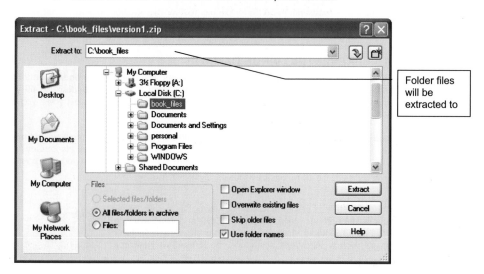

Folder files will be extracted to

Once the files are extracted we can quit WinZip and use the extracted files as normal.

EXERCISES TO PROVE YOU KNOW

1. Download and install the WinZip application if it is not already installed on your PC.
2. Create a new Zip file called **MyFiles.Zip**
3. Add the Notepad text file **Headers.txt** created earlier to the **MyFiles.Zip** file.
4. What is the difference in size between the original *headers.txt* file and the *MyFiles.Zip* file? Would you expect to see a larger difference if the file was bigger? Why?
5. Close **WinZip.**
6. Double-click the **MyFiles.Zip** file to re-open the archive inside WinZip.
7. Extract the *headers.txt* Notepad file back to the Desktop.

SECTION 2.7:   VIRUSES

We introduced *Computer Viruses* on Page 55 – please review this section to learn what damage Viruses can cause and how they spread onto your computer. In this section we will learn what we can do to help prevent a Virus getting onto our PCs and how we can remove a Virus if we become infected.

LESSON 2.7.1:   PREVENTING VIRUS DAMAGE

Viruses pose a REAL threat to your computer and our businesses. What would you do if all your PCs lost their data and you couldn't use any of them? What if you sent a Virus accidentally to all your customers, suppliers and friends? How much would it cost you? How much would it cost you if you lost all of your data and you could never recover it?

Until you have really been infected by a Virus you won't realise how bad they can be and you might treat them lightly. There are many "soft" Viruses that are only irritating but there also many very dangerous and destructive Viruses that will wipe out your entire systems faster than you can possibly imagine.

There are a number of anti-Virus products available. Most of these are better than the rather rudimentary products available within DOS and Windows. We recommend you to buy a reputable Virus checker from a major manufacturer such as *Symantec's Norton AntiVirus Toolkit* or the *MacAfree AntiVirus Toolkit.*

The most important thing to remember about a Virus checker is that it should be kept up to date. Most companies supply updates on a regular basis on CD-ROM or allow us to receive updates through the Internet automatically. Without updates anti-Virus software becomes redundant and useless.

We will look next at using *Norton AntiVirus*, which is one of the most popular Virus checking tools available. Norton AntiVirus is available online in trial format from **www.symantec.com**.

LESSON 2.7.2:   IDENTIFYING A VIRUS ON YOUR PC

So how do you know if you have a Virus? Well hopefully your Virus checking software will detect the Virus for you automatically and tell you that you have been infected. If however you don't have a Virus checker or the Virus checker needs updating you may not know until it's too late.

Some things to watch out for that *might* indicate that your PC is infected with a Virus:

- ❑   Your PC has started to Run very slowly
- ❑   Your Internet connection is extremely slow and nearly unusable
- ❑   Cutting and pasting does not work as you expect
- ❑   Programs that used to Work on your PC do not work any more or crash when they start
- ❑   Your keyboard or mouse does not respond correctly
- ❑   There is an unusual amount of disk activity when your computer should be doing nothing.
- ❑   You cannot login to your computer
- ❑   Someone you sent an e-mail to tells you that you sent them a Virus
- ❑   You received a message from the Virus telling you that your system is infected or your entire computer system is wiped.

LESSON 2.7.3: REMOVING VIRUSES

Viruses can be very painful to remove even if they are discovered early. The chances are some of your files will have to be permanently deleted and restored from a backup – if the backup is not infected itself.

If you have been infected with a Virus you should:

- ❑ Notify your IT manager or PC support company
- ❑ Consult your Virus protection manual for the procedures to follow for your Virus software
- ❑ Shut down or turn off your PC
- ❑ Disconnect the PC from the Network and the Internet
- ❑ Notify your colleagues – they are likely to be infected as well if they share files with you
- ❑ Buy an updated Virus checker or download one from the Internet
- ❑ Run the Virus checker on all the machines on your network only re-connecting them to the network when all Viruses are removed and Virus protection is installed on the PC.

LESSON 2.7.4: SCANNING FOR VIRUSES AND DISINFECTING FILES

Assuming a Virus checker is installed on our PC we can scan for Viruses. We will start up Norton's anti-Virus toolkit and scan for Viruses.

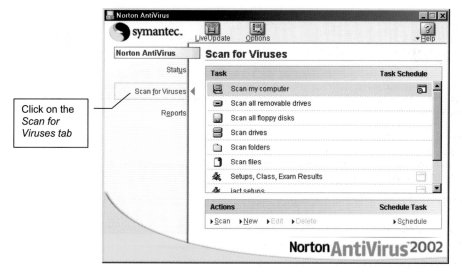

Using the Virus checker is much like using Windows Explorer. It will allow us to scan individual files, folders, hard disks or network drives.

- ❑ Select the drive to scan – if you are not sure which to scan choose "Scan all files" or "Scan my computer" and click on the Scan button.

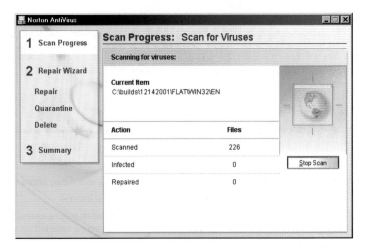

Norton's Anti-Virus software now starts scanning the drives connected to the computer. As it scans it records how many files it has found which are infected and how many it has been able to repair.

Hopefully the number repaired and infected are the same. However sometimes it may not be able to repair the file. In this case Norton places the files into a *Quarantine* where they can be inspected for possible later repair or disinfection (files infected with a Virus are said to be *Disinfected* once the Virus has been removed and the file repaired).

LESSON 2.7.5:   QUARANTINE

Files that couldn't be repaired or *Disinfected* but that are still infected should end up in *Quarantine*. It is possible that a later update to the Virus checker might be able to fix the problem and repair the file. Under **no circumstances** should the file be restored from Quarantine if it is infected – the risks of the Virus are far too great.

❑   To view the items in *Quarantine* click on the **Reports** button and click **View Report**

Any files in the Quarantine will appear in the list on the right hand side.

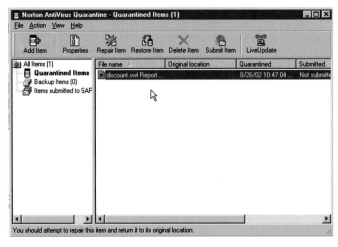

We can choose to permanently *delete*, attempt to *repair* or choose to submit the item for inspection as a potential new Virus. Norton will then attempt to repair the file and identify the Virus that is attached.

Updating the Virus software

Remember - Virus software is useless unless it is kept up to date. The **Live Update** button on the Norton AntiVirus toolbar will allow the Anti-Virus toolkit to update the program and Virus definitions over the Internet. Ensure that your Virus checker software is updated whenever new disks arrive or automatically over the Internet to protect your computer against the threat of Viruses.

EXERCISES TO PROVE YOU KNOW

1. Name three ways in which a Virus can infect a PC

2. Visit the website www.symantec.com and read the announcements section.

3. What might make us suspicious that our PC was infected with a Virus?

4. Outline the steps involved in identifying and removing a Virus from a PC

5. How frequently should we scan for Viruses?

6. Which of the following statements are TRUE?

    a) Viruses can infect PCs through the choice of bad (easy) passwords

    b) We should never open an attachment in our e-mail unless we are sure of the source of the attachment

    c) Downloading files from the Internet can infect our computer with Viruses.

    d) Viruses can infect my PC when it is turned off.

    e) If a file has been quarantined by our Virus checking software it is infected with a Virus

    f) If we leave a Virus-riddled PC alone for long enough it will cure itself.

SECTION 2.8:   EXAM OVERVIEW AND TIPS

In the File Management exam, Module 2, you will be asked to create a folder structure and to carry out various operations associated with manipulating files and folders within the folder structure.

The exam will be broken down into a sequence of 32 questions.

You will be given a floppy disk, it will have all the folders and files that you will need to answer the questions. Be sure to hand the disk up at the end of the exam.

Points to note:

- ❑   Time allowed: 45 minutes
- ❑   To pass you must get 24 marks out of a possible 32.

In this exam you will be asked to open an answer file. This is a Word document that you will type the answers into. It looks like this:

Candidate Identification :_____

Question No.	Response
1.	
2.	

You will need to be able to locate this answerfile.doc on the floppy disk, open it and type into it. Insert your candidate identification number at the top of the answer file. You will be asked to enter your answer beside the relevant question number.

It is important that you remember to save this file as you go along and at the end of the exam.

All of the topics covered in this Module could be asked in the exam.

For further tips on examinations visit **http://www.iactonline.com/ecdl**

Module 3
WORD PROCESSING

The complete IT training provider

MODULE 3: WORD PROCESSING

The invention of the typewriter made a tremendous difference to the way we produce documents. Prior to the typewriter everything was hand-written or painstakingly typeset by hand. With the invention of the typewriter – the quality of writing was no longer a problem – but early typewriters left a lot to be desired.

The traditional typewriter was invented by *Christopher Sholes* in 1874. His keyboard layout is rumoured to have been designed to *slow down* the typist. Early typewriters would jam regularly as the typist became more proficient – so **QWERTY** keyboards became the standard.

There are alternative layouts –**DVORAK** being the most well known which arranges the keys for comfort and speed of access – but it may be some time if ever before we see these in any kind of wide use.

QWERTY *Keyboard layout*

DVORAK *Keyboard layout*

Up until the 1980s producing letters and reports in companies hadn't really changed that much and typewriters (although now mainly electronic) were the norm. The biggest manufacturer of electronic typewriters was IBM. IBM brought out their first IBM PC – the forerunner of today's PCs in the early 1980's. One of the first programs written for the IBM was a word processor that allowed the PC connected to a printer to print documents. It had most of the features we have today – although it was crude by comparison.

Word processors provide two major advantages over typewriters:

1. An ability to *save* documents for later editing and retrieval means enormous savings in time and effort

2. *Advanced editing* – word processors allow us to edit whole paragraphs that can be moved and shuffled easily around a document.

Today *Microsoft Word* is the leading word processor followed by *Corel Word Perfect*. Both these programs support similar features and their latest incarnations even allow us to dictate text through a microphone!

NOTE: This is one of the most important modules of the ICDL/ECDL syllabus and also one of the longest. Master Word and the other modules will fall neatly into place.

SECTION 3.1:   INTRODUCTION TO WORD

Microsoft Word is a fantastic word processor and is now by far the most widely used word processor for Windows today. Mastering Word will help with using all the other programs that run on Windows.

In this section we will look at:

- ❑ Starting Microsoft Word
- ❑ Touring Word
- ❑ Typing text
- ❑ Working with menus
- ❑ The formatting toolbar
- ❑ Saving a document
- ❑ Exiting Word

LESSON 3.1.1:   STARTING MICROSOFT WORD

To start Word we need to go to:

- ❑ **Start** menu choose **All Programs** and choose **Microsoft Office** and click on **Microsoft Office Word 2003**

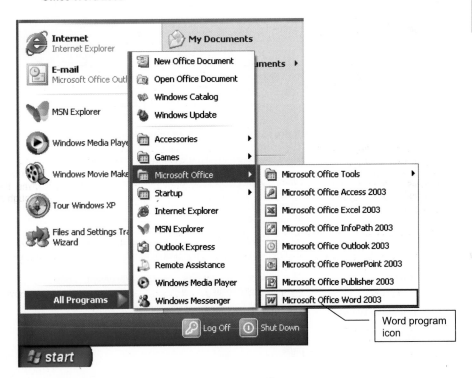

Word will start after a few moments and the opening screen will appear.

Touring Word

Now that we have successfully opened Word, we are now going to have a look at the main Word window.

Word opens with a blank document open on screen.

There are certain areas of this window that we need to be able to identify and use very well. Below is the basic Word window:

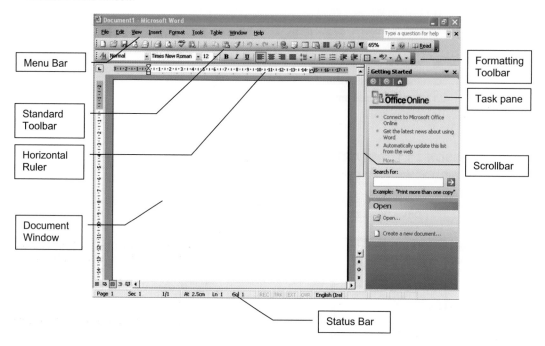

We need to be familiar with the location of each of these items on our screen:

MENU BAR	Gives us access to all the commands in Word
STANDARD TOOLBAR	Offers us quick access to frequently used commands /SHORTCUTS
FORMATTING TOOLBAR	Offers quick access to character and paragraph formatting features
TASK PANE	Provides tools for different tasks – the task pane changes depending on the task at hand.
RULER	Give the measurements of the document area currently being used
DOCUMENT WINDOW	This is where we type our text
VERTICAL SCROLL BAR	Allows us to scroll up and down a page or from page to page
STATUS BAR	Displays information about our document, such as the page number and the insertion point position.

LESSON 3.1.2:   CREATING A NEW DOCUMENT

We can open a new blank document from scratch or we can use one of the built in templates as a new document. Normally we would open the document using the new blank document option. Word comes supplied with several pre-designed templates and Wizards for many common tasks. When we create a new document we are presented with a list of all available templates and wizards.

- From the **File** menu choose **New**.

The *New Document* panel will appear.

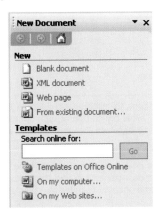

From the **New Document** panel we can choose to create a new document from either a *Blank Document, an XML document, a Web Page, from an existing document or* by using a *template* that is either on the computer or available on the Internet.

- ❑ To create a new blank document click on the *Blank Document* option

Alternatively we can open a new document using a built in template:

- ❑ Click on the **On my computer...** option from the **New Document** panel and the templates window will appear:

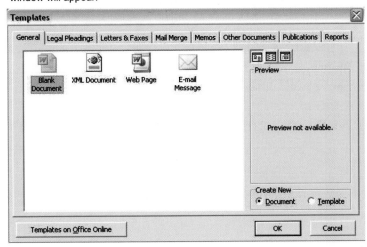

Now we can choose the tab that matches the type of document that we want to create.

- ❑ Choose the template and click **OK**

The document panel will automatically close after we have created our new document.

LESSON 3.1.3: INSERTING TEXT

Next we are going to type text into our document.

Typing with a word processor is similar to typing with a typewriter. One big difference is that with a word processor, we do **not** need to press the **Enter** key at the end of every line - the text automatically wraps to the next line as we write.

We only ever use the **Enter** key when we wish to create a new *paragraph*.

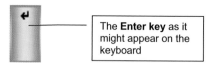

The **Enter key** as it might appear on the keyboard

We will type the following into Word:

I am writing these two paragraphs to test the text-wrapping feature that is automatically built into all word processors. This is my first paragraph completed and in order to create a new paragraph with a blank line between this one and the new one I need to press the Enter key twice.

This is paragraph two, so let's now revise how we got here. We just kept typing until we specifically wanted to create a new paragraph and then we pressed the Enter key twice, once to move to the next line and once more to leave a blank line.

NOTE: to create the new paragraph and to leave a blank line between the two paragraphs we need to press the Enter key twice.

When we've finished, the screen should look something like this:

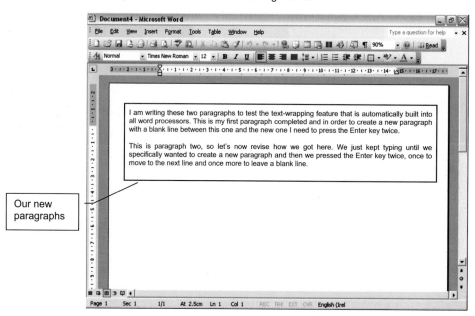

Our new paragraphs

Notice the blank line between the paragraphs created by the **Enter** or **Return** key.

LESSON 3.1.4: PRINTING AND PREVIEWING A DOCUMENT

Printing options are usually located in the **File** menu.

To Print our document

❑ Click on **File | Print**.

As well as printing the entire document - we can specify the range of pages to print – by entering the start and end pages – as well as specifying the number of copies we wish to print

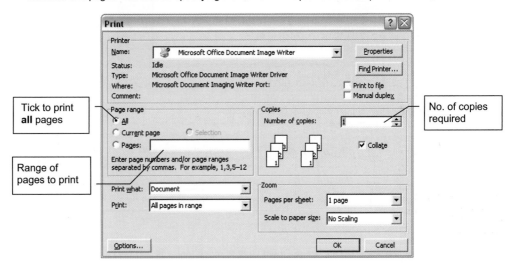

*The **Print** window*

Before printing the document ensure the printing defaults are correct and press **OK**.

Review *Lesson 2.5.4: Page setup and Printing on page 135* for more information on printing and page setup.

Previewing our document

We can also preview our document prior to printing it – that way we can check if the page breaks for the document are ok.

To preview the document:

- ❏ From the **File | Print Preview**

This will display the page as it will be printed:

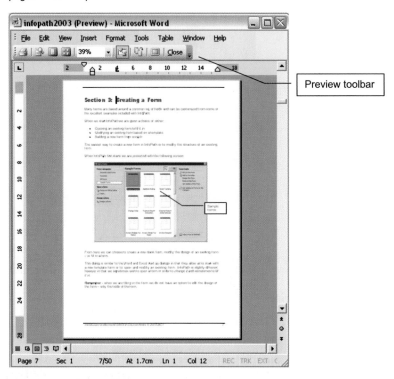

The *Preview* toolbar will appear at the top of the screen.

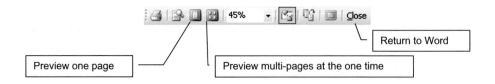

- ❏ Use the **Page Up** and **Page Down** keys to move forwards and backwards through pages in the document.
- ❏ To return to edit our document press the **Close** button on the toolbar.

LESSON 3.1.5: WORD'S TOOLBARS

We can open or close any toolbar by going to the **View** menu and choosing **Toolbars**. Here we can see the toolbars that are open have ticks beside their names. Those that are closed have no ticks. To open or close a toolbar, simply click on the name of the toolbar.

It is useful to always have the *Standard* and the *formatting toolbar*s open by default.

❑   To turn on or off the toolbars go to the **View** menu and choose **Toolbars**:

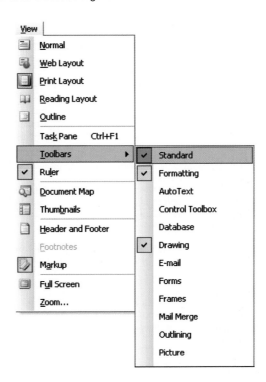

Saving a document
Saving documents is very important since when we turn off our PCs – any unsaved documents will be lost forever. The document that we typed appears on screen, but it has not been saved to disk. Unless we save the document, it will no longer exist when we exit Word.

File Structure
We looked at how directories and folders are organised in *Module 2 – File Management*. Let's take a quick review to see what our options are.

To start with we need to decide where we would like to save our document. Generally, we will have a choice of two different places (or two different drives).

1. We have a **C: drive** – the computers *hard drive*. This would save the document into the Desktop PC itself.

2. We have an **A: Drive** – which is a floppy disk. This would save the document onto a floppy disk that we can then take away, to access this document from another PC.

Once we have decided on a drive, we then need to decide where on that drive to put the document. If we were just to put all our documents into the **C** drive or the **A** drive, we would have problems finding them later on.

To guard against this, we file our documents into folders. For example, on our **C** drive we might have a folder that holds all our *personal* documents and then another folder that holds all our *work* documents. When we are saving our files we store them into the appropriate folders for retrieval later.

Here are the steps involved in determining where to save a file:

- ❑ Choose a drive
- ❑ Choose a folder on that drive
- ❑ Choose a subfolder (if necessary) and repeat this step as many times as needed
- ❑ Give the file a suitable name
- ❑ Save the document

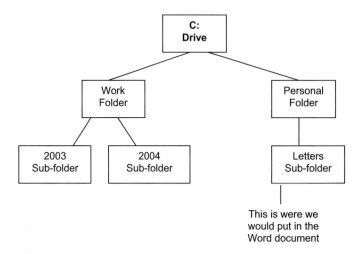

The full name, or *path name* of a file includes the drive letter, the folder, the subfolders (if there are any) and the file name. A colon (:) separates drives from their folders and filenames. A backslash (\) separates folders from subfolders and filenames.

C : \ personal \ letters \ test.doc

| *Drive* | *Folder* | *Sub-folder* | *Document name* |

Now we are going to save our document in the **letters** folder.

- ❑ Choose **File | Save As**

The following window will appear:

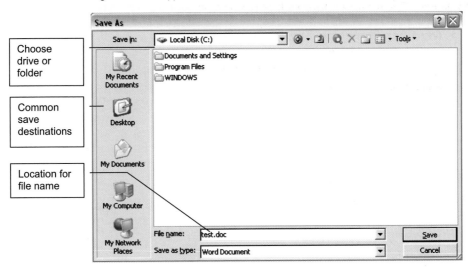

Choose drive or folder

Common save destinations

Location for file name

Firstly we need to locate the correct drive, by clicking on the drop-down of the **Save in** drop down. Click on the **Save in** drop down list to reveal the folders and drives on this PC.

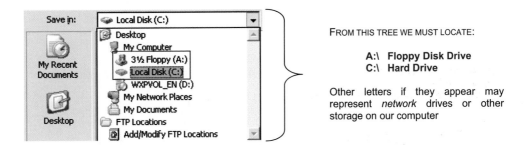

FROM THIS TREE WE MUST LOCATE:

A:\ Floppy Disk Drive
C:\ Hard Drive

Other letters if they appear may represent *network* drives or other storage on our computer

Once we've chosen the drive to save to we open the folder on the drive we want to save into.

❏ Double click on the folder that we want to save into, in this case it's the **personal** folder. Once open we can choose a subfolder to save in. Choose the **letters** folder.

Now that we have decided *where* we are going to save our file - we need to give the document a name.

❑   Click into the *file name* box and type the name **test**.

The **Save As** screen should now look like this:

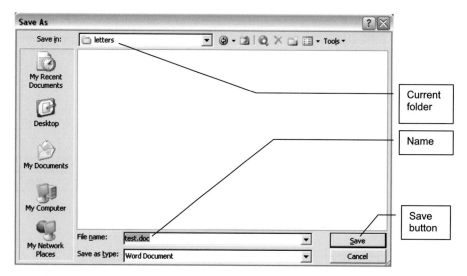

❑   Click the **Save** button.

We have now successfully saved our document, called **test.doc** into the **C** drive, in a folder called **personal** and into a sub-folder called **letters**.

NOTE: This is a very important process. Practice this technique until you are happy saving documents to both the C drive and the A floppy disk drive. This will be integral to your exam. Review this in Module 2 to see more detail.

LESSON 3.1.6: OPENING A DOCUMENT

We will open the document that we created in the previous section.

Start Word if it is not already running.

❑ Choose **Open** from the **File** menu or press the icon on the standard toolbar

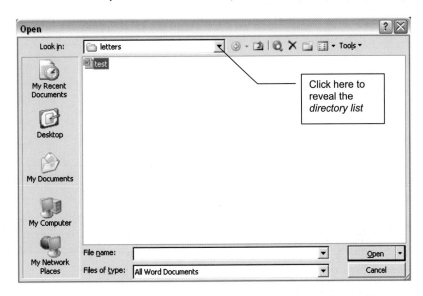

❑ Choose the **C:** drive from the directory list.
❑ Double click on the **Personal** directory in the folders list to display its contents.
❑ Double click on the **Letters** directory to display its contents
❑ Double click on **test** to display its contents.

LESSON 3.1.7: OPENING SEVERAL DOCUMENTS

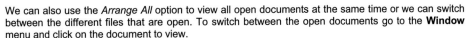

We can open several documents and work with them together. To open another document simply go to the **File** menu and choose **Open**. The new document will open *on top of* the existing document. But the previous file is still accessible. This is useful if we want to move or copy information between different files.

We can also use the *Arrange All* option to view all open documents at the same time or we can switch between the different files that are open. To switch between the open documents go to the **Window** menu and click on the document to view.

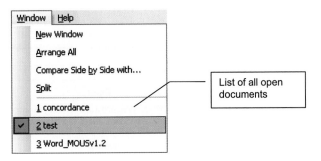

LESSON 3.1.8:   SAVING A DOCUMENT WITH A NEW NAME

To get some more practice saving – we'll resave our document – but this time with a new name. That way we have a "copy" of the document.

❑   Choose **Save As** from the File menu.

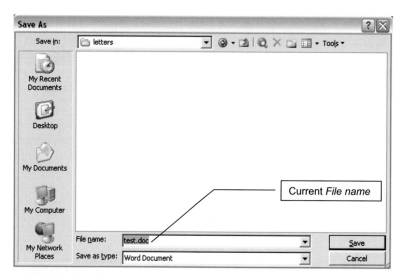

The window automatically opens in the last folder accessed – which is our `c:\personal\letters\` folder.

❑   We are going to resave this document as **"Typing Skills".** Enter its name into the File name box.

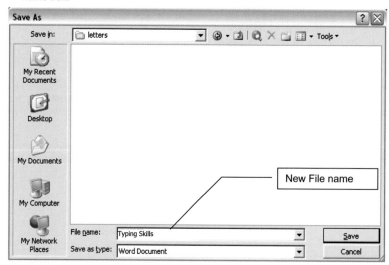

❑   Press the **Save** button or press **Enter**.

The original file *test.doc* still exists. We are now editing a *copy* of the file which is called **Typing Skills.doc**. Changes made to this file will **not** effect the original.

Saving the document with the same name

To save the document with the same name that it already has choose **Save** from the **File** menu (or press **Ctrl+S**). This will over-write the existing file with the changes in the current document.

LESSON 3.1.9: CLOSING OUR DOCUMENT

To close a document without exiting from Word,

❑ Choose **Close** from the **File** menu.

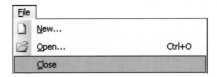

❑ When prompted choose **Yes** to save changes to the file.

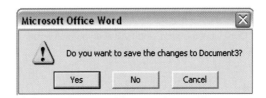

We are now left with a blank screen. We may open an existing document or create a new document.

LESSON 3.1.10: EXITING WORD

Before we finish this section, we will *exit* Word. Choose **Exit** from the **File** menu. As our document has been saved, Word will immediately exit and we will automatically be returned to our Windows screen.

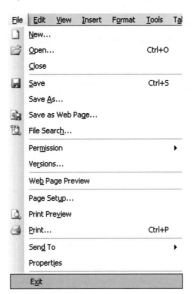

Exiting from Word closes it completely – but Word will prompt to save any unsaved documents. Make sure to save any files that haven't been saved before exiting.

EXERCISES TO PROVE YOU KNOW

1. Open a new blank document in Word.

   Type in the following text:

   > Hi Sam,
   > While I am in **Italy** this week it would be great if you could do the following for me:
   > Phone Hertz and book the car for next **Friday**
   > Alfa Romeo, Blue, Power Steering.
   > Tell Mary to go ahead with the project
   > Order more stationery
   > *Pens*
   > Marker *pens* for white board
   > Fluorescent *highlighters*
   > *Envelopes*
   >
   > Thanks! Don't work too hard, and I will see you next week!
   > Regards,
   > Sandra.

2. Save the document in your *My Documents* folder as **letter_to_Sam.doc.**

3. Close the document.

4. Open the **letter_to_sam.doc** created in the last question.

5. Close the Word document and then close the Word application.

SECTION 3.2: EDITING OUR DOCUMENT

In this section we will learn how to do the following:

- Move the cursor or insertion point
- Delete text
- Use Undo and Redo
- Delete text
- Cut, copy and paste text in our document
- Close a document

LESSON 3.2.1: MOVING THE CURSOR OR INSERTION POINT

Before we edit the document, we must know how to move the insertion point through the document. We can move the insertion point by clicking with the mouse or by using the *arrow keys* on the keyboard.

Let's try this out:

- Move the mouse pointer anywhere within the second paragraph and click.

Notice that the flashing insertion point moved.

- Experiment with all four arrows keys until you feel comfortable moving through the document.

Inserting New Text
Next we will add a sentence to the middle of the second paragraph.

- Place the insertion point before the word "This" in the first paragraph:

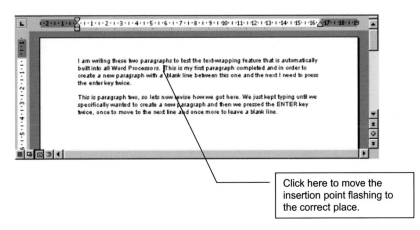

Click here to move the insertion point flashing to the correct place.

❑ Next enter the following sentence:

> It is so easy all I have to do is type.

The new text appears at the insertion point position. Existing text is pushed forward and reformatted as we type.

LESSON 3.2.2: DELETING TEXT

We can remove characters to the left of the insertion point by pressing the **Backspace** key. We can remove characters to the right of the insertion point by pressing the **Delete** key.

❑ Move the insertion point between the words "paragraph" and "completed" in the first paragraph.

❑ Now press the **Backspace** key until the word "paragraph" is deleted.

❑ Press the **Delete** key until the Word "completed" is deleted.

LESSON 3.2.3: USING *UNDO* AND *REDO*

Word provides us with a very useful tool that allows us to *undo* or *reverse* our last action. Wouldn't it be nice if we had one of these for everyday living!

We can use **Undo** to reverse just about anything (except *saving* and *opening*) including deletions, insertions, formatting and so on.

If we delete a section of text and then press **Undo** button ↻ ▾ or use the shortcut key **Ctrl + Z** the last action we perform will be reversed.

There are several levels of *undo* available in Word depending on the amount of memory we have. Each time we press the **Undo** button the previous action is undone. Press it a few times to see what happens.

If after we have *undone* an action we wish to Redo it simply press the **Redo** button ↺ ▾ or use the shortcut key **Ctrl+Y** .

LESSON 3.2.4:   SELECTING TEXT

Selecting text is a vital skill which we need making changes to text already in a document. Once we have selected text we can *delete* it, *move* it, or *change* its appearance.

Suppose we wanted to select the word "paragraphs" in the first paragraph below:

> This word is
> selected

I am writing these two paragraphs to test the text-wrapping feature that is automatically built into all Word Processors. This is my first paragraph completed and in order to create a new paragraph with a blank line between this one and the new one I need to press the ENTER key twice.

This is paragraph two, so let's now revise how we got here. We just kept typing until we specifically wanted to create a new paragraph and then we pressed the ENTER key twice, once to move to the next line and once more to leave a blank line.

- ❑ Select the Word by putting the mouse pointer directly on the word, and double-clicking on it.

The word will become highlighted to show it is selected.

To select using the mouse

- ❑ Hold down the left mouse button and move it across any text to select it.

To deselect the text

- ❑ Click anywhere outside the selected area to deselect it.

To select a word in a document

- ❑ Double click any word to select it and then click anywhere to deselect it.

To select a line

- ❑ Click once in the left-hand margin, adjacent to the line that is to be selected, this will select the entire line. Hold down the mouse in the margin and drag and this will select consecutive lines.

To select using the cursor keys

- ❑ Hold down the **Shift** key and press any of the cursor keys to select text in that direction.

Common ways of selecting text

There are many ways to select text. The following table shows some of them:

Drag using the mouse	Selects text as the mouse is moved
Double click	Selects a word
Click in left margin	Select a line
Shift+cursor keys	Extends selection in direction of cursor or arrow keys
Ctrl+Click	Select a sentence
Ctrl+A	Select entire document

Practice each of these methods until they become second nature.

LESSON 3.2.5: SELECTING AND REPLACING/CHANGING TEXT

In this lesson, we will learn that when we highlight a word, phrase or paragraph, we can easily replace or edit the selection. The cut/copy/paste feature can also be used in other applications covered in the ICDL/ECDL, namely Excel, Access, PowerPoint, Windows Explorer and Outlook.

Selecting to replace text:
When we select text and then type, the typed text replaces the selected text.

- ❑ Select the text "Word Processors".
- ❑ Type "Microsoft Word".

The selected text disappears and the text "Microsoft Word" replaces it.

Selecting to delete text:
When we select text and press **Delete** the selected text is deleted.

- ❑ Select the text "Word Processors"
- ❑ Press **Delete**

The selected text disappears.

Selecting to change text:

- ❑ Select "Microsoft Word" in the first paragraph.
- ❑ Press the I button on the formatting toolbar or press **Ctrl + I**.

The text becomes *italicised*.

LESSON 3.2.6: CUTTING, COPYING AND PASTING

We can use the cut, copy and paste features of Word to move and copy text and graphics from one location to another.

When we *cut* text with the cut ✂ tool or *copy* text with the copy 🗐 tool, it is stored in the *clipboard*, which is a temporary storage area in the computer's memory. When we *paste* with the paste 📋 tool it is retrieved from the clipboard and inserted into a new location.

Document One

Without its software, a computer is basically a useless lump of plastic and metal. However, with added software, a computer can store, process, and retrieve information, find spelling errors in manuscripts, play games, and engage in other valuable activities to earn its keep.

Computer software can be roughly divided into two types: the *system programs*, which manage the operation of the computer itself, and the *application programs*, which solve problems for their users.

Cut or **Copy**

✂   🗐

The Virtual Clipboard

Computer software can be roughly divided into two types: the *system programs*, which manage the operation of the computer itself, and the *application programs*, which solve problems for their users.

Document Two

Computer software can be roughly divided into two types: the *system programs*, which manage the operation of the computer itself, and the *application programs*, which solve problems for their users.

Paste

📋

The most fundamental of all the system programs is the **operating system**, which controls all the computer resources and provides the base upon which the application programs can be written.

LESSON 3.2.7:   CUTTING AND PASTING TEXT

Suppose we wanted to move a sentence to a different location. One option is to delete the sentence and then retype it. But a faster way is to cut and paste the sentence.

- ❑ Select the text *"This is paragraph two, so let's now revise how we got here."* including the full stop and space after the sentence using the mouse.

> I am writing these two paragraphs to test the text-wrapping feature that is automatically built into all Word Processors. This is my first paragraph completed and in order to create a new paragraph with a blank line between this one and the new one I need to press the ENTER key twice.
>
> This is paragraph two, so let's now revise how we got here. We just kept typing until we specifically wanted to create a new paragraph and then we pressed the ENTER key twice, once to move to the next line and once more to leave a blank line. |

Select this sentence

- ❑ Go to the **Edit | Cut** *or* press **Ctrl + X** *or* press the cut button ✂ on the standard toolbar.

The selected text will **disappear**. It is stored on the *Windows Clipboard*, ready to be pasted. The text remains on the clipboard until we Cut or Copy again, or until we exit Windows.

- ❑ Next we'll move the insertion point to the end of the document, after "blank line."

- ❑ Now choose **Edit | Paste** *or* press **Ctrl + V** *or* press the paste button 📋 on the standard toolbar.

The sentence that was cut reappears at the insertion point position.

LESSON 3.2.8:   COPYING AND PASTING TEXT

We have just **Cut** and **Paste** text. Now we will copy and paste the words *"Microsoft Word"* to a different location in the same sentence.

- ❑ Select the words *"Microsoft Word"* using the mouse or keyboard.

- ❑ Choose **Edit | Copy** *or* press **Ctrl + C** *or* press the copy button 📋 on the standard toolbar.

The text remains selected and it is copied to the clipboard, replacing previous text.

- ❑ Move the insertion point between *"test the"* and *"text-wrapping feature"* in the first sentence.

- ❑ Choose **Edit | Paste** *or* press **Ctrl + V** *or* press the paste button 📋 on the standard toolbar.

The text we copied has reappeared at the insertion point position.

LESSON 3.2.9: COPYING AND MOVING BETWEEN DOCUMENTS

Occasionally we may need to copy or move text between one document and another. Perhaps when quoting a previous letter or amending existing text. To move text between open documents:

- ❑ Select the text to move or copy

- ❑ If copying between documents press **Ctrl + C** or press **Ctrl + X** if moving the text.

- ❑ Go to the **File | New** or click on the ⬜ button to create a new document.

or

- ❑ To copy/move text to another open document choose the document from the **Window** menu if it is already open, or open it.

A new document window will now appear. Notice that the Title bar will show the name of the active document. The document we were working on is now hidden behind this window.

- ❑ Next go to **Edit | Paste** or press **Ctrl + V** or press the paste button 🖺 on standard toolbar.

Notice that the paragraph is pasted into the document window.

Shortcut keystrokes

Most menu items have shortcut keystrokes (or can have them easily assigned to them). These can make accessing the commands much faster. As we work with the tools we'll get to know these shortcuts better. For the moment notice where the shortcut appears in the menu.

For example:

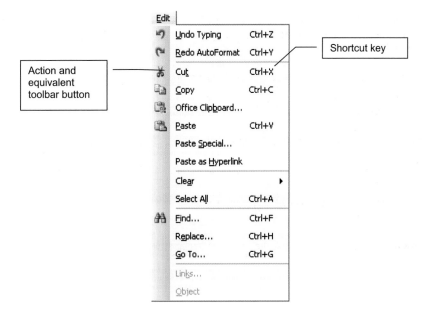

These shortcut keys offer quicker ways to perform tasks. For example, instead of choosing **Cut** from the **Edit** menu, we can press **Ctrl + X**. We have met this before.

LESSON 3.2.10: ARRANGING DOCUMENT WINDOWS

Word makes it easy to move between document windows. The names of all open documents are listed in the **Window** menu.

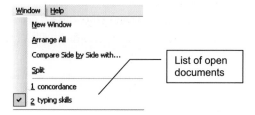

We have two files open at the moment – **typing skills** and now **concordance**.

Don't worry if this document has a different number as it will depend on how many files we have opened while using Word.

❑ Choose **typing skills** from the Window menu.

The **typing skills.doc** window becomes active.

❑ To view both documents simultaneously choose **Arrange All** from the **Window** menu.

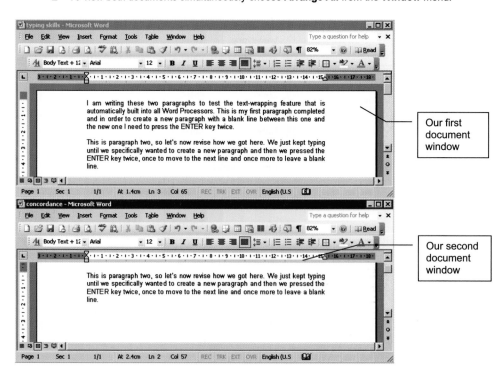

Results of arranging the two open documents

❑ To Restore, press the *Maximise* button on the top right corner of each document window.

EXERCISES TO PROVE YOU KNOW

1. Open the file that was created in the last exercise called *letter_to_sam.doc*.

2. Re-save the document into a new folder on your **C:** drive (your hard drive) and call the new folder **Letters**.

3. Save the document as **letter_to_joe.doc.**

4. In the new document, change the letter so that it says Hi Joe.

5. Delete the following text:

   > Order more stationery
   > Power Steering

6. Insert the following text:

   > The car should be an ...

   After the text "…..next Friday"

7. Open the document **letter_to_sam.doc** and arrange both document windows on-screen.

8. Copy the text *The car should be* from the **letter_to_joe.doc** to **letter_to_sam.doc**

9. Undo the last action.

SECTION 3.3:   FORMATTING TEXT AND PARAGRAPHS

The formatting features of Word allow us to change the appearance and arrangement of text in the document. In this section we will learn how to:

- ❑ Work with the formatting toolbar
- ❑ Change the colour, font and size of text
- ❑ Change text case
- ❑ Align paragraphs
- ❑ Adjust paragraphs indentation
- ❑ Adjusting line and paragraph spacing
- ❑ Border and shade paragraphs

LESSON 3.3.1:   FORMATTING TOOLBAR

Using the formatting toolbar is a quick way to perform formatting tasks in Word.

The formatting toolbar usually looks like this:

We will now use the formatting toolbar to type some text that will be formatted as **bold**.

We can move the cursor to the end of the last paragraph, after the text that says "blank line."

> I am writing these two paragraphs to test the text-wrapping feature that is automatically built into all Word Processors. This is my first paragraph completed and in order to create a new paragraph with a blank line between this one and the new one I need to press the ENTER key twice.
>
> This is paragraph two, so let's now revise how we got here. We just kept typing until we specifically wanted to create a new paragraph and then we pressed the ENTER key twice, once to move to the next line and once more to leave a blank line.

Insertion point is here

- ❑ Click the **B** button on the formatting toolbar or press **Ctrl+B** and start typing

Notice that the icon shows an outline and colour change to show that it is selected.

B I U

As we type our text will come out in **Bold**.

Let us now create another new paragraph.

Notice that the text you type is darker than the previous text. Now we will turn off bold.

- ❑ Click the **B** button again on the toolbar to turn bold off or press **Ctrl+B**

Experiment with the other icons on the formatting toolbar to determine what each does. Holding the mouse over on the icons will tell us what each icon is supposed to do.

LESSON 3.3.2: CHANGING THE TEXT COLOUR

We can change the colour of text in our document using the *Font colour* icon 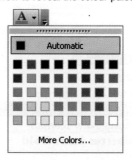 on the formatting toolbar.

- ❑ Select the text to change
- ❑ Click on the downward arrow to reveal the colour palette

- ❑ Click on the desired colour and the selected text will then change colour

LESSON 3.3.3: CHANGING FONT STYLE AND SIZE

A *font* is a set of characters with a specific design. Different printers have different fonts. However, Word has included many common fonts that work with almost any printer. Here is what some of them look like:

Courier

Arial

Times New Roman

CASTELLAR

Curlz

Bradley Hand

Blackadder

Palace Script

There are thousands of different fonts available for Windows

Each font is available in different *point sizes*. 72 points equals 1 inch.

This is a 10 point font

This is an 18 point font

We will now change the font and size of our memo title.

- ❑ Select the text "Memo".
- ❑ From the formatting toolbar select the *font* drop down list

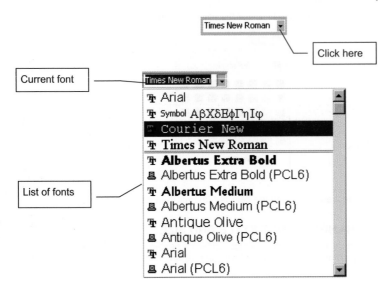

- ❑ From the list of available fonts choose **ARIAL**.
- ❑ From the formatting toolbar select the *font size* drop down list

A list of available font sizes will appear:

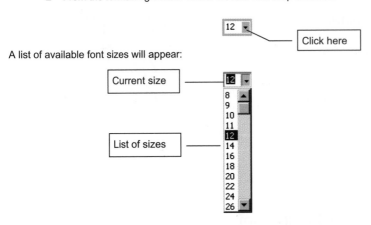

- ❑ Choose 18 from the list of available sizes.
- ❑ Click anywhere else in the document window to de-select the text.

An alternative method for changing the text attributes is to choose **Font** from the **Format** menu.

- ❑ Select the text "Memo".
- ❑ From the **Format | Font**.

The Font dialog will appear. This allows us to change the font type and size as well as setting other font attributes such as

Double Underlining	**Bold Face**
SMALL CAPS	*Italics*
Superscript	SUBSCRIPT

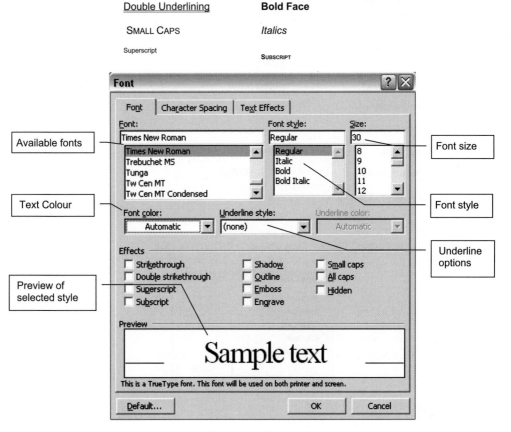

The standard font window

❑ Choose **ARIAL** from the fonts list.

❑ Choose **18** from the font size list and click **OK**.

LESSON 3.3.4: CHANGING SENTENCE CASE

Occasionally WE MIGHT TYPE ACCIDENTALLY WITH THE CAPS LOCK KEY ON without realising it or have a large amount of text all in a particular 'case'. If we've typed a lot of text – having to re-type it all to change its 'case' can be a nuisance. Word allows us to change the sentence case of a word or paragraph in one go.

Here are the results of applying each of the available options to the following sentence:

Typing is fun.

SENTENCE CASE.	Typing is fun.
LOWER CASE	typing is fun.
UPPER CASE	TYPING IS FUN.
TITLE CASE	Typing Is Fun.
TOGGLE CASE	tYPING IS FUN.

To change the case of a paragraph:

❑   Select the paragraph

❑   Choose **Format | Change Case** and select the required case

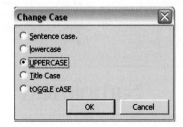

❑   Click **OK** to convert the text.

LESSON 3.3.5: CHANGING PARAGRAPH ALIGNMENT

Text can be aligned on the left, or right margin, centred, or fully justified (straight on both sides, like newspaper columns).

> This text is left aligned. It will be jagged on the right but always straight on the left.
>
> This text is right aligned. This text will be ragged on the left but always straight on the right.
>
> This text is centred.
>
> This text is fully justified. It will be straight on both the left and the right margins of the page. This is achieved automatically by Word adding extra spaces to each line.

The formatting toolbar contains four buttons for aligning text:

Button:	Action:
≣	Left align selected paragraph.
≣	Centre selected paragraph.
≣	Right align selected paragraph.
≣	Fully justify selected paragraph.

Experiment with the different alignment buttons.

Create a new document in Word.

- ❑ From the formatting toolbar press ≣ to *centre* the current line.

- ❑ Type "Memo" and select the text and press **U** to underline the text and **B** to put it in bold (**Ctrl+U** and **Ctrl+B** are the short cut keys to do the same task).

Our document will now look something like this:

> **<u>Memo</u>**

When we press return, our insertion point will stay in the centre of the page and the bold and underline attributes will remain **on**. In order to turn these settings off, click on each of the icons. These icons work as toggle buttons, a single click turns them *on*, another click turns them *off*.

> **To:**   Donald
> **From:**   Lorraine
> **Date:**   20th November
> **Subject:** Holidays

- ❑ Type the word "To:" press the **Tab** key

The **Tab** key is on the left of the keyboard and looks like this:

- ❑ Type "Donald", then press **Enter**.
- ❑ Highlight the Word "To:" and make it **bold** (press **Ctrl + B**)

Inserting a horizontal line

Now we will insert a line that divides the memo information from the body of the memo.

- ❑ Place the insertion point on a new line by pressing **Enter**.
- ❑ Press and hold the **Shift** key and press on the **underscore** key on the keyboard. Keep pressing the underscore key until the line is complete.

LESSON 3.3.6:   INDENTING PARAGRAPHS

Occasionally it is useful to indent paragraphs away from the main body of a document's text. Type the following text into the document:

> I would like to confirm all details of our Christmas holidays. I believe that we are closing down all operations for two week period commencing on Tuesday 22nd December and ending on Tuesday 5th January. This implies all employees are due back to work on Wednesday 6th January.
>
> With the above in mind I have a special request, as I am going home to my family in Australia for the Christmas festivities I would like to have permission to take some extra leave. I wish to take an extra 2 weeks holidays.
>
> I would appreciate your consideration in this matter and look forward to hearing from you at your earliest convenience.

Paragraph to indent.

- ❑ To indent the second paragraph select the paragraph and press the button. To indent it further press the button again.
- ❑ To "unindent" text, which is already indented, highlight the text and press the button.

> I would like to confirm all details on our Christmas holidays. I believe that we are closing down all operations for two week period commencing on Tuesday 22nd December and ending on Tuesday 5th January. This implies all employees are due back to work on Wednesday 6th January.
>
> > With the above in mind I have a special request, as I am going home to my family in Australia for the Christmas festivities I would like to have permission to take some extra leave. I wish to take an extra 2 weeks holidays.
>
> I would appreciate your consideration in this matter and look forward to hearing from you at your earliest convenience.

Result of indenting.

LESSON 3.3.7:   ADJUSTING PARAGRAPH INDENTATION USING THE RULER

We can also adjust the indentation of a paragraph by using the ruler. Click on the ruler markers and drag left or right to adjust the left, right or hanging indent of the selected paragraphs.

Holding down the left **and** right mouse buttons while clicking on any of the ruler markers will show the distances relative to the page margins like this:

Alternatively we can use the **Format | Paragraph** options to change these paragraph settings.

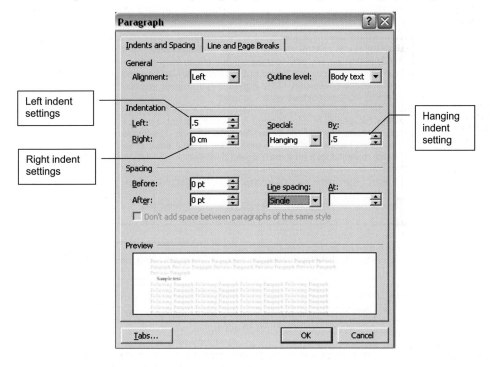

LESSON 3.3.8: CHANGING LINE SPACING

When we create a new document the line spacing is always *single-spaced*. We will now double-space the last paragraph of the memo. Sometimes double-spacing is required for published documents or articles – and can be useful in formatting certain types of documents.

❑   Select the last paragraph of the memo. Go to **Format | Paragraph**

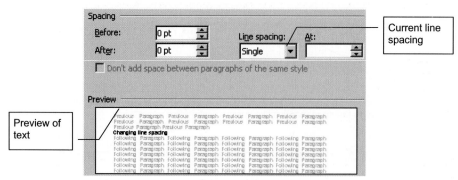

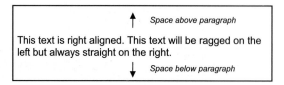

❑   Select **Double** from the line spacing drop down list menu and press **OK**.

The paragraph selected is now double-spaced.

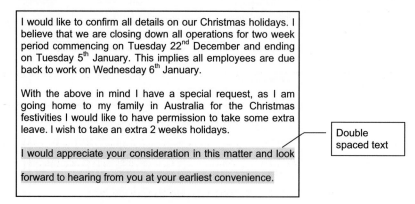

Changing spacing above and below paragraphs

We can also adjust the space above and below the current paragraph using the paragraph dialog box.

To change the spacing above or below the current paragraph range

❑   Enter values into the *Before* and *After* text boxes in the **Format | Paragraph** dialog box.

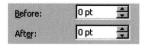

❑   Press **OK**.

LESSON 3.3.9: BORDERING AND SHADING PARAGRAPHS

We can use paragraph borders and shading to enhance the appearance of our document. It creates blocks of text. We can create a border around an entire page (see *Page Borders* on page 221) or we can create a border around a paragraph only.

    ❑   Highlight the paragraph

    ❑   Go to **Format | Borders and Shading** and click on the **Borders** tab

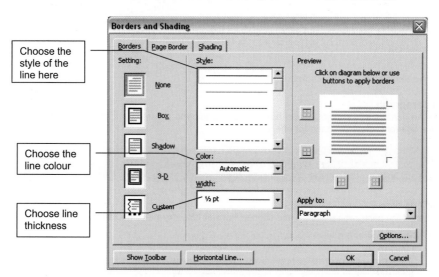

Choose the style of the line here

Choose the line colour

Choose line thickness

We can choose the style of our border first, then the colour of the border as well as the thickness and style for the border.

This paragraph has a 2 pt border all around it.

To place a border or partial border (line above, below or on the sides) of a paragraph:

    ❑   Select the style, colour and thickness of the line to use.

Now click on the preview area to apply the border to the top, bottom, left and right parts of the paragraph.

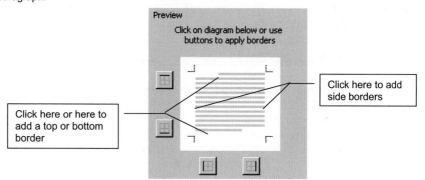

Click here to add side borders

Click here or here to add a top or bottom border

- ❏ Click on the preview area to choose where to put the borders or use the corresponding buttons below

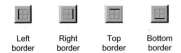

| Left border | Right border | Top border | Bottom border |

- ❏ The preview area will show where the border will appear around the paragraph. We can mix different line colours and styles in the one border.
- ❏ Press **OK**

The paragraph selected will now be bordered.

Shading a paragraph

We also use the borders and shading dialog box to apply shading to a paragraph. We can highlight a paragraph in a different colour or shade for effect.

This paragraph is shaded 30% grey.

To shade a paragraph

- ❏ Select the paragraph to shade and choose **Format | Borders and Shading**
- ❏ Choose the **Shading** tab

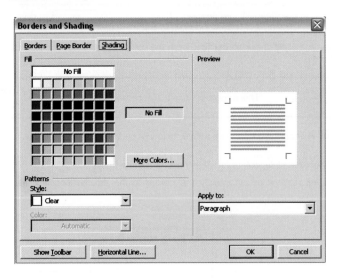

- ❏ Pick a colour or shade - we can also add a pattern style with a different colour
- ❏ Press **OK**

The paragraph selected will now be shaded.

LESSON 3.3.10: THE FORMAT PAINTER

The Format Painter is a handy feature in Microsoft Office – and particularly handy in Word. This feature allows us to copy the *formatting* information from one piece of text onto another.

For example, if we have a piece of text that is already centred, red and in Arial size 14, we can use the *Format Painter* to automatically change other pieces of text to look the same. This can save a lot of time.

The *Format Painter* icon is found on the standard toolbar – it looks like a paintbrush!

To use Format Painter:

- ❑ Select the text with the formatting to copy
- ❑ Click on the *Format Painter* icon
- ❑ Select the text to change into the format

Double clicking on the format painter will allow us to repeat these steps without selecting the original text each time. To turn off the format painter just click again on the Format Painter icon.

EXERCISES TO PROVE YOU KNOW

1. Open the file called *Music_flyer.doc* (available on the CD-ROM)
2. Increase the font size of the title to 22 points, apply small caps. Right align the paragraph.
3. Change the first paragraph to be double-line spaced. Indent the paragraph one tab space.
4. Change the second paragraph first line indent to .5"
5. Change paragraph spacing on all paragraphs to be 12 points
6. Shade each of the paragraphs of text using different shades of grey.
7. Save the document as *Music_flyer2.doc*
8. Highlight the heading "music". Change it to size 16 and colour Pink.
9. Use the format painter to change the other six headings in the document to match the *music* heading.
10. Change the case of the entire document to UPPER case.
10. Save the document.

SECTION 3.4: BULLETS AND NUMBERING

In this section we will:

- ❏ Create a bulleted list
- ❏ Create a numbered list

LESSON 3.4.1: BULLETING TEXT

A bulleted list is a list that looks something like this:

- Video Projections of various Christmas movies
- A ceiling camouflage with Christmas goodies
- Tables dressed with seasonal goodies
- Artists, face painters and magicians

Each bulleted point is made up of a separate paragraph of text.

- ❏ Select the text shown in the above letter
- ❏ Press the ⠿ button on the formatting toolbar.
- ❏ Indent the bulleted points by pressing ⫯.
- ❏ Deselect the text.

Changing the bullet
We can change the bullet symbol too if we want.

- ❏ Select the bulleted text.
- ❏ From the **Format** menu choose **Bullets and Numbering**.

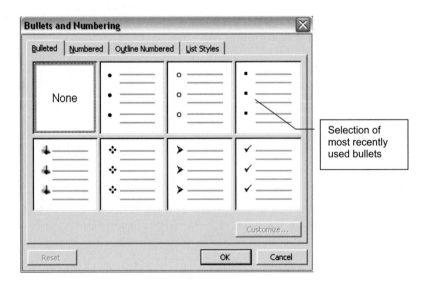

Selection of most recently used bullets

❑ Press **Customize…** to view additional bullet options

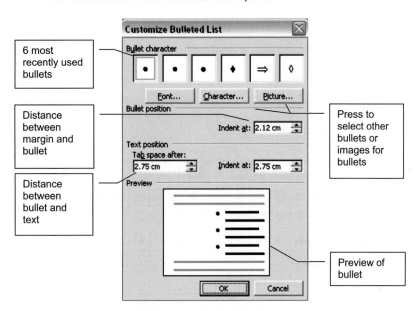

6 most recently used bullets

Distance between margin and bullet

Distance between bullet and text

Press to select other bullets or images for bullets

Preview of bullet

❑ Press Character… or Picture… to view the full range of available symbols or images that we can use for bullets.

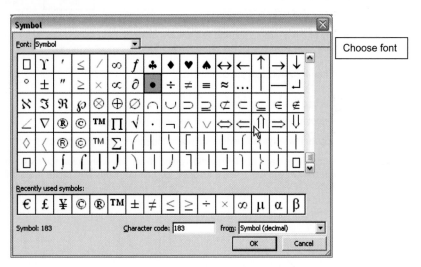

Choose font

Most of the bullets live in the *Symbol* and *Wingdings* fonts – although there are sometimes useful symbols in the regular fonts as well.

❑ Press on the desired symbol to use as a bullet and click **OK**.

Removing Bullets

❑ To remove bullets simply select the bulleted text and press the ⊟ button.

LESSON 3.4.2: INSERTING SYMBOLS AND SPECIAL CHARACTERS

Sometimes we will want to insert a special symbol – like a bullet – directly into the text of our document.

Symbols like bullets come from specially designed fonts which contain useful symbols and graphics.

□   To insert a symbol into Word choose **Insert | Symbol**.

The **Symbol** window will appear:

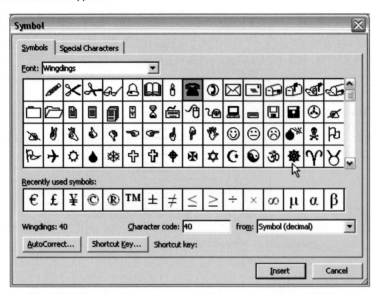

Clicking on any of the characters in the window will magnify the character to make it easier to see. By choosing different fonts we can pick a wider range of characters or symbols.

We will insert the ♠ symbol into our document.

□   Choose **Insert | Symbol**

□   Select the **Wingdings** font from the drop-down menu

□   Locate the ♠symbol and select it with the mouse and click **Insert**

The ♠ character will appear at the insertion point. If we select the character we will notice that it is formatted in the *Wingdings* font. Once inserted we can cut, copy and paste the symbols just like any other character.

LESSON 3.4.3:   NUMBERED LISTS

We can number text in a similar manner to the way in which we bullet text. To create a Numbered List:

❑   Select the text we had previously bulleted in the letter.

❑   Press the ▤ button on the formatting toolbar.

❑   Indent the bulleted points by pressing ▦ and deselect the text.

This will create a numbered list like this:

1. Video Projections of various Christmas movies
2. A ceiling camouflage with Christmas goodies
3. Tables dressed with seasonal goodies
4. Artists, face painters and magicians

We can also change the way we number the lines.

❑   Select the bulleted text and from the **Format** menu choose **Bullets and Numbering**

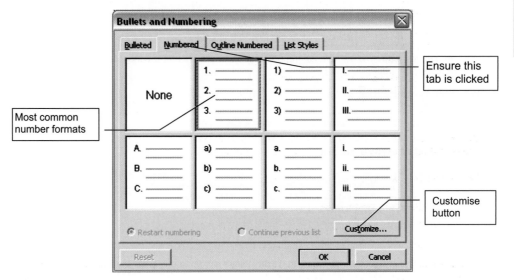

❑   Select one of the available number styles and click the Customize... button.

The **Customize Numbered List** window will now appear:

Style for
numbering
1,2,3 etc.

Distance
between
margin and
bullet

Distance
between
bullet and
text

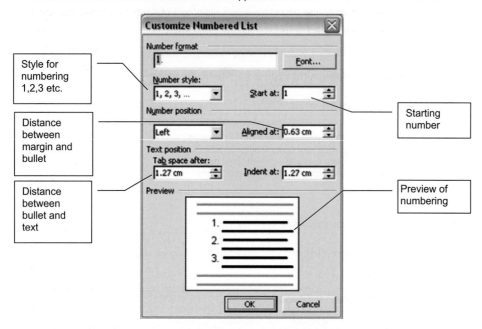

Starting
number

Preview of
numbering

We can use this window to set the starting point for our numbers and the indentation of the numbers relative to the paragraph.

Let's start our numbering at 3.

❑ Type "3" as the starting number and click **OK** to continue.

The numbered list will now start at 3.

> 3. Video Projections of various Christmas movies
> 4. A ceiling camouflage with Christmas goodies
> 5. Tables dressed with seasonal goodies
> 6. Artists, face painters and magicians

We can adjust the style of the numbering to display letters or roman numerals as required.

Change the
style here

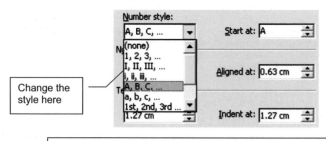

> a. Video Projections of various Christmas movies
> b. A ceiling camouflage with Christmas goodies
> c. Tables dressed with seasonal goodies
> d. Artists, face painters and magicians

EXERCISES TO PROVE YOU KNOW

1. Create a new document like the one below and format it according to the instructions:

> | Right align and set the font to 10pt *Times New Roman* | ———————— | Joanne Keating,
General Manager,
Keats Hotel,
Co. Limerick,
Ireland. |
>
> 10 November, 2010.
>
> Donald Murphy,
HR Manager,
FQ Systems, ——————— **Bold** 'FQ Systems'
Co. Dublin,
Ireland.
>
> Dear Mr. Murphy,
>
> Thank you for your enquiry regarding our Christmas Parties here at Keats Hotel. This year we present a *Funky Christmas theme* for your company party. This will include:
>
> - Video Projections of various Christmas movies —— Bullet and indent
> - A ceiling camouflage with Christmas goodies   Set to 1.5 line spacing
> - Tables dressed with seasonal goodies
> - Artists, face painters and magicians
>
> Why not take the option of staying over with our special party night rate of €145.00 mid-week and €155.00 weekend per person sharing.
>
> If you would like this party night "with a difference", please contact one of our sales team and we will arrange it all.
>
> Looking forward to hearing from you soon.
>
> Yours Sincerely,

2. Save the document as **Christmas.doc**

3. Open a new blank document and type in the following using bullets and numbers:

> ### The Contacts and Links Database Manual
>
> 1. Definition of an *Individual Contact*:
>   - An Individual Contact is <u>one</u> person. That person might have several addresses, e-mail contact numbers, phone numbers or work addresses.
>
> 2. Contact Database keeps track of the individual's:
>   - Home and work addresses
>   - E-mail and fax information
>   - Information on their membership to groups and projects
>   - Correspondence sent to them
>   - Notes assigned to them

SECTION 3.5: SPELLING, THESAURUS AND GRAMMAR

The spelling checker and thesaurus in Word are tools that help us *proof* our documents. 'Proof reading' our document includes searching for spelling errors, repeated words, overlapping graphics and correct page layout and orientation. Proofing a document is an important part of preparing our document for printing and final production. Properly proofing our document will help make it more professional and avoid costly printing and presentation errors. Properly presented reports and proposals can mean the difference between winning and losing business or passing and failing an exam!

The *spell check* option in Word allows us to check a document for misspelled words as well as add our own words to its custom dictionary. Word's *thesaurus* allows us to view the synonyms of a word and can usually suggest good alternatives. Both these tools are very useful in proofing our document and we will look at these next.

In this section we will learn to:

- ❑ Spell check a document.
- ❑ Add words to a custom dictionary.
- ❑ Find an alternative to a word using the thesaurus.

LESSON 3.5.1: SPELL-CHECKING A DOCUMENT

We will use the spell checker option to check the spelling of our open document. When a misspelled word is found, the spell checker offers possible spelling choices so that we can replace the word. The spell checker will also search for duplicate words, words containing numbers and irregular capitalisation.

Type the word "Kindley" and position the cursor anywhere within the word.

- ❑ From the **Tools** menu choose **Spelling** or press the ![AEC] button or press **F7** on your keyboard.

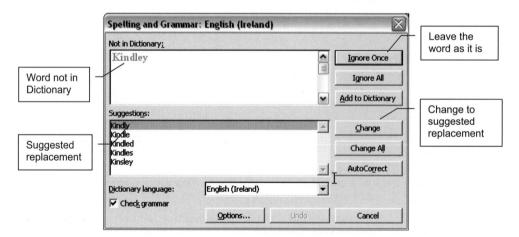

The spell checker compares each word in the document to the list of words in the program's dictionary to ensure that every word is spelt correctly. Whenever it comes across something that is not in the dictionary, the speller stops and displays suggested spellings, if any are available.

Word's spelling checker underlines spelling errors with a red wavy line.

Changing a misspelled word

If one of the suggested words offered by the dictionary has the correct spelling, you may select it and choose *Change*. The speller will then replace the word in the document. The spell checker will then continue checking the rest of the document for errors. To replace all occurrences of a misspelled word choose *Change All*.

Ignore All

To keep the current spelling of a word and to have the spell checker skip over any other occurrences of the word choose *Ignore All*.

Adding a word to a custom dictionary

There may be many correctly spelt words in your document that Word's spell checker does not recognise. These are usually company names, place names or people's names. We can **Add** these words to our own custom dictionary in these cases. Be warned however, that if a misspelled word is added to the dictionary it will never again detect the incorrect spelling of that word!

To add a word to the dictionary:

❑ Start the spelling checker – choose **Tools | Check Spelling and Grammar** or press **F7**

When the spelling checker finds a word not in its dictionary the main spelling and grammar window will appear.

❑ To add the word to the dictionary click the **Add to Dictionary** button.

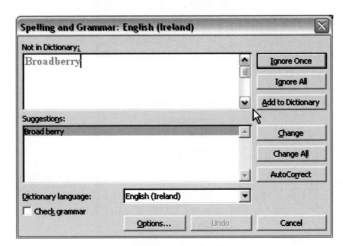

If you find you have inadvertently added words to your dictionary which are incorrectly spelt – you can edit the dictionary.

❑ Choose **Tools | Options** and click on the **Spelling and Grammar** tab.
❑ Click on **Dictionaries** and select **Edit**

Word will open a new document showing a list of words in the custom dictionary. When we edit these words and save the file, the dictionary will be changed and the spelling checker updated.

LESSON 3.5.2:   WORD'S THESAURUS AND RESEARCH TOOLS

Word 2003 has expanded Word features beyond a basic Thesaurus. In Word 2003 we are given a special *Research* panel that lets us search for text in a variety of different research archives – including the traditional thesaurus.

The *Research* tool allows us to:

- Reference research sites such as *Encarta* and *MSN* to look for related information
- Search business and financial sites for information
- Search reference books including online Thesauruses in different languages.

This is very useful when we're stuck for a word or when completing a crossword or if we are carrying out general research for a publication. Let's use Word's research tool to find alternative words for the word "affable".

- Type the word "affable" and position the cursor anywhere within the word.

- Choose **Tools | Research** and press the ➡ button or press the research icon 📖 or press **Shift + F7**

The *Research Panel* will appear and a list of alternatives for the word will appear:

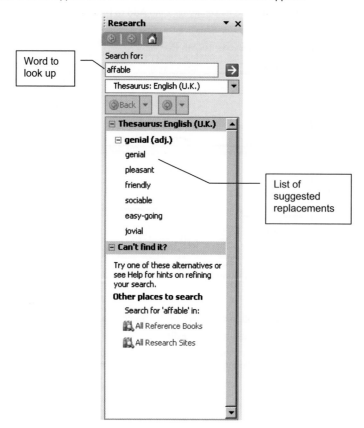

A list of suggested alternatives for the word are displayed.

- Select "pleasant" and click on the drop-down arrow to reveal the list of options

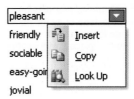

- Choose **Insert** to replace the word in the document, **Copy** to copy the word to the clipboard or **Lookup** to perform another search this time on the word "Pleasant"

Experiment with the Research panel and lookup meanings and references for other words.

EXERCISES TO PROVE YOU KNOW

1. Run the spelling checker on the *Christmas.doc* file create earlier.
2. Add any names found to the custom dictionary
3. Using Word's Thesaurus find alternatives for the following words:
   a) Entertainment
   b) Arrangements
   c) Cute

SECTION 3.6: FINDING AND REPLACING

Searching for and replacing words or phrases in a document is very useful. Sometimes we'll find we need to use an abbreviation of a word instead of its full name – or we'll have mis-typed it consistently throughout a document. *Find* allows us locate a word or phrase in our document and the replace tool allows us find a word or phrase and then replace it with another Word or phrase.

In this section we will:

- ❑ Find text
- ❑ Find and replace text

We are going to work with the file **christmas.doc.**

LESSON 3.6.1: FINDING TEXT

Suppose we wanted to find the word "funky" in our document.

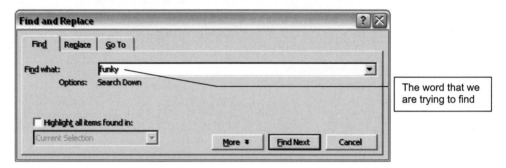

The word that we are trying to find

- ❑ From the **Edit** menu choose **Find** or press **Ctrl+F**
- ❑ Type "funky" into the *Find what:* text box.
- ❑ Choose **Find Next** to begin the search.

The first occurrence of "funky" is selected. If we wish to continue the search and find other occurrences of the word we can press **Find Next** again.

Finding formatted text

We can also ask Word to find text in a particular format, for example to find all words in **Bold.**

- ❏ From the **Edit** menu choose **Find**.
- ❏ Press the ⎓ More ⎓ button on the **Find and Replace** window to show additional search options.

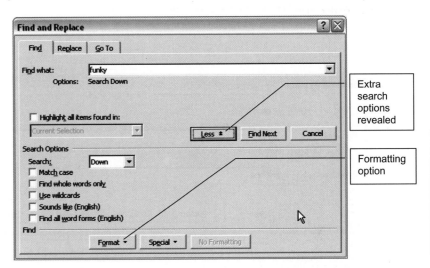

- ❏ Choose **Format Font** and select **Bold** from the list of available styles and click **OK**.
- ❏ Press **Find Next**.

Word will locate the next piece of text in bold face. If there is a word in the *Find what* text box it will search for that word with the specified formatting.

LESSON 3.6.2: FINDING AND REPLACING TEXT

We can use the **Replace** tool to find text and exchange it with something else. Suppose we wanted to replace several occurrences of the word "funky" with the word "exciting".

- ❏ Move the insertion point to the start of the document.
- ❏ Choose **Replace** from the **Edit** menu
- ❏ Type "funky" into the *Find what* text box.
- ❏ Type "exciting" into the *Replace with* text box.

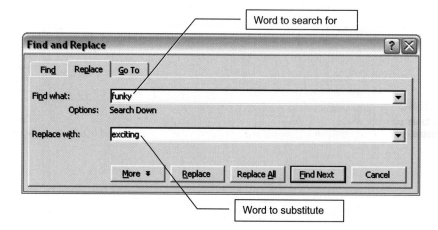

Word to search for

Word to substitute

- ❏ Press **Find Next** to begin the search
- ❏ Choose **Replace** to replace the first occurrence.
- ❏ Choose **Find Next** to leave the word the way it is and continue the search.
- ❏ Choose **Replace All** to replace all occurrences of the word "funky" with "exciting".

EXERCISES TO PROVE YOU KNOW

1. Open the *Christmas.doc* file created earlier.
2. Find all occurrences of *Donald* in the **Christmas.doc** file and replace them with *Michael*
3. Replace all **Bold** text in the document with *Italic* text

SECTION 3.7:   TABLES AND TABS

Tables allow us organise information into columns and rows. Once the table is created, we can add text and numbers and align the text in any way we choose. Tables are one of the most powerful and versatile layout tools we have in Word.

In this section we will:

- ❑   Create a table
- ❑   Type text into a table
- ❑   Re-size a table
- ❑   Add borders and shading to a table
- ❑   Add columns and rows to a table
- ❑   Learn to work with tabs

LESSON 3.7.1:   INSERTING A TABLE

A table consists of *rows* and *columns*. Rows and columns intersect to create *cells*. Each cell can be resized and formatted to suit our needs and can contain text or graphics and formatted in many ways.

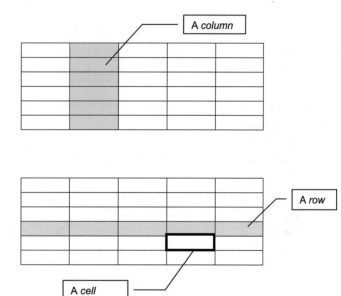

A column

A row

A cell

We will create a table with six rows and five columns.

❑   Place the insertion point on a blank line.

There are two ways of inserting a table:

Method 1:

❑   Go to the **Table | Insert Table**

❑   Type **5** for the number of columns and **6** for the number of rows and click **OK**

Word will insert a 6 x 5 table into our document.

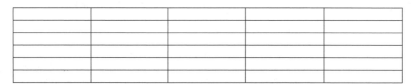

Method 2:

❑   Select the desired table size by pressing the table 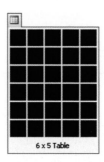 button on the standard toolbar and dragging to choose a table of the same size, we must keep our finger down on the mouse when dragging over the cells.

6 x 5 Table

Either method will insert a table like this with a ½ point black border around each cell:

If we remove the borders from the table we will usually see the table's *gridlines* that define the table's layout. To remove the border from a table:

- ❑ Select the entire table and choose **Table | Table Properties** and click on the **Borders and Shading** button
- ❑ Select **None** from the list of border settings and press **OK**

The table will now appear in our document with just gridlines similar to the image below:

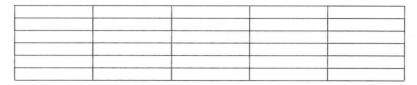

Creating a table that does not show borders can be very useful in laying out more complex documents.

Showing and hiding gridlines
What we can see in the table above are *gridlines*. Gridlines do not print[2] - making them very useful for laying out complex documents. We can hide or show our gridlines using the 📅 **Hide Gridlines** option in the **Table** menu.

Navigating the table
We can move from cell to cell by clicking on the cell with the mouse button or by pressing **Tab** or **Shift+Tab** to move forward and backwards through the cells or by using the **Cursor** keys.

Experiment by moving the insertion point throughout the table.

LESSON 3.7.2:   SELECTING SECTIONS OF A TABLE
When working with tables we often need to be able select parts of the table – usually a whole row, a column or the whole table. We do this using mouse with a slight different technique for each requirement:

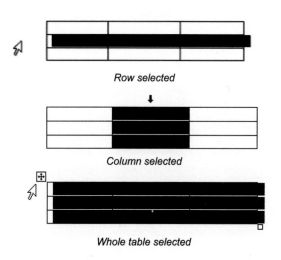

Row selected

Column selected

Whole table selected

To select a row of a table – move the mouse to the left of the row until it changes to a left-pointing arrow 𝔞. Now click with the mouse to select the row.

To select a column from a table – move the mouse pointer above the column to select until the ↓ arrow appears. Click to select the column.

To select the whole table click on the ⊞ icon at the top-left of the table. This will select the whole table.

---

[2] *We have changed the colour of the gridlines here so that they will print.*

LESSON 3.7.3: ADDING ROWS AND COLUMNS TO A TABLE

Once we have inserted a table, we may find that we want to make changes to the number of columns or rows we have in the table.

Take, as an example, the following table:

It has 2 rows and 3 columns.

Adding a column:

❑ Click in a cell – in this case we'll select the second cell on the first row

❑ Go to the **Table** menu and click on the **Insert** option

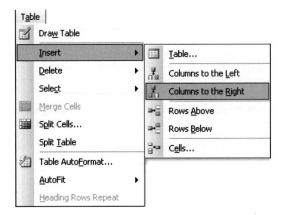

From here we can insert a column to left **or** a column to right of the current cell.

❑ Click on **Columns to the Right** to insert a column to the right of the current cell.

A new column will appear to the right of the cell that we had clicked in.

New Column

This works the same for new columns to the left.

Adding rows

Adding a row is easy.

- ❑ Select a row in the table
- ❑ Go to **Table | Insert**

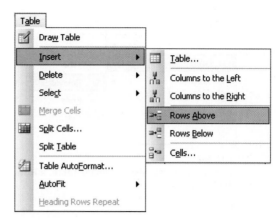

From here we can choose to insert a new row above or below our selected row:

- ❑ Click on **Rows Above**

A new row will appear *above* the selected row in our table.

Resizing Columns

To resize a cell move the mouse pointer over the cell column or row to resize:

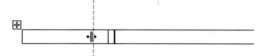

Then drag left or right to resize the cell.

Resizing Rows

To resize a row either press **Enter** within the cell or position the mouse at the row to enlarge and drag with the mouse.

We can also set width and height precisely using the **Table Properties** option from the **Table** menu and selecting the **Cells** tab.

Deleting Rows or Columns

- ❑ Select either the row or column that needs to be deleted.
- ❑ Go to **Table | Delete**

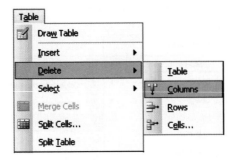

- ❑ From here we can choose whether it is the entire **Table,** a **Row**, a **Column** or just a **Cell** that we need to delete.

Note: Remember the Undo button will bring back any errors that we may make while doing this.

Merging Cells

Merging cells allows us to join numerous cells together to become one. This is very useful for headings at the top of tables.

- ❑ Highlight the cells that need to be merged

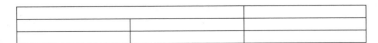

We do this by placing our mouse in one cell, hold down the left mouse button and dragging over the other cell(s). We may find that the cell does not become highlighted until we drag completely over it.

- ❑ Go to **Table | Merge Cells**

In this table the first two cells of the first row have been merged to become one big cell.

Splitting Cells

Splitting cells allows us to split an existing cell into more than one row or column.

- ❑ Click inside the cell that we need to split
- ❑ Go to the **Table** menu and click on **Split cells**

The following window appears:

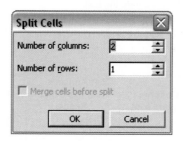

- ❑ Choose 2 columns and 1 row

Our result is as follows:

The first cell in this table has been split into 2 columns. We can repeat this procedure to split single cells into multiple rows as required.

LESSON 3.7.4:   FORMATTING TEXT IN A TABLE

Let's look at what is involved in formatting a newly created table. To start with let's recreate the following table which will contain cost analysis information. Notice that this is a **5 column x 6 row** table with the first row of cells merged together. To create it:

- ❑ Insert a new table with 5 columns and 6 rows using the **Table | Insert | Table** option
- ❑ Merge all the cells in the top row into one cell by selecting the cells and choosing **Table | Merge Cells**

Cost Analysis				
	Cost per square foot	Average Office Space	Employee Count	Total Cost
Low Rise	$95	150 Sq. Ft.	2,500	
(Remodel)	$90	100 Sq. Ft.	3,500	
High Rise	$190	140 Sq. Ft.	3,500	
	$192	90 Sq. Ft.	3,500	

- ❑ Now type the corresponding text and numbers into each of the cells

Notes:

When we **Tab** to get from cell to cell, we may tab too many times and notice that an extra row appears at the end of our table. If this accidentally happens and we insert an additional line, press **Undo** to delete it.

If we press the **Enter** key by a mistake, it will place the insertion point on the next line in the same cell, press **Backspace** to delete it.

Changing the table's appearance

The next thing we wish to do is change the appearance of the table heading "Cost Analysis" by formatting it in **bold** and centring it.

- ❑ Select the text "Cost Analysis" in the top row

- ❑ Press the **B** button on the formatting toolbar to format the text as bold.

- ❑ Press the ≣ button to centre the text.

Do the same for the headings in cells in row 2.

The table will now look like:

Cost Analysis				
	Cost per square foot	**Average Office Space**	**Employee Count**	**Total Cost**
Low Rise	$95	150 Sq. Ft.	2,500	
(Remodel)	$90	100 Sq. Ft.	3,500	
High Rise	$190	140 Sq. Ft.	3,500	
	$192	90 Sq. Ft.	3,500	

Now right align all the figures in each column:

- ❑ Select all of the numbers in the table and choose ≣ from the formatting toolbar menu.

The numbers should now be right justified as in the table below:

Cost Analysis				
	Cost per square foot	**Average Office Space**	**Employee Count**	**Total Cost**
Low Rise	$95	150 Sq. Ft.	2,500	
(Remodel)	$90	100 Sq. Ft.	3,500	
High Rise	$190	140 Sq. Ft.	3,500	
	$192	90 Sq. Ft.	3,500	

LESSON 3.7.5: AUTOFORMATTING A TABLE

There is a clever feature in Word that allows us to automatically format our table. This means that it will add shading and border colours for us based on a predefined style. In the next section, we will learn how to do this manually, however, here we will use the *AutoFormat* options.

Auto Formatting the table

❑ Select the entire table

We can do this by clicking anywhere in the table and then going to the **Table** menu and choosing **Select | Table**

❑ Go to the **Table | Table AutoFormat**

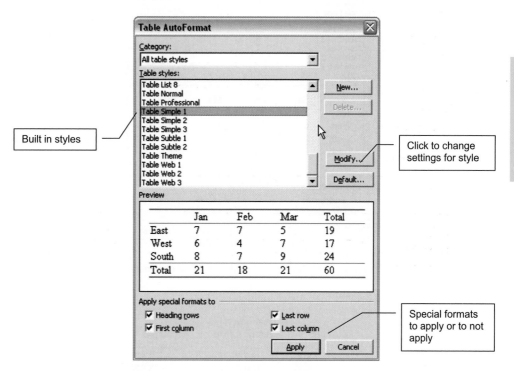

The Table AutoFormat window allows us to choose from a list of built in settings on the left hand side of the screen.

❑ Choose a setting and press the **OK** button

The table will now take on the format that we applied

Here is the result of choosing one of the *autoformat* settings for our table:

Cost Analysis				
	Cost per square foot	Average Office Space	Employee Count	Total Cost
Low Rise	$95	150 Sq. Ft.	2,500	
(Remodel)	$90	100 Sq. Ft.	3,500	
High Rise	$190	140 Sq. Ft.	3,500	
	$192	90 Sq. Ft.	3,500	

To remove an AutoFormat from a table:

- ❑ Select the table
- ❑ Go to the **Table | Table AutoFormat**

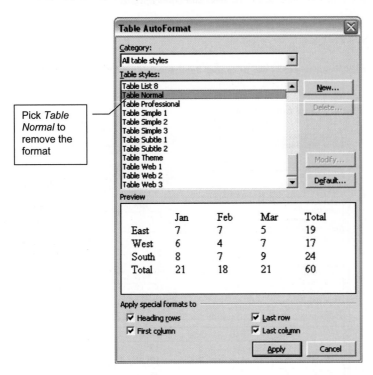

Pick *Table Normal* to remove the format

- ❑ Choose the option: *Table Normal* - this style will delete all formatting from the table.

Our table will now look like this:

	Cost per square foot	Cost Analysis Average Office Space	Employee Count	Total Cost
Low Rise	$95	150 Sq. Ft.	2,500	
(Remodel)	$90	100 Sq. Ft.	3,500	
High Rise	$190	140 Sq. Ft.	3,500	
	$192	90 Sq. Ft.	3,500	

LESSON 3.7.6: BORDERING, COLOURING AND SHADING

Word provides very flexible options for bordering and shading our tables. We can create very elaborate tables quickly and easily using Word's bordering and shading options. We can modify or remove the border around selected cells in our table as well as shading or colouring cells to meet our requirements.

Setting borders on a table

To modify or remove the border on a table:

- ❑ Highlight the table (or the cells within the table around which to place a border).
- ❑ Choose **Format | Borders and Shading**.

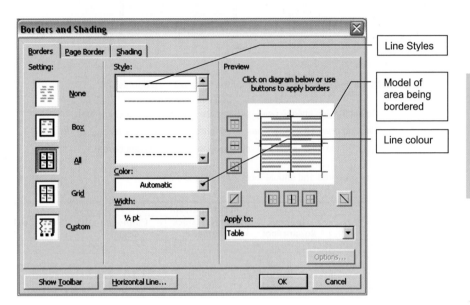

We may choose from a range of different line types and line colours.

The figure below represents the selected cells within the table. The outer lines represent a *bounding box* around the selected text. The inner lines represent the *inside border* within the selected cells.

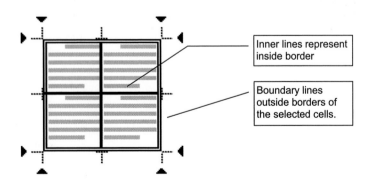

- ❑ Select the ¾ point double line (════════)

- ❑ Click on each of the **border lines** in the model window once in turn.

The model will now look something like:

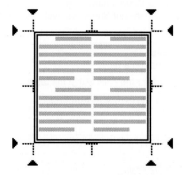

This indicates that the surrounding border for the table will be a double line.

- ❑ Select the line style to use – in this case select a ¾ point single line (‾‾‾‾‾‾)
- ❑ Click on one of the inner lines representing the inside border.
- ❑ Click on the other inner line representing the other inside border.

Our table is now bordered and should look something like this:

Cost Analysis				
	Cost per square foot	Average Office Space	Employee Count	Total Cost
Low Rise	$95	150 Sq. Ft.	2,500	
(Remodel)	$90	100 Sq. Ft.	3,500	
High Rise	$190	140 Sq. Ft.	3,500	
	$192	90 Sq. Ft.	3,500	

Shading cells in a table

We can also use the borders and shading window to shade the cells in our table.

❑ Select the top line of the table.

❑ Return to the **Format** menu and select the **Borders and Shading** option.

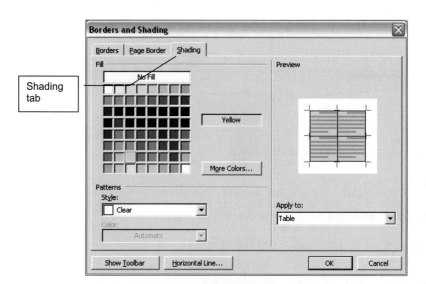

Cost Analysis				
	Cost per square foot	**Average Office Space**	**Employee Count**	**Total Cost**
Low Rise	$95	150 Sq. Ft.	2,500	
(Remodel)	$90	100 Sq. Ft.	3,500	
High Rise	$190	140 Sq. Ft.	3,500	
	$192	90 Sq. Ft.	3,500	

❑ Click on the '*Shading*' tab as seen above and choose a shade of grey.

❑ Click on a **shade** of grey and click **OK**.

The selected cells are now shaded grey.

LESSON 3.7.7: TABS

Tabs were often used to perform many of the operations now carried out by tables – but they are still useful in their own right. Tabs are often used as a method of aligning text and numbers in Word. Tabs appear as markers on our ruler in Word.

In order to work with tabs we need to make sure that the Ruler is visible.

Viewing the ruler

❑ Click on the **View** menu and choose **Ruler**.

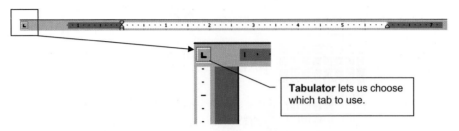

Tabulator lets us choose which tab to use.

There are a number of parts to our ruler that allow us to work with tabs. Firstly notice the **Tabulator** on the left hand corner of the ruler. Clicking on it changes the images representing the different types of tabs we can use. These symbols represent the different tabs available.

L	Left Alignment
⊥	Centre Alignment
⌐	Right Alignment
⊥	Decimal Alignment

Adding a tab to a paragraph

To use these tabs, we simply

❑ Select the correct tab from the **Tabulator**

❑ Click on the ruler at the point that the tab is needed

Left Tab	**Left Tab**	**Centre Tab**	**Right Tab**

Here the ruler shows a left tab at the 1" and 2" mark, a centre tab at the 3" mark and a right tab at the 4.5" mark.

We can add as many tabs as we want onto the ruler. The tabs will apply for the current or selected paragraphs. We use the **Tab** key on the keyboard to move from tab to tab. Text placed at a particular tab position will align according to the type of tab.

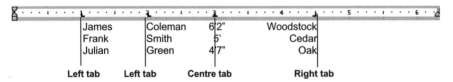

James	Coleman	6'2"	Woodstock
Frank	Smith	5'	Cedar
Julian	Green	4'7"	Oak
Left tab	**Left tab**	**Centre tab**	**Right tab**

Notice the text for the left tab is straight along the left edge. Text is centred along the centre tab position and right aligned with the right tab.

Decimal tabs

Decimal tabs are used for aligning on a specific character – usually a decimal point or comma. We use decimal tabs to ensure numbers are correctly aligned in columns.

Here are two lists of numbers – one aligned on a right tab and one aligned using a decimal tab:

A	B
123.33	123.00
124.3	124.3
45.9999	45.999

Column **A** is aligning the numbers using a right tab – column **B** is aligning the numbers with a decimal tab – notice it is much easier to read the numbers in column **B**.

Inserting tabs into a paragraph

We insert a tab by clicking the tabulator to select the type of tab we wish to insert and then clicking on the ruler at the tabs position. We can move the tab after it is positioned by dragging with the mouse or by double-clicking on the tab symbol.

We are going to place two decimal tabs into a document positioned at 6" and 9" positions.

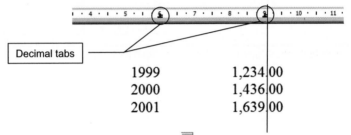

Decimal tabs

1999	1,234.00
2000	1,436.00
2001	1,639.00

- ❑ Choose the decimal tab symbol 📃 from the tabulator and click on the ruler at the 6 and 9cm marks.
- ❑ To move to the first tab position press the **Tab** key and then enter the first number.
- ❑ Press **Tab** to move to the next tab position and enter the next number.
- ❑ Pressing **Enter** or **Return** will copy the tab settings to the next line automatically and we can repeat the steps.

Experiment with *left, right* and *centre* tabs.

To Remove a Tab

- ❑ Click on the tab that needs to be removed and drag it off the ruler

The tab disappears off the ruler and will not affect the current paragraph any longer.

EXERCISES TO PROVE YOU KNOW

1. Layout the following Invoice template using tables and whatever other formatting is required - the light grey lines are table gridlines only and should not print.

DLTV Ltd. TVs and Videos for tomorrow… 91 Lr. George's Street, Dun Laoghaire Co. Dublin Tel: +353 1 2808-869 Fax: +353 1 2808-870	**INVOICE** INVOICE NO: 001 DATE: October 3rd

To:	**Ship To:**

Salesperson	Date Shipped	Shipped via	terms

QTY	description	unit price	amount

SUBTOTAL	
VAT	
SHIPPING and HANDLING	
TOTAL DUE	

Make all cheques payable to: **DLTV Ltd.**
If you have any questions concerning this invoice, call: Joe Murphy

THANK YOU FOR YOUR BUSINESS!

2. Save and close the document.

3. Open a blank new document and type in the following text:

> Computer Book
> By buying components and assembling them yourself, you can save a little money and gain a lifetime of free technical support. *Building a PC for Dummies* removes the intimidation factor from building your own Intel-based personal computer, explains what you need, and shows you how to put everything together. It's a fine place to start if you've never assembled your own machine before and want to give the process a try.

4. Save the document as **book.doc**

    Insert the following tabs:

    >   3" centre tab on the first line
    >   1.5" left align tab on the second line

5. Insert the following at the end of the document, using the decimal tab:

    >   Desktop $456.52
    >   Monitor $378.25
    >   Sound Card $85.00
    >   Network Card $75.50

6. Save and close the file.

SECTION 3.8: PAGE SETTINGS

In this section we will look at the options provided by Word to help us format the pages in our document. Headers and footers are very common in documents – they save considerable effort in renumbering or reorganising the information in a document. Page numbers, the date, time of creation, author and document name all appear in headers and footers. A **header** is text or graphics appearing in the top margin of a document page[†]. It usually contains text which is common to all pages, or all pages in a group or section (for example all odd numbered pages).

A **footer** consists of text or graphics which appear at the bottom part of a document page, it may contain a date, a page number or reference name for example.

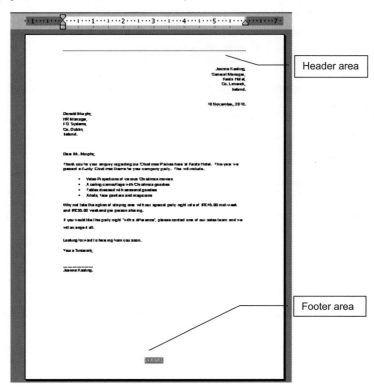

In this section we will:

- ❑ Create a header and footer for our document
- ❑ Insert automatically updating information into our document
- ❑ Adjust the page settings for our document
- ❑ Adjust the documents margins and page orientation ad size
- ❑ View our document in two page mode
- ❑ Add and view page breaks and other hidden characters
- ❑ Hyphenate our document

[†] Word does not actually restrict the location of a header or footer, but by convention a *Header* appears at the top of a document page, and a *Footer* appears at the bottom.

LESSON 3.8.1:   CREATING A HEADER OR A FOOTER

To work with headers and footers we need to use the *Header and Footer* toolbar.

❑   This toolbar will appear when we choose **Header and Footer** from the **View** menu.

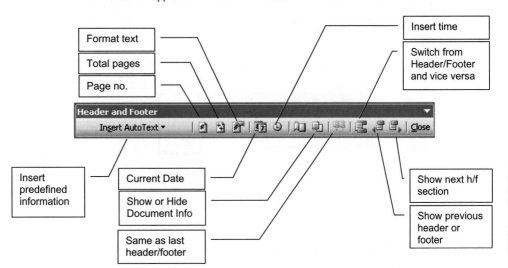

The document will switch to *header-footer* mode and our cursor will appear in either the header or footer section. The dotted line shows the current bounds of the footer area. We can type into this area, placing text, graphics or tables just like any other part of Word. The difference is that once completed – the text will appear on all pages with the same header-footer section.

❑   Press the [#] button to insert the current page number this will be updated automatically by Word as the pages change.

❑   To align the page number on the right of the page press the ≡ button on the formatting toolbar.

To switch between header and footer press the button.

We can use all of the standard editing and alignment menu options and toolbar buttons to insert text or graphics into our header or footer.

Page numbers

As well as inserting page numbers into the header and footer directly – Word also allows us to insert a page number into our document automatically.

To insert a page number directly into the header or footer of a document:

- ❏ Choose **Insert | Page Numbers…**

The following window will appear:

From here we can choose the *position* of the page number (either in the header or footer of the document) and its alignment on the page (left, right or centred).

- ❏ To omit the page number from the first page of the document un-tick the *"Show number on first page"* check box. This can be useful as we will often have a cover sheet or letter on the first page of a long document for which we do not wish to show a page number.

To change the format of the page numbering – the starting number for the pages and the display format – click on the **Format** button.

AutoText

Word allows us to insert special text or fields into our document. This is particularly useful if placed in the headers and footers of our document because it changes automatically without us having to edit the header/footer section each time. We can define fields in our document that we can insert as *autotext* entries into our document. AutoText entries also include *filenames* and other statistical information which can act as a useful summary for our documents.

- ❏ Open the document to edit and choose **Properties** from the **File** menu.

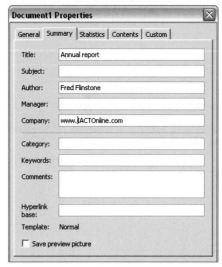

- ❏ Fill in appropriate information into the fields, such as *Author* and press **OK**.

Now choose an *AutoText* entry from the header/footer toolbar.

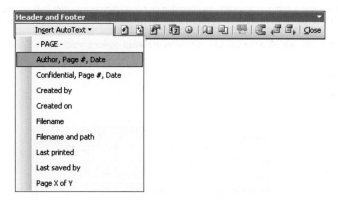

Word will insert the field into the document and it will be updated automatically whenever the document properties change.

We can also insert a document's *filename* or its *filename and path* into the document using autotext fields –this can act as a useful reference on the document when it is printed.

Autotext entries and field entries appear as **grey** when we attempt to edit them. This is to indicate that they will update automatically.

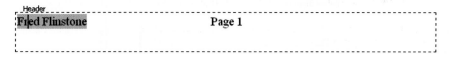

LESSON 3.8.2: PAGE OPTIONS FOR HEADERS AND FOOTERS

When we change the header or footer for a particular page Word assumes that we want to change the header and footer on all pages in this section of the document unless we tell it otherwise.

We can change this and other options from the **Page Setup** options from within Word.

❑   Press the ⬚ button.

This will display the **Page Setup** window:

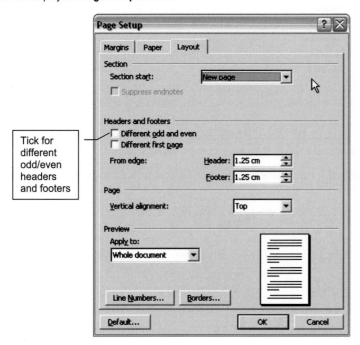

Tick for different odd/even headers and footers

The page setup dialog also allows us to set the page dimensions and add borders to our document pages.

Even and odd pages

From this window we can tell Word how we wish to organise our headers and footers.

With a double-sided document it is important to ensure that odd and even pages have different headers and footers. Odd pages might show the page number on the right corner of the page whereas even pages might show them in the left hand corner.

❑   To ensure different odd and even headers and footers, tick the **Different Odd and Even** check box.

Quite often it is also necessary to have a different header and footer on the *first page* of a document. The first page is often a title page and doesn't need a page number. To request a different header and footer for the first page of a document tick the **Different First Page** check box.

Copying headers and footers

Although we can create different headers and footers for all of our documents – usually we'll want to copy the settings from the previous section into the current one.

❑ To ensure the current section's header or footer is the same as the previous sections, press the ⊞ button on the *headers and footers* toolbar.

❑ To view the **previous** sections' header or footer press the ⊏ button.

❑ To view the **next** sections' header or footer press the ⊐ button.

Next we'll see how we can preview our multiple headers / footers using different preview modes.

LESSON 3.8.3:   ADJUSTING PAGE MARGINS, ORIENTATION AND SIZE

Margins are the surrounding region of a page in which text does not appear.

For example:

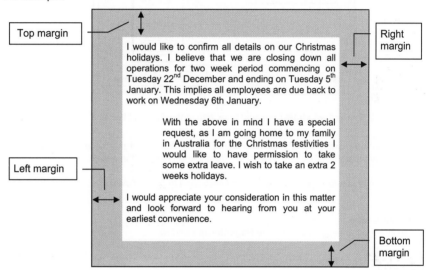

It is often necessary to change margins, for example if we *bind* a document it is necessary to leave a larger left margin on the page. Similarly if we wish to leave a space at the top and bottom of each page for a heading, title or page number. We will adjust the margins of our memo:

❑ Choose **Page Setup** from the **File** menu.

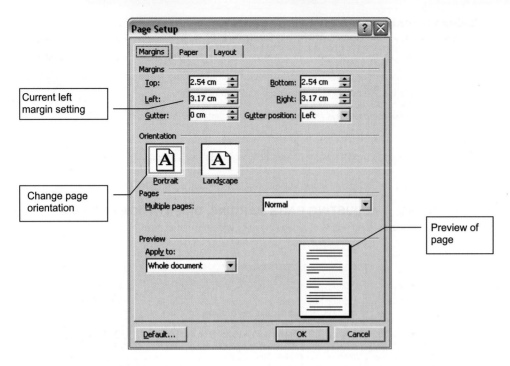

Current left margin setting

Change page orientation

Preview of page

□ Type 2.5cm in the **Left** text box and type 2cm in the **Top** text box and choose **OK**.

When printed, the top margin of the document will be offset 2cms from the top edge of the paper on every page. The left margin will be offset by 2.5cm from the left edge of the paper.

Use the *orientation* option to switch the page from *Landscape* to *Portrait* view.

Changing page size
We can also change the page size using the **Page Setup** Window.

□ Click on the *Paper* options tab:

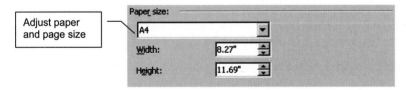

Adjust paper and page size

Choose different paper sizes from the list or specify them directly by entering the width and height of the page.

LESSON 3.8.4: PAGE BORDERS

We can also place a border around a page of our document.

    ❑   Choose **Format | Borders and Shading** and click on the **Page Border** tab.

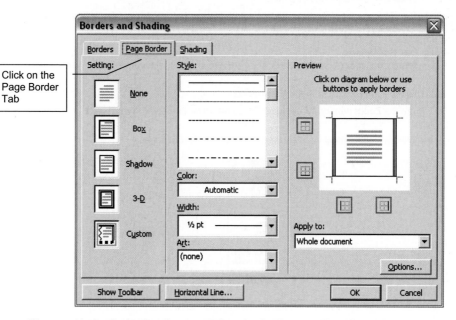

We can add a border by choosing presets from the **Setting** area. To add a border to the page:

    ❑   Choose the page border type to use.

We can modify the style and thickness of the border used by modifying the settings in the preview area

    ❑   Click **OK**

A border will appear around the current page based on the settings that we made.

LESSON 3.8.5: PAGE VIEW MODES

We can view our document in five different modes. *Normal, Web Layout, Print Layout, Reading Layout* and *Outline* modes.

These options are available from the **View** menu:

    ❑   **Normal** mode shows us the main body of text, but it does not display items such as margins, headers and footers.

    ❑   **Web Layout** previews our document as it would appear in a web browser

    ❑   **Print Layout** lets us see headers and footers and edit the text as it will appear when printed.

    ❑   **Reading Layout** resizes our document to make it easier to read onscreen and is useful when previewing or proofreading a long document

    ❑   **Outline** lets us view and organise large documents in sections.

Changing view modes

To change between view modes:

- ❑ Choose the view mode to switch to from the **View** menu – for example to switch to *Print Layout* view choose **Print Layout**

Word will change the page view mode to that selected. Notice that the appearance of our document can change dramatically in different view modes.

Magnifying our document

We can also magnify our view of the document and view two pages of a document at the same time.

- ❑ Choose **Print Layout** from the **View** menu.
- ❑ From the **Zoom** drop down menu on the standard toolbar select **Two Pages**

Any other selection will either magnify or shrink the size of the current page.

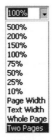

The document will now be displayed in **Two Page** mode.

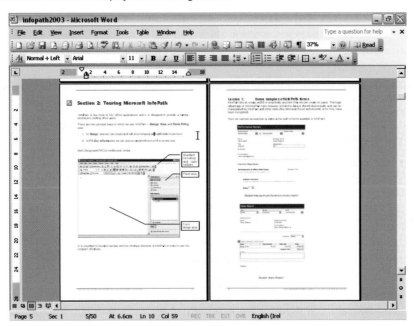

To return to normal viewing select **Page Width** from the **Zoom** drop down menu button.

LESSON 3.8.6:   INSERTING THE CURRENT DATE

Word lets us insert the current date into a document in two different ways. As *text* or as a *field*. If the date is inserted as *text* it appears in the document as it's typed. If the date is inserted as a *field* the date will be updated each time the document is opened.

- ❑   Delete the date from "memo.doc".
- ❑   Make sure the insertion point is placed where the old date was located.
- ❑   Choose **Date and Time...** from the **Insert** menu.

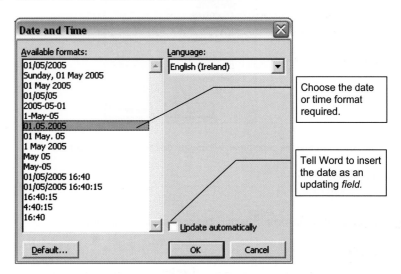

Choose the date or time format required.

Tell Word to insert the date as an updating *field*.

The current date should appear in the document.

If the date is incorrect, this means the computers internal date and time are incorrect. This can be set from within the *Control Panel* in Windows.

LESSON 3.8.7: ADDING AND REMOVING PAGE BREAKS

Adding a page break
We can add a page break to a document to force a new page at any point in the document.

- ❑ To force a page break choose **Insert | Break** or press **Ctrl + Enter**

- ❑ Click **OK** and the page break will appear directly after the cursor.

Removing a page break
To remove a page break

- ❑ Press the show/hide ¶ button. The page break will be visible

¶

--Page Break--

- ❑ Select the page break and press **Delete**

The page break will disappear.

LESSON 3.8.8: DISPLAYING AND HIDING NON-PRINTING CHARACTERS

As we create our documents, Word embeds many special hidden or *non-printing* characters along the way. These special characters represent keys like "tab" and "end of paragraph". We don't normally need to see these characters but sometimes it can be useful.

To display or hide non-printing characters in a document press the ¶ button on the standard toolbar.

Copying & Moving between documents

Occasionally we may need to copy or move text between one document and another. Perhaps when quoting a previous letter or amending existing text. Lets try this out:

- Select the second paragraph of the document.

    - If copying between documents press **CTRL + C** *or* press **CTRL + X** if moving the text.

- Go to the **File** menu and choose **New** or click on the button to create a new document.

Original paragraph

Copying·&·Moving·between·documents¶

Occasionally· we· may· need· to· copy· or· move· text· between· one· document· and· another. ·Perhaps· when· quoting· a· previous· letter· or· amending· existing· text. ·Lets· try· this· out:¶
¶
- → Select· the· second· paragraph· of· the· document.¶
¶
    - → If· copying· between· documents· press· **CTRL·+·C** ·*or*· press· **CTRL·+·X**· if· moving· the· text. ·¶
¶
- → Go· to· the· **File**· menu· and· choose· **New**· or· click· on· the· button· to· create· a· new· document.¶
¶
¶
¶

Same paragraph showing hidden characters

Inserting and removing hidden characters

We insert hidden characters into our document automatically as we type into Word. For example the hidden paragraph mark is inserted when we press the **Enter** key. To remove or delete a hidden character we simply select and delete the character when the hidden characters are revealed – just as if they were regular pieces of text in the document.

SYMBOL	WHAT IT MEANS	KEY TO INSERT
¶	End of paragraph	**Enter**
↵	Line break (or soft return)	**Shift+Enter**
→	Tab	**Tab Key**
·	Space	**Space key**

LESSON 3.8.9: HYPHENATING A DOCUMENT

Sometimes we will want Word to hyphenate our document. Hyphenation provides a professional finish to paragraphs which are fully justified.

Compare these two paragraphs with hyphenation on and off. You will notice that the hyphenated paragraph looks neater.

When you have played each lesson twice practice the examples demonstrated. Follow the instructions in the training book to lead you to the same end point. If you get stuck refer to the CD again looking at that particular lesson. Remember you can *pause, stop and* replay any lesson as often as you like.

When you have played each lesson twice practice the examples demonstrated. Follow the instructions in the training book to lead you to the same end point. If you get stuck refer to the CD again looking at that particular lesson. Remember you can *pause, stop and* replay any lesson as often as you like.

Paragraph A
(no hyphenation)

Paragraph B
(hyphenation turned on)

These two paragraphs look very similar but there is a subtle difference. Paragraph **B** is hyphenated. The word "**instructions**" is spread across two lines which makes a difference in the spacing (or tracking) between the words on the following line. Notice the last line of the paragraph only has two words on it compared to 3 in paragraph **A**.

We can turn on Hyphenation by going to the **Tools | Language** menu and choosing **Hyphenation**.

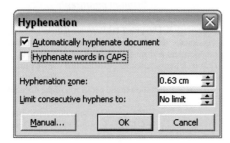

Tick the box to have the document hyphenated automatically. Usually capital letters are not hyphenated but to override this feature click on the "Hyphenate words in CAPS" option. Alternatively highlight the text to hyphenate and press on the **Manual** button.

EXERCISES TO PROVE YOU KNOW

1. Open a new blank document . Change the margins to the following settings:

Top	2.5 inches	Left	1 inch
Bottom	1 inch	**Right**	2 inches

2. Format the *Headers and Footers* in the document as follows:

Page	Header	Footer
1	None	Copyright © 2001 Euro Information
2 onwards	Welcome to the Euro	Page Number

4. Add a manual page break at the bottom of page 1 of the document.

5. View hidden characters in the document.

6. Delete the manual page break.

7. Add the current date to the footer of all pages.

SECTION 3.9:   TEMPLATES AND WIZARDS

Templates are a very clever idea. They allow us to build a "blue print" or "master copy" for documents we regularly use – and save us time in recreating documents.

A *template* document can be used repeatedly to create documents of the same type. For example we might have a template for our company letter headed paper or for timetables or invoices.

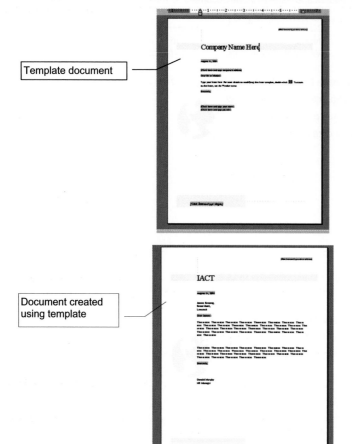

Template document

Document created using template

The built in templates in Word usually have generic text on them so that they can be modified to suit our needs.

When we have configured the built in templates for our purposes we can then save them as our own template documents.

In this section we will:

- ❑ Open a template document
- ❑ Create a *Résumé* using a Wizard
- ❑ Save a customised template

LESSON 3.9.1:   OPENING WORD TEMPLATES

Word comes supplied with several pre-designed templates and Wizards for many common tasks. When we create a new document we are presented with a list of all available templates and wizards.

❑   From the **File** menu choose **New**. The **New Document** panel will appear.

From the New Document panel we can choose to create a new document from either a *Blank Document, an XML document, a Web Page, From an existing document… or* by using a *template* that is either on the computer or available on the Internet.

The **Normal** template is Word's default template. It contains the settings that are used each time we choose to create a new document. These settings include details such as:

❑   Page size and orientation

❑   Default font style and size and page margins

❑   Paragraph spacing and alignment

If we open this template and modify these settings they will be changed forever in our new blank documents.

By creating our own template with the settings precisely matching those we use all the time we save ourselves a considerable amount of repetitive and tedious work.

Firstly we will examine some of the existing templates:

❑   Click **On my computer…** from the list of template options

The following dialog box will appear:

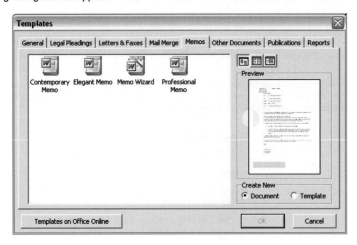

- ❑ Click on the **Memos** tab and choose "Contemporary Memo" from the list in the Memos tab.
- ❑ Click **OK**

Word creates a new document, but instead of being empty it has copied the contents of the template into the file. We can now update the file using as much of the pre-written text as we like. We have created a new document based on this template.

Many templates contain no text at all, merely styles and settings that can be used by the user. We will look at styles and their connection to templates later on.

LESSON 3.9.2: THE WORD WIZARDS

Word provides us with a more powerful type of template called a "Wizard". A Wizard helps and guides us through choices with simple questions and answers. There are Wizards for a number of interesting documents. To create our Wizard we would need to learn Visual BASIC (programming language), but using them is easy.

We will look at the "Resume" Wizard.

- ❑ Click **On my computer...** from the **New Document** panel
- ❑ Choose the **Other Documents** tab and choose **Resume Wizard**

After a few moments the following screen will appear.

- ❑ Click **Next**.

This step asks us which style we would like to make our Resume in:

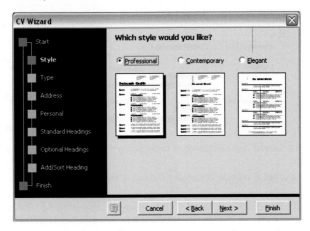

- ❑ Choose the *Contemporary style*. Click **Next**.

The next step asks us to choose a type of Resume.

- ❑ Choose *Entry Level Resume*. Click **Next**.

This next step is asking us to fill in the information that we want to appear at the top of our document.

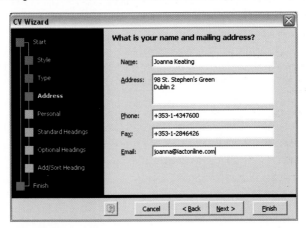

The next three steps ask us to choose headings and to add any additional headings into our Resume. Click **Next** after each of these steps.

- ❑ Click on **Finish** to see the final product:

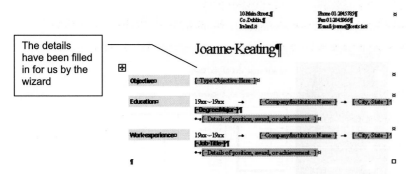

The details have been filled in for us by the wizard

As we can see, the wizard has completed a large amount of the document, leaving refinements and modifications to us.

❏ Save the newly created document and call it "Resume".

Any changes made to a document based on a template or created using a Wizard will not effect the original template or wizard. To change the template we must edit the template directly. **This is worth remembering**.

LESSON 3.9.3: CREATING A NEW TEMPLATE

Suppose we wanted to re-use the invoice we created in an earlier lesson. We have two choices:

1. We could locate our original invoice and open it and then we could *re-save* it with a new name.

or

2. We could create a **template** for the invoice.

We are going to create a template:

❑ Open up "invoice.doc" created earlier.

This document is ready to be used as a template as it contains the minimum amount of information common to all invoices that we may want to print.

❑ Choose **File | Save As** and choose **Document template** from the list of file types.

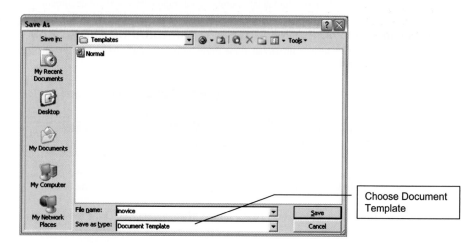

Choose Document Template

❑ Type "Invoice" into the file name window and choose *Document Template* from the **Save As Type** selection box.

Automatically the document will be saved into the correct folder called Templates. *It is important that we do not change this.*

❑ Choose **OK**, and then **Close** the current document.

We have now created a template called "Invoice" and it will appear in the list of available templates when we wish to create a new document (see *Lesson 3.9.1:Opening Word Templates* on page 229).

EXERCISES TO PROVE YOU KNOW

1. Open a new blank document.

2. Change the page margins to the following settings:

Top	2.5 inches	**Left**	1 inch
Bottom	1 inch	**Right**	2 inches

3. Add the date to the top of the page and right align it.

4. Save the document as a template called **headed_paper**

5. Create a new document based on the **headed_paper** template.

SECTION 3.10:   STYLES

Styles provide an easy way to format similar types of text, such as headings and lists. We can use the same style repeatedly to save time and to ensure that the document has a consistent format.

For example, suppose we want the first level headings of a report to be *italicised, bold, centred* and 16pts in size. Instead of having to choose these options each time for each first-level heading in the report, we can create a *single style* that contains all of these codes. Then we can apply this style to each of the first-level headings.

Styles are attached to, or associated with, *templates.* Each template has its own set of styles. Styles can be copied between templates.

In this section we will:

- ❏ Apply existing styles to paragraphs
- ❏ Modify and create new paragraph styles
- ❏ Create a style to automatically number paragraph sections in our document

LESSON 3.10.1: APPLYING STYLES TO PARAGRAPHS AND WORDS

The current style we type in is displayed in the **Style** drop down edit box on the formatting toolbar. The default style is called *Normal.*

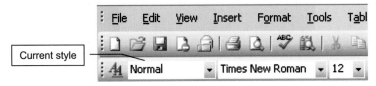

Current style

Each style has a unique name. The list of all styles available to the document can be accessed from the style drop down list. We can apply a different style by selecting one from this list.

- ❏ Create a new document based on the "Normal" template. Type the following extract into the document:

> Compilers and Interpreters
>
> The Synthesis Phase:
> As translation progresses, the compiler's internal representation of the source program changes. This can be seen on the diagram over the page.
> After syntax and semantic analysis some compilers generate an explicit intermediate representation of the source program.
>
> Intermediate code generation
> We can think of this intermediate representation as a program for an abstract machine. This intermediate representation has two important properties: it is easy to produce and it is easy to translate to the target language.
> The intermediate code is like an advanced assembly language. In the example over the page it can be taken to be that of a three address machine. With this machine the compiler must consider the order in which the operations are to be performed and it must generate temporary variables to hold intermediate results.
>
> Code optimisation:
> This phase attempts to improve the previous phase so that faster running machine code will result. Some optimisations are trivial some are very difficult. This would include removal of assignments to variables, which are not used, removing constant assignments in loops, eliminating tail recursive functions and many more.

We are now going to format this document by applying the templates built in styles.

❑ Select the phrase *"Compilers and Interpreters"* and choose "Heading 1" from the *styles* in the drop down list box.

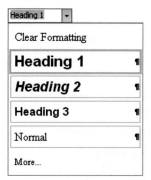

❑ Select the phrase *"Synthesis Phase"* and choose "Heading 2" from the list of available styles.

"Heading 1" and "Heading 2" are two styles we have now applied to our document.

❑ **Heading 1** is usually reserved for chapter or section titles.
❑ **Heading 2** is usually reserved for sub-section titles.
❑ **Heading 3** for sub-sub-section titles and so on.

It is a good idea to adopt the same policy when creating reports or other long documents.

LESSON 3.10.2: MODIFYING PARAGRAPH STYLES

The main benefit of styles is the ability to be able to change the formatting of similarly styled paragraphs instantly once a style has been applied. If we adjust the **Heading1, Heading2** or **Heading3** styles we have just used we will see changes reflected throughout the document straightaway.

To modify or create a new style:

    ❑   From the **Format** menu choose **Style**.

This will display the *Style and Formatting* panel:

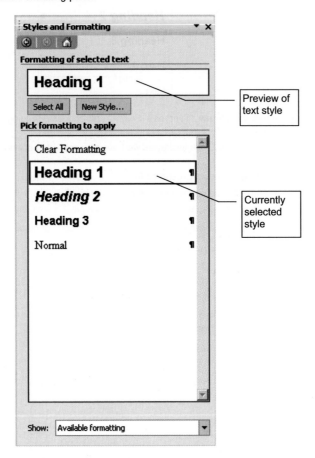

    ❑   Select "Heading 1" from the list of available style and choose **Modify** from the drop-down menu

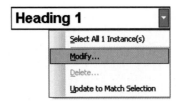

The *modify style* window will open:

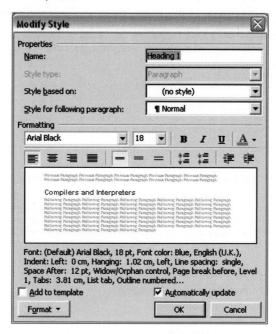

- ☐ Change the text colour to **Blue**
- ☐ Now click the **Format** button and select **Paragraph**.

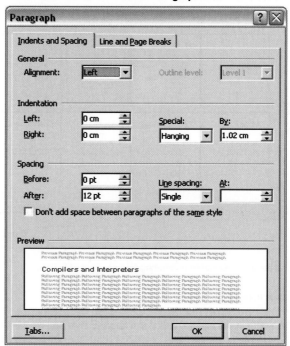

We can now change the alignment and other settings for this style.

- ☐ Select "Centred" from the **Alignment** drop down list.

❑   Choose **OK** and exit from the paragraph window and choose **OK** again.

We have now modified the Heading 1 style and our document should now look like this:

<table>
<tr>
<td>

Compilers and Interpreters

The Synthesis Phase:
As translation progresses, the compiler's internal representation of the source program changes. This can be seen on the diagram over the page.

After syntax and semantic analysis some compilers generate an explicit intermediate representation of the source program.

</td>
<td>

Heading1 style automatically centred and now blue

</td>
</tr>
</table>

LESSON 3.10.3:   CREATING A STYLE TO NUMBER SECTIONS

It is sometimes useful to number paragraphs and sections in a document – particularly long documents. Word can help us do this automatically if we adopt the scheme we have been using for formatting sections. If we ask Word to number the sections and paragraphs we no longer have to keep track of the numbering ourselves. So if we choose to re-organise a section or chapter we will not have to renumber the entire document manually. To automatically number the heading styles in our document:

❑   Click inside the first paragraph formatted in the *Heading 1* style

❑   Choose **Format | Bullets and Numbering**.

❑   Choose the *Outline Numbered* tab

Choose the option that has the *heading 1* and *heading 2* references.

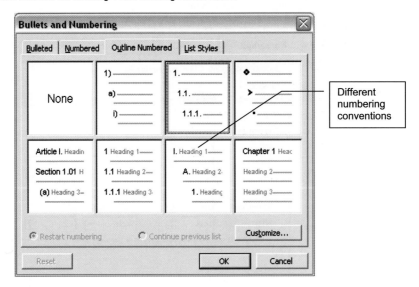

We can select from the list of available numbering formats or modify them.

❑   Select an appropriate numbering style and click **OK**.

When we click **OK** word applies our changes to the heading style and we can see that all our heading paragraphs are automatically numbered and indented according to the numbering format chosen.

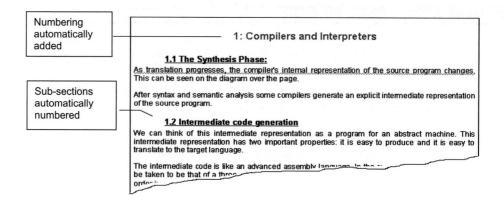

Numbering automatically added

Sub-sections automatically numbered

1: Compilers and Interpreters

1.1 The Synthesis Phase:
As translation progresses, the compiler's internal representation of the source program changes. This can be seen on the diagram over the page.

After syntax and semantic analysis some compilers generate an explicit intermediate representation of the source program.

1.2 Intermediate code generation
We can think of this intermediate representation as a program for an abstract machine. This intermediate representation has two important properties: it is easy to produce and it is easy to translate to the target language.

The intermediate code is like an advanced assembly language. In the ... be taken to be that of a three ... order ...

Changing the style settings will then automatically update all text in the document using that style.

EXERCISES TO PROVE YOU KNOW

1. Open a new blank document. Modify the existing styles for Heading1, Heading2 and Heading 3 so that they now look like this:

Heading 1	Blue, Centred, Comic Sans, 16pts
Heading 2	Red, Left Aligned, Comic Sans, 14pts
Normal	Black, Justified, Arial, 12pts

2. Apply the styles to a paragraph and test them.

3. Modify the *heading 3* style so that:

Font Size	10pt
Font Colour	Red
Alignment	Right aligned
Font Style	Courier New

4. Apply the style to a paragraph.

5. Save and Close the document.

SECTION 3.11:   MAIL MERGE

When we need to send the same document to a lot of different people we will often use a mail-merge in order to personalise the document. For example if sending out an invitation to 100 guests we might create a mail-merge document which personalises the name on each invitation.

In this section we will learn how to create a mail-merge document in order to personalise letters and labels when sending information to a group.

LESSON 3.11.1: WHAT IS A MAIL MERGE?

Mail merge is a tool in Word that lets us create personalised letters, envelopes, or mailing labels when we merge or combine one *document* with a *data source*. The document contains the text and other items that remain constant in each version of the letter. The *data source* contains the list of names and addresses that will change for each letter.

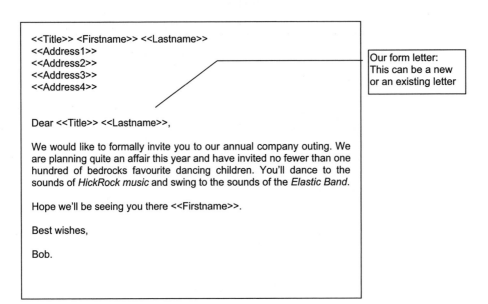

Title	firstname	Lastname	Address1
Mr.	Fred	Flinstone	Bedrock
Mr.	Barney	Flood	Greystones
Ms.	Wilma	Flinstone	Bedrock
Ms.	Cathy	Flood	Greystones

Our datasource could be a Word table...

<<Title>> <Firstname>> <<Lastname>>
<<Address1>>
<<Address2>>
<<Address3>>
<<Address4>>

Dear <<Title>> <<Lastname>>,

We would like to formally invite you to our annual company outing. We are planning quite an affair this year and have invited no fewer than one hundred of bedrocks favourite dancing children. You'll dance to the sounds of *HickRock music* and swing to the sounds of the *Elastic Band*.

Hope we'll be seeing you there <<Firstname>>.

Best wishes,

Bob.

Our form letter:
This can be a new or an existing letter

To create a mail-merge we need to have the *records* (in this case the list of names and addresses) that we will be sending letters to.

Generally there are two scenarios when creating a mail-merge.

1) Where we must create the names and addresses from scratch.

2) Where the names and addresses already exist.

LESSON 3.11.2: CREATING A MAIL MERGE FROM SCRATCH

Creating a mail-merge from scratch is easy but involves a number of different steps.

Firstly let's open up a new blank document and type the letter that will be sent to each individual, but leave out any *personal* information.

The letter might look something like this:

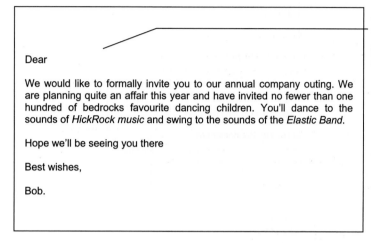

Dear

We would like to formally invite you to our annual company outing. We are planning quite an affair this year and have invited no fewer than one hundred of bedrocks favourite dancing children. You'll dance to the sounds of *HickRock music* and swing to the sounds of the *Elastic Band*.

Hope we'll be seeing you there

Best wishes,

Bob.

> We've left a blank for any personal information

❑   Now from the **Tools | Letters and Mailings** menu choose **Mail Merge**.

The **Mail Merge** panel will appear:

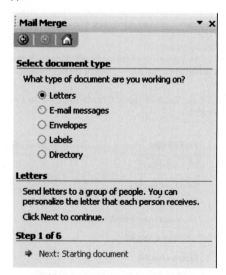

We are going to use the letter we have just written as our mail-merge letter. However, we could just as easily have used an existing document.

Now we must choose the type of document we are going to create.

❑ Select **Letters** from the *Mail Merge* panel and then click **Next**

We will be asked if we want to create a new document to achieve the mail merge or use the document we have already open. We're going to use the document we have open already, which is in the *current document.*

❑ Click **Next** to continue.

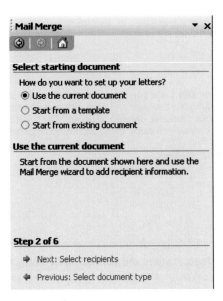

We have now completed stage one of our mail-merge and can progress to *Step 3*. Step 3 involves creating the names and addresses that will be merged into our form letters.

Selecting or creating a datasource

Next we need to create or open the list of names and addresses that will be merged into our letter or choose a list of names and addresses that have already been created.

❑ Choose **Type a new list** and press **Create** to continue or choose **Use an existing list** if the list already exists.

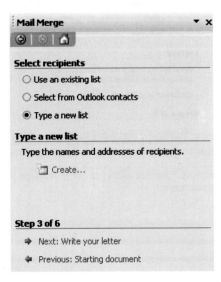

The following window will appear allowing us to enter the names and addresses of the recipients of our letter:

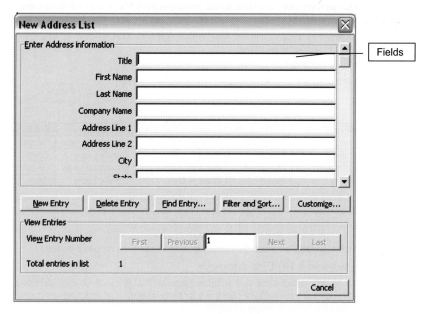

This window gives us the default fields used for names and addresses. We can change the order of these fields, add extra fields or remove the fields by clicking **Customize...**

When we click **Customize...** the following window will appear:

To **Delete** a field:	Select it and press **Delete**
To **Add** a field:	Press **Add** and give the field a name
To **Rename** a field:	Select the field and press **Rename**
To **Reorder** a field:	Use the **Move Up** and **Move Down** buttons

Creating the right list of fields and ensuring the list is in the correct order is critical to making sure our mail merge runs smoothly.

We can now enter the names and addresses that we wish to merge with our document.

- ❑ If required we can use the **Customize Address List** window to adjust the list of fields so that they appear as above.
- ❑ Type in the details of 4 individuals.
- ❑ Press **New Entry** for each new name and address

Fields

Title	First Name	Last Name	Company Name	Address1	Address2	Address3
Mr.	Fred	Flinstone	Bedrock Ltd.	Mountain View	Greystones	Co. Wicklow
Mr.	Barney	Flood	Roks R Us	Sandy Lane	Bray	Co. Wicklow
Ms.	Wilma	Flinstone	Bedrock Ltd.	Mountain View	Greystones	Co. Wicklow
Ms.	Cathy	Flood	Roks R Us	Sandy Lane	Bray	Co. Wicklow
....	....	....		....	....	....
....	....	....		....	....	....
....	....	....		....	....	....

- ❑ Click **CLOSE** when all the names and addresses are properly entered.

We will now be asked to **SAVE** the *datasource*.

- ❑ Save the datasource in a suitable place so that it can be easily identified and recovered and give it a meaningful name – e.g. *party_guests*. For example we might choose to store the data in the **C:\party** directory.

Our screen will now look like:

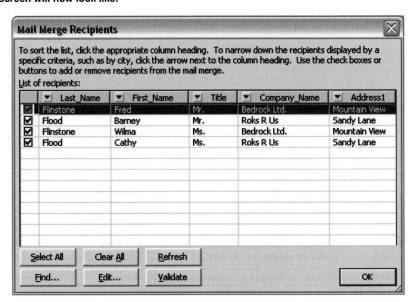

Word now displays the full list of names and addresses of those that will receive the letter. From here we can remove names from the list, change the sort order or edit them directly.

- ❑ Click **OK** to continue.

❑ The *Mail Merge* panel should now look something like this – Word is telling us that we have selected a data source called "party_guests.mdb" (which we just created) and we are now ready to *Write your letter* (or edit the one we created earlier).

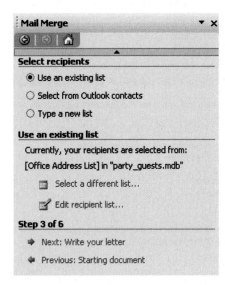

Notice that we have a new toolbar, the **Mail Merge** *toolbar:*

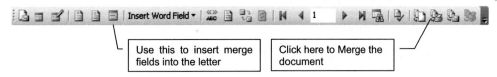

| Use this to insert merge fields into the letter | Click here to Merge the document |

❑ Move the cursor to where the address would normally be on the letter and press the **Insert Merge Field** button 📄 on the mail-merge toolbar.

The Insert Merge Field dialog box with all the available fields will appear something like this:

❑ Choose **Title** and press **Insert**

The field will be inserted into the document like:

<<Title>>

- ❏ Now insert the field **Firstname,** and **Lastname** fields and press **Cancel** on the **Insert Merge Fields** dialog box.

- ❏ Now insert a space between the **Title, Firstname** and **Lastname** fields by moving between the fields and pressing the **Space** bar.

- ❏ Press **Enter** to create a new paragraph after the **Lastname** field.

- ❏ Now we can press the ▤ button again and repeat this until the address is complete and looks as follows

> **<<Title>> <Firstname>> <<Lastname>>**
> **<<Company Name>>**
> **<<Address1>>**
> **<<Address2>>**
> **<<Address3>>**

- ❏ Now press the ⟪⟫/ABC button on the mail merge toolbar. The field names will be replaced by the actual data of the first record.

For example:

Mr. Fred Flinstone
Bedrock Ltd.
Mountain View
Greystones
Co. Wicklow

Experiment with the ⟪⟫/ABC button and the ◄◄ ◄ 1 ► ►◄ navigation buttons to see how it is possible to move between records.

Performing the mail merge
To perform the mail merge and print the personalised letters:

- ❏ Press the ▤ button to merge to a new document

or

- ❏ Press the ▤ button to merge directly to the printer

We are asked to decide whether we wish to merge all records, the current record or a range of records.

- ❏ Press the **OK** button to perform the mail merge.

Printing individual pages of a Mail Merge

We can print individual pages of our letter by moving between the records and choosing *PRINT* as normal. This can be useful if we need to reprint a certain letter.

That's essentially it!

Now although there seem to be lots of steps involved in setting up the initial mail-merge, the good news is that once the document is saved, it can be re-opened and it will appear exactly as it was, merge fields and all.

LESSON 3.11.3:   LABELS

Another common use of the mail merge feature in word is to generate labels. Labels can be tricky to produce and are not usually the favourite part of a mail shot! Let's see how we would produce labels for our mail-merge document. For the purpose of this lesson we will be using a sheet of 3 x 8 labels – giving us 24 labels per sheet.

To create labels for our mail-shot we follow the same steps to building the mail-merge letter but in step one we choose **Labels** as the type of document we are going to produce.

> **Select document type**
>
> What type of document are you working on?
>
> ○ Letters
> ○ E-mail messages
> ○ Envelopes
> ● Labels
> ○ Directory

❑   Click on **Next**

Word handles labels by using carefully sized tables. Getting the size of the tables right at the beginning and ensuring they match the label is crucial to lining the text and graphics that appear on the label later on.

> **Change document layout**
>
> Start from a ready-to-use mail merge template that can be customized to suit your needs.
>
> 🗐 Label options...

❑   Click on **Label options...** to choose the label size and format

❑   To following label setup window will appear:

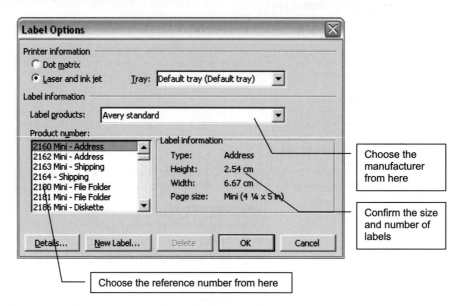

Choose the manufacturer from here

Confirm the size and number of labels

Choose the reference number from here

The first step in setting up the document is to choose the label manufacturer. **Avery™** make the most common labels available. These are the easiest labels to setup as Microsoft have configured the program to recognize the particular Avery reference numbers that appear on the label boxes. Compatible labels will often provide their equivalent "Avery" number. If you work a lot with labels check out www.avery.com for useful tips on working with labels and for some handy templates.

In Europe ensure the label option is set for **Avery A4** and **A5** sizes or we won't find the correct reference number from the list.

In the US use the **Avery Standard** size which is set to use the standard **Letter** paper.

We are using sheets of labels with 24 labels per page. From the Avery list and from our label sheet we can see this is **L7159** label type.

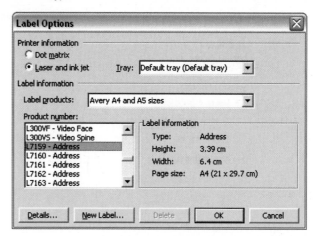

To confirm the settings click on the **Details** button to show the settings for this label.

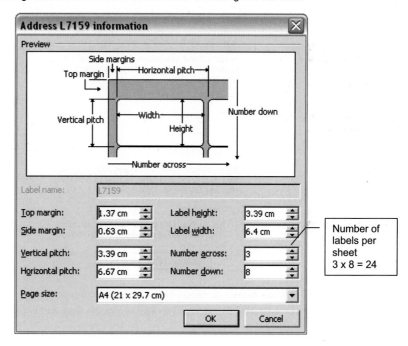

This window shows the page size, the margins around the page for this label sheet as well as the number of labels across and down that will appear on the page.

It is possible to modify the settings by hand here for unusual label styles. However practically every label ever made has a reference number built into Word and it is much easier to find the matching label number than modify these settings by hand as it is difficult to get the figures exactly right for different printers.

 ❑   Click **OK** to confirm the label type

❑   Next we must select the data source for the labels. Click **Next**

We should use the same data source as was used to create the addresses for letters earlier.

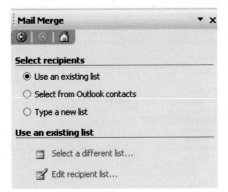

❑   Select the datasource and press **Next**

Once we have selected our data source we need to tell Word what is to appear on each label.

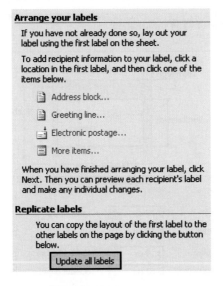

❑   Click on **More items…** to display the list of fields in the data source.

In the same way as we inserted the address information onto the letter earlier – create the address on the first label.

❑ Once the address information is correct press **Update all labels** and Word will add the address information onto every label.

Word will now update the table with merge fields like this:

«Title» «First_Name» «Last_Name» «Company_Name» «Address1» «Address2» «Address3»	«Next Record»«Title» «First_Name» «Last_Name» «Company_Name» «Address1» «Address2» «Address3»	«Next Record»«Title» «First_Name» «Last_Name» «Company_Name» «Address1» «Address2» «Address3»

The **Next Record** field ensures that each label contains the next address to display on the label. We can now merge the document to a printer to print the labels the same as we did with our mail-merge document.

Pressing the **View Merged Data** button on the mail merge toolbar will display the contents of the labels. Our first 3 labels should look like this:

Mr. Fred Flinstone Bedrock Ltd. Mountain View Greystones Co. Wicklow	Mr. Barney Flood Roks R Us Sandy Lane Bray Co. Wicklow	Ms. Wilma Flinstone Bedrock Ltd. Mountain View Greystones Co. Wicklow

EXERCISES TO PROVE YOU KNOW

1. Create a template letter to send to three potential clients requesting business.

2. Create a new data source with all the default fields for a mail-merge letter. Save this data source as *New customers* data source.

3. Add three records to the data source.

   Insert merge fields above the body of the letter as follows:

   «FirstName» «LastName»
   «Address1»
   «Address2»
   «City»

   Dear «FirstName»

4. Merge the letter and records to a new document.

5. Return to the original letter and reopen the mail merge helper.

6. Produce labels for the letters (use *Avery code 2662* Mini-Address labels) using the same data source.

SECTION 3.12: PICTURES, IMAGES AND CHARTS

In this section we are going to learn how to insert pictures, images and charts into a Word document. Graphic images might be scanned, taken with a digital camera or come from a clipart gallery. We will learn how to work with these types of images in Word.

Microsoft's graphics toolbar is the same in *Word, Excel* and *PowerPoint. Module 6 – PowerPoint on page 480* covers this toolbar in detail.

LESSON 3.12.1: IMPORTING AN IMAGE FROM CLIPART OR A FILE

We can insert a ClipArt image or we can insert an image file that we have created ourselves.

For either option we'll work with a blank Word document:

❑ From the **Insert | Picture** menu choose **Clipart** *or* **From File**

To insert the *ClipArt* image:

❑ Choose **Insert | Picture | ClipArt**
❑ Type a keyword that describes the clipart to search for
❑ The clipart gallery will display a list of matches

Note: to view all clipart in the gallery leave the search field blank

❑ Hover the mouse over the image to reveal a drop-down arrow like this:

❑ Click on the drop-down arrow and choose **Insert**
❑ The image will now be in our Word document
❑ Repeat this for each image

To insert an image from a file:

❑ Choose **Insert Picture | From File…**

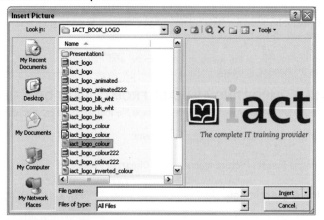

❑ Locate the folder that holds the image that we need to insert.

To preview the image before inserting it make sure the **Preview** view is selected from the view drop down list:

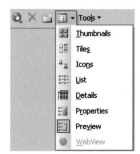

❑ Click on **Insert**

❑ The image will now be in the Word document

LESSON 3.12.2: INSERTING A CHART INTO WORD

We can insert other objects into our Word document, *Spreadsheets*, *slides* in fact any program that supports OLE (object linking and embedding) can have its components embedded into Word.

We are going to insert an Excel Chart into Word.

❑ Choose **Insert | Object**.

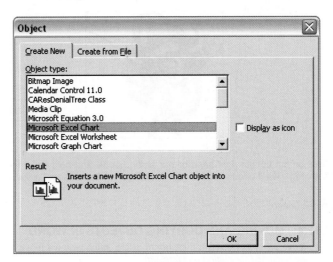

❑ To insert a chart object choose *Microsoft Excel Chart* and click **OK**.

or

❑ To import an existing chart or spreadsheet choose **Create from File** and browse to locate the spreadsheet to import.

LESSON 3.12.3: SELECTING AND RESIZING GRAPHIC OBJECTS

Once the image is in Word, we can move and resize the image to suit our needs.

❏   We select an image by clicking anywhere on the image with the *left* mouse button.

We will see that when selected the image will show small black boxes on each corner of the image. These are *sizing* handles and also show that the image has been selected.

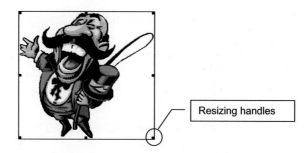

Resizing handles

❏   Click on the bottom *right hand* corner sizing handle and hold down the left mouse button and drag inward or outward to make the image smaller or bigger respectively.

This will resize the image.

LESSON 3.12.4: MOVING AND COPYING OBJECTS IN WORD

We can copy or move an image using the clipboard in the same way we move regular text or other objects in word (see page 167 for *cutting and pasting*)

❏   Select the object by clicking on it with the mouse

❏   To move the object press ✂ or press **Ctrl+X**

❏   To copy the object press 📋 or press **Ctrl+C**

❏   Move to the location where we want the image and press 📋 or press **Ctrl+V**

Alternatively we can *drag* the image using the mouse to a new location in the document. Click on the object and hold down the mouse button. Then drag to the new location.

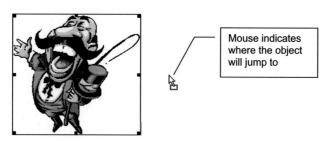

Mouse indicates where the object will jump to

Deleting objects in Word

To delete objects like images and charts in word

❏   Select the object and press **Delete** or cut object onto the clipboard.

EXERCISES TO PROVE YOU KNOW

1.   Open the *Christmas.doc* file created earlier and insert some appropriate clipart into the document.

2.   Create a chart in Microsoft Excel and copy the chart into a blank Word document.

SECTION 3.13: USING HELP

One of the most useful facilities offered by Windows is its *Help* utility. Most Windows products come with excellent help facilities usually containing as much if not more information than the accompanying reference guides. The help system uses a technique called "hypertext" to access information relating to a particular topic. This system allows the reader to follow a *thread* through the help database, constantly looking up and referring to related information.

LESSON 3.13.1: STARTING HELP

The help system in Word (and in Office generally) works like an Internet browser. We search for help by providing a keyword or phrase and we can follow links and threads much as we would do inside Internet Explorer. Some of the information for Word's help can in fact come from online resources in order to stay up to date.

Help can be started by pressing **F1** or selecting from the **HELP** menu and this will display the **Word Help** panel (shown below).

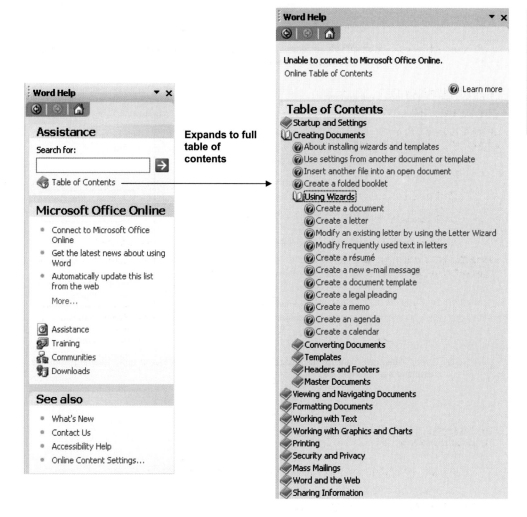

LESSON 3.13.2:   SEARCHING FOR HELP

The search tool allows us to search directly for a particular feature or facility of Word

Let's find information about Word's thesaurus.

❑   Type "Thesaurus" into the search box and press **Enter**

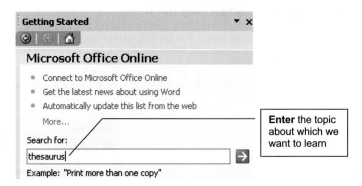

The following list of topics will appear:

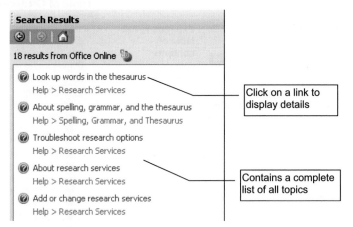

❑   Type "Thesaurus" and press **Search.** Choose the most relevant topic heading from the results to see the help file.

❑ Click on "Look up Words in the thesaurus". The Help system will now display detailed information on "Look up Words in the thesaurus".

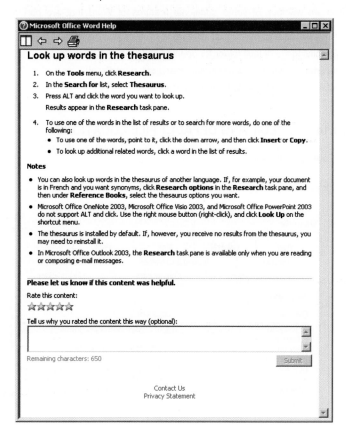

❑ This information can then be printed for later reference.

EXERCISES TO PROVE YOU KNOW

1. Use Word's Help tool to find out information on *Line Spacing* and *Customising the toolbar*
2. Copy the text into a new blank document and print it out.
3. Close the Help Panel.

SECTION 3.14: ADVANCED FEATURES

In this section we will look at some additional features of Word that are part of the ICDL/ECDL examination.

- ❑ Specifying the default folder for opening and closing files
- ❑ Inserting External Files (importing charts etc. from Excel)
- ❑ Alternative File Formats for Word documents.

LESSON 3.14.1: SPECIFYING DEFAULT FILE LOCATIONS

We can specify the default location Word uses to open and save our documents. These settings are stored in the **Tools | Options** menu.

- ❑ Click on **Tools | Options** and click on the **File Locations** tab

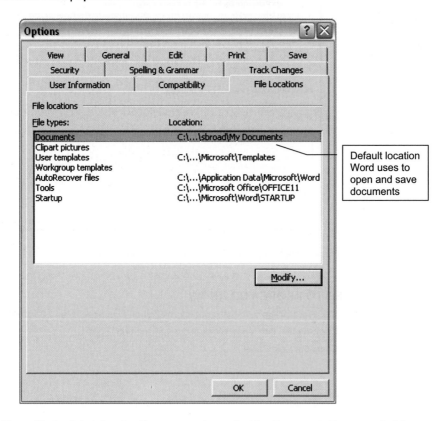

- ❑ To modify the default location files are saved to, select the *Documents* file type and click **Modify**. The default location can be a local folder or a network folder.

Word will look first in this location when opening and saving files.

We can also specify the *user information* from the options dialog box. The user information is saved with all documents created using Word and can help identify the author of a document.

To modify the user information stored by Word – click on the *User Information* tab in the options dialog box.

- ❑ When all the changes have been made press **OK**

LESSON 3.14.2: INSERTING AN EXTERNAL FILE

Quite often we will want to insert a chart into our document. Let's suppose we have a chart in Excel. We can import the chart into our Word document.

- ❑ Open Excel and then open or create a new chart (see page 321 for detailed instructions)
- ❑ Select the chart

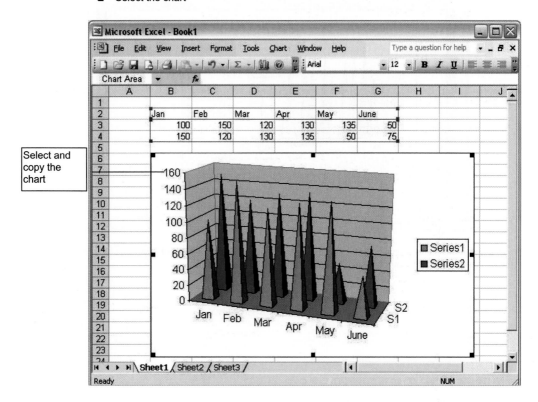

- ❑ Go to the **Edit** menu and choose **Copy** or press **Ctrl+C** to place the chart on the clipboard.
- ❑ Minimise the Excel screen and re-open Word.
- ❑ Locate the cursor in the document where the chart is required and choose **paste** or press **Ctrl+V**

Pasting will place the chart into the Word document page.

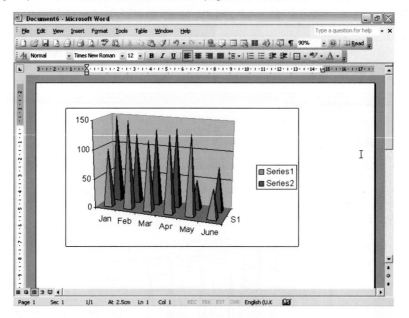

This copy and paste feature can be done between *Word, Excel* and *PowerPoint* in exactly the same way. We can use it to move tables from Word into PowerPoint or Excel.

LESSON 3.14.3: SAVING WORD IN DIFFERENT FILE FORMATS

So far we have saved our documents as Word documents with the file extension ***.doc**.

Word can save documents in a variety of different formats, which means that we can open and read a Word document in different applications. Many people use *Corel WordPerfect* as their word processor or may need the text of the document in a plain format. Or we might like to convert our document for viewing on the web.

Note: Before saving the file in a different format, we should always save it in its native word format to avoid losing any information.

Saving a document as a Web page
To save as a web page – we save it as a HTML document.

- ❏ Open a Word Document to convert
- ❏ Click on the **File** menu and choose **Save As** and from the **Save as type** box select **'Web Page'**

The *save as* window will appear:

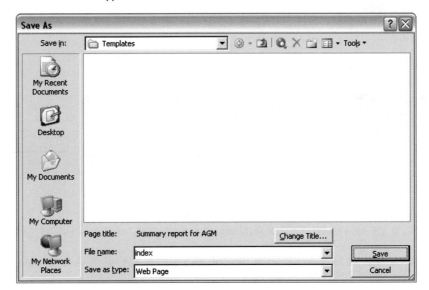

- ❏ Give the file a name, keep the name of the file in lowercase and do not use any spaces in the file name.

Word will create additional files if your document contains graphics or sound files. When publishing to a web site all these additional files should also be copied.

This can now be opened in an Internet Browser like Explorer

Saving to different versions of Word
Each new release of Word introduces a slightly different file format. It is useful to be able to save our file into a different version in order to have the program correctly translate our document. To save the file into these formats simply choose the word version number from the list of available file formats.

Different file formats support different features available in Word – and some conversion/translation will take place – so we may find that some formatting may be lost in the process. Be aware of this and always save a copy in the original Word version so as not to lose your work.

Document Templates
Saving a document as a template allows it be re-used as a standard "boiler-plate" for our document which we met earlier (See page 233).

Saving in other file formats.

Sometimes we'll want to save our documents in different formats so that we can use them in earlier versions of Word or in different word-processing applications or programs. For example we might want to save our document in "WordPerfect" format so that we can give it to someone using WordPerfect to edit and update. To save the document in a different file format – we proceed as we would when normally saving the document.

- ❑ Click on the **File** menu and choose **Save As**
- ❑ The usual save window will appear:

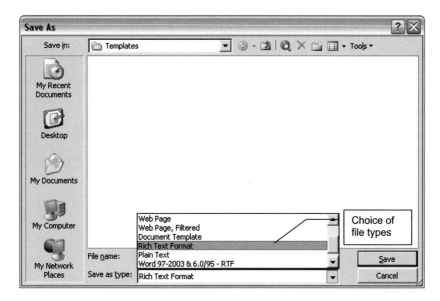

- ❑ From the **Save as type:** textbox click on the arrow.
- ❑ Here we are able to choose the type of file that we need.
- ❑ To save the file as a *Rich Text Format* file choose *Rich Text Format* and click **Save**

By saving our Word file as an **RTF** (Rich Text File) we convert to a format which can be read by nearly all word processing software.

EXERCISES TO PROVE YOU KNOW

1. Open the *Christmas.doc* file created earlier and re-save the file in the following formats:

    o   Save as a Rich Text file - in **RTF** format.

    o   Save as a Plain Text file

    o   Save as a Web Page document

SECTION 3.15:   EXAM OVERVIEW AND TIPS

In the exam for Module Three, Word Processing, you will be given a disk. The disk will hold all files needed for this exam plus an answer file – **answerfile.doc**. The answer file is a Word document that you will type the answers into. It looks like this:

Candidate Identification :_____

Question No.	Response
1.	
2.	

You will need to be able to locate this answerfile.doc on the floppy disk, open it and type into it. It is important that you remember to save this file as you go and at the end of the exam. There can be up to 30 questions and each question will ask you to edit an existing Word document testing all the areas covered in the Module. You will be asked to open a Word document with text already in it and asked to edit that text.

Points to Note:

- Time allowed: 45 minutes
- Answer all Questions:
- Marking System
    - Questions vary from 1 pt to 3pt (marks will be shown)

Topics Checklist:

- Opening and Closing Word Documents
- Formatting a Font
- Aligning text
- Deleting Text
- Paragraph and line spacing
- Setting page Margins
- Setting and removing tabs
- Inserting Tables
- Page Breaks
- Headers and Footers
- Inserting Images
- Creating a Mail Merge
- Performing a Spelling Check

All of the topics covered in this Module could be asked in the exam.

For sample examinations visit **http://www.iactonline.com/ecdl**

Module 4
SPREADSHEETS

iact

The complete IT training provider

MODULE 4: SPREADSHEETS

Next to word processors the most widely used application is the Spreadsheet. The father of the modern spreadsheet is *Dan Bricklin*. He released VisiCalc in 1979 which sold over 1 million copies! *Lotus* bought the *VisiCalc* rights in 1985 having developed *Lotus 1-2-3*. Bricklin has gone on to design other successful, though more specialised products, but none has revolutionised computing like the spreadsheet.

Spreadsheets replace the paper based accounting systems traditionally used in business and their key to success is their ability to recalculate nearly instantly any changes to the information making up the spreadsheet.

Spreadsheets have many different uses – ranging from handling lists of data to creating financial reports and charts.

*Dan Bricklin
Inventor of the
Spreadsheet*

In this module we will learn about *Excel* but the theory and capabilities of Excel are similar in all spreadsheet packages.

SECTION 4.1:   INTRODUCTION TO EXCEL

In this section we will learn how to:

- ❏ Start Microsoft Excel
- ❏ Open a New Workbook
- ❏ Tour Excel
- ❏ Enter and Edit Data
- ❏ Save a Workbook
- ❏ Exit Excel

LESSON 4.1.1:   STARTING EXCEL

To start Excel we need to go to:

- ❏ **Start** menu and choose to **All Programs** and choose **Microsoft Office** and click on **Microsoft Office Excel 2003**

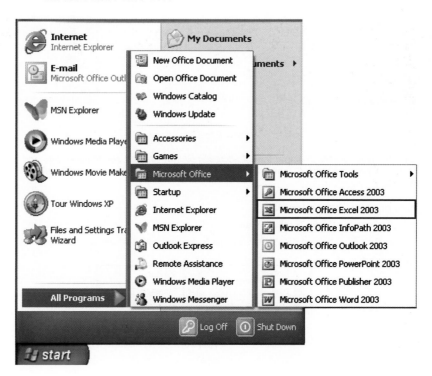

After a few moments the Excel application will start and the opening screen will appear.

LESSON 4.1.2:   TOURING EXCEL

Microsoft Excel opens with a blank Workbook and the *Getting Started* pane is visible.

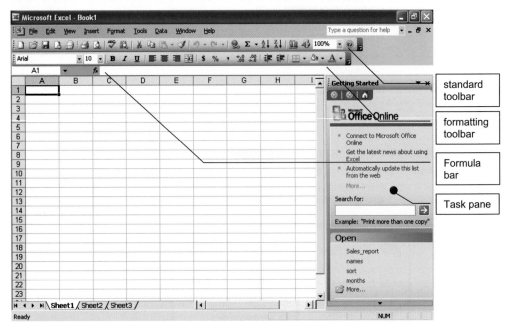

A Blank Excel Workbook

The screen layout is very similar to that of *Microsoft Word*. We can see the *Standard* and *formatting toolbar*s. If we are missing any toolbars, we can go to the **View** menu and select **Toolbars** to open or close them.

To hide or show Excel's toolbars

- ❑   Go to the **View | Toolbars** menu
- ❑   Tick or un-tick the name of the toolbar to display or hide a toolbar.

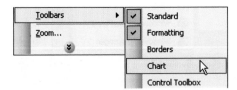

Cells, Workbooks and Worksheets

In Excel, the *worksheet* or *spreadsheet* is divided into columns (represented by letters) and rows (represented by numbers). The gridlines on the screen help us to see the cells. Each cell is named by the column and the rows that it resides in.

For example, the cell that is selected here is cell **A1**. This is known as the ***active cell***.

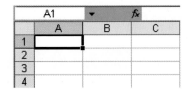

The active cell is always highlighted in this way.

The formula toolbar is also visible and it shows the *Name Box* and *Formula Box*.

Name of current cell

Formula or contents cell **A1**

The **Name Box** – shows the name of the cell that is active

The **Formula Box** – shows the contents of the cell

At the bottom of the screen we can see that this Excel workbook has three sheets.

We will learn later in this module how to add, delete and rename these sheets. For the moment, we need to be able to click on the sheets and to realise that they are all part of the same workbook.

LESSON 4.1.3: ENTERING AND EDITING DATA

To enter data into a cell

- ❑ Select the cell
- ❑ Type the word "Sales" into the cell and press **Enter**

The word "Sales" appears in the cell **A1**. We can also see the word "Sales" in the *Formula Bar* at the top of the screen.

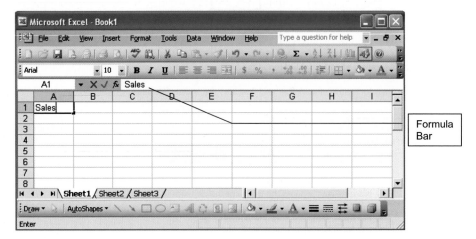

We enter numbers in exactly the same as we enter text. Text will always appear left aligned and numbers by default will always appear right aligned.

Editing contents of a cell:

In order to edit data that has already been entered, we click on the cell that the data is in to make the cell active.

- ❑ Click into the cell and press **F2**. We can then edit the cells contents as required using the cursor keys.

or

- ❑ Click into the cell and then edit the text that appears on the *Formula Bar*. The insertion point appears in the formula bar and we can edit the contents as required.

or

- ❑ Double click on the cell and type to change the content.

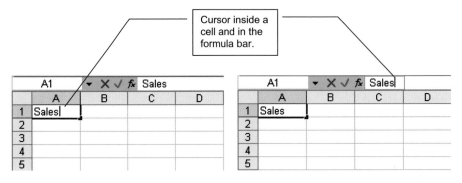

| *Editing inside a cell* | *Editing on the formula bar* |

LESSON 4.1.4:   SAVING A WORKBOOK

When we have entered data into a workbook, we must then save it. We will usually save our workbook
to the **My Documents** folder or to the **C:** drive or a floppy drive (**A:** drive).

To save to the Hard Drive (or **C:** drive)

- ❑   Click on the **File** menu choose **Save As**

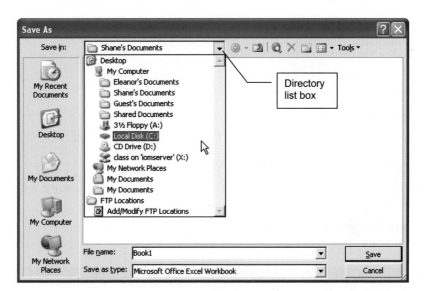

- ❑   Choose the **C:** drive from the directory list.

Once we have chosen the **C:** drive, we can then choose to save to any folder in the **C:** drive.

- ❑   Give the file a name by typing into the **File Name** box.

An Excel workbook automatically saves with the file extension ***.xls**. There are alternative file formats
that we can save to and these will be discussed later.

Saving a spreadsheet with a new name

Once the spreadsheet has been saved, we can save it again with a new name. We might do this if we planned to make changes to the spreadsheet but wanted to keep the original, or if we wanted to keep a backup of the spreadsheet we had created.

- ❏ Click on the **File** menu and choose **Save As**
- ❏ Type a new name for the spreadsheet
- ❏ Choose the drive and folder to save the spreadsheet to and press **Save**

The spreadsheet is now saved with a new name.

Creating a new Workbook

To create a new Excel Workbook or *spreadsheet*

- ❏ Press the *New Workbook* icon 🗋 or press **Ctrl+N**

Excel will create a new blank workbook.

Opening a Workbook

- ❏ To open an Excel Workbook choose **File | Open** and locate the file to open and click **OK**.

Opening Several Spreadsheets (or Workbooks)

Excel also allows us to open more than one spreadsheet at a time. This powerful feature is very useful with large spreadsheets. To open more than one spreadsheet simply press **Ctrl+O** and locate the spreadsheet to open.

To save a Spreadsheet to a floppy disk:

- ❏ Click on the **File** menu and choose **Save As**

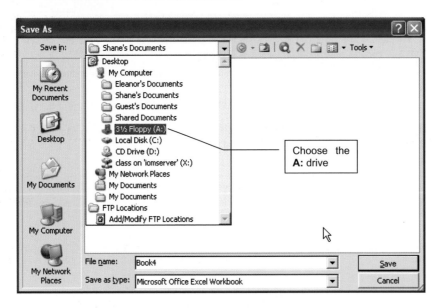

Choose the **A:** drive from the directory list and give the file a name. This allows us to bring our Excel file with us onto another computer.

Saving the file after modifications

- ❏ To re-save the spreadsheet after editing it – choose **File | Save**.

This will save the file with the same name and overwrite the existing file.

LESSON 4.1.5: SAVING EXCEL INTO DIFFERENT FILE FORMATS

Saving an Excel workbook is easy. We simply click on the **File** menu and choose **Save**. The default file extension is ***.xls**

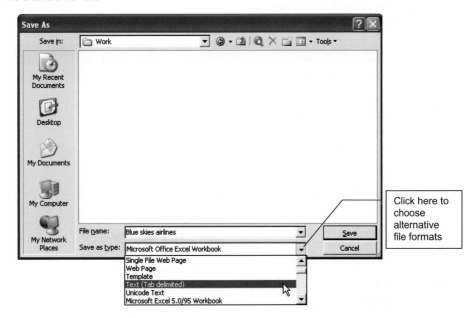

Click here to choose alternative file formats

We can however save our spreadsheet into alternative file formats. We might do this for example if we need to give the spreadsheet to someone with a different spreadsheet package (the most common are the *Lotus 1-2-3* and *Corel QuattroPro* packages) or if we needed to save to an earlier version of Excel. We also sometimes export into different file formats if we wish to export the data into a database or another program that cannot directly work with Excel files.

Here are the most important **Save As** options:

Saving to a previous version of Excel
This allows us to **save** the Excel workbook in a previous version of Excel. This is important if we are sending an *Excel 2003* file to a colleague that has *Excel 97* or an even earlier version (95 or v5.0 etc.)

Saving as a Template
Choosing to save a spreadsheet as a template causes the spreadsheet to be saved into the templates folder automatically. Once it is saved as a template we can open it by going to the **File** menu, choose **New** and then we will see the template file. Templates are useful for files that have a basic shell that we use repeatedly.

Saving a spreadsheet as a Text Files (TXT file)
This option saves the Excel sheet as a text file that can be opened in Notepad or a word processor. We might choose to do this if we were creating a mailing list or a report. This option will only save the *active* worksheet.

If we have multiple worksheets, we need to save each worksheet individually.

Saving as a HTML document (or publishing as a web page)
Saving a spreadsheet as a web page means we can view it in a browser like Internet Explorer.

To save the spreadsheet as a web page:

❑ Go to the **File** menu and choose **Save as Web Page**

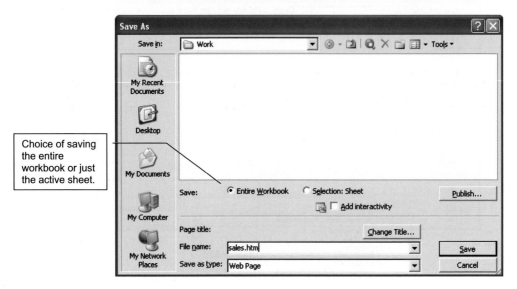

Choice of saving the entire workbook or just the active sheet.

Excel will publish the pages to a directory. We can then copy or upload these pages to an intranet or web site to view them. Open the published page in *Internet Explorer* to preview it.

LESSON 4.1.6: CLOSING A WORKBOOK AND EXCEL

Once a workbook has been saved we can close it. To close a workbook:

- ❑ Click on the **File** menu and choose **Close**

Excel will always prompt us to save if we need to do so.

- ❑ To close the Excel application itself, simply click on the **File** menu again and this time we choose **Exit.**

LESSON 4.1.7: SETTING FILE DEFAULTS

We can modify some of the default settings Excel uses when opening and creating new workbooks. We can modify the default font used in our worksheets as well as the number of sheets in new workbooks. We can also change the default folder used when opening and saving workbooks. This can make it faster to open and save files – as we won't usually have to navigate to a new folder.

- ❑ To modify Excel's default settings choose **Tools | Options** and click on the **General** tab

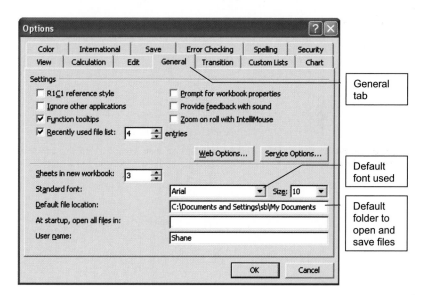

To change the default font

- ❑ Click on the *Standard font* list box and choose a font.

To change the default folder used by Excel when opening and saving files:

- ❑ Click into the *Default file location* text box and enter the default file path for spreadsheets.

An example path might be:

C:\Documents and Settings\Shane\My Documents

Now whenever we go to save or open a file Excel will open this folder by default.

We can also set the default *User name* used when creating spreadsheets. The username is saved in the properties of the file and helps identify the author of the spreadsheet later on. It is also used when sharing workbooks.

To change the default username for all spreadsheets

- ❑ Type the name and initials into the *username* text box.
- ❑ When all of the settings are correct press **OK**.

EXERCISES TO PROVE YOU KNOW

1. Open Excel and enter the following data onto *Sheet1*

Jan	Feb	Mar	Apr	May
100	200	130	150	180

2. Change the figure for **Feb** from **200** to **242**

3. Save the spreadsheet to a floppy disk as *Rainfall.xls*

4. Show the *chart* toolbar.

5. Set the default path for spreadsheet files to **c:\My Documents\Spreadsheets**

6. Save the spreadsheet into Excel 5.0 format.

SECTION 4.2:   SELECTING CELLS AND RANGES

In this section we will learn to manipulate and format the cells in our workbook.

We will learn to:

- ❑ Select cells
- ❑ Move, copy and delete cells
- ❑ Search and replace the values in cells
- ❑ Perform a spell check on our workbook

LESSON 4.2.1:   SELECTING CELLS, ROWS AND COLUMNS

Its important to be able to select cells and ranges of cells in our workbook.

- ❑ **To select a cell**, we simply click on it once. We can tell that it is selected because there is a thick black border around the cell.

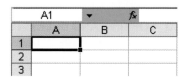

- ❑ **To select a row**, we simply click on the row number at the far left of the row. By clicking on the number, the entire row becomes highlighted.

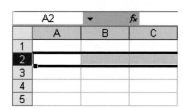

- ❑ **To select a column**, we simply click on the letter that denotes the column. By clicking on the letter, the entire column becomes highlighted.

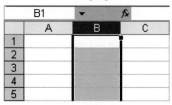

Selecting non-adjacent rows and columns

- ❑ **To select a series of rows or columns** which are non-adjacent hold down the **Ctrl** key and click on the column or row headings to select them.

Selecting a range of cells

- ❑ **To select a range of cells**, we click on the first cell in the range of cells, hold down the left mouse button and then move to the last cell in the range. This will highlight every cell in-between.

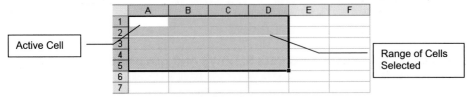

Active Cell

Range of Cells Selected

The cell that is left white in the range (the first cell) is the cell that is 'active', even though all are highlighted. When we type our text will appear in the active cell.

LESSON 4.2.2: MOVING, COPYING AND DELETING CELLS

We can delete, move and copy cells within a worksheet, between worksheets and between open Spreadsheets (workbooks) using the clipboard.

In all cases:

- ❑ We must first select the cell or range of cells to move or copy and press **Ctrl+C** (if we are copying the cells) or **Ctrl+X** (if we are moving the cells).

We then do one of the following depending on the required result:

To delete the cells

- ❑ Press the **Delete** or **DEL** key

To move or copy cells within the same sheet:

- ❑ Click on the destination cell and press **Ctrl+V**

or

To move or copy cells to a different sheet:

- ❑ Select the sheet to move to by clicking on its tab

|◄ ◄ ► ►|\ **Sheet1** ╱ Sheet2 ╱ Sheet3 ╱

- ❑ Now click on the destination cell and press **Ctrl+V**

or

To move or copy cells to a different workbook or spreadsheet

- ❑ Open the destination workbook (press **Ctrl+O** and locate the file) or select the workbook from the **Window** menu if it is already open. Click on the destination cell and press **Ctrl+V**.

LESSON 4.2.3:   USING *UNDO* AND *REDO*

Excel also provides us with the very useful **Undo** and **Redo** commands we met in Word. These tools allow us to *undo* or *reverse* our last action. We can use **undo** to reverse just about anything (except *saving* and *opening*) including deletions, insertions, formatting and so on.

> ❑ For example if we delete a range of cells and then press **Undo** button ↺ ▾ or use the shortcut key **Ctrl + Z** the deletion will be reversed.

There are several levels of *undo* available in Excel depending on the amount of memory we have. Each time we press the **Undo** button the previous action is undone.

Note: The Undo command can only reverse actions up to the last time the document was saved

If after we have *undone* an action we wish to Redo it simply press the **Redo** button ↻ ▾ or use the shortcut key **Ctrl+Y.**

LESSON 4.2.4:   FINDING AND REPLACING VALUES

Finding and replacing is a useful feature in Excel as we use it regularly when updating large spreadsheets. **Find** allows us locate a word or number in a cell in our workbook. **Replace** allows us to find a word or number and then replace it with another word or number.

Let's try this out:

> ❑ Click on the **Edit** menu and choose **Find** or **Replace**

This works in the same way as the *Find and Replace* feature in Microsoft Word. In Excel though, we need to watch out when we are looking for numbers. When we search for the number 10, we do not want to find 100 or 1000.

To ensure only whole cell matches are found, click on the **Options** button and ensure that the *Match Whole Cell* option is turned on.

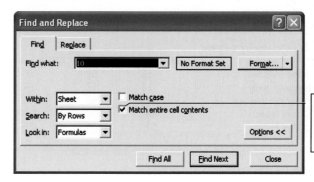

Click here to ensure that we only find entire cells that match

---

LESSON 4.2.5: SPELL CHECKING A SPREADSHEET

Spell Check in *Excel* works just like it does in *Microsoft Word*. Once we have completed our worksheet, we should always do a spell check.

❑ Go to the **Tools** menu and select **Spelling** or press **F7**

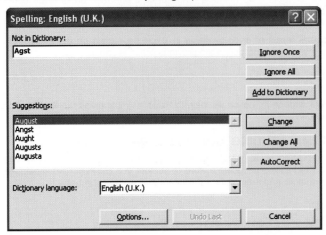

The above screen will appear giving us suggestions for correct spelling. We can *ignore* or *change* spellings as required.

EXERCISES TO PROVE YOU KNOW

1. Open a new workbook in Excel and type in the following data:

	A	B	C	D	E
1	Sales figures for the year				
2		QTR1	QTR2	QTR3	QTR4
3	James O'Brien	50	52	60	65
4	Margaret Kelly	56	57	59	60.5
5	Peter Woodhouse	215	250	215	250
6	Ciaran Jones	850	850	850	850
7	Jackie Phillips	515	500	485	470

a) Replace all occurrences of the number **850** with **852**

3. Check the spelling of the spreadsheet

4. Copy the contents of *sheet1* onto *sheet2*

5. Save the workbook as *Sales.xls* and close Excel.

SECTION 4.3: FORMATTING CELLS AND THEIR CONTENTS

In this section we will learn how to:

- ❑ Format the appearance of cells data
- ❑ Change the alignment, bordering and colour of cells
- ❑ Merge and centre cell contents
- ❑ Format numbers in cells
- ❑ Add borders to our cells

LESSON 4.3.1: SELECTING AND FORMATTING CELLS

To format a cell or range of cells, we need to highlight or select the cell or range of cells first. In order to highlight cells that are not adjacent:

- ❑ Click on the first cell and hold down the **Ctrl** key on the keyboard.
- ❑ Now click on all the other cells that need to be selected

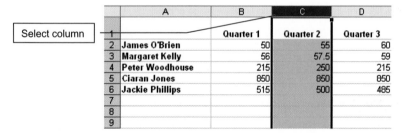

	A	B	C	D
1		Quarter 1	Quarter 2	Quarter 3
2	James O'Brien	50	55	60
3	Margaret Kelly	56	57.5	59
4	Peter Woodhouse	215	250	215
5	Ciaran Jones	850	850	850

Non-adjacent cells selected

To select rows or columns click on the rows or columns headings.

Select column

	A	B	C	D
1		Quarter 1	Quarter 2	Quarter 3
2	James O'Brien	50	55	60
3	Margaret Kelly	56	57.5	59
4	Peter Woodhouse	215	250	215
5	Ciaran Jones	850	850	850
6	Jackie Phillips	515	500	485
7				
8				
9				

To select a series of rows or columns which are non-adjacent hold down the **Ctrl** key and click on the column or row headings to select them.

The formatting toolbar

Once we have highlighted the cells, rows or columns we wish to change we can format them using the formatting toolbar just as in *Microsoft Word*.

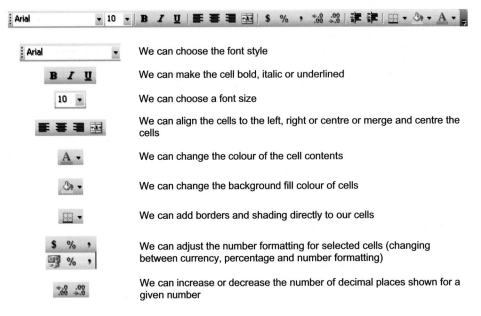

Arial	We can choose the font style
B *I* <u>U</u>	We can make the cell bold, italic or underlined
10	We can choose a font size
align buttons	We can align the cells to the left, right or centre or merge and centre the cells
A	We can change the colour of the cell contents
fill	We can change the background fill colour of cells
borders	We can add borders and shading directly to our cells
$ % ,	We can adjust the number formatting for selected cells (changing between currency, percentage and number formatting)
.0 .00	We can increase or decrease the number of decimal places shown for a given number

Aligning data within cells

We can align data horizontally within a cell and across a range of cells.

Left Aligned		
		Right Aligned
	Centre Aligned	

❑ To **CENTRE** the data within the cells press the ≡ button.

❑ To **LEFT ALIGN** the data within the cells press the ≣ button.

❑ To **RIGHT ALIGN** the data within the cells press the ≣ button.

Merging Cells and adding titles

We will often want to place a title across our spreadsheet or merge a number of cells into one. To merge cells together we use the ⊞ button on the formatting toolbar.

❑ Select the range of cells that we wish to merge and press the merge and centre button ⊞ to merge the cells.

	A	B	C	D
1		Sales		
2				
3	Jan	Feb	Mar	
4	10	50	50	
5	20	40	20	
6	30	10	10	
7				

Merged Cells

LESSON 4.3.2:   CHANGING CELL ALIGNMENT

We can alter the alignment of data in a cell using options in the formatting menu. Let's have a look at some of the options available.

❑   Select a range of cells and go to the **Format | Cells** menu.

In this dialog box there are many tabs to choose from. For the moment we will concentrate on the *Alignment Tab*

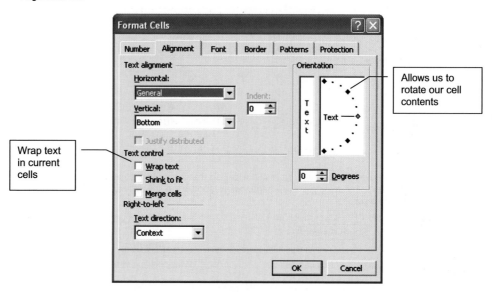

From Alignment tab we can *align* a cell's contents horizontally and vertically.

❑   Use the *Horizontal* alignment option to change the alignment of the cells between left, centred or right (remember though, that numbers are normally aligned on the right of a cell).

❑   Use the *Vertical* alignment option to change the up/down alignment within a cell. **Note the row height may need to be adjusted to see this properly.**

Here we can see the results of the different cell alignment options:

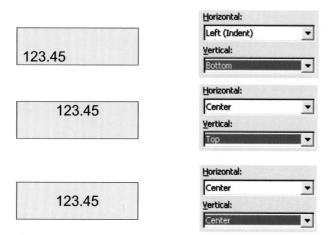

Changing a cells orientation

We can also change the rotation of text in a cell from 0 to 90 degrees.

❑ Select the months in cells **A3:C3** and then select the **Rotate** option from the **Format | Cells** menu. By setting this to 45 degrees we can rotate the date headings.

By rotating the text 45 degrees we end up a spreadsheet like this:

Text Wrapping

Sometimes it is useful to be able to *wrap* text in a cell so that longer text appears underneath and not beside the other text. For example the image below shows the difference between wrapped and unwrapped text into a cell.

South America

Unwrapped text in a cell

South America

Wrapped text in a cell

We can wrap the text in a cell by turning on the **Wrap text** option in the Format cells menu.

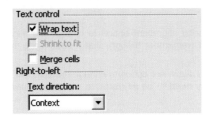

Once activated, this option will allow the text to flow or wrap onto more than one line.

LESSON 4.3.3: FORMATTING NUMBERS AND DATES

Being able to correctly display numbers in a spreadsheet in the correct number format is very important. Clearly there is a big difference between displaying **Monday** in a cell and displaying **6th June** or similarly displaying **10 or 10,000,000** in a cell - but to Excel the difference can be just the formatting of the numbers.

In this lesson we will learn some of the powerful features available in Excel to format the contents of cells.

Formatting cells to display currencies

Often our spreadsheets will contain amounts relating to currencies. To indicate this clearly we often format the cells to display the currency symbol. To do this:

❑ Select the cell to format and click the **$** or 🔳 button.

Excel applies the default currency number format to the selected cells. Sometimes, the cell will display the symbols ###### instead of values. This is because the columns are too narrow to display the full numbers in the new format. (Later in this section we will see how to widen columns). If the default currency is not the correct one, we need to go to:

❑ **Format** menu and choose **Cells**

❑ Make sure that the **Number** tab is selected

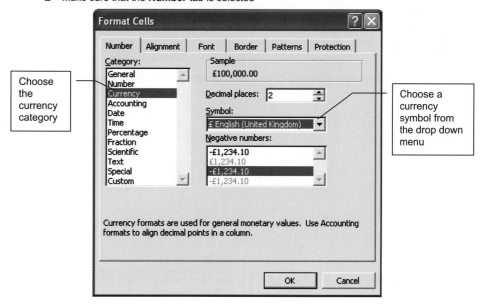

Choose the currency category

Choose a currency symbol from the drop down menu

❑ From here, we can choose from a list of currency symbols. Then click **OK**.

Formatting cells to restrict the number of decimal places

To display numbers without the currency symbol, to control the number of decimal places, and choose whether a thousand's separator is used, click on the **Number** category:

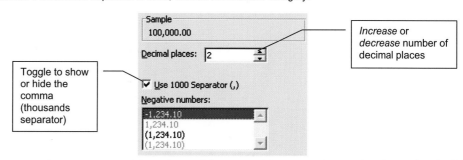

Toggle to show or hide the comma (thousands separator)

Increase or decrease number of decimal places

Formatting cells to display a date
The date category allows us to format a cell in a date or time format

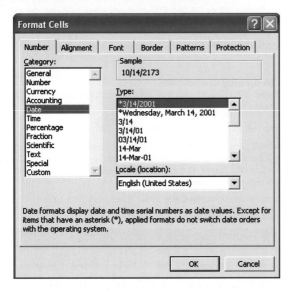

Here, we can choose from a series of different date formats depending on our requirements.

Formatting cells to display percentages

The percentage category allows us to format decimal numbers as percentages

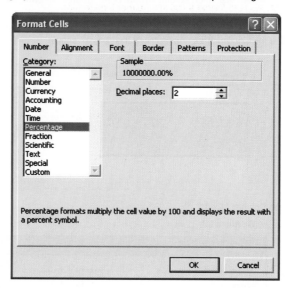

Here we can choose how many decimal places we need in the percent cell. Excel will round off the figure correctly.

When we apply a percent format to a cell, it will put both the % sign and it will also multiply the contents of the cell by 100 – watch out for this!

LESSON 4.3.4: CELL BORDERS AND PATTERNS

Usually the gridlines that are visible on screen will not print. In order to print the grid borders, we need to add them ourselves.

- ❑ Recreate this spreadsheet and highlight the cells as shown

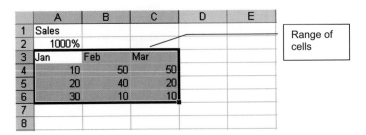

Range of cells

- ❑ Go to the **Format | Cells**
- ❑ Click on the **Borders** tab

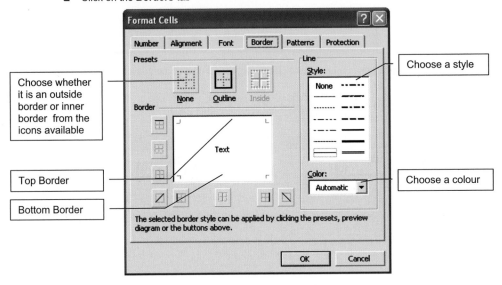

Choose whether it is an outside border or inner border from the icons available

Top Border

Bottom Border

Choose a style

Choose a colour

- ❑ Choose the style of line needed and the colour of the line

Choose where to place the border by selecting from the icons surrounding the preview box. Here, we will choose a thick, red, top border line and a bottom border line

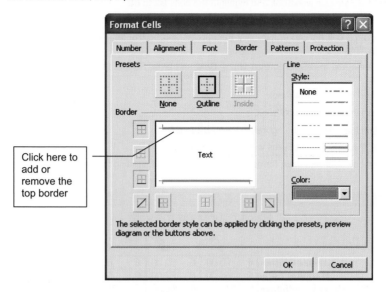

Click here to add or remove the top border

The resulting cells should look like this:

We have now put a top and bottom border around the cells that we had highlighted

	A	B	C	D
1	Sales			
2	1000%			
3	Jan	Feb	Mar	
4	10	50	50	
5	20	40	20	
6	30	10	10	
7				

Borders and shading are very similar to their Word counterparts. If we are editing the borders frequently we can use the useful Excel toolbar icon ▦ ▾ .

EXERCISES TO PROVE YOU KNOW

1. Open the *Sales.xls* workbook and highlight the cells **B2** to **E2**

2. Rotate the contents in the cells by 45 degrees

3. Click on the cell **A1** and ensure that the vertical and horizontal alignment of the cells are both centred

4. Format the text in cell **A1** to size 16pts, Bold and blue. Format the background colour to yellow.

5. Save and close the Workbook.

6. Re-open the *Sales.xls* workbook.

7. Highlight the cells with the figures in them, **B3** to **E7**

8. Format the cells to hold Euros with 2 decimal places

9. Highlight all cells with data, format the cells borders and shading to mirror the following:

	A	B	C	D	E
1	Sales figures for the year				
2		QTR1	QTR2	QTR3	QTR4
3	James O'Brien	€ 50.00	€ 52.00	€ 60.00	€ 65.00
4	Margaret Kelly	€ 56.00	€ 57.00	€ 59.00	€ 60.50
5	Peter Woodhouse	€ 215.00	€ 250.00	€ 215.00	€ 250.00
6	Ciaran Jones	€ 850.00	€ 850.00	€ 850.00	€ 850.00
7	Jackie Phillips	€ 515.00	€ 500.00	€ 485.00	€ 470.00

10. Open a new blank Workbook.

11. Enter the following into the cells:

	A	B
1	Date	
2	02/02/74	
3	06/10/85	
4	07/08/03	
5		
6		
7	Percentages	
8	0.01	
9	0.1	
10	0.05	
11		

12. Change the format of the cells so that the data changes to:

	A
1	**Date**
2	2-Feb
3	October 6, 1985
4	7-Aug-2003
5	
6	
7	**Percentages**
8	1%
9	10%
10	5%
11	

13. Save the file as *section4_3.xls*

SECTION 4.4:   BUILDING SIMPLE FORMULA

The power of spreadsheets starts to become apparent when we start to add formulae to our workbooks. Excel has a huge range of powerful built in functions that are easy to learn and can perform any calculations we desire. In this section we will learn how to build a formula in Excel.

We will learn to:

- ❏ Use common mathematical operators **+ - / ***
- ❏ Use the Sum() function
- ❏ Use AutoSum
- ❏ Use the Average(), Count(), Max(), Min() and IF() functions
- ❏ Identify common error messages

LESSON 4.4.1:   MATHEMATICAL OPERATORS + - / *

On paper we might write the addition of two numbers like this:

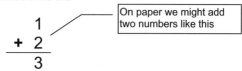

On paper we might add two numbers like this

To accomplish the same results in Excel we use the grid references of the cells we wish to add:

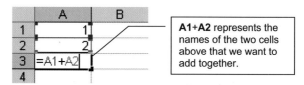

A1+A2 represents the names of the two cells above that we want to add together.

By using grid references in our formula we ensure that whenever the values in the cells change the calculation to work out the sum will automatically be updated!

Recreate the above spreadsheet and type **=A1 + A2** into cell **A3**

This formula says *"Calculate the sum of the contents of cell A1 and A2 and put the result into cell A3"*

Notice that our calculation to add the contents of cell **A1** and cell **A2** starts with an '**=**' sign.

Once a formula has been typed, we must press **Enter** to save our changes.

Here are the standard mathematical operators in Excel

Function	Symbol	Example
Addition	**+**	**=A1 + A2**
Subtraction	**-**	**=A4 – C9**
Division	**/**	**=C2 / C3**
Multiplication	*****	**=C1 * E2**

NOTE: REMEMBER ALL OUR FORMULAE Start WITH '='

When we enter a formula into a cell we usually just see the *result* of the calculation in the cell itself. However once we click in the cell to make it active the formula entered originally into the cell will appear both in the cell and in the formula bar.

It is best to edit a formula from the formula bar as there is more space to view the full formula.

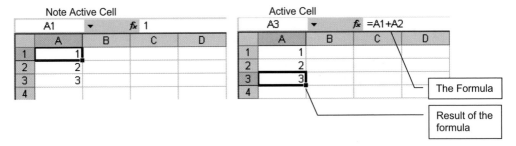

We can use any combination of the standard mathematical operators as the basis of our spreadsheet calculations.

LESSON 4.4.2: USING THE SUM() FUNCTION

SUM is a built in function that allows us to quickly and easily add a range of cells. The function has a set format:

=SUM(first cell in range:last cell in range)

Let's look at an example.

❑ Type the following into a blank worksheet:

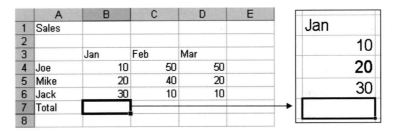

In the cell **B7**, we need a formula that will add the above three cells, **B4**, **B5** and **B6**.

Type in the formula:

=SUM(B4:B6)

The result of the calculation will appear in the cell, once we press **Enter**.

The next two formulae in cells C7 and D7 respectively would be:

=SUM(C4:C6)

=SUM(D4:D6)

4
Spreadsheets

Our final spreadsheet should look like this:

	A	B	C	D	E
1	Sales				
2					
3		Jan	Feb	Mar	
4	Joe	10	50	50	
5	Mike	20	40	20	
6	Jack	30	10	10	
7	Total	60	100	80	

=SUM(B4:B6)

=SUM(C4:C6)

=SUM(D4:D6)

There is another, faster way of adding numbers in Excel. It is called *AutoSum* and it is a shortcut to creating the formulae that we have just used. In the next lesson we'll see how we can use the **AutoSum** button.

LESSON 4.4.3: USING AUTOSUM

Excel has an alternative way of adding cells and that is to use the *AutoSum* button **Σ**. The button is found on the standard toolbar. Let's use AutoSum to total the numbers above cells **B7**.

❑ Firstly delete the formulae in cells **B7** to **D7**

❑ Now click on cell **B7** (the cell that we want the formula to go into) and then click on the AutoSum button **Σ** on the standard toolbar. The following appears:

SUM	▼ ✕ ✓ ƒx	=SUM(B4:B6)			
	A	B	C	D	E
1	Sales				
2					
3		Jan	Feb	Mar	
4	Joe	10	50	50	
5	Mike	20	40	20	
6	Jack	30	10	10	
7	Total	=SUM(B4:B6)			
8		SUM(**number1**, [number2], ...)			
9					

Excel automatically enters the sum formula into the cell and shows the range of cells that are being added!

❑ Press **Enter** to accept the formula

Excel is guessing the cells that we need to add. If we are happy that the guess is correct, looking at the formula, we press the **Enter** key.

If, however, the guess in incorrect, we need to click on the first cell in the range, hold down our left mouse button and drag to the last cell in our range.

Release the mouse button on the last cell. The formula will change automatically and the *marching ants* (the dotted black line) will change to highlight the new range. When we are happy that the formula is correct, press **Enter**.

NOTE: Be sure to check that the formula is correct when using AutoSum.

LESSON 4.4.4: USING THE AVERAGE() FUNCTION

AVERAGE is a built in function that allows us to quickly and easily get the average of a range of cells. The function will usually look like this:

=AVERAGE(first cell in range:last cell in range)

Let's look at an example.

- ❑ In cell **A9**, type in the word **Average** as our title heading
- ❑ **B9** is going to be the average of cells **B4**, **B5** and **B6**.
- ❑ Type in the formula as follows:

=AVERAGE(B4:B6)

SUM		▼ ✗ ✓ ƒx =AVERAGE(B4:B6)				
	A	B	C	D	E	F
1	Sales					
2						
3		Jan	Feb	Mar		
4	Joe	10	50	50		
5	Mike	20	40	20		
6	Jack	30	10	10		
7	Total	60	100	80		
8						
9	Average	=AVERAGE(B4:B6)				
10						
11						

- ❑ Press the **Enter** key to see the result

Repeat this step to get the average for the next two cells C9 and D9.

A9		▼	ƒx Average			
	A	B	C	D	E	F
1	Sales					
2						
3		Jan	Feb	Mar		
4	Joe	10	50	50		
5	Mike	20	40	20		
6	Jack	30	10	10		=AVERAGE(**C4:C6**)
7	Total	60	100	80		
8						
9	Average	20	33.33333	26.66667		=AVERAGE(**D4:D6**)
10						
11						

If we change the values in any of the cells used to calculate the average the average will change automatically.

LESSON 4.4.5:   USING THE COUNT() FUNCTION

The **COUNT** function will count the number of non-blank entries in a range of cells. The function looks like this:

=COUNT(first cell in range:last cell in range)

This could be useful when creating a tally or when using some statistical functions.

Let's look at an example.

- ❑ Reproduce the spreadsheet shown below – including the blank cells.
- ❑ Cell **C7** is going to be the count of all the non-blank cells in the range **A1:C6**
- ❑ Type in the formula as follows:

=COUNT(A1:C6)

For example:

	A	B	C	D
1	1	1		
2		1	1	
3	1	1	1	
4	1	1	1	
5	1	1	1	
6	1			
7			=count(A1:C6)	
8				

This function returns the value **14** in this case - the number of **1's** in the range of cells.

LESSON 4.4.6:   USING THE MAX() FUNCTION

The MAX() function is used to find the largest value in a range of cells. The function takes a range of cells and returns the largest value in the range.

=MAX(first cell in range:last cell in range)

Let's look at an example.

- ❑ In cell **C1**, type "**Total Sales**" as our title heading
- ❑ **C7** is going to be the maximum of cells **C2**, **C3**, **C4** and **C5**.
- ❑ Type in the formula as follows:

=MAX(C2:C5)

	A	B	C	D
1			Total Sales	
2	Computers		€ 5,000.00	
3	Hi-Fi		€ 45,000.00	
4	Television		€ 33,000.00	
5	Video		€ 2,500.00	
6				
7			=MAX(C2:C5)	
8				

This function will display the value **€33,000.00** as this is the maximum value in the range of cells.

LESSON 4.4.7:   USING THE MIN() FUNCTION

This **MIN** function finds the minimum value in a range of cells – and works precisely as the **MAX** function in reverse.

=MIN(first cell in range:last cell in range)

In the above example it would display the value **€2,500.00** as this is the smallest value in the range.

LESSON 4.4.8:   USING THE IF() FUNCTION

The **IF()** function allows us to test the value in a cell and carry out two different formulae based on the result of the test. The function uses a condition to perform the test and performs the **TRUE** part if the condition is true and the **FALSE** part otherwise.

=IF(<condition>, <true part>, <false part>)

The best way to see this working is to look at a couple of examples.

Example 1:

	A	B	C
1	Cost of Sales	€ 25,000.00	
2	Sales	€ 38,000.00	
3			
4		*Net Profit*	
5			=IF(B1 < B2, "Net Profit", "Net Loss")

In this case if the contents of cell **B1** is less than the contents of cell **B2** cell **B4** will display the text **"Net Profit"** otherwise it will display the text **"Net Loss"**. The *condition* is the test for whether **B1 < B2**. If the condition is **TRUE** the function will display **"Net Profit"** otherwise it will display **"Net Loss"**.

Example 2:

	A	B	C	D
1	**Unit Price**	**VAT Rate**	**VAT Due**	
2	€ 100.00	A	€ 21.00	
3	€ 100.00	B	€ 15.00	
4	€ 200.00	A	€ 42.00	
5	€ 200.00	A	€ 42.00	
6				
7				

=IF(B5 ="A", A5 * 21%, A5 * 15%)

In this case the **IF** statement is used to determine whether the VAT[3] due should be calculated at the **A** rate or the **B** rate. The appropriate **IF** statement is entered into cells **C2** to **C5**.

The example above assumes any VAT rate other than **A** will give a value of 15%. The *condition* is the test **B5="A"**. If the condition is **TRUE** the function calculates the VAT at a rate of 21% otherwise at a rate of 15%. In order to have additional VAT categories we have to use a nested **IF** something like:

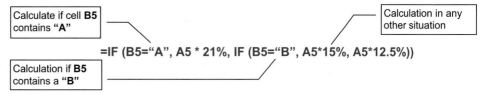

Calculate if cell **B5** contains **"A"**

Calculation in any other situation

=IF (B5="A", A5 * 21%, IF (B5="B", A5*15%, A5*12.5%))

Calculation if **B5** contains a **"B"**

This formula now handles VAT rates **A, B** and another. **A** is calculated at a rate of 21%, **B** is calculated at a rate of 15% and any other rate is calculated at 12.5%

---

[3] *Please note that VAT rates vary between different countries. These rates are based on current Irish VAT rates – in the UK these rates are 17.5% and 8% respectively.*

LESSON 4.4.9: COMMON FORMULA ERRORS

Sometimes when we are using formulae in Excel, we get an error message. Here are some of the most common errors that might occur.

Circular References

If the following error message appears on screen, we have created a circular reference.

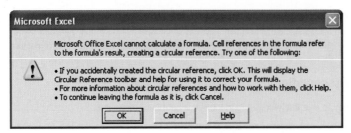

When we click in the cell with the error we should see **Circular: D7** appear in the status bar – indicating a 'circular' reference in the formula.

A *circular* reference means that we have included the answer cell in the original formula. In the above example, look at the formula bar.

Here is the formula in cell **D7**:

=SUM(D4:D7)

D7 is the cell that will hold the formula, so therefore it cannot be included in the answer. This is a *circular reference* and is easily fixed. To resolve this, click in the formula bar and edit the formula so that it no longer includes this cell:

=SUM(D4:D6)

Other Formula Errors

#VALUE!
The #VALUE! error occurs when we have entered a text type field into a formula when it needs a number

#DIV/0!
The #DIV/0! error value occurs when a formula divides by 0 (zero) or a blank cell.

#NAME?
The #NAME? error value occurs when Microsoft Excel doesn't recognise text in a formula.

EXERCISES TO PROVE YOU KNOW

1. Open the *Sales.xls* workbook and type in the correct formulae to calculate the results indicated below

	A	B	C	D	E	F
1		Sales figures for the year				
2		QTR1	QTR2	QTR3	QTR4	Total
3	James O'Brien	€ 50.00	€ 52.00	€ 60.00	€ 65.00	Formula
4	Margaret Kelly	€ 56.00	€ 57.00	€ 59.00	€ 60.50	Formula
5	Peter Woodhouse	€ 215.00	€ 250.00	€ 215.00	€ 250.00	Formula
6	Ciaran Jones	€ 850.00	€ 850.00	€ 850.00	€ 850.00	Formula
7	Jackie Phillips	€ 515.00	€ 500.00	€ 485.00	€ 470.00	Formula
8	Total sales	Formula	Formula	Formula	Formula	
9						
10	Average Sales	Formula				
11	Largest Sale	Formula				
12	Lowest Sale	Formula				
13	Total Sales for year	Formula				

2. Save the workbook and close it.

3. What is wrong with the following formulae:

Function with error	Reason for error
=sum(a:b9)	
=average(9b:8c)	
=count()	
=maximum(a1:a10)	
=minimum(a12:b13:)	
=if(a1>0, "profit, "loss")	

4. Explain why we might get the following errors appearing in our spreadsheet:
   a) **#VALUE!**
   b) **#DIV/0!**
   c) **#NAME?**

Solutions:

1.

	A	B	C	D	E	F
1		Sales figures for the year				
2		QTR1	QTR2	QTR3	QTR4	Total
3	James O'Brien	50	52	60	65	=SUM(B3:E3)
4	Margaret Kelly	56	57	59	60.5	=SUM(B4:E4)
5	Peter Woodhouse	215	250	215	250	=SUM(B5:E5)
6	Ciaran Jones	850	850	850	850	=SUM(B6:E6)
7	Jackie Phillips	515	500	485	470	=SUM(B7:E7)
8	Total sales	=SUM(B3:B7)	=SUM(C3:C7)	=SUM(D3:D7)	=SUM(E3:E7)	
9						
10	Average Sales	=AVERAGE(B3:E7)				
11	Largest Sale	=MAX(B3:E7)				
12	Lowest Sale	=MIN(B3:E7)				
13	Total Sales for year	=SUM(B3:E7)				

3. Correct formulae as follows:

Function with error	Reason for error
=sum(a:b9)	**Missing row reference e.g. a9**
=average(9b:8c)	**Illegal reference to cell 9b – should be b9 and c8**
=count()	**No range specified e.g. =count(a3:a7)**
=maximum(a1:a10)	**Invalid formula should be max**
=minimum(a12:b13:)	**Invalid formula should be min and extra colon after b13**
=if(a1>0, "profit, "loss")	**Missing closing quote after the word Profit**

4. See previous page for causes of these errors.

4
Spreadsheets

SECTION 4.5: THE AUTOFILL TOOL

The *AutoFill* tool in Excel is one of its most endearing. AutoFill will save us many hours of repeated entries of formulae in our spreadsheets.

AutoFill allows us to automatically fill in data, based on the content of adjacent cells. Often formulae in many cells are related to those above or beside them. We also tend to type in the months of the year and the days of the week frequently. Using AutoFill all we need do is show the pattern of information we are entering and Excel will fill in the rest for us.

In this section we will learn:

- ❏ To use AutoFill with text
- ❏ To use AutoFill with numbers
- ❏ To use AutoFill with functions and formulae
- ❏ About absolute and relative referencing

LESSON 4.5.1: USING AUTOFILL

Using AutoFill with text

- ❏ Open a new blank workbook and in cell A1, type in *January* and press **Enter**
- ❏ Click back on the cell A1 so that it is active

In the corner of the cell there is a little black box, this is called the *Fill Handle*

Fill handle

- ❏ Put the mouse pointer over the fill handle and it will change into a black cross

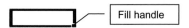

Mouse pointer changes into a black cross

- ❏ Hold down mouse button to drag it either to the right or downwards

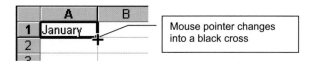

- ❏ Drag to the right and stop at cell **F1**
- ❏ When we release the mouse, Excel will have automatically filled in the cells for us with the months February to June.

This works for *days of the week* and *months of the year* automatically. We do not even have to start at the first day or month, it will continue the list from any start point and we can drag in any direction!

Using AutoFill with Numbers:

We can also use AutoFill to complete a sequence of numbers. Go onto a new worksheet –

❑ Type numbers in the first two cells in a sequence and select them both.

	A	B
1	10	
2	20	
3		

❑ Put the mouse pointer on the fill handle, to get the black cross
❑ Hold down the left mouse and drag to row 10

Drag and drop to Row 10   *It fills in the sequence in all cells*

	A	B
1	10	
2	20	
3		
4		
5		
6		
7		
8		
9		
10		
11		100
12		

	A
1	10
2	20
3	30
4	40
5	50
6	60
7	70
8	80
9	90
10	100
11	

This works when the fill handle is dragged either horizontally or vertically.

If we use the fill handle on only one number cell, it will copy that number into the cells that we drag over.

❑ Select only the one cell A1

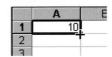

	A	E
1	10	
2		
3		

❑ Click on the fill handle and drag to row 10

❑ This time, because Excel sees no sequence it just copies the number down into the cells

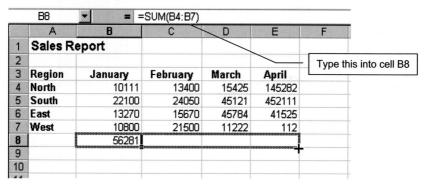

To use AutoFill when using formulae:

AutoFill becomes very useful when we are working with formulae. We can use the fill handle to copy formulae horizontally or vertically on our workbook.

Take a look at the following worksheet:

	A	B	C	D	E	F
B8	▼	=	=SUM(B4:B7)			
1	**Sales Report**					
2						Type this into cell B8
3	**Region**	**January**	**February**	**March**	**April**	
4	**North**	10111	13400	15425	145282	
5	**South**	22100	24050	45121	452111	
6	**East**	13270	15670	45784	41525	
7	**West**	10800	21500	11222	112	
8		56281				
9						
10						

Instead of having to type the formula into **C8**, **D8** and **E8**, we can use the fill handle to copy the formula across and it will automatically fill in the data – adjusting the formula as it does so.

LESSON 4.5.2: RELATIVE REFERENCING

When using AutoFill in a formula, we should notice that the fill handle is not simply copying the formula but changing the formula relative to where it is moved to.

Let's have a look at the Excel sheet again, this time looking at the formulae closely:

	A	B	C	D	E
B27			=		
1	Sales Report				
2					
3	Region	January	February	March	April
4	North	10111	13400	15425	145282
5	South	22100	24050	45121	452111
6	East	13270	15670	45784	41525
7	West	10800	21500	11222	112
8		=SUM(B4:B7)	=SUM(C4:C7)	=SUM(D4:D7)	=SUM(E4:E7)
9					
10					
11		*The formulae are changing as we move across*			
12					
13					

The formula that we copied was

=SUM(B4:B7)

We moved that formula one **column** to the right, hence the formula changed to:

=SUM(C4:C7)

The only change was that 'B' turned into 'C'. That is, the formula changed relative to where it was moved to.

The AutoFill feature does this automatically!

If we were to move a formula down a row, then it would be the row number in the formula that would change.

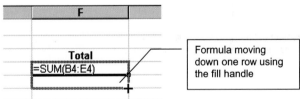

F
Total
=SUM(B4:E4)

Formula moving down one row using the fill handle

The formula changes to:

=SUM(B5:E5)

LESSON 4.5.3: ABSOLUTE REFERENCING

When we do not want Excel to make adjustments to our formulae when they are copied or moved we have to make the references to cells in our formulae *absolute*. In this lesson we will learn how to make a cell reference absolute.

Recall that a cell is named by column and then by row, e.g. cell **A1** is the top left cell on a worksheet. Usually we refer to this cell in a formula just as **A1** – and if we move or copy the formula containing this reference it will change as we saw in the last lesson.

To make cell **A1** *column* absolute we need to:

❏ Type a $ symbol in front of the column name – e.g. **$A1**

To make cell **A1** *row* absolute we need to:

❏ Type a $ symbol in front of the row number – e.g. **A$1**

To make cell **A1** column and row absolute

❏ We type a $ symbol in front of the column and row number – e.g. **$A$1**

Take a look at the Excel sheet below:

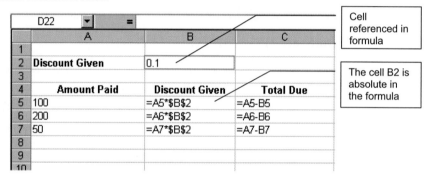

The cell B2 is absolute in the formula contained in cell **B5**. When we copy or move the formula it does not change the reference to cell **B2**. Notice that we left the reference to cell **A5** relative and it changed to **A6** and **A7** as the formula was copied downwards.

Tip: By pressing F4 in the formula bar we can toggle the cell reference to make it Absolute.

EXERCISES TO PROVE YOU KNOW

1. Open a new blank workbook and type *Monday* into the cell **B1**. Using the AutoFill tool, complete the days of the week across the columns

2. Type January into cell **A2**. Using the AutoFill tool, complete the months of the year down the rows

3. Save the Workbook.

4. Type in the following figures (**Hint: use your AutoFill to help fill in the figures**):

	A	B	C	D	E	F	G	H
1		Monday	Tuesday	Wednesday	Thursday	Friday	Saturday	Sunday
2	January	100	5	1	10	20	0	0
3	February	200	10	2	10	20	0	0
4	March	300	15	3	10	20	0	0
5	April	400	20	4	10	20	0	0
6	May	500	25	5	10	20	0	0
7	June	600	30	6	10	20	0	0
8	July	700	35	7	10	20	0	0
9	August	800	40	8	10	20	0	0
10	September	900	45	9	10	20	0	0
11	October	1000	50	10	10	20	0	0
12	November	1100	55	11	10	20	0	0
13	December	1200	60	12	10	20	0	0
14								

6. In cell B14 insert a formula to add all figures for Monday.

7. Using the *AutoFill* tool and relative referencing, drag the formula to fill in the formulae for the rest of the week days

8. Which of the following are *absolute* references?

     a) $A$1   b)   A3   c) $A$1:$B$10   d) $C4:$G4

4
Spreadsheets

SECTION 4.6:   MODIFYING A WORKSHEET

Workbooks consist of many parts and we need to be able to change the configuration of our workbook, such as adding sheets, columns or rows as required. In this section we'll look at:

- ❑ Inserting, deleting and renaming worksheets
- ❑ Changing our worksheet views
- ❑ Deleting cells, rows and columns
- ❑ Modifying the width and height of columns and rows
- ❑ Freezing rows and columns in a worksheet

LESSON 4.6.1:   WORKSHEETS

So far we've selected cells from just the first worksheet. To select cells on the next worksheet *click* on the worksheet tab. To select cells on **Sheet 2**

- ❑ Position the mouse pointer over the **Sheet 2** tab and click with the left mouse button.

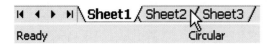

Inserting a new worksheet
We can insert a new worksheet easily.

- ❑ Move to the worksheet tab and click the **RIGHT** mouse button.

The following menu will appear:

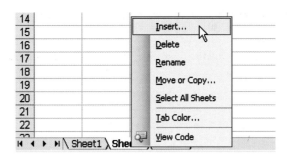

- ❑ Click on the **INSERT** option

Excel will prompt us with the type of sheet we want to insert. Choose *Worksheet* and press **OK**.

We can now rename the worksheet or rearrange its position in the workbook if required.

Renaming a worksheet

We can rename a worksheet easily.

  ❏ Move to the worksheet tab and click the **RIGHT** mouse button.

The following menu will appear:

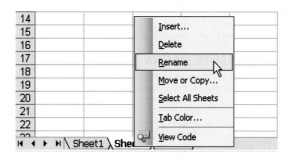

  ❏ Select **RENAME** from the pop-up menu.

  ❏ Type the new name for the Worksheet and press the **Enter** key.

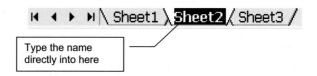

Type the name
directly into here

Moving and copying worksheets

We can move and copy worksheets within a workbook or to another workbook.

To move or copy a workbook

  ❏ Right-click on the worksheet tab to move or copy and choose **Move or Copy..**

The following dialog will appear

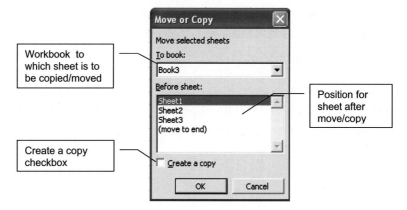

Workbook to
which sheet is to
be copied/moved

Position for
sheet after
move/copy

Create a copy
checkbox

  ❏ To move the sheet to a new position in the current workbook select the sheets' new position by clicking on a sheet name from the *Before sheet* list and press **OK**.

or

  ❏ To move the sheet to a new workbook choose the workbook to move to from the *To Book* list and press **OK**

To create a *copy* of a worksheet in the current workbook or in another workbook click on the **Create a copy** check box and follow the same steps above for moving the sheet.

Deleting a worksheet

We can easily delete a worksheet from our workbook.

- ❏ Right-click on the sheet to remove and choose **Delete**

Excel will prompt us to confirm the deletion.

- ❏ Choose **OK** to delete the sheet

Note: Be careful deleting sheets as a deleted sheet cannot be recovered – even with Undo!

LESSON 4.6.2:   WORKSHEET VIEWS

Excel supports two commonly used *views* that allow us to work with the document in different ways. We can switch between these modes by using the View menu:

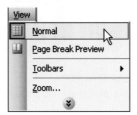

Normal View

Excel opens by default in the *Normal View*. We can zoom in and out of the normal view by using the % Zoom box.

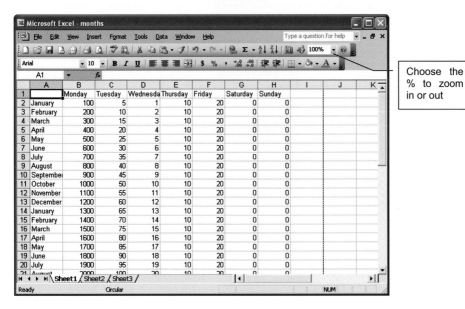

Choose the % to zoom in or out

This will allow us to see a large worksheet all at once on the screen. Most of our work will be done from the *Normal View*.

Page Break View

This view allows us to view all pages within the one worksheet at once, in miniature. This is a good view to choose before we print our worksheets as we can see how many pages will print and also we see the information that is on each page.

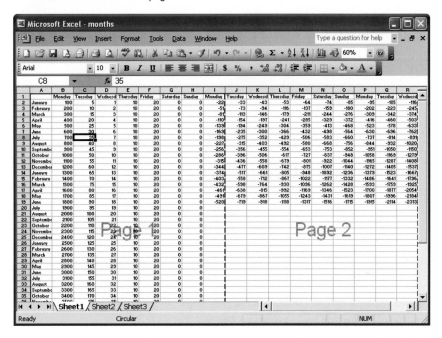

The Zoom box works here as well so we can zoom in on areas of the page as we did in the *Normal View*.

LESSON 4.6.3:   DELETING CELLS OR CELL RANGES

There is a difference between deleting the contents of a cell and deleting the cell itself. Deleting the contents only leaves a blank cell. Let's look at the difference.

- ❑ Click on a cell to make it active or select a range of cells
- ❑ Press the **Delete** key on the keyboard – this will clear the cell contents of the selected cells.

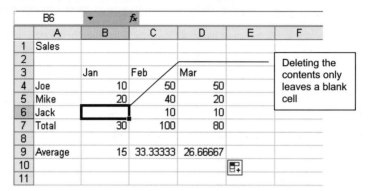

If we delete the cell itself, it will move the other cells to fill the gap that it will leave behind (in effect changing the cell reference of the entire row or column).

- ❑ Click on the cell, to make it active
- ❑ Go to the **Edit** menu and choose **Delete**
- ❑ The following dialog box appears:

- ❑ Choose the option that best suits the data. All cells will move in that direction. For example, Choose **Shift Cells Left**.

The two cells from the left will move into the blank cell position.

B6	▼		*fx* 10		
	A	B	C	D	E	F
1	Sales					
2						
3		Jan	Feb	Mar		
4	Joe	10	50	50		
5	Mike	20	40	20		
6	Jack	10	10			
7	Total	30	100	70		
8						
9	Average	15	33.33333	35		
10						
11						

These cells have moved left into B6 and C6

LESSON 4.6.4:   INSERTING AND DELETING ROWS AND COLUMNS

We can also insert extra rows and columns into our worksheet.

To insert a Row

❏   Click on the row number that we want the new row to go above

❏   From the **Insert** menu and choose **Rows**

This will insert a blank row, **above** the row selected

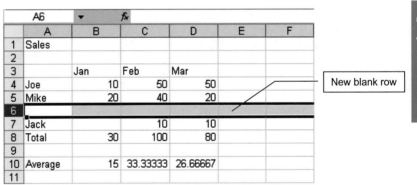

A6	▼		*fx*		
	A	B	C	D	E	F
1	Sales					
2						
3		Jan	Feb	Mar		
4	Joe	10	50	50		
5	Mike	20	40	20		
6						
7	Jack		10	10		
8	Total	30	100	80		
9						
10	Average	15	33.33333	26.66667		
11						

New blank row

All the existing rows are moved down to accommodate the new row.   All formulae also update appropriately.

Inserting a Column

- ❑ Click on the column heading
- ❑ Go to the **Insert | Columns** menu.

This will insert a blank column to the **left** of the selected column

	A	B	C	D	E	F
1	Sales					
2						
3		Jan		Feb	Mar	
4	Joe	10		50	50	
5	Mike	20		40	20	
6						
7	Jack			10	10	
8	Total	30		100	80	
9						
10	Average	15		33.33333	26.66667	
11						

New Blank column

All other columns have been moved to the right to accommodate the column. All formulae have also updated themselves.

To delete a row or a column

- ❑ Highlight the row(s) or column(s) that need to be deleted by clicking on the row or column heading
- ❑ Go to the **Edit** menu and choose **Delete**

This will delete the entire row or column. Excel will not warn us that it is about to delete all of the information in the rows or columns – but we can press ↩ ▾ **undo** to reverse the deletion if we make an error.

LESSON 4.6.5: MODIFYING COLUMN AND ROW SIZE

We can adjust the width of the columns and the height of rows using the mouse pointer.

To adjust a row's *height* position the mouse between the rows to be resized and then click and drag with the mouse:

	A	B	C	D
1	Height: 18.00 (24 pixels)	Jan	Feb	Mar
2	Mon	£ 343.00	£ 125.00	£ 343.00
3	Tues	£ 234.00	£ 256.00	£ 234.00
4				
5				
6				

C4   *fx*

To adjust the *column widths* position the mouse pointer between the column headings and then click and drag with the mouse:

C4   *fx*   Width: 12.43 (92 pixels)

	A	B	C	D
1		Jan	Feb	Mar
2	Mon	£ 343.00	£ 125.00	£ 343.00
3	Tues	£ 234.00	£ 256.00	£ 234.00
4				
5				
6				

To adjust the column or row widths to automatically fit their contents we can use the *autofit* tool

- ❑ Select the row or column to resize
- ❑ Choose **Format | Column | AutoFit Selection**

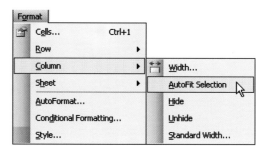

The cells will be automatically adjusted to the correct width for the contents of the column (or row) selected.

LESSON 4.6.6: FREEZING AND UNFREEZING ROWS AND COLUMNS

When a worksheet is so large that we cannot view all of it on screen at once, we can *freeze* a worksheet's columns and/or rows. The frozen column or row remains on the screen even when we scroll down and across the worksheet. This is very useful when dealing with multiple rows/columns of numbers as it means we don't have to keep scrolling up and down to identify which row or column is which.

To freeze a row or column:

❑ Click in the cell one below and one to the right of the row and column you wish to freeze. For example – to freeze the first row of our spreadsheet we would click in cell A2.

Frozen row

	A	B	C	D	E	F	G
	A2	▼	= 1				
	Membership No	Category No	Surname	Forenames	Title	Street	Town
1	Membership No	Category No	Surname	Forenames	Title	Street	Town
2	1	2	Walker	Andrew J	Mr	16 Dovecot Close	Dublin
3	2	1	Cartwright	Denise	Mrs	27 Bowling Green Rd	Dun Laoighaire
4	3	6	Perry	Jason R	Mr	59 Church Street	Dublin
5	4	2	Forsythe	Anne	Miss	2 Ferndale Close	Dublin

❑ Go to the **Window** menu and click on **Freeze Panes**

Frozen row stays put as user scrolls down

	A	B	C	D	E	F	G
	A7	▼	= 6				
1	Membership No	Category No	Surname	Forenames	Title	Street	Town
7	6	3	Robinson	Petra	Miss	16 Lowton Lane	Dun Laoighaire
8	7	5	Harris	David J	Mr	55 Coven Road	Dublin
9	8	2	Shangali	Imran	Mr	47 High Street	Newcastle
10	9	1	Barrett	Martha	Mrs	7 Oldcott Way	Dublin

Any rows above the cell that we clicked on and to the left of the cell we clicked on will be 'frozen' when we use the scrollbar to move around the screen.

To Unfreeze a row or column:

❑ Go to the **Window | Unfreeze panes**

EXERCISES TO PROVE YOU KNOW

1. Open a new blank workbook and insert three new sheets.

    a) Rename the sheets in order to **Jan 02, Feb 02, March 02, April 02, May 02, June 02**.

    b) Change **June 02** to **Dec 01**.

    c) Move this sheet to go in front of **Jan 02**.

    d) Save this workbook as *Months.xls*.

2. Open the workbook *Months.xls*, and click on the sheet March 02.

    a) Type in the days of the week across the worksheet in cells A1 to A7.

    b) Resize column B and column D so they are no longer visible.

    c) Type in the following data:

	A	C	E	F	G
1	Monday	Wednesday	Friday	Saturday	Sunday
2	€ 150.00				
3	€ 450.00				
4	€ 650.00				
5	€ 150.00				
6	€ 120.00				
7	€ 560.00				

    d) Freeze the first row of the worksheet so that when you scroll you can always see the days of the week at the top

    e) Save the workbook and close.

SECTION 4.7: SORTING DATA

Much of the data we use and keep in spreadsheets is a list or *database* of some sort. An employee list, a directory, a telephone log, a sales list and so on. Excel includes several facilities that make it easy to manipulate data in lists. In this section, we will learn how to:

❑ Sort lists of data

LESSON 4.7.1: SORTING DATA

❑ Open a new blank workbook and type in the following:

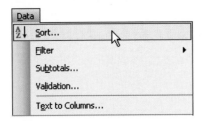

	A	B
1	**Name**	**Amount**
2	Derek	34
3	Eleanor	54
4	Shane	23
5	Chad	543
6	Chris	23
7	Brian	43
8	Steve	12
9	Cara	43
10	Fiona	23
11	Joe	55
12	Leonie	66
13	Breffni	32

Data to sort

❑ Select the cells A1 to B13 (it is very important to include all the columns which are part of the data range – or we might end up sorting just one column).

❑ Go to the **Data** menu and choose **Sort**

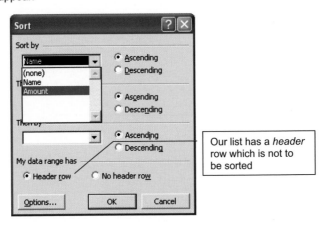

The following window will appear:

Our list has a *header* row which is not to be sorted

We choose *Header Row* if our list has a row at the top that we do not want sorted (this is often the case where the field names appear at the top of a list) as with our list.

Sorting alphabetically or numerically

Excel's sort options allow us to sort alphabetically or numerically. An alphabetic sort sorts a list based on the correct alphabetic position of each word in the list. A numerical sort sorts by the numeric value of the list. We can choose whether to sort alphabetically or numerically depending on the column we choose to sort by.

To sort the list *alphabetically* we need to sort by the *name* field. Choose *name* from the drop down list box in the **Sort** dialog box and click **OK**.

To sort the list *numerically* we need to sort by the *Amount* field. Simply choose *Amount* from the drop down list box in the **Sort** dialog box and click **OK**.

Our data is now sorted. The list below is sorted numerically from the lowest number upwards (ascending order). Note that the names correspond to the same amounts as in our original list.

	A	B
1	**Name**	**Amount**
2	Steve	12
3	Shane	23
4	Chris	23
5	Fiona	23
6	Breffni	32
7	Derek	34
8	Brian	43
9	Cara	43
10	Eleanor	54
11	Joe	55
12	Leonie	66
13	Chad	543

Data sorted numerically by *Amount* in ascending order

The data is sorted by the second column (Amount). If we add or amend the data in the list it will need to be re-sorted.

From the sort dialog box we can select up to three columns to sort by in either *ascending* or *descending* order.

4
Spreadsheets

EXERCISES TO PROVE YOU KNOW

1. Open a new blank workbook and enter in the following data:

	A	B	C	D	E	F	G	H
1	Employee ID	Last Name	First Name	Title	Dept Name	Office #	Ext	Salary
2	1	Hughes	Joe	Mr	Sales	1	101	€ 22,000.00
3	2	Maxwell	Matt	Mr	Operations	2	102	€ 34,000.00
4	3	Byrne	Paul	Mr	Sales	1	103	€ 22,000.00
5	4	Jacobs	Peter	Mr	Admin	3	104	€ 20,000.00
6	5	Andrews	Brian	Mr	Sales	1	105	€ 24,000.00
7	6	Fox	David	Mr	Marketing	3	106	€ 34,000.00
8	7	Wall	Fred	Mr	Sales	1	107	€ 40,000.00
9	8	Flynn	Frank	Mr	Admin	3	108	€ 25,000.00
10	9	O'Brien	Emma	Mrs	Sales	1	109	€ 21,000.00
11	10	Cullen	Sally	Miss	Sales	1	110	€ 22,000.00
12								

2. Save the Workbook as employees.xls

3. Sort the information by Last name (ascending order)

4. Sort the information by *Last Name*, then by *Dept Name* and then by *Salary* (all in descending order)

5. Save the workbook.

SECTION 4.8: CHARTS AND GRAPHS

A **chart** is a visual representation of worksheet data. Charts are dynamic; when we change the data a chart is based on, Excel updates the chart.

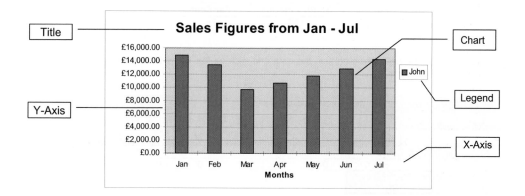

Showing data in a chart can make the data clearer, more interesting and easier to read. Charts also help evaluate data and make comparisons between different worksheet values.

This is how the following worksheet translates into a Chart.

	1993	1994	1995
Japan	$ 3.70	$ 4.30	$ 4.90
Korea	$ 2.40	$ 2.70	$ 4.20
China	$ 3.20	$ 3.90	$ 4.60

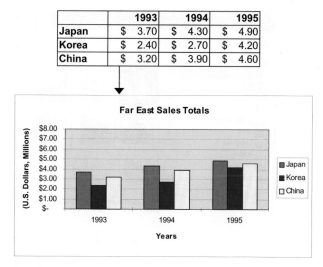

In this section we will learn how to:

- ❑ Create charts in Excel,
- ❑ Move and Resize Charts
- ❑ Edit a Chart
- ❑ Format Charts
- ❑ Insert other objects into Excel

LESSON 4.8.1: CREATING A COLUMN CHART

We are now going to create a column chart to graphically display the data in our spreadsheet.

❑ Open a blank new workbook and type in the following data.

Europe	South America	Far East
100	125	75

❑ Highlight the cells which contain the data and click on the *Chart Wizard* Icon 📊 on the *standard toolbar*

This will open the *Chart Wizard* Dialog box. The wizard has *four* steps, let's go through them.

❑ Select a *chart type* and *sub-type* – pick the column chart.

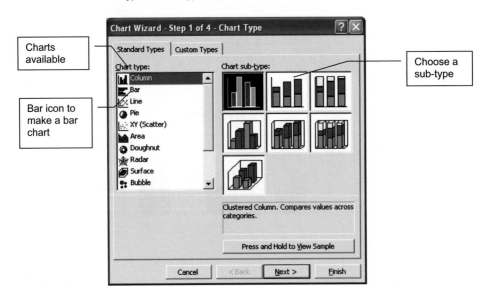

❑ Click **Next**.

Creating a Bar Chart

We can change our chart type at this point to any other type. For example to create a **Bar Chart** we simply click on the *Bar* icon in the dialog box.

We now need to check that we are graphing the correct data range and the wizard is working correctly. Notice the data range and compare it to the correct range on the worksheet.

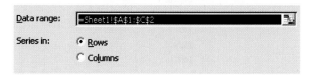

❑   If the data range looks correct – press **Next**

Now we configure the chart *options.* We can add a *title* to the chart, an *x-axis* category and *y-axis* category.

❑   Give the chart the title **"Sales"** and label the X-Axis **"Regions"** and the Y-Axis **"Amount"**

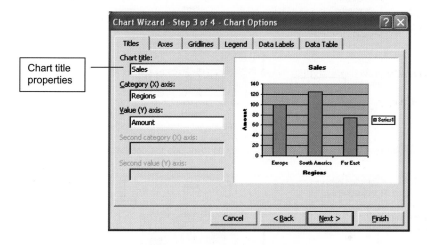

❑   Click on the Axes tab. Here we can choose to show or hide each of the chart axes

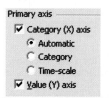

❑   Click on the *Gridlines* tab. Here we can choose to show or hide major or minor gridlines.

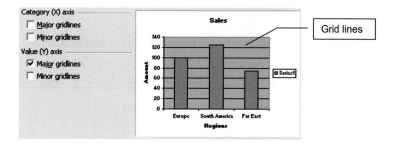

❑ Click on the *Legend* tab. Here we can choose to *show* or *hide* the legend and where we want it positioned.

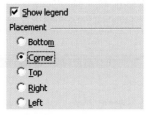

As the legend is repositioned the graph will rearrange itself.

❑ Click on the *Data Labels* tab. Here we can choose to show the values of each of the column bars in our chart.

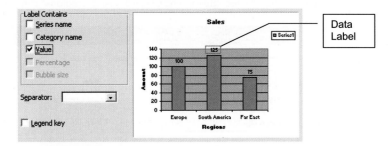

❑ Click on the *Data Table* tab. This tab allows us to include the data table in the chart

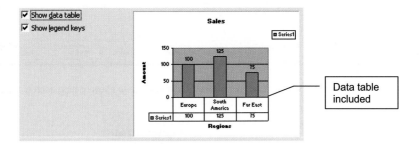

❑ Next we have to specify the *Chart Location*. Here we decide where we would like the chart to appear. We can either *embed* the chart on the current sheet or create a new *sheet*.

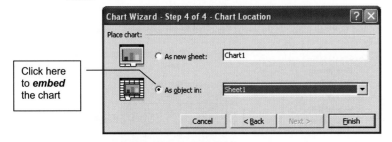

We're going to embed the chart onto the current sheet so

❑ Choose *As object in* and click **Finish**.

And that's it! We should now have the following chart on our worksheet:

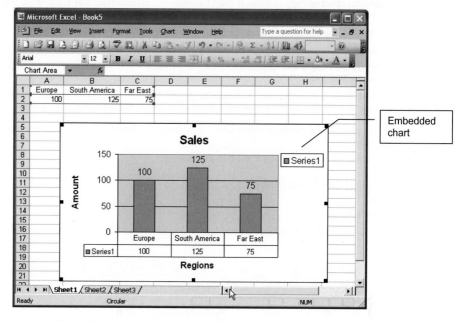

It is important to be able to move this chart and resize it on the sheet. We'll look at this next.

LESSON 4.8.2:   MOVING AND RESIZING A CHART After inserting a chart onto a sheet
we will often need to move and resize it.

Moving a chart on a worksheet

❑   Select the chart – by clicking on the chart area (aim at the white part of the chart).

When the chart is selected successfully, we will see little black *sizing handles* on each corner of the
chart.

❑   Place the mouse pointer directly over the white chart area and *drag* the chart into position.

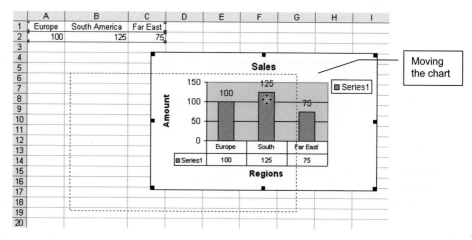

The chart will show a *ghost* outline of the chart as it is moved.

Moving a chart between open spreadsheets

Occasionally we may need to copy or move a chart between one spreadsheet and another. To move a chart between two open spreadsheets:

- ❑ Select the chart to move or copy by clicking on it once with the mouse.
- ❑ If copying between spreadsheets press **Ctrl + C** *or* press **Ctrl + X** if moving the chart.
- ❑ Choose the destination spreadsheet from the **Window** menu if it is already open, or open it from the **File** menu.

The destination spreadsheet window will now appear. Notice that the Title bar will show the name of the active spreadsheet. The spreadsheet we were working on is now hidden behind this window.

- ❑ Next go to **Edit | Paste** *or* press **Ctrl + V** *or* press the paste button 🖻 on the standard toolbar.

The chart has now been moved or copied into this spreadsheet.

Resizing the chart on the worksheet

To resize a chart

- ❑ Select the chart.

When the chart is selected successfully, we will see little black sizing handles on each corner of the chart.

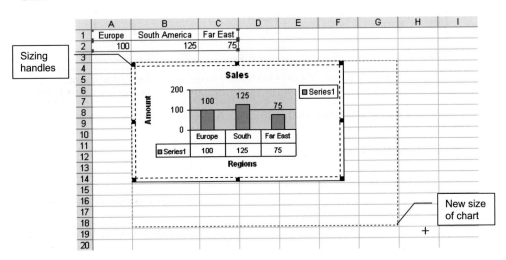

- ❑ Place the mouse pointer directly over one of the sizing handles. Notice that the mouse pointer changes to a double-headed arrow.
- ❑ Drag the mouse inwards to make the chart smaller, drag outwards to make the chart bigger.

When the mouse button is released the chart will be resized.

LESSON 4.8.3: EDITING THE CHART TYPE

Once a chart has been created, we can make further changes to it – change its style, colours and other options. Before we can change the chart's settings we must first select the chart.

❑ Select the chart to modify.

When the chart is selected successfully, we will see little black sizing handles on each corner of the chart.

❑ Go to the **Chart** menu and choose **Chart Type**

This brings up the Chart Type dialog box and allows us to choose from the list of different charts.

The *chart type* dialog box will then appear:

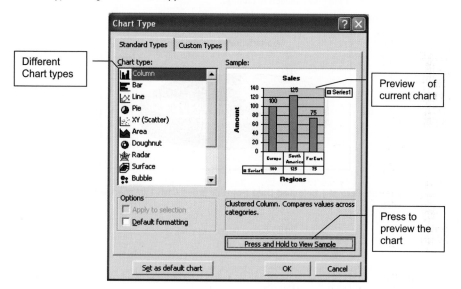

❑ Choose the *pie chart* option and press **Press and Hold to View Sample** to preview the changes.

❑ Press **OK** to commit the changes and change the chart to a **3D Pie chart**.

LESSON 4.8.4: FORMATTING CHART SECTIONS

Formatting a chart is easy, once we select the correct area in the chart to change.

- ❑   Select the chart to modify.
- ❑   Click again on the chart area.

Excel will select all of the pieces of the chart

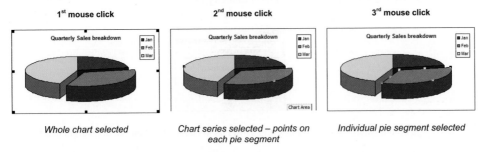

1st mouse click	2nd mouse click	3rd mouse click
Whole chart selected	*Chart series selected – points on each pie segment*	*Individual pie segment selected*

- ❑   Now click on the chart section to change.

Handles will appear when the section is selected.

- ❑   Choose **Format | Selected Data Point** or press **Ctrl+1** to change the settings for the pie slice.

The charts formatting options allow us to change the colour and style of the chart and its parts:

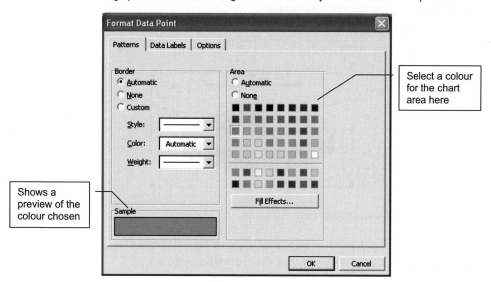

Shows a preview of the colour chosen

Select a colour for the chart area here

❑ Select a colour from the patterns tab.

To create a more elaborate fill effect click *Fill Effects* button. From here we can blend two or more colours together to create a gradient fill effect.

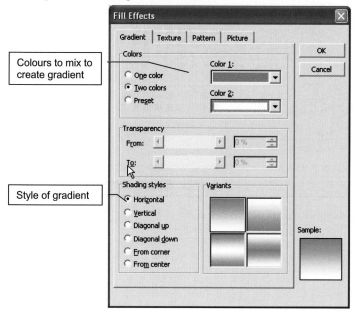

Colours to mix to create gradient

Style of gradient

Note: We can change the colour and pattern used in any section of the chart using this technique. Remember to make sure to *select* the item to change before choosing the formatting options.

❑ Press **OK** to confirm the changes.

Changing the chart background colour

We can also change the background colour in our chart. This can be useful if we are printing the chart or using it in a presentation. To change the background colour of a chart:

❑ Select the chart by clicking on it once with the mouse.

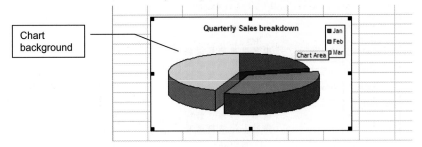

Handles around the chart indicate that it is selected.

❑ Press **Ctrl+1** to change the settings or choose **Format | Chart Area**

❑ Select a colour and pattern from the fill dialog box and press **OK**

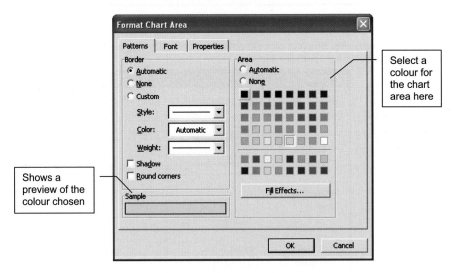

The chart background colour will change with the new settings.

LESSON 4.8.5:   ADDING AND REMOVING A CHART TITLE

We can add a title to our graph after it has been created by modifying the charts settings.

To add a title to a chart

    ❑   Select the chart and choose **Chart | Chart Options**

The following dialog will appear

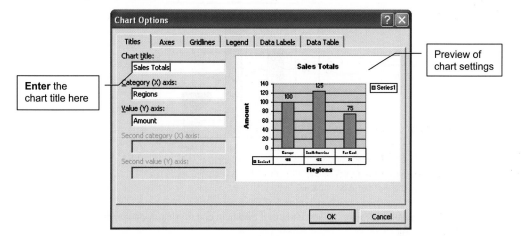

    ❑   Type the chart title into the *Chart Title* text box.

We can also add **X** and **Y** axis labels by filling in the <u>**Category (X) axis**</u> and <u>**Value (Y) axis**</u> text fields.

    ❑   Click **OK** to confirm the changes and add the title

If we later wish to remove the title or axis labels from the chart

    ❑   Select the chart

    ❑   Choose **Chart | Chart Options** and delete the text in the *Chart Title* box and press **OK**

LESSON 4.8.6: CHANGING THE CHART SCALE

The scale used on a chart can greatly affect how the chart is perceived – a small scale will amplify small changes – where as a large scale will smooth out differences.

To adjust the chart's scale:

❑ Double-click on the chart's Y-Axis (up-down axis)

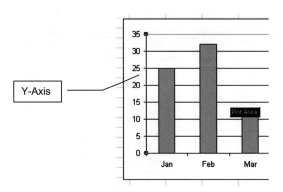

This will display the *Format Axis* window.

❑ Click on the **Scale** tab and enter new minimum and maximum values for the Y-axis.

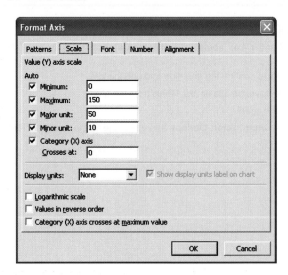

❑ Click **OK** to confirm the changes and adjust the scale.

LESSON 4.8.7:   ADDING DATA LABELS TO A CHART

Data labels show the value a particular point in a chart represents. We can add a data label to a chart from the *Chart options* dialog box.

- ❑ Select the chart to modify and choose **Chart | Chart Options**
- ❑ Select the **Data Labels** tab and click **Category Name** and press **OK**

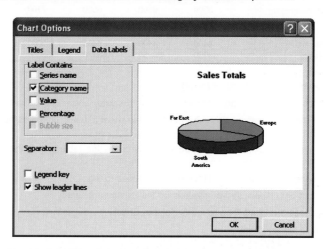

When *Category Name* is ticked Excel displays the regions around the pie chart.

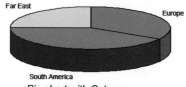

Pie chart with Category name
data labels showing

Same pie chart with no data labels

To remove the data labels from a chart

- ❑ Select the chart and choose **Chart | Chart Options**
- ❑ Select the *Data Labels* tab and choose **None** from the list of options and press **OK**

LESSON 4.8.8:   DELETING A CHART AND CHART DATA

To delete a chart, we simply select it and click on the **Delete** button on the keyboard or cut it onto the clipboard by pressing **Ctrl+X**.

EXERCISES TO PROVE YOU KNOW

1. Open a new workbook and type in the following data:

	A	B	C	D	E	F	G
1				Dublin Hotel			
2				BUDGET FOR 6 MONTHS			
3							
4	Department	January	February	March	April	May	June
5	Housekeeping	6500	6500	6500	7100	7100	7100
6	Restaurant	13600	13600	13600	14200	14200	14200
7	Sports & Rec	8750	8750	8750	9350	9350	9350
8	Marketing	4400	4400	4400	5000	5000	5000
9	Totals	33250	33250	33250	35650	35650	35650

2. Save the workbook as Hotels.xls.

3. Create a 3-D bar chart on a new sheet for this data, showing the chart title and a legend.

4. Change the location of the chart from a new sheet to being on the same sheet as the table above

5. Move the chart so that it appears directly below the table and is the same width as the table

6. Change the colour of the Housekeeping series to red

7. Insert data labels, showing values for the Restaurant series

8. Change the Chart Type to a 3-D Column Chart

9. Save the workbook.

SECTION 4.9: IMPORTING TEXT AND GRAPHICS

Excel allows us to insert and import other objects such as images (clipart and other graphics) and text files into our spreadsheet. In this section we will learn how to:

- ❑ Import clipart and graphic files
- ❑ Import text files into Excel

LESSON 4.9.1: GRAPHICS FILES

Inserting clipart into our workbook

To insert a picture (photograph or clipart image) into our spreadsheet:

- ❑ Click on the **Insert | Picture | Clip Art**

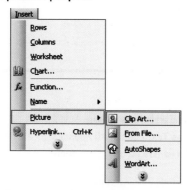

- ❑ Pick a category and an image and choose **Insert**.

The clipart image does not go into a cell - it floats over the cells. We can move and resize the picture once it has been inserted.

Resizing and moving a graphic image

Resizing and moving a graphic image is the same as resizing and moving a chart (see *page 325*).

Importing GIF, JPG and other graphic formats

To import a .GIF or .JPG image file into our spreadsheet choose:

- ❑ **Insert | Picture | From File**

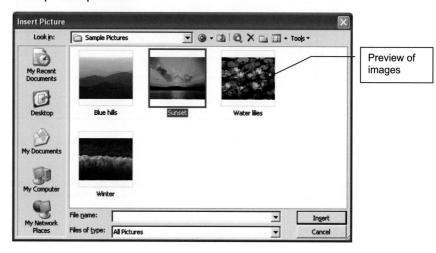

Preview of images

- ❑ Locate the file to import and click **Insert**.

LESSON 4.9.2: IMPORTING TEXT FILES (*.TXT FILES)

Much data generated by phone systems, accounts packages and other reporting tools is produced as a text file (often called an *ASCII* text file). It is useful to be able import a text file into Excel for reporting and charting purposes.

Take for example the text file below opened in *Notepad* – it shows two columns of data and 6 rows.

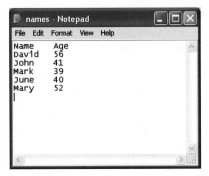

To open this text file in Excel

- ❑ Go to the **File** menu and choose **Open**
- ❑ Choose files of type **Text Files** or **All Files** and locate the text file to import.
- ❑ Locate the text file **names.txt** and press **open**

A wizard appears on screen to help us convert the file.

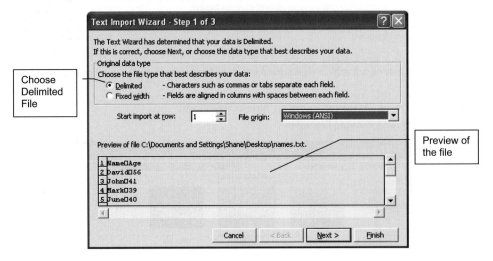

- ❑ Click **Next** and the wizard will choose *tab separated* as the conversion format. Click **Next** and then choose **Finish**

The file is now open in Excel. When this file is saved we will have the option of saving it as a **.TXT** file or as an Excel spreadsheet. If we add formulae or charts to this sheet these will be lost if we save it as a plain text file.

SECTION 4.10:   PRINTING AND PAGE SETUP

We can print sections of a worksheet, an entire worksheet or workbook in Excel. In this section we will learn how to:

❑   Proof and preview a document

❑   Modify the page setup

❑   Create Headers and Footers

❑   Print selections or areas of a workbook

LESSON 4.10.1: PROOFING AND PREVIEWING

Before printing a workbook or sending it to a colleague or client it is important to properly proof and preview our spreadsheet. The layout and appearance of our spreadsheet can make a big difference to how easy it is to understand and follow and how professional it is. Spell checking the spreadsheet, properly spacing and laying out pages and cross checking any calculations is also an important part of proofing our spreadsheet.

We can start proofing our spreadsheet by previewing it. To preview a spreadsheet:

❑   Choose **File | Print Preview** or click the print preview button 🔍

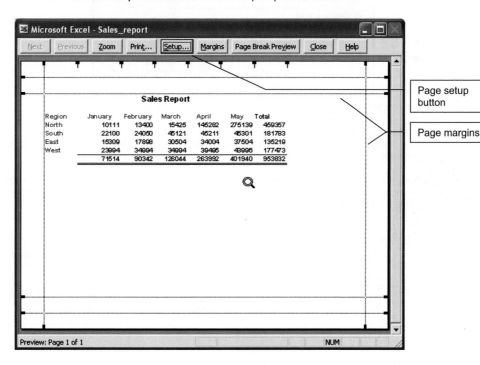

❑   Use the **Zoom** button to zoom in and out of the spreadsheet.

❑   Use the **Margins** button to show and hide the document margins. These can then be adjusted from within the page setup window (which we see later) or by dragging the margin lines with the mouse. Remember margin changes affect all pages.

❑   Use the **Next** and **Previous** buttons to go forwards and backwards through the pages in the document. Check for blank pages and 'lost' numbers or calculations on pages.

❑   Click **Close** to return the spreadsheet and leave print preview mode.

LESSON 4.10.2: ADJUSTING THE PAGE SETTINGS

Often when printing from Excel we will want to change the page orientation and page size and adjust the page margins and footers. We do all of this from the *page setup* dialog. This is usually easiest to do when we are already previewing the document.

To preview the document and view the page setup dialog:

❑ Choose **File | Print Preview** and click on **Setup**

The **Page Setup** dialog will appear

Click to change the page orientation

Click here to make document fit on a specified number of pages (default is 1 page)

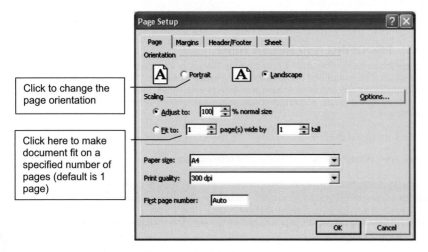

The first tab in this dialog box is the **Page** tab. Here we can set the orientation of the page and also adjust the scaling of the data on the page.

Adjusting the scale of our spreadsheet

We can scale our spreadsheet to increase or decrease the print size on the page (just like using the *zoom* feature on a photocopier).

Modifying the print *scale* of the spreadsheet is very useful when we have data that is just a little too big to fit on one page or needs to be made slightly larger. If we reduce the scaling by ten or fifteen percent, we will see that the page contents reduce in size and might just fit within the page boundaries.

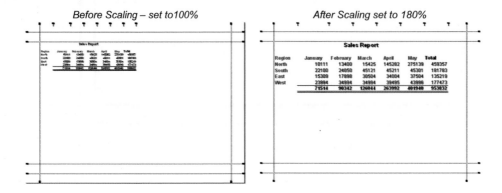

Before Scaling – set to100%   *After Scaling set to 180%*

To adjust the scale or magnification of our spreadsheet:

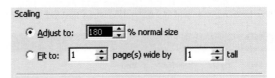

- ☐ Use the up/down arrows to change the scaling (values larger than 100% will enlarge the printout size and values smaller than 100% will decrease the printout size).
- ☐ Press **OK** to preview the document with the new scaling.

Fitting a document to a specific number of pages

Sometimes we will want to squeeze our spreadsheet into a certain number of pages. We can do this from the scaling options in the page tab of the **page setup** menu.

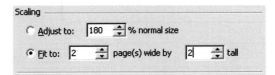

- ☐ Click **Setup** and click on the **Fit to** option in the scaling area of the window
- ☐ Specify how many pages to fit the spreadsheet into and click **OK**

Excel will then reduce the scale of the spreadsheet to fit the number of pages specified. It will not magnify the spreadsheet however to stretch it across multiple pages.

Changing document margins

The second tab in the setup dialog box is the **margins** tab.

This section is used to change any of the page margins and also to centre the page either vertically or horizontally.

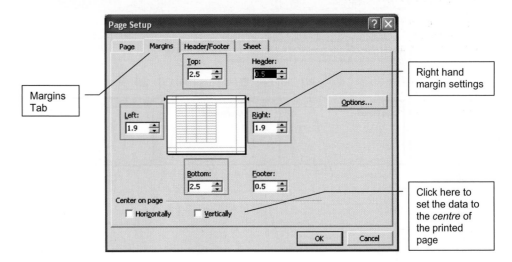

These setup changes will not be seen in the main spreadsheet, they are only visible in print preview mode or when the page is finally printed.

Adjusting the page margins can help squeeze additional information onto the page or help space out a spreadsheet better improving its overall presentation.

Headers and Footers

The third tab in the setup dialog box is the *Headers and Footers* tab. Headers and footers are important as they allow us to number and identify pages when they are printed.

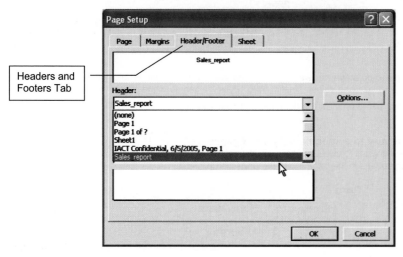

Headers and Footers Tab

In the *Headers and Footers* section, we can set the headers and footers for the active sheet. We can choose a preset header or footer by clicking on the drop down arrow or we can choose to make our own header or footer.

❑ Click on the *Custom Header* or *Custom Footer* buttons.

Creating a custom header or footer

To create a custom header/footer click **Customer Header/Footer** and type into the three white text areas shown below (called *Left Section, Centre Section and Right Section)*. To include a special field (such as the date, page number or sheet name) click on the appropriate icon.

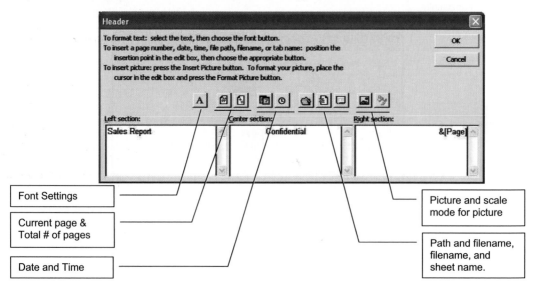

Font Settings

Current page & Total # of pages

Date and Time

Picture and scale mode for picture

Path and filename, filename, and sheet name.

LESSON 4.10.3: PRINT OPTIONS

Excel gives us quite a number of options when printing out our spreadsheet. Since spreadsheets can become very big – it is important that when printing them the contents look good and make sense.

For example we might wish to print out the row and column headings for our spreadsheet so we can see exactly where we are in the spreadsheet when looking at the printout. Similarly we might want to repeat a particular row or column across a number of pages (similar to *freezing* rows and columns which we saw earlier).

Let's have a look at how we can do this.

❑ Choose **File | Page Setup** and click on the **Sheet** tab

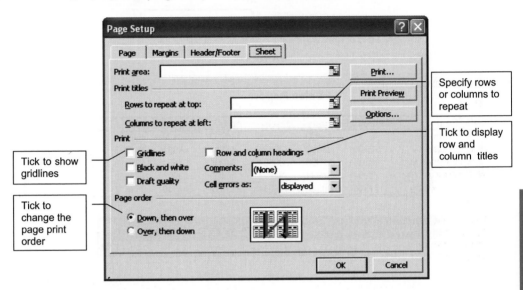

❑ To print the row and column headings in our document tick the **Row and column headings** check box.

Sales Report

Region	January	February	March	April	Total
North	10111	13400	15425	145282	184218
South	22100	24050	45121	452111	543382
East	13270	15670	45784	41525	116249
West	10800	21500	11222	112	43634
	56281	74620	117552	639030	887483

Typical preview of spreadsheet

	A	B	C	D	E	F
1			**Sales Report**			
2						
3	Region	January	February	March	April	Total
4	North	10111	13400	15425	145282	184218
5	South	22100	24050	45121	452111	543382
6	East	13270	15670	45784	41525	116249
7	West	10800	21500	11222	112	43634
8		56281	74620	117552	639030	887483

Preview of spreadsheet showing gridlines and row & colun headings

Printing spreadsheet titles

When printing a large spreadsheet we will often need to repeat rows and columns on multiple pages. Repeating rows and columns by hand in our document leads to all sorts of problems as our spreadsheet gets bigger and makes our spreadsheet harder to edit and work with.

To repeat rows or columns:

- ❑ Choose **File | Page setup** and click on the **Sheet** tab

- ❑ To print row titles click on the 🔲 icon next to the *Rows to repeat at top* text box.

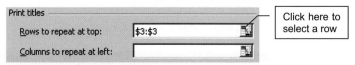

Print titles	
Rows to repeat at top:	$3:$3
Columns to repeat at left:	

Click here to select a row

- ❑ Click on the row or rows to repeat.

Excel will display the selected rows in a window like this:

	A	B	C	D	E	F	G	H
1				**Sales Report**				
2								
➡3	Region	January	February	March	April	May	Total	
4	North	10111	13400	15425	145282	275139	459357	
5	South	22100	24050	45121	45211	45301	181783	
6	East	15309	17898	30504	34004	37504	135219	
7	West	23994	34994	34994	39495	43996	177473	
8		**71514**	**90342**	**126044**	**263992**	**401940**	**953832**	
9								
10								
11	**Page Setup - Rows to repeat at top:**						? X	
12	$3:$3							
13								
14								
15								

Here we have selected row 3 to repeat.

- ❑ When the area is selected press **Enter** to return to the page setup dialog.

Excel will now repeat this row at the top of the page each time a new page is displayed.

We can repeat a column or a number of columns in the same way. Use the 🔲 icon next to the *Columns to repeat at left* text box to specify the column to repeat and follow the same steps as before.

Printing a workbook

Once we have configured the page setup we can then proceed to print.

❑ Click on the **Print** button on the toolbar of the print preview screen.

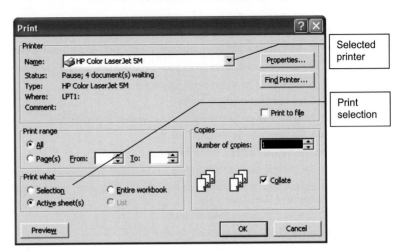

By default, we can print the active sheet. We can however, specify that we only want the cells that we selected printed (selection) or that we want the entire workbook printed.

❑ To print the spreadsheet press **OK**

EXERCISES TO PROVE YOU KNOW

1. Open *sales.xls* workbook.

2. Change the page setup to show the following changes:

   a) Change the page size to A4, landscape

   b) Change the scaling to 70%

   c) Ensure that the data is centred horizontally and vertically on the page when printed

3. Create a header and footer on all pages in sheet one that will show the following:

   a) Name of the File and sheet at top centre

   b) Page number on bottom centre

   c) Today's Date on the top right (date to update automatically)

4. Save the workbook as *section4_10a.xls*.

5. Change the print options to the following:

   a) Ensure that the *first row* of sheet 1 is repeated at the top of every page when printed

   b) Ensure that the numbering on the pages is *Over, then down* as apposed to the default setting of Down, then over

   c) Ensure that the gridlines *will* print

6. Save the workbook as *section4_10b.xls*.

SECTION 4.11:   USING HELP IN EXCEL

One of the most useful facilities offered by Windows is its *Help* utility. Most Windows products come with excellent help facilities usually containing as much if not more information than the accompanying reference guides. The help system uses a technique called "hypertext" to access information relating to a particular topic. This system allows the reader to follow a *thread* through the help database, constantly looking up and referring to related information.

LESSON 4.11.1: USING THE HELP FUNCTION

Help can be started in Excel by pressing **F1** or choosing **Microsoft Excel Help** from the **Help** menu.

This will display the Microsoft Excel help panel:

We can search for help on any feature in Excel – including all the formulae and functions. The help feature in *Microsoft Excel* works exactly the same as it does in *Microsoft Word*. Review Using Help on *page 257*.

EXERCISES TO PROVE YOU KNOW

1. Search for help on "Pivot Tables" in Excel to learn about consolidating data.
2. Search for help on "Conditional formatting" and try using it in a new workbook.

SECTION 4.12:   EXAM OVERVIEW AND TIPS

In the exam for Module 4, Spreadsheets, you will be given a disk. The disk will hold all files needed for this exam plus an answer file – **answerfile.doc**. The answer file is a Word document that you will type the answers into. It looks like this:

Candidate Identification :_____

Question No.	Response
1.	
2.	

There are 32 questions and each question will ask you to edit an existing Excel spreadsheet testing all the areas covered in the Module.

POINTS TO NOTE:
- Time allowed: 45 minutes
- Answer all 32 Questions:
- Marking System
    - Each question is awarded 1 mark, with exception to question 2, which is awarded 4 marks.

Topics Checklist:
- Opening and Closing Workbooks
- Enter and Edit Data
- Text Formatting
- Number Formatting
- Changing Column Width/Row height
- Deleting Data/Cells/Rows/Columns
- SUM / AVERAGE Formulae
- Borders
- Headers and Footers
- Copy and Paste
- Creating Charts
- Formatting Charts
- Spell Check

All of the topics covered in this Module could be asked in the exam.

For sample examinations visit http://www.iactonline.com/ecdl

Module 5
DATABASES

iact

The complete IT training provider

MODULE 5: DATABASES

We live in the information age – databases are all around us and our details probably exist in dozens, if not hundreds, of different databases. Everything from our tax affairs to our hair colour is stored on a database somewhere. The amount of information available about every one of us is quite dazzling.

Think of these to start with:

- ❑ The tax man tracks our RSI number and knows where we work, what we earn and where we live and what we drive. All this is stored on a database
- ❑ Our travel movements are recorded on travel agents computers with vast databases of knowledge about our destinations, flight times and companions
- ❑ Our movement on the Internet is recorded on databases
- ❑ Supermarkets watch what we buy and when we buy it
- ❑ Our schools record our results, our IQ and our career options
- ❑ Our video store records what we watch and when we watch it
- ❑ Our hairdresser might record our preferred style and colour
- ❑ Doctors and hospitals store our health and fitness records

Databases are the most widely used application in business. Most systems are really front-ends to vast databases. The Internet in fact could be viewed as a giant interconnected database.

There are many different database systems (or *database management systems)* which have evolved from the earliest days of computing. On PCs today the most common databases are:

- ❑ Microsoft Access
- ❑ Lotus Approach
- ❑ Foxpro
- ❑ Dbase
- ❑ Oracle
- ❑ Microsoft SQL Server
- ❑ Sybase
- ❑ Ingres

Although different to use and of varying degrees of power, the fundamentals of all these systems is much the same. We will be working with *Microsoft Access* for the duration of this course but the skills we learn will be applicable to most other databases.

SECTION 5.1:   STARTING ACCESS

In this section, we will learn how to:

- ❑ Start Access
- ❑ Open and logon to a database
- ❑ Create a Database
- ❑ Understand the concept of a *Table, Record* and a *Field*
- ❑ Delete, update and edit a record
- ❑ Modify table layout
- ❑ Exit Access

LESSON 5.1.1:   STARTING ACCESS

Firstly, we must turn on our computer and logon to Windows.

- ❑ Once Windows has loaded, go to the **Start Menu** and choose **Microsoft Office** and then choose **Microsoft Office Access 2003**.

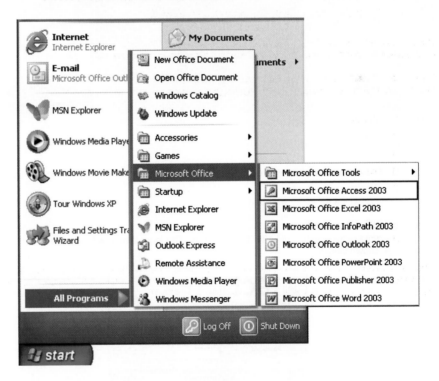

After a few moments the Access application will start.

LESSON 5.1.2: OPENING AND LOGGING ONTO A DATABASE

When Access first starts we see a blank screen with the *Getting Started* panel visible:

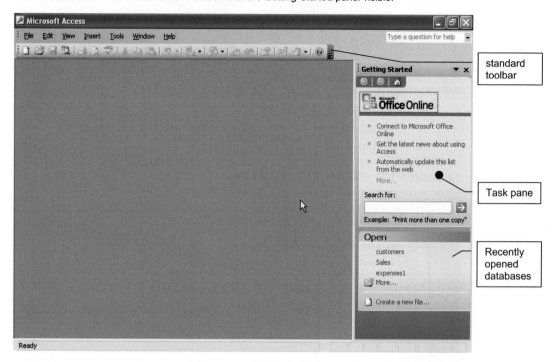

To open an existing database:

  ❑   Click **More...** or choose a recently opened database from the list or choose **File | Open**.

After a short period the database will open.

Logging onto a database
Some databases require us to *login* after they open up. The login screen will vary but here is a typical login screen shown below:

To logon to the database we will usually need a username and a password. Usernames and passwords are usually case sensitive – a username *John* is different to *JOHN*. Check the CAPS LOCK key is not pressed accidentally when you are trying to login.

Note: You should keep your username and password secret as it allows access to a secure system – and unauthorised access can lead to data loss or worse!

LESSON 5.1.3: CREATING A NEW DATABASE

To create a new database:

- ❑ Choose **Create a new file...** from the **Getting Started** panel or press the *New Database* icon 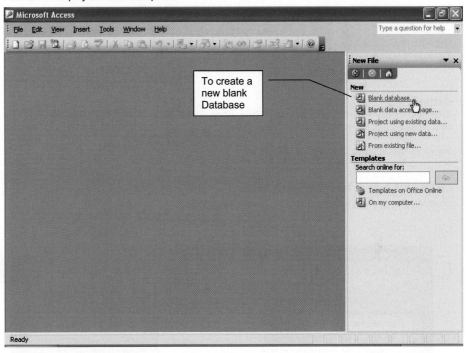 on the standard toolbar.

Access will display the **New File** panel:

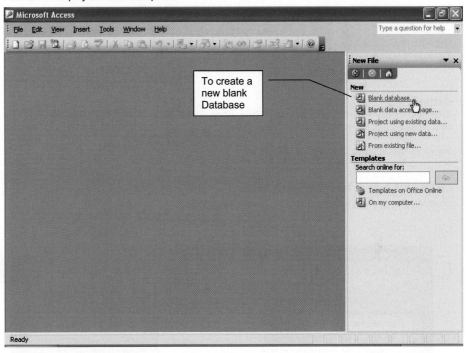

The New File panel invites us to create a **Blank Database** or *data access page...* or to use an existing project or file to build our new database. Usually we will open an existing database and work with it but on this occasion we will create a blank database.

- ❑ Click **Blank Database** from the **New File** panel.

Access now needs to know where we plan to save our database.

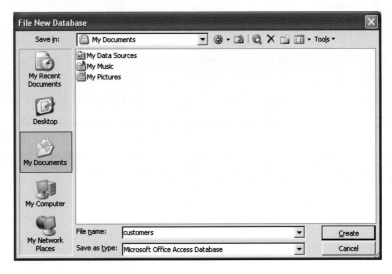

The **File New Database** is the same as all other save dialog boxes.

❑ Call the database *Customers* and save it into the **My Documents** folder.

Access files can be identified with the .MDB file extension.

NOTE: this is different to most other applications which usually allow us to *save* our documents when we are finished – <u>Access needs to save, right from the start</u>.

Closing the database
To close the database:

❑ Choose **File | Close**.

Getting Help
Microsoft Access includes comprehensive help which works as in other Office applications. To start help press **F1** and follow the onscreen instructions.

For further details on using help see page 257.

LESSON 5.1.4:   TOURING ACCESS
When Access opens a database, we see the following screen.

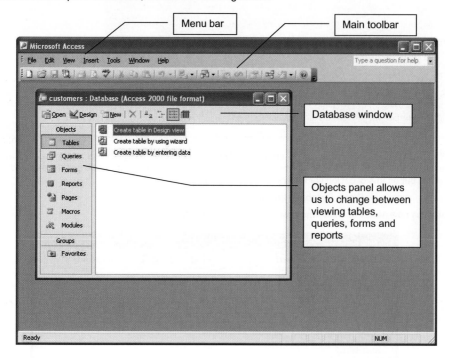

The *Database Window* is made up of several parts which change in appearance as the application is used in different ways. The *Objects panel* is a very important part of the Database window. It will allow us to navigate through the different parts of our database.

Customising Toolbars

To turn on and off the different toolbars in Access:

❑ Choose **View | Toolbars | Customise**.

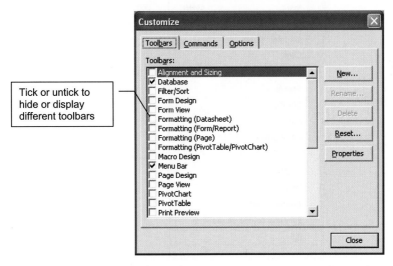

Tick or untick to hide or display different toolbars

We can turn on and off toolbars by ticking next to the toolbar to display.

Switching view modes

As we work with Access we will see that there are a number of ways of working with objects. We'll see that we can view a table in *Design view* – where we are able to edit the structure of the table and we can also view it in *Datasheet view* – where we can view, edit and update the information stored in the table. We can do the same with queries, forms and reports.

Once a table, form, report or query has been opened we can change view modes by using options on the main toolbar:

Clicking on the down-arrow reveals the available view modes for the current object. Select the option required and the object will switch to that mode.

LESSON 5.1.5:   EXITING ACCESS

To exit or quit Access, go to the **File** menu and choose **Exit**.

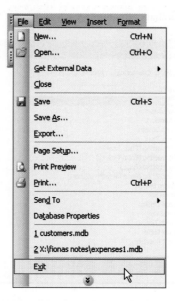

Note that data stored in the database is already saved.

EXERCISES TO PROVE YOU KNOW

1.   Open Access and create a new blank database using the Wizard.

2.   Use the navigation bar to switch to table view mode

3.   Use the built in help to search for information on *Tables*.

SECTION 5.2:   MANIPULATING TABLES

In order to work with Access we must first learn to work with tables – the fundamental building blocks of our database. In this section we will learn:

- ❑   To open and close tables
- ❑   To recognise the structure and make up of a table
- ❑   How to add, delete and change records in a table
- ❑   How to navigate through a table
- ❑   How to sort and filter records in a table

LESSON 5.2.1:   TABLES

All of the data held in our database lives in one or more *tables*. A table will look rather like a spreadsheet but is more precise in its design. When we create a table, we can specify the *type* of information we wish to store in each of the table's *fields.*

Opening and Closing a table
To open an existing table

- ❑   Select it and then double-click on it from the database window.

Here is what the **tblCustomers** table looks like when we open it. This table holds information about Customers; their name, address and phone numbers.

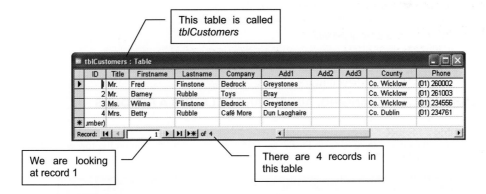

This table is called *tblCustomers*

ID	Title	Firstname	Lastname	Company	Add1	Add2	Add3	County	Phone
1	Mr.	Fred	Flinstone	Bedrock	Greystones			Co. Wicklow	(01) 260002
2	Mr.	Barney	Rubble	Toys	Bray			Co. Wicklow	(01) 261003
3	Ms.	Wilma	Flinstone	Bedrock	Greystones			Co. Wicklow	(01) 234556
4	Mrs.	Betty	Rubble	Café More	Dun Laoghaire			Co. Dublin	(01) 234761

We are looking at record 1

There are 4 records in this table

To close the table

- ❑   Press the ☒ button in the top right hand corner of the window.

Information in a table is made up of repeated records of information. Each line in the table is called a record and each record consists of a set of fields.

ID	Title	Firstname	Lastname	Company	Add1	Add2	Add3	County	Phone
1	Mr.	Fred	Flinstone	Bedrock	Greystones			Co. Wicklow	(01) 260002
2	Mr.	Barney	Rubble	Toys	Bray			Co. Dublin	(01) 261003
3	Ms.	Wilma	Flinstone	Bedrock	Greystones			Co. Wicklow	(01) 234556
4	Ms.	Betty	Rubble	Café More	Dun Laoghaire			Co. Dublin	(01) 2347611

Record ◄

Field

Some Definitions
It is important at this point to understand some key terms:

- ❑ A *Field* is defined as the smallest indivisible part of a table. In our table **ID, Firstname** and **Lastname** are all examples of fields (as are **Add1**, **Add2** etc.). Fields hold different *types* of data and should be setup to hold that data in the most efficient way possible.

- ❑ The *Field/Data Type* determines the kind of information that can be held in a field. For example a "Text Field" can hold textual information whereas a "Date" field can hold date information. By correctly assigning field types to our fields we make it much easier to sort, group and summarise the data that is held in our tables. We will look at the field types Access provides us with later

- ❑ A *Record* is an individual line or row of data in a table.

- ❑ A *Table* is a set of records

Remember these terms as we will use them throughout this section.

LESSON 5.2.2:   CHANGING, ADDING AND DELETING A RECORDS

Changing a record
Changing a record in a table is easy. Firstly, we select the record by clicking on the row we wish to change – in this case let's select the second record (in this case its *Barney's* record)

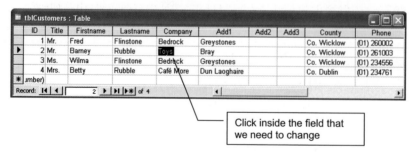

Click inside the field that we need to change

www.iactonline.com

Let's suppose we wish to change the name of the company from "Toys" to "Bricks'R'Us":

❑ Simply move to the field by pressing the **Tab** key or by clicking in the field with the mouse

❑ Overwrite the field with the new text "Bricks'R'Us" and press **Enter**.

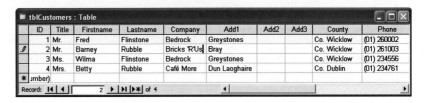

When we move from this record the changes are automatically saved to the table and database.

Adding a record
To add a record to the table place the cursor on the last line of the table

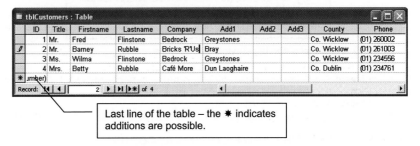

Last line of the table – the ✱ indicates additions are possible.

Fill in the fields with the new information for new record. When we press **Enter** the record will be saved and added to the end of the table.

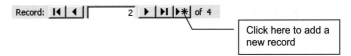

Click here to add a new record

Another way of adding a record is to click on the ▶✱ button in the record navigator, this will automatically place the insertion point on a brand new row, to begin entering a new record.

Navigating through a table
We can navigate through a table using the navigation toolbar which is at the bottom of the table window. The icons work much like those on a CD or tape player.

◄		Move to *First* record in table
◄	Move to *Previous* record in table
►	Move to *Next* record in table
►		Move to *Last* record in table
►✱	Add a *New* record to the table

5
Databases

Deleting a Record

To delete a record select the record by clicking on the record select arrow ▶, this will highlight the entire record or row. Then press the **Delete** key or go to the **Edit** menu and choose **Delete Record**.

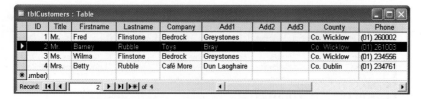

Access will prompt with the message:

❑ Click on the **Yes** option to permanently delete the record.

NOTE: Once a record is deleted it cannot be recovered – there is usually NO Undo like in Word or Excel.

To delete more than one record at a time highlight all the records to delete and press the **Delete** key.

LESSON 5.2.3:   SORTING AND FILTERING RECORDS

We can sort our table easily by using the ⒜↓ button to sort in *ascending order* or the ⒵↓ button to sort in *descending order*.

To sort the records in a table:

❑ Open the table to sort

❑ Select the field to sort by placing the cursor in the field or clicking on the field name (in our case it's the *firstname* field)

❑ Press the ⒜↓ or the ⒵↓ buttons on the toolbar.

	ID	Title	Firstname	Lastname	Company	Add1	Add2
▶	4	Mrs.	Betty	Rubble	Café More	Dun Laoghaire	
	1	Mr.	Fred	Flinstone	Bedrock	Greystones	
	3	Ms.	Wilma	Flinstone	Bedrock	Greystones	
✳	ımber)						

This table is sorted in *ascending order* by the *firstname* field

	ID	Title	Firstname	Lastname	Company	Add1	Add2
▶	4	Mrs.	Betty	Rubble	Café More	Dun Laoghaire	
	3	Ms.	Wilma	Flinstone	Bedrock	Greystones	
	1	Mr.	Fred	Flinstone	Bedrock	Greystones	
✳	ımber)						

This table is sorted in *descending order* by the *ID* field

Filtering Records

When we open our Table we can also *filter* it to restrict the information that it shows. Access has a special *filter* button that allows us to select the records we are interested in – highlighting for example those in a particular country or region.

To tell Access that we only want to see customers from the **UK** we need to filter our table giving it an *example* of the data that we want.

❑ Open the table

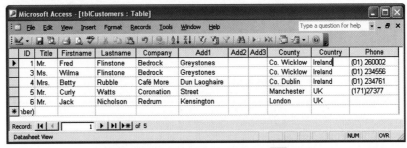

❑ Select the **Country** field and press the *Filter by Form* button

The records disappear and just the field headings and a blank row remain.

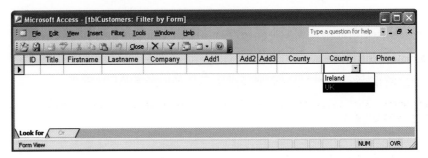

Specify the criteria to filter using the drop-down arrows

We can now select the types of records we want to see by choosing them from the drop-down list or by typing into the filter box.

This is very like using filters in Excel. We can also use the wildcard operators (*, ? etc.) that we use in queries later on.

Filtering by selection

❑ Choose or type "**UK**" from the drop-down box and press the **Filter** button.

Access will now show the list of customers in the UK.

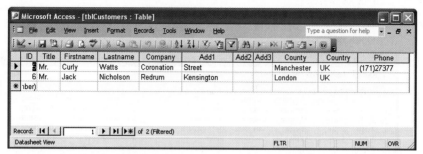

❑ We can turn on and off the filter by toggling the filter button.

Filtering on multiple fields

We can apply the filter to several fields at once specifying multiple 'criteria'.

❑ Select the *Filter by Form* button and specify additional requirements from the other field headings

❑ Press the *Filter* button to apply the filter.

When we make changes to the table (even if filtered) the changes are saved to the table.

Removing the filter

To remove the filter - ensure that the filter button is *de-pressed* on the toolbar.

LESSON 5.2.4: CUSTOMISING TABLE LAYOUT

Adjusting Column Width

To make the data in a table easier to view, it is useful to be able to alter the widths and heights of the columns and rows of a table.

To alter a column width:

- ❏ Move the mouse pointer to the "Field Name" row (at the top of the table).
- ❏ Move the Pointer to the dividing line between the column you wish to change and the column to the right, it should change shape to a ✛
- ❏ Click and drag the column to the desired width.

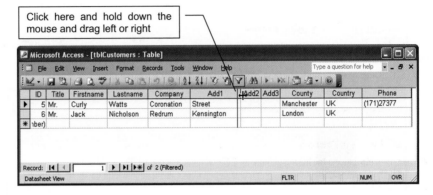

Adjusting Row Heights

We can adjust the height of rows in a similar way.

To alter a row's height:

- ❏ Move the pointer to the row selector (at the left edge of the table).
- ❏ Move the pointer to the dividing line between the row you wish to change and the row below, it should change shape to a ✛
- ❏ Click and drag the row to the desired height.

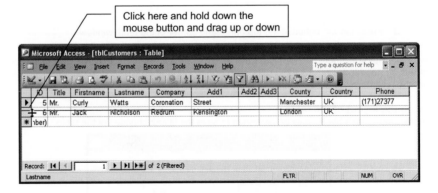

Rearranging columns in a table

We can rearrange the order of columns in our table by dragging using the mouse.

  ❑ Click the column to move with the left mouse button

This will select the column.

  ❑ Drag the column to its new position and release the mouse button.

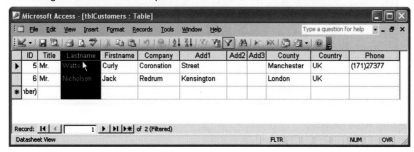

Changing the font used in a table

To change the font used to display records:

  ❑ Go to the **Format** menu and choose **Font**.
  ❑ Select the required font and size from the **Font** dialog box and press **OK**

Closing the table

To close a table:

  ❑ Press the  button in the top right hand corner of the table window.

If we have made changes to the *layout* of the table Access will prompt us to save those changes. There is no need to "save" the table data as information in the database is automatically saved as we enter the records in the table.

Saving the layout of the table

When we close the table we may be prompted to save the layout changes of the table.

If we save our changes the column order, column width, row height and font settings will be the saved and used the next time we open the table.

EXERCISES TO PROVE YOU KNOW

1. Which of the following statements are true?

   a. Tables are made up of fields

   b. Records consist of one or more fields

   c. A database must have at least one table

   d. There can be at most 1000 records in a table

2. Open the database called *Employees.mdb* and open the customers table:

   i. Sort the records, in ascending order, by the employee's last name.

   ii. Filter the records by selection using the surname "Byrne".

   iii. Filter the records by form using the country "USA".

   iv. Close the table and close the database.

3. Adjust the column width of the **Name** field

4. Rearrange the **Lastname** and **Firstname** fields.

5. Add a new record to the employees table for a new employee "John Wayne"

SECTION 5.3:   CREATING TABLES

All the data in a database, is stored in a table or a set a of tables. So to build a database, we have to construct tables and fill those tables with data. Tables are the most important part of a Database, we must ensure that they are designed properly as all other database objects, such as forms and queries, are built from tables.

Before we create a table we must first think about the information it will contain. Let's suppose we want to create a table to contain *customer information.*

Firstly think about the type of information we need to store about our customers. This will give us an idea for the fields we should be creating in our table. To help us understand this, we need to know what we will be using the information for. This is often called *data analysis* and is a detailed process.

Let's suppose we want to build a table to hold customer details so that we can easily contact them by phone, fax, e-mail or by post.

As a starting point we know we need at least the following information:

Customer ID
Customer Name
Address
Phone
Fax
E-Mail

When we think about how we plan to use this data – our first thoughts might reflect on creating a *mail-merge* document in Word. If you recall when we created a mail-merge we needed to create or open a *data source.* Our table could be one such data source.

To build the table we must sub-divide the items which are to be stored in the table into their *atomic* parts. So the *Customer Name* will be broken in to *Title, First name* and *Last name* fields. This might seem fiddly at first but we'll get used to it.

This makes the data much more useful and flexible. In the case of a letter being written to our customer we could start our letters:

Dear Fred,

Dear Mr. Flinstone,

or even

Dear Mr. Fred Flinstone.

By sub-dividing our Customer name into three separate fields, we gain this flexibility. We'll also do this with the address fields and other fields where appropriate.

In this section we will learn:

- ❑   How to create a table and modify a table's layout
- ❑   How to define fields
- ❑   How to specify field types
- ❑   How to create and define an index and a primary key
- ❑   How to set field properties
- ❑   How to create masks and validation rules

LESSON 5.3.1: DESIGNING AND SAVING A TABLE

In this lesson we will design and save a new table. Our table will be made up of the following fields:

Field Name	Purpose
Customer ID	To hold a reference number for our customer
Title	To hold the customers title (Mr./Ms. Etc.)
Firstname	To hold their first name
Lastname	To hold the last name
Add1	To hold address information
Add2	
Add3	
County	
Telephone	To hold their phone number
E-Mail	To hold their e-mail address

❑ To create the table click on the **Tables** tab in the database window choose and press the
❏ **New** button.

When the following dialog appears choose **Design View** and click **OK**

We are now in the tables *design view*.

To add fields to this table, type in the list of field names into the left hand window as follows:

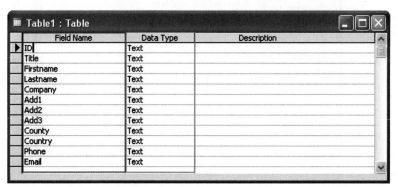

Field names   **Field types**

❑   To save the table, go to the **File | Save**

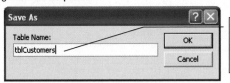

Prefix all table names
with **tbl**, so that they are
easily recognisable as
tables

❑   Save this table as **tblCustomers**.

Prefixing table names with **tbl** makes them easier to identify later on. When we save a table, the
following dialog box may appear:

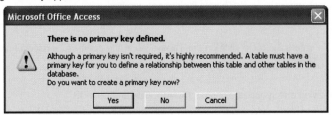

Primary keys are explained in *Lesson 5.3.5:Indexes and primary keys* on *page 368*, so for the moment
we will click on the **No** button to continue.

LESSON 5.3.2:   DELETING A TABLE

We don't often delete our tables – all of the data in the table as well as the structure of the table is lost
if we do so – but occasionally when building a database we create temporary tables we no longer
need. To delete a table :

❑   Select it from the database window and press **Delete**.

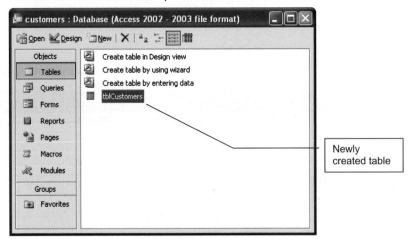

Newly
created table

Access will ask us to confirm that we wish to delete the table

❑   To confirm the deletion press **Yes**.

LESSON 5.3.4: CHOOSING FIELD TYPES

Now that we know the fields we need – we need to consider the type of information that is going into each field so that we can choose the field types.

We can choose the field types from the drop-down list box next to the field name in table design view.

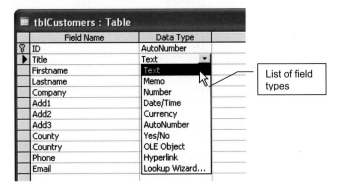

We have a number of different fields types to choose from. Here is a full list – but we'll usually work with **TEXT, NUMBER, DATE** and **AUTONUMBER** fields.

Field Type	Used for
Text	Text and numeric information. A text field can contain up to 255 characters. Examples include names, addresses and phone numbers.
Memo	Lengthy text and numbers. A memo field can store thousands of characters. For example, comments about a hotel, in a travel company's database, letters etc.
Number	Numerical data on which we intend to perform mathematical calculations, except calculations involving money. Example, number of items in stock.
Date/Time	Dates and times. A variety of display formats are available, or we can create our own. Example, date of joining.
Currency	Money. Don't use the Number data type for currency values because numbers to the right of the decimal may be rounded during calculations. The currency data type maintains a fixed number of digits to the right of the decimal. Example, membership fee.
Autonumber	Sequential numbers automatically inserted by Access. Numbering begins with one. Example, customer ID.
Yes/No	Yes/No, True/False, On/Off. Example, smoker/non-smoker.
OLE Object	Used to hold binary data/inserted objects – examples include photographs, graphs, Word documents.
Hyperlink	Used to hold links to web pages or other documents

Modify the field types of our table so that they look as follows:

Field Name	Data Type
🔑 ID	AutoNumber
Title	Text
Firstname	Text
Lastname	Text
Company	Text
Add1	Text
Add2	Text
Add3	Text
County	Text
Country	Text
Phone	Text
▶ Email	Text

The *AutoNumber* field will automatically assign a unique ID to each customer

LESSON 5.3.5:   INDEXES AND PRIMARY KEYS

We create an index on a field in a table in order to help Access search, sort and organise the information in that table. This means that where a table has a field indexed it should find the information in the table much faster than it might otherwise be able to do.

We use indexes in the real world all the time. Consider a regular telephone directory. This is *indexed* by the *Lastname* and *Firstname* fields. Essentially from our point of view it is sorted in order. If we need to find someone in the directory we need only know their last name and first name to be able to quickly find them.

But what about finding someone based on their phone number? This would involve searching through at least half the entries in the phone book most of the time. Quite a task. Thankfully we don't need to lookup phone numbers in this way – the Police however probably have phone books indexed by region and phone number as well as by last name and first name to make this job possible.

In theory adding an index to every field should make Access's job easier – but it doesn't usually work that way. Only fields which are going to be searched or sorted regularly should have an index. Otherwise our database may become too large and slow down considerably.

To add an index to a table open the table in design view:

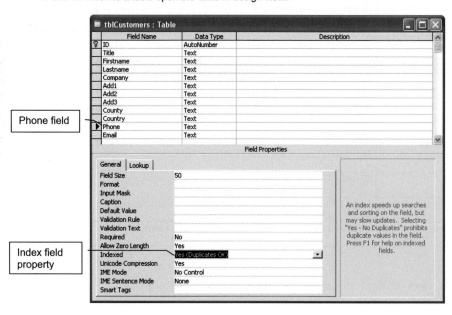

Choose the field to index (in this case we are indexing the *phone* field in the **tblCustomers** table).

In field properties,

❑ Choose the index property

❑ Choose **Yes (Duplicates OK)** – to create an index on the field with non-unique entries.

or

❑ Choose **Yes (No Duplicates)** - to create an index that prohibits duplicates in the field.

Specifying *No Duplicates* is useful if we are sure there should never be a duplicate item in the field as it acts as a safety check. Primary keys – which we meet next - are *always unique*.

We must save the table to apply the index.

❑ Click **SAVE** and call the table **tblCustomers**.

We have now added an index to the phone field.

Primary Keys

The primary key is a field or combination of fields that uniquely identifies each record in a table. The primary key is the main index for the table and it is used to associate data between tables. Though not required, a primary key is highly recommended for every table we create.

A primary key speeds up data retrieval and helps us define default relationships between tables. In the case of our customer table the **Customer ID** uniquely identifies each customer – this is an ideal *Primary Key*.

Setting or changing the primary key

To set or change the primary key:

❑ In the table's *Design view*, select the field or fields to define as the primary key.

To select one field, click the row selector ▶. To select multiple fields, hold down the **Ctrl** key, and click the row selectors for each field.

❑ Click the **Primary key** button on the tool bar, or go to **Edit | Primary Key**.

Access places the primary key icon in the row selector column.

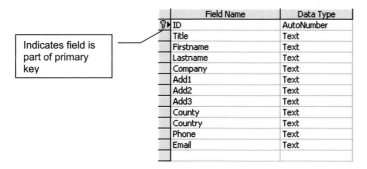

❑ **Save** the table to commit the changes and create the primary key.

LESSON 5.3.6:   COMMON FIELD PROPERTIES

Each field has a set of properties that can be used to modify it's behaviour. For instance we might wish to restrict the number of characters in a field or specify that a field is compulsory. In the case of our customer table for example – we might consider the customer's name a *required* field since we must have this information for the data to be of any use.

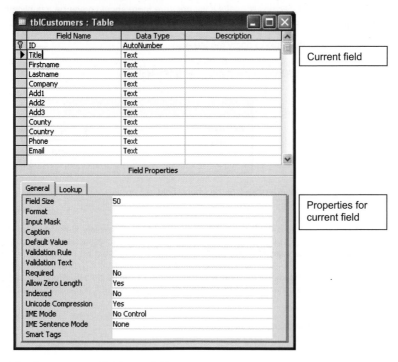

Current field

Properties for current field

Let's have a look at the common properties for our fields:

The **Field Size** property allows us to place a maximum on the number of characters we can enter into a text field. By limiting the number of characters we reduce the wasted space in the database and make it faster.

The **Caption** property allows us to specify a detailed name for a field, which makes it more user friendly. This caption will be used as a label in forms and reports. If we do not enter a caption, the field name will be used as the fields caption.

The **Default Value** property allows us to set a default for new records inserted into the table. We might set the default to be today's date, a number or the most common value to be entered into a field.

The **Validation Rule and Validation Text** allow us to specify a simple validation for the data going into a field (for example, we may have three department types, Sales, Admin and Ops – the validation rule would only allow one of those options).

The **Required** field if set to YES forces the field to have an entry in it or it will not accept changes or additions to a record.

Note: Changing the *Field Size* property after the table has been created can have serious side-effects. If we *shorten* the number of characters in a field we may save space but we will permanently lose any information held in the field which was longer than the new field size. Data in the field will be *truncated* (shortened) to the new field size.

LESSON 5.3.7: CHANGING DISPLAY FORMATS

The *Format property* allows us to display the data in a field in the format that is specified regardless of the way in which the field's data was originally entered. For example we can view a date as a day of the week or as a month by changing the display format. Changing the display format doesn't change the data stored in the field just the way it is presented.

Access gives us different display format options depending on a field's *type*. We can change to any of the built in formats by clicking on the format drop down arrow.

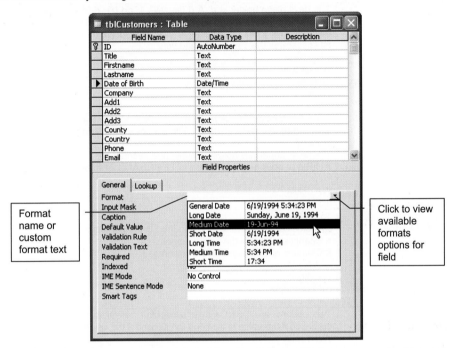

For example a display format can be created which will show all telephone numbers using a particular format e.g. (0777) 565656 or 0777-565656.

Let's have a look at some options for customising display formats:

Numeric Format	The # indicates the place for a digit but if the place is not used then leading and trailing zeros are not shown. The **0** indicates a place for a digit and if the place is not used a 0 is shown. The comma may be used as a thousands separator.
Examples	Will display :-
##,###.00	56.98 6.90 5,890.07 100.00
#0.000	0.020
Date Format	The days place holder is **d**. A **d** displays 1, **dd** 01, **ddd** Mon, **dddd** Monday. The months placeholder is **m.** An m displays 1, **mm** 01, **mmm** Jan, **mmmm** January. The years placeholder is **y**. A **yy** displays 01 and **yyyy** 2001. The **/** or **-** separates the day, month and year.
Examples	Will display :-
dddd d mmmm yyyy	Tuesday 26 April 2004
dd/mm/yy	28/06/04
Time Format	The hours placeholder is **h**. An **h** displays 3, **hh** 03. The minutes placeholder is **m.** An m displays 6, **mm** 06. The seconds placeholder is **s**. An **s** displays 7, **ss** 07. The colon separates hours, minutes and seconds. **AM/PM** or **am/pm** displays time in 12 instead of 24 hour format
Examples	Will display :-
h:mm AM/PM	6:34 PM
hh:mm:ss	15:07:46
Text Format	@ indicates that a character is required in the particular position.
	> Changes all text in the field to uppercase. < Changes all text in the field to lowercase.
Example	Will display :-
(@@@@)@@@@ @@	(0777)565656
Yes/No Format	Two options are typed with a semicolon before each. The first option is displayed if the value is true and the second if the value is false.
Example	Will display :-
"Female";"Male"	"Female" for **true** and "Male" for **false.**

LESSON 5.3.8:   CREATING INPUT MASKS

The *Input Mask* property allows us to simplify data entry. The input mask is a particular format or pattern in which the data must be entered. An input mask is only suitable where all the data for that particular field has the same pattern.

Here are some example candidates for input masks showing the input mask required to allow the sample values to be input and restrict invalid entries.

Input Mask	Sample Values
\ABM-000-0000->L	ABM-372-4950-C
0000-000000	0777-567890
>L<???????????	Jackson

An input mask is created using the following special mask symbols:

Character	Indicates
0	a digit **must** be entered.
9	a digit **may** be entered
#	a digit, + or - sign or space **may** be entered
L	a letter **must** be entered
?	a letter **may** be entered
A	a letter or digit **must** be entered
a	a letter or digit **may** be entered
&	any character or space **must** be entered
C	any character or space **may** be entered
.,:;-/	decimal point, thousands, date and time separators
<	characters to the right are converted to lower case
>	characters to the right are converted to upper case
\	character following is not to be interpreted as a mask character. It is inserted automatically without keying.

Revisit the properties of the **Lastname** field and set the mask to:

Input Mask	Sample Values
>L<???????????	Jackson

LESSON 5.3.9: CREATING A VALIDATION RULE

The **Validation Rule** and **Validation Text** properties allow us to specify a simple validation rule for the data going into a field.

The validation rule is checked before data is entered into a field. If the rule is broken – the validation text is displayed and the data is not entered into the field. If the new data satisfies the validation rule the field will be updated.

Here are some sample validation rules and validation text messages:

Field type	Sample validation rule	Sample validation text
Number	>0	Number of items ordered must be larger than 0
Date	<1/1/2000	Your date of birth must be before 1st January 2000
Text	"Sales" or "Admin" or "Ops"	Type either Sales, Admin or Ops
Currency	> 1000 and <1000000	Your salary range must be between 1,000 and 1,000,000

We enter the validation rule and validation text into the properties of the field we wish to validate. Below we are changing the settings for the **Dept** field.

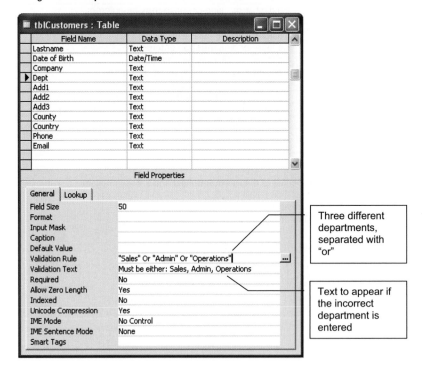

When we update or add a record to this table Access will apply the validation rule. If the validation rule is broken the validation text will be displayed and we won't be allowed enter that value into the field.

Validation rules can be a useful way of ensuring the correct data is entered into fields in our database.

www.iactonline.com

EXERCISES TO PROVE YOU KNOW

1. Create a new database called *Staff.mdb*

   a) Add a table called *tblEmployee* to the database with the following fields and field types:

Field name	Field Type
EmployeeID	Number
Fname	Text
Lname	Text
Phone	Text
Ext	Text
Country	Text

   b) Enter in the following records into the table:

Employeeid	Fname	Lname	Phone	Ext	Country
5	Dan	Jones	78542111	125	UK
6	Julie	Duggan	65498777	156	USA
7	Greg	Downs	96385236	895	USA

   c) Delete the record with EmployeeID 6 from the table.

   D) Use the office assistant to help you find out more information about tables.

2. Create a new database called *bankstaff.mdb*

   a) Create a table, in this database, with the following fields

   Field name
   EmpID
   Firstname
   Lastname
   DOB
   Startdate
   Dept
   Salary
   Parking
   Photo
   CV
   Car_reg
   Swipe_no
   Contract_type
   Starttime

   b) Make the **EmpId** field the primary key.

   c) Use appropriate data types for each one of the above fields.

   d) Save the table as **tbl_Employees**.

   e) Enter in three records into this database.

   f) Close the table.

5
Databases

3. Create a new database called **blinddate.mdb**

  a) Create a table with the following field names and data type properties;

Client_ID	Use this as the unique identifier which increments automatically
First_name	Capital first letter then small case
Last_name	Capital first letter then small case
Add1	
Add2	
County	
Phone	
DOB	Medium Date
Gender	
Marital_status	
Height	Use an input mask so that the height is displayed in metres
Hair_colour	
Eye_colour	
Occupation	
Dollar_Salary	$
Euro_Salary	€
Photo	OLE

  b) Add a validation rule to ensure the salary is above $0 but below $1,000,000

  c) Save the table as **tbl_clients**.

SECTION 5.4:   TABLE RELATIONSHIPS

One of the golden rules of database design is that data should exist only in one place. That is to say in order to make a change to the information stored in the database it should only need to be done in one place.   The main tactic employed to achieve this goal is to split data into tables and specify the relationships between them.

In this section we will learn:

- ❏   Why information is split into separate tables
- ❏   How to link tables in Access

LESSON 5.4.1:   SPLITTING TABLES

Consider a typical spreadsheet or table that contains a list of orders placed by customers. It might look something like this:

CustomerID	Name	Phone	OrderID	Date
4	Fred Flinstone	876345	33	1/2/01
15	Barney Rubble	345666	443	1/3/01
33	Wilma Hogsworth	234553	34	2/3/01
23	Jamie Lee	231231	23	2/4/01
21	Pamela Anderson	432321	44	2/4/01
4	Fred Flinstone	876345	233	4/4/92

This system is fine but flawed. The problem rests with the repetition of data. Customer **4** (*Fred Flinstone*) appears twice in this list – in fact Fred will appear each time he places an order. Each time *Fred* places an order his **phone** details are recorded along with the **date** and **orderID.**

What happens when Fred changes his phone number?

Well if we just change the current record and we find later that we have a problem with a previous order – the details we will see will refer to his old phone number. So we've got to change ALL of Fred's phone numbers. If we forget to do so or if the system is unable to find all the occurrences correctly our database is now wrong and we can no longer trust its accuracy.

There really isn't an easy way around this – to stick with the existing system will hurt in the long run as the database gets bigger. We'll have much more work to update it and we won't be able to rely on the data that is in it.

To overcome this problem, we **split the data into separate pieces** – referring to Fred's details in one place only. When Fred needs to update his details they just get changed once.

To do this, we will create two tables:

- ❏   One containing the customer orders
- ❏   The other containing the customer details.

5
Databases

It might look like this:

Orders table holds order information   *Customers table holds customer details*

OrderID	Date	CustomerID
33	1/2/01	4
443	1/3/01	15
34	2/3/01	33
23	2/4/01	23
44	2/4/01	21
233	4/4/92	4

CustomerID	Name	Phone
4	Fred Flinstone	876345
15	Barney Rubble	345666
33	Wilma Hogsworth	234553
23	Jamie Lee	231231
21	Pamela Anderson	432321

Both records in the *orders* table refer to the same *customer* record. A change in the *customer* record will be correctly found by both records in the *orders* table.

This *splitting* of information into different tables is called **normalization** and is a fundamental part of database design. We can always re-combine the data together once separated to return to our original data – so nothing is lost – but we avoid our update and repetition problem.

LESSON 5.4.2:   LINKING TABLES IN ACCESS

Let's set up these tables and define this relationship in Access.

Firstly we must design the two tables.

- ❑   Open a new blank Database and Save it to the **C:** drive as *Purchase_Orders.mdb.*
- ❑   From Database window, click on **Tables** in the objects panel and choose **New**.
- ❑   Select **Design View** and press **OK**

- ❑   Create the *tblCustomers* table with the following fields and field types:

Field name	Field Type and size
CustomerID	Autonumber
Firstname	Text (30 characters)
Lastname	Text (30 characters)
Phone	Text (30 characters)

- ❑   Make the **CustomerID** the primary key.
- ❑   Save the table as **tblCustomers**

Next create the *tblOrders* table with the following fields and data types:

Field name	Field Type and size
OrderID	Autonumber
CustomerID	Number*
Date	Date field

*NOTE: The CustomerID in this table is a NUMBER field and it will be set to a Long Integer format in order to link to the Orders Table

- ❏ Make **OrderID** the primary key.
- ❏ Save this table as **tblOrders**

LESSON 5.4.3: RELATIONSHIP TYPES

There are two main types of relationship between tables:

- ❑ **One-to-one relationship**
  - o In this type of relationship there is just one matching record in each table
  - o To create a one-to-one relationship, the tables must share a primary key field that contains a unique value for each record in the database

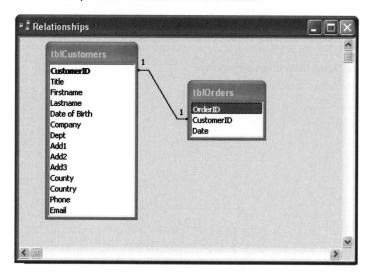

Graphic representation of a one-to-one relationship – there is one record in the tblCustomers table and one matching record in the tblOrders table.

- ❑ **One-to-many relationship**
  - o With this type of relationship a record in one table has one or more matching records in another table
  - o To create a one-to-many relationship, one table will contain a primary key field (unique in that table) and will link to a field in other table that is not the primary key (not unique).

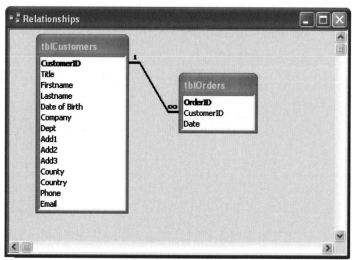

One customer can purchase as many times as they like

The most common type of relationship is a one-to-many relationship.

LESSON 5.4.4:   CREATING TABLE RELATIONSHIPS

Let's define the relationship between the *tblCustomers* table and the *tblOrders* table.

- ❑ To define a one-to-many relationship between these two tables in Access click on the ▣ icon on the toolbar or choose **Relationships** from the **Tools** menu.

- ❑ Access needs to know which tables we wish to add to the relationships window. Choose both tables and click **Add**

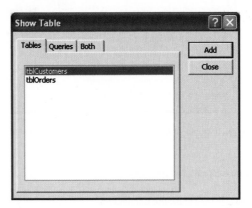

- ❑ Choose **Close** and the following window will appear:

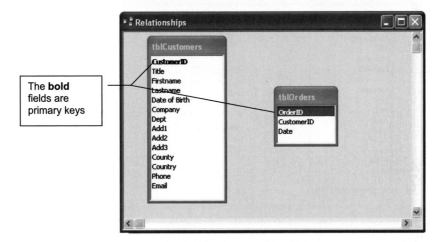

The **bold** fields are primary keys

- ❑ To *link* or relate the two tables click on the **CustomerID** field in the **tblOrders** table then *drag it* and *drop it* on top of the **CustomerID** field in the **tblCustomers** table.

Note: Be careful to link the right fields together – incorrectly linked fields can cause serious problems. Only indexed fields should be related. Primary keys are automatically indexes.

The following dialog appears asking about the relationship between the two fields in the two tables:

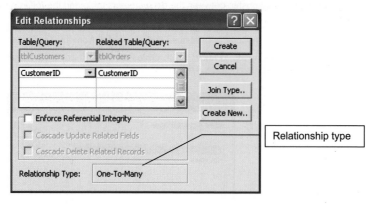

Relationship type

This is a *one-to-many* relationship and this is identified by the relationship type shown in the bottom window.

❑ Click **Create** to create this relationship.

The relationship window will now show the connection.

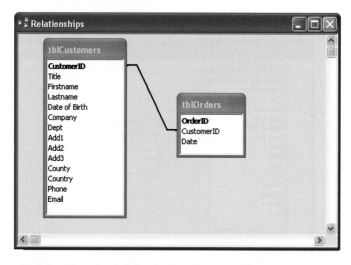

Access will use this information when building Queries, Forms and Reports.

One-to-many and one-to-one relationships

Access determines the type of relationship between the two tables based on the allowable values between the two tables. To create a one-to-one relationship we must ensure that only one field matches a corresponding field in another table. We can do this by linking two uniquely indexed fields.

Subdatasheets

When we have two or more tables in a database related to each other, we will see a sub datasheet in the table datasheet view showing the contents of the linked table. A sub datasheet is a table within a table.

Clicking on the **+** icon on the left hand side, will change it into a − symbol, this is a sub datasheet and we can use it to enter data.

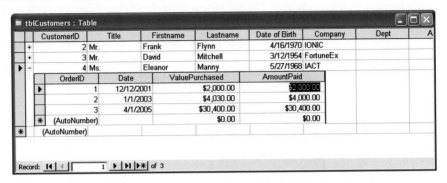

This feature in Access makes it much easier to enter data across two or more tables.

LESSON 5.4.8: ENFORCED REFERENTIAL INTEGRITY In the **Edit Relationships**

Window, there is an option to *Enforce Referential Integrity*. This will apply a system of rules that Access uses to prevent inaccurate values from being entered into fields in related records and prevents the creation of 'orphan' records. We usually 'tick' this option when we create a relationship.

By enforcing referential integrity Access prevents us from entering records where there is no related record in the main table – creating an orphan record. Access also prevents us from deleting parent records where child records still exist. The two options *cascade delete* and *cascade update* help us manage these options.

We can reinforce the referential integrity rules by also setting the *cascade update* and/or *cascade delete* options.

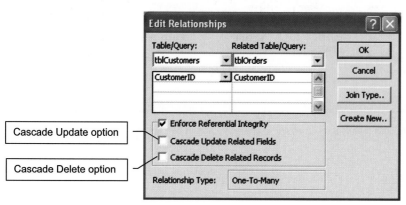

Cascade Update option

Cascade Delete option

Cascade Update changes the contents of the table on the *many* side of the relationship. It reflects any changes in the primary key of the *one* side of the relationship.

For example: If the contact name of a customer changes, the name would be changed in the customer table. This name change would then be reflected in all sales for this customer in the sales table.

Cascade Delete removes records from the table on the *many* side of the relationship whenever a related record on the one side is deleted.

For example: If a customer is deleted from the customers table, any related sales for that customer would also be deleted.

LESSON 5.4.9: DELETING TABLE RELATIONSHIPS To delete a relationship created between two tables we open the relationships window

- ❑ Click on the ⊞ icon on the toolbar or choose **Relationships** from the **Tools** menu.
- ❑ Select the relationship to delete (it will be become a heavier line to indicate it is selected)

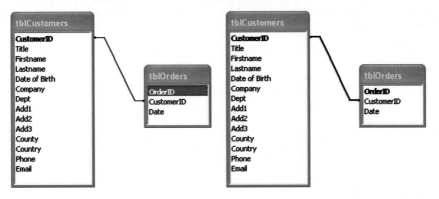

Relationship not selected   *Relationship selected*

- ❑ Press the **Delete** key

The relationship is now deleted.

EXERCISES TO PROVE YOU KNOW

1. Create a database called *library.mdb* that has the following three tables:

   Tbl_Authors, **Tbl_Books** and **Tbl_publishers**.

TblAuthors	TblBooks	tblPublishers
AuthorID	ISBN	PubID
AuName	Title	PubName
AuPhone	PubID	PubPhone
	Price	City
	AuthorID	

   Create the fields as shown ensuring they have the correct field properties, data type, field size, format, etc.

2. Type in three publisher records and three author records as follows:

   Publishers records:

PubID	PubName	PubPhone	City
1	Small House	7894561	Dublin
2	Big House	9876541	Berlin
3	Medium House	3216544	Paris

   Author records:

AuthorID	AuName	AuPhone
1	Blyton	4445555
2	Green	6541233
3	Que	6665455

   Create the following relationships between the tables:

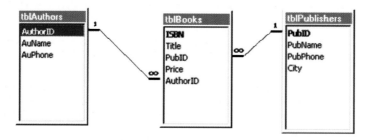

SECTION 5.5: QUERIES

Databases often contain millions of different pieces of data. To get value from that data and in order to make sense of it we need to be able to extract the information that it contains. Queries or filters are the tools we use to extract the answers to questions that we have about the data.

In this section we will learn:

- ❏ How to define a Query
- ❏ How to filter and print a Query
- ❏ How to hide fields with a Query
- ❏ How to Query results
- ❏ To understand Query parameters
- ❏ How to specify Query criteria
- ❏ About different types of Queries

LESSON 5.5.1: WHAT IS A QUERY?

A query is basically a question that we need to ask the database. Basic queries are similar to applying a filter to a table. Queries allow us to:

- ❏ Filter the data and extract information from what remains
- ❏ Remove unnecessary fields from view
- ❏ Summarise data held in tables
- ❏ Update, delete and append information

Access supports a querying technique invented by IBM – called *Query By Example* (or QBE for short). The QBE system is very clever and works on the idea that we provide an *example* of the information we want.

The Queries built in this way are then converted into a language called SQL, which is the universal language of databases. It is much easier usually to use the QBE tools however rather than writing SQL directly.

We often use the *example* technique in the real world. If we were trying to match the paint colour of our walls with the paint colour of a new pot of paint we might bring along a "sample" of the paint and compare it against suitable matches. We are trying to get as good a match as possible.

Similarly Access allows us to specify the type of records we *want:*

"All correct records will have 'John' as the author"
"All correct records will start with an S"
"All correct records are between 1970 and 1995"

or the types of records we *don't want*:

"Don't give me any dates after 2005"
"Don't give me any amounts over $1000"
"Don't give me any records for 'Mary'"

By combining the information we know we want and the information that we know we don't want we give Access a picture of the information to return.

LESSON 5.5.2: BUILDING A QUERY

To build a query we must firstly, switch to the **Queries** tab in the database window.

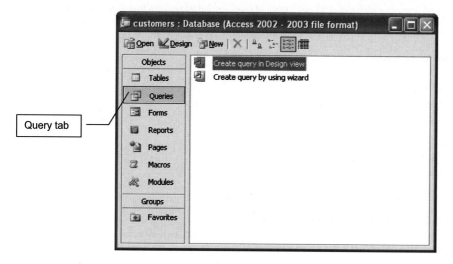

- ❑ Now double-click **Create Query in Design View**

Access needs to know the tables that contain the data we plan to query.

- ❑ Choose the table *tblCustomers* and click **Add**

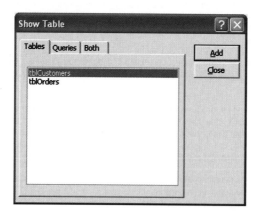

- ❑ Close the *Show Table* window

We should see the query window something like this:

Tables which form part of query

Query options and criteria for query

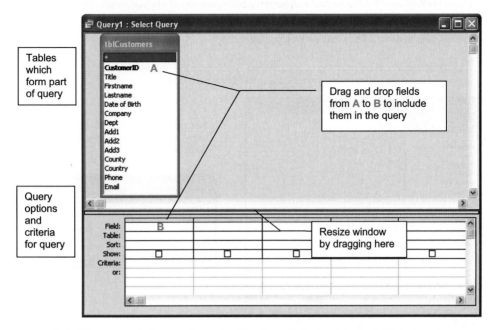

Drag and drop fields from **A** to **B** to include them in the query

Resize window by dragging here

Note: The query window can be resized to allow all the fields in the table to be seen

The top section of this screen shows the tables that will be queried. In our case just the *tblCustomers* table.

The bottom section is the "example" or *criteria* section that allows us to specify the records that we are extracting. It is here that we add the fields that we need to see and provide samples for the records we are looking for.

Adding fields to a query

Suppose we want to view just the contact names and phone numbers of our customers. We need to view the *Firstname, Lastname* and *phone* fields from the table.

To do this we need to add the fields we need to our query.

❑ Drag the *Firstname, Lastname* and *Phone* fields from the tblCustomers table into the criteria section of the query (from **A** to **B** in the diagram below).

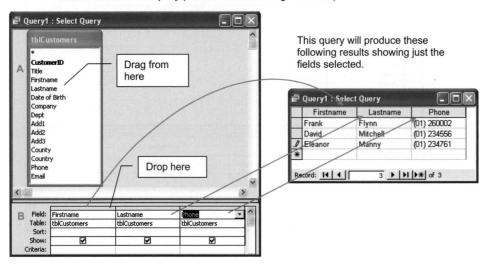

Note: The order in which we drag the field names will affect the order in which they appear in the output window.

Removing a field from a query

We can remove a field from a query.

❑ Move the mouse pointer just above the field name, we will see a black arrow pointing down.

❑ Click to select the field.

❑ Press **Delete** to remove the field from the query.

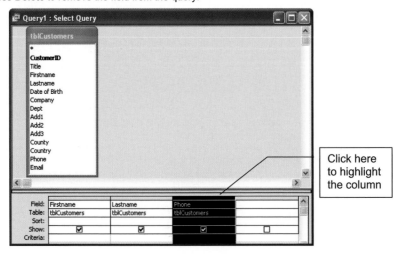

Now the column will disappear from the query window.

Hiding and unhiding query fields

We can also hide the fields in our query by un-ticking the **show** check box under the field name. If the check box is ticked the field will be displayed in the query results – if it is un-ticked it will not be displayed.

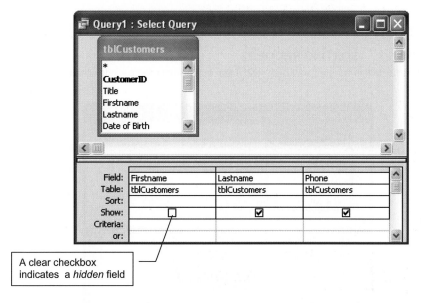

A clear checkbox
indicates a *hidden* field

Hiding a field in this way is useful if we want to use the field as part of the query but we don't want it to display in the query results. By default the check box is ticked to display the field.

Running a query

To view the results of the query we have to run it.

❑ To run it click the ! icon or choose **Run** from the **Query** menu. To return to design view and re-edit the query press the ✎ icon.

Saving a query

So that we can re-use the query at a later time we can save it.

❑ Choose **Save** from the **File** menu or click on the 🖫 icon.

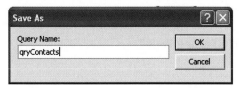

Call the query *qryContacts* so that it can be easily found later and identified as a query.

Every time we Run a query, it refreshes. That is, if new data has been entered into the database, when we run a query, the new data will appear in the answer. This means that queries, once made, can be reused over and over again. To run a query, we can simply double click on it from the database window.

Deleting a query
If we wish to delete a query

- ❑ From the database window select the query.
- ❑ Press **Delete** and confirm that you wish to delete the query.

Access will then delete the query.

LESSON 5.5.3: SORTING RECORDS

We can sort the data in our query by choosing the sort option from criteria window in the design view of the query:

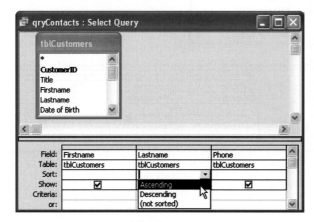

Let's sort these records in *Ascending* order by *lastname*.

- ❑ Run the query by clicking on the icon.

The results should look something like this:

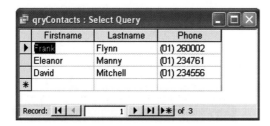

Notice that *Flynn* is now at the top of the list.

LESSON 5.5.4: SPECIFYING CRITERIA AND FILTERING RECORDS

To work with additional queries we are going to open the *Northwind* sample database that comes with Access. This table contains more records and will allow us to perform more complex queries. Its structure is very similar to the table we created earlier although there are some additional fields.

To open Northwind sample database:

- ❑ Go to the **Help** menu and choose **Sample Databases | Northwind Sample Database** or locate the *Northwind* database file and choose **File | Open**

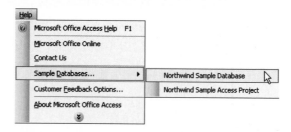

When it opens – close the opening screen and the *Northwind* database looks like this:

It consists of several tables. The *customers* table contains many different records for customers from around the World.

In this example we wish to see just those customers which are based in the UK. For those customers we wish to view:

- ❑ The customer's name
- ❑ The customer ID
- ❑ The contact name in the company and their job title
- ❑ Their phone number

To do this we need to create a *query* which includes just those fields and restricts the list of names to customers in the UK.

❑ Go to the query tab in the objects panel, click on *create query in design view*

❑ Add the *Customers* table to the query window.

❑ Add the following fieldnames - *CustomerID, CompanyName, ContactName, ContactTitle* and *Phone* fields

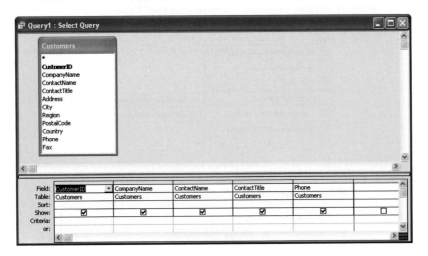

The query window should look something like that above.

When we run this query by clicking 🍷 the results show a table with 91 records (your version of Access may show more or less depending on the version of Access you have).

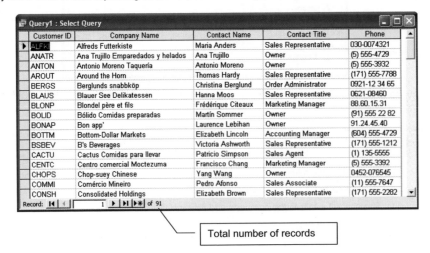

Total number of records

Filtering Data with a Query

Our Query is displaying records from many different countries.

To tell Access that we only want to see customers from the "**UK**" we need to add a filter to the data giving it an *example* of the data we want.

❑ Add the field called **Country** to the query window.

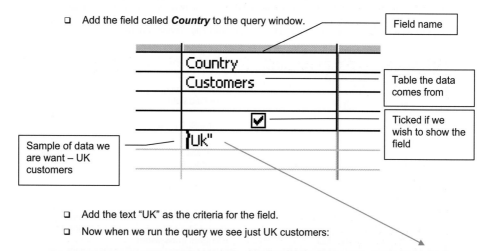

Field name

Table the data comes from

Ticked if we wish to show the field

Sample of data we are want – UK customers

❑ Add the text "UK" as the criteria for the field.

❑ Now when we run the query we see just UK customers:

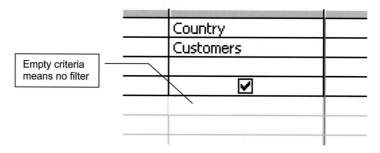

	Customer ID	Company Name	Contact Name	Contact Title	Phone	Country
▶	AROUT	Around the Horn	Thomas Hardy	Sales Representative	(171) 555-7788	UK
	BSBEV	B's Beverages	Victoria Ashworth	Sales Representative	(171) 555-1212	UK
	CONSH	Consolidated Holdings	Elizabeth Brown	Sales Representative	(171) 555-2282	UK
	EASTC	Eastern Connection	Ann Devon	Sales Agent	(171) 555-0297	UK
	ISLAT	Island Trading	Helen Bennett	Marketing Manager	(198) 555-8888	UK
	NORTS	North/South	Simon Crowther	Sales Associate	(171) 555-7733	UK
	SEVES	Seven Seas Imports	Hari Kumar	Sales Manager	(171) 555-1717	UK

Record: ◀◀ ◀ 1 ▶ ▶◀ ▶＊ of 7

In this case that is just 7 records.

Hiding fields

To hide the field but still use it to filter data untick the ☑ box. It will be used to help filter the data but will no longer appear when the query is run.

Removing the Query criteria

To view all the records again we need to clear the criteria from all occurrences of the field or delete the field from the query window. Ensure that all of the criteria rows are clear.

Empty criteria means no filter

LESSON 5.5.5:   DIFFERENT QUERY CRITERIA

Sometimes we won't be able to provide an *exact* match for the data we are looking for – but we will be able to provide a *pattern* against which we want to match our records.

For example we might want records that fit between a range of dates, or want to know about records that occurred "around" a particular time. In these cases we specify a range of values to match against.

Access gives us a set of operators to use to help match records. These are the most common:

Operator	Example in criteria	Explanation
*	801*	Locate all records which **start with** 801 in the specified field. Example: **801**-2234
*	*123	Locate all records that **end with** 123 in the specified field. Example: 341-2**123**
*	456*123	Locate all records that **start with** 456 and **end with** 123 and have 0 or more characters or numbers in between. *Example: 456*4453458012*123*
?	AB?DE	Match all records which **start with** AB followed by any character or digit and end in DE *Example: AB*C*DE*
>	> 1/4/1970	Locate all records which occur **after** 1st April 1970
<	< 10/2000	Locate all records which occur **before** 1st October 2000
>=	>= 1/4/1970	Locate all records which occur **on or after** 1st April 1970
<=	<= 31/12/2000	Locate all records which occur **on or before** 31st December 2000
Between	Between 31/1/2000 and 30/4/2000	Locate all records that occur between 31/1/2000 and 30/4/2000 (not inclusive)

LESSON 5.5.6: BOOLEAN LOGIC

Boolean logic is named after the famous mathematician *George Boole.* Professor Boole lived in Cork, Ireland where he worked in UCC and greatly contributed to modern mathematical logic. He generated the fundamental rules for combining logical expressions using the operators *AND*, *OR* and *NOT*.

Boole's rules form truth tables which are the basis of all logic programming and are used in all computer systems right down to the smallest microprocessors.

We will use Boole's logic and the keywords **AND**, **OR** and **NOT** to join query criteria together to create more complex queries.

George Boole
1815–1864

Consider the following cars and their descriptions:

> A black Renault 5 bought in 1993 with an engine size of 1,300cc
> A silver BMW Z4 bought in 2003 with an engine size of 3,500 cc
> A black Jaguar XK8 bought in 2005 with an engine size of 4199cc
> A blue Ford Escort bought in 2001 with an engine size of 1900cc

The AND truth table

When combining conditions using the AND operator only where both statements are TRUE will the whole expression be true.

AND	TRUE	FALSE
TRUE	TRUE	FALSE
FALSE	FALSE	FALSE

Suppose we wanted to see cars bought AFTER 2001 with an engine size >2000 cc

We would use AND to describe this type of query

YEAR >= 2001 AND ENGINE >= 2000

This would display the BMW Z4 and Jaguar XK8.

The OR truth table

When combining conditions using the OR operator if either statement is true or both statements are true the whole expression is true.

OR	TRUE	FALSE
TRUE	TRUE	TRUE
FALSE	TRUE	FALSE

YEAR > 2002 OR COLOUR = "BLACK"

This would display the BMW Z4, Jaguar XK8 and the Renault 5.

The NOT truth table

The **NOT** operator reverses the state of any given logical expression. So whatever is TRUE becomes FALSE and vice versa. It is sometimes easier to say what we *don't* want rather than what we do want.

NOT	
TRUE	FALSE
FALSE	TRUE

NOT YEAR >= 2001

This would display the Renault 5.

Specifying additional required matches (AND)

Let's revisit the *Northwind* Database and ask Access some more questions.

❑ Create a new query based on the *Customers* table.

Suppose we wanted a list of *Sales Managers* who lived in the *USA*. Here we have two criteria to meet - that of living in the USA and of being a 'Sales Manager'. The more criteria we must satisfy at any one time the shorter our resulting list will be. When we are specifying a number of criteria that must be matched *at the same time* we are specifying an **AND** condition.

Generally, whenever we specify multiple criteria that must be matched together the list will stay the same length or get shorter.

We can write this into our query window like this:

Field:	CompanyName	ContactName	ContactTitle	Phone	Country
Table:	Customers	Customers	Customers	Customers	Customers
Sort:					
Show:	☑	☑	☑	☑	☑
Criteria:			"Sales manager"		"USA"
or:					

By having multiple criteria on the **same line**, we specify **AND** criteria and both conditions must be met to find a match.

❑ Run the query to view the results.

Specifying alternative matches (OR)

Now suppose we wanted to view records for customers that came from the *UK, France* or *Germany*. Here we have a list of alternatives that we are interested in viewing. This is a candidate for Boole's **OR** operator.

We can write this into our query window like this:

Field:	CompanyName	ContactName	ContactTitle	Phone	Country
Table:	Customers	Customers	Customers	Customers	Customers
Sort:					
Show:	☑	☑	☑	☑	☑
Criteria:					"UK" Or "France" Or "Germany"
or:					

Alternatively we could lay it out on **separate lines** and omit the **OR** keyword:

Field:	CompanyName	ContactName	ContactTitle	Phone	Country
Table:	Customers	Customers	Customers	Customers	Customers
Sort:					
Show:	☑	☑	☑	☑	☑
Criteria:					"UK"
or:					"France"
					"Germany"

Both queries will give the same results.

❑ Run this query to view the results.

Specifying what we don't want (NOT)

Sometimes its easier to say what we don't want instead of what we do want. For example if we want all customers outside the USA its easier to say "Give me all countries except the USA". This is done using the **NOT** operator (sometimes written **<>**).

We can write this into our query window like this:

Field:	CompanyName	ContactName	ContactTitle	Phone	Country
Table:	Customers	Customers	Customers	Customers	Customers
Sort:					
Show:	☑	☑	☑	☑	☑
Criteria:					Not "usa"

❑ Run this query to view the results.

By combining Boole's logical operators **AND OR** and **NOT** in our queries we can extract any information contained in our database.

LESSON 5.5.7: PARAMETER QUERIES

Sometimes it is useful to prompt the user for a parameter value when a query runs. In this way we don't have to manually alter the criteria in the query.

To add parameters to a query, we insert the criteria in square brackets [ ] with an appropriate prompt inside the brackets. When the query is run, the user will be asked for a value for the parameter.

Let's see how it works.

❑ Open a new query based on the *Customers* table.

❑ Add the *Country* field to the query and save the query as *qryCustomer*

Suppose we want to let the user decide which country's customers they wish to view when they run our *qryCustomer* query. We can do this by specifying a query parameter. In the country criteria box type:

[Enter country to view]

Note we must include the square brackets around the parameter name.

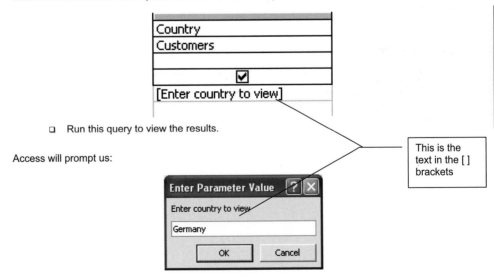

This is the text in the [ ] brackets

❑ Run this query to view the results.

Access will prompt us:

Depending on the value that we enter, the query will filter the appropriate country.

We can add multiple criteria to different fields simply by adding additional parameters in [] brackets.

Other types of query

There are several different types of query known as *action queries* supported by Access. These types of queries usually perform updates or deletions on large sets of data. The most common form of action queries are:

- ❑ Deletion queries
- ❑ Update Queries
- ❑ Append Queries
- ❑ Make Table Queries

To learn more about these types of query look at Access's **Help** tool.

EXERCISES TO PROVE YOU KNOW

This exercise is based on the *Clients* table in the *BlindDate* Database.

Make sure you include the *firstname* fields and the *lastname* fields for each question.

1. Create a query that finds all the males in the table. Save it as *qry1*.

2. Using a *parameter query*, create a query that will ask you to enter the sex type of the client that you are searching for. Save it as *qry2*.

3. Find all the clients that live in Dublin 2. Save it as *qry3*.

4. Find all the Females that live in Dublin 6. Save as *qry4*.

5. Find all clients that live in any part of Dublin. Save it as *qry5*.

6. Find all the men that have blue eyes and brown hair. Save it as q*ry6*.

7. Find all the females that are employed. Save as *qry7*.

8. Find all men that are divorced. Save as *qry8*.

9. Using a *parameter query*, create a query that will ask you to enter the marital status and eye colour of the client. Save it as *qry9*.

10. Find all of those that where born in the 60's. Save it as *qry10*.

11. Find all of the females from Dublin born in the 70's with blue eyes. Save it as q*ry11*.

12. Find all those born between 1965 and 1975. Save it as *qry12*.

13. Find all females that enjoy playing tennis as a hobby. Save it as *qry13*.

SECTION 5.6: FORMS

Databases usually consist of lots of related tables. Entering data correctly into each of these tables by hand would be very difficult, error prone and time consuming.

To make data entry and retrieval easier, and to allow us to use other tools available from Access, we usually build **Forms**. Forms help prevent inconsistencies in the database and errors with data entry.

In this section we will learn:

- ❑ What a form is and how to enter, edit and delete data using a form
- ❑ How to create a form using a form wizard
- ❑ How to modify the forms layout
- ❑ How to use the wizards to automate common tasks on a form

LESSON 5.6.1: INTRODUCTION TO FORMS

Forms provide the *front end* or interface to our database. Data entered or updated on a form directly updates the contents of our tables.

Below is a form showing customer information from the **tblCustomers** table in the *Sales* database. Notice that the layout of the form makes it easier to see the important information quickly and we have added buttons to run common tasks such as *mail-merge* and *printing*.

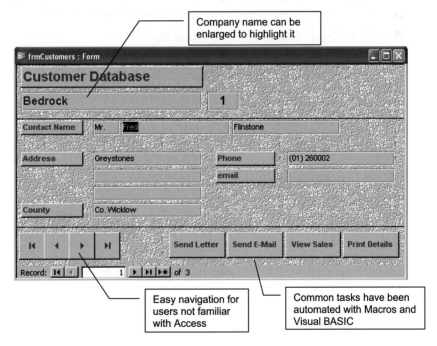

LESSON 5.6.2: BUILDING A FORM

Building a form with the wizard is pretty straightforward and we can customize the form's layout when the wizard has finished.

❑ Firstly switch to the *Form* tab in the database window:

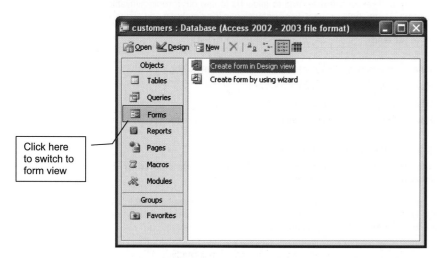

Click here to switch to form view

❑ Next double-click **Create form by using Wizard**

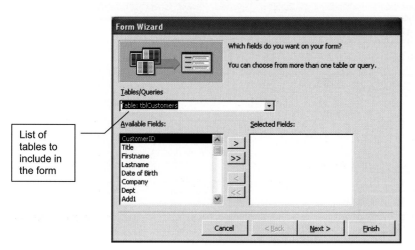

List of tables to include in the form

❑ Choose the table *tblCustomers* from the drop down list as we intend the form to be based on this table.

❑ Click on the right pointing >> arrow to move all the fields to the right hand window.

❑ Now press **Next**

❑ Now we are asked for the layout of our form window. We can experiment with these options later – for the moment we will pick the default *Columnar* option.

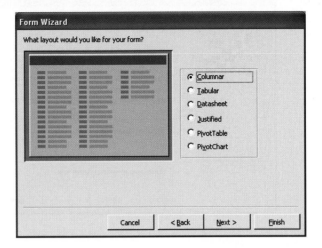

❑ Press the **Next** button

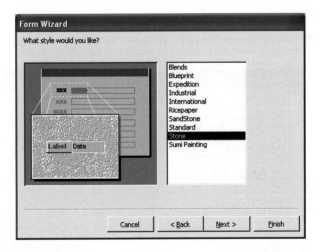

❑ Pick a style for the form – this will affect the background image and colour of our form but not how it behaves.

❏ Next we'll be asked for a name for our form – type ***frmCustomers*** and press **Finish**

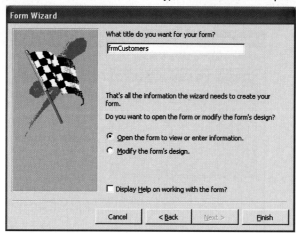

NOTE: The default name is the same name as the table name – to avoid confusion make sure the prefix TBL is replaced with FRM

The form will now be created and saved by the wizard

LESSON 5.6.3:   ENTERING DATA INTO A FORM

When we open a form we can use it to view, update and delete information stored in the database. If we open the form we just created the default view should look something like this:

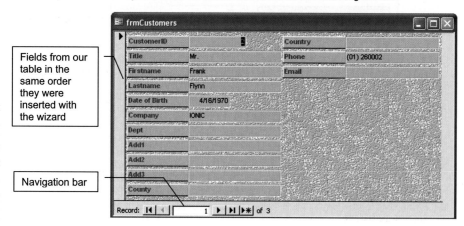

Fields from our table in the same order they were inserted with the wizard

Navigation bar

Navigating through records

We use the *navigation toolbar* at the bottom of the form to move between records and add new records

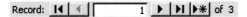

This is the same toolbar we see on tables and in queries.

I◄	Move to *first* record in table
◄	Move to *previous* record in table
►	Move to *next* record in table
►I	Move to *last* record in table

Moving to a specific record on a table or form

To move to a specific record number we can type into the navigation bar the record we want to go to:

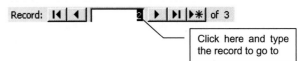

Click here and type the record to go to

❑ Type the record number to go to and press **Enter**

Modifying and updating records

We can modify or update a record using the form.

❑ Navigate to the record to update using the navigation toolbar

❑ Click into a field to change and type – exactly as we would if updating data in a table directly.

The form will update the record in the table once we leave the current record by either closing the form or moving to another record.

Adding records using the form

We can **Add** a new record to a table using our form by using the navigation buttons at the bottom of the form window.

❑ To add a new record using the form press the **►*** button

or

❑ Choose **Edit | Goto | New Record** or press **Ctrl + +**

A new blank record will be displayed in the form.

❑ Enter data directly into the fields by typing.

❑ Use the **Tab** key to move between the fields.

5
Databases

Deleting a record using a form
To delete a record using the form

- ❑ Navigate to the record to delete using the navigation toolbar
- ❑ Choose **Delete Record** from the **Edit** menu

Access will prompt with the message

- ❑ Click on the **Yes** option to permanently delete the record.

Practice entering data into the form and navigating through the records using the navigation bar.

Finding a record
We often need to move to a specific record in a table or a form. In order to find a particular record we need to use the **Find** tool.

- ❑ From the **Edit** menu choose **Find** or press **Ctrl+F**

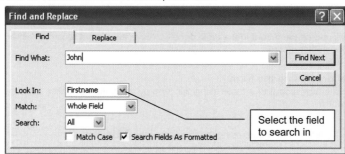

- ❑ Type the text or number to search for into the **Find What** field
- ❑ Choose the field to search through from the **Look In** list box (choose **Form** to search all fields in the form)
- ❑ Click **Find Next**

If a record matching the search is found the form will display the record. If it is not found Access will display a failure message:

NOTE: Try to help Access find the record for you as quickly as possible by choosing the field to search in and matching against an entire field. Searching through all the fields in each record and looking for partial matches makes the search much slower.

LESSON 5.6.4: OPENING, CLOSING AND DELETING A FORM

Opening the form
To open an existing form in the database

- ❑ Select the form from the database window

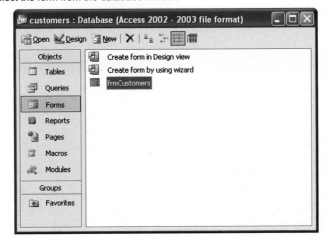

- ❑ Double-click on the form or select it and choose **Open**

The form will open in view mode and display the contents of the table on which it was built.

Closing a form

- ❑ Close the form by pressing the ☒ button in the form window.

Deleting a form
To delete the form

- ❑ Select the form from the database window and press **Delete**

Access will prompt for confirmation

- ❑ Click **Yes** to delete the form.

LESSON 5.6.5: MODIFYING A FORM'S LAYOUT

A form created by the wizard can be modified to include extra features and to change the general layout of the form.

- ❑ To edit the form select it from the database window and press the 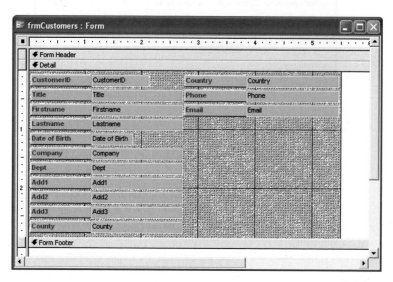 Design button.

The form will go into *Design view* mode. When a form is in design mode we can make changes to it. A form in design mode shows the names of the fields in text boxes – not the *values* contained in the fields.

- ❑ Maximise the window to see the edges of the form.

The Access toolbox can be turned on or off, by going to the **View** menu and clicking on **Toolbox**.

The Toolbox contains controls to allow us to customize the form.

We can add images, tabs, combo-boxes and other controls to a form.

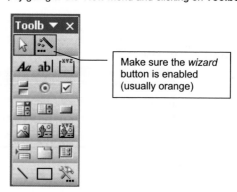

Make sure the *wizard* button is enabled (usually orange)

Moving fields on the form

We can move fields to improve their layout simply by clicking and dragging the field to a new location.

- ❑ Choose the  tool from the toolbox and select the textbox to move.
- ❑ Now drag the textbox to its new location.

Once the form is saved, the textbox will always appear in this location.

Inserting text onto the form header or footer

Let's insert text into the forms header giving the form a title.

The top of the form shows a grey bar titled "form header" and the bottom of the form shows the "form footer":

Drag to expand

- ❑ Expand the gap between the form header or footer and the detail section by stretching the space with the mouse. It should look something like this when finished:

This gives us space to insert some text. The text in the form header will always be visible. We can insert text onto the form by using the label tool shown by the Aa icon in the toolbox. Select the tool and the mouse will change to a *cross hair*.

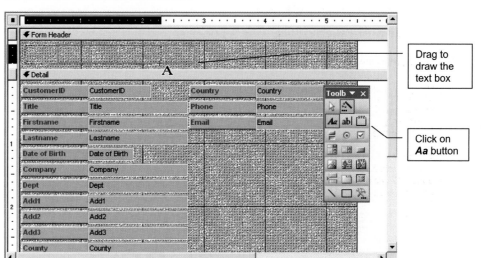

Drag to draw the text box

Click on
Aa button

- ❑ Click and drag with the mouse to draw a rectangular box like that below:

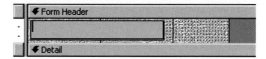

A cursor should appear in the box into which we can type text.

❑ Type "Customer Details":

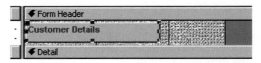

If we select the text box (not the text itself) we can change the font style and colour using the formatting toolbar at the top of the page.

❑ Adjust the font size to 12 pt and change the colour to navy blue.

The standard font formatting toolbar appears when we select the label control.

The field descriptions are also labels and their formatting, appearance and text can be changed in the same way.

Other labels automatically inserted

Inserting a graphic

We can insert a graphic on to the form using the image control .

❑ Select the image tool with the mouse
❑ Now click and drag with the mouse to draw a box.

We will be asked then to choose a graphic to insert.

❑ Locate the file to insert and press **OK**

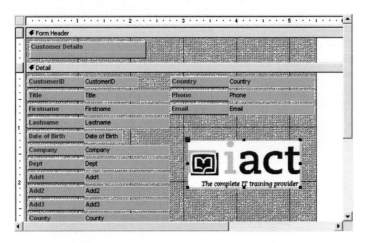

We might use the image control to place a company logo or a photograph onto the form.

Changing a form's background colour

We can change the form's background colour in the *Design View*. To change the background colour:

❑ Right click on the detail section of the form while in design view and choose Properties.

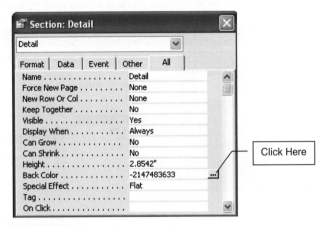

Click on the **Back Color** attribute and choose the expand button. This will bring up a colour window and from here we can choose the colour scheme that we want.

LESSON 5.6.6:   AUTOMATING COMMON TASKS

Access provides a wizard to help us automate common tasks such as navigating through records, printing, deleting and so on. We can place buttons into the form and choose the action that we wish the button to perform. Access assigns "macros" to the buttons to make them perform these tasks.

Let's add navigation buttons to the bottom of our form to make navigation easier. These buttons will look like:

They will allow us to go to the *First, Previous, Next* and *Last* records in the database by clicking on them.

❑ Select the command button ⬛ from the toolbox

❑ Click and drag in the form footer to draw a small box

The command button wizard will appear.

The wizard provides a whole host of powerful and regularly used features that can be assigned to this button.

- ❑ Select the *Record Navigation* category
- ❑ Choose *Goto First Record* from the list of actions in the right hand window.

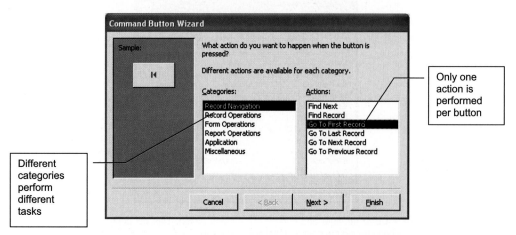

Different categories perform different tasks

Only one action is performed per button

- ❑ Choose **Next** and then pick and appropriate icon to display on the button:

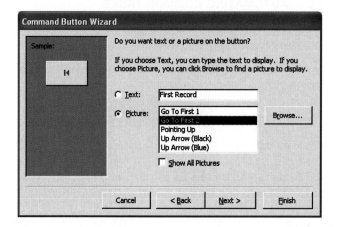

- ❑ Click **Next**

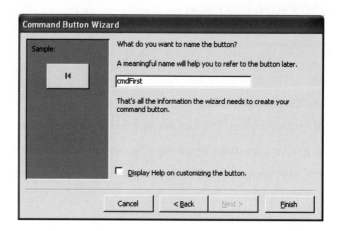

❑ Name the button **cmdFirst** and click *Finish*

Repeat these steps for the next 3 buttons (choosing *previous, next* and *last* as the navigation options and the corresponding button name).

To see the command buttons working, save the form and then close it. Now double-click on the form to re-open it in form view mode. In this mode our newly created command buttons will be operational.

5
Databases

EXERCISES TO PROVE YOU KNOW

1. Open the Library database.

Create the following forms:

  a) A form to view all the publications by author.

  b) A form to view a list of authors

2. Add titles to each of the forms

3. Add navigation buttons to the form and place them in the forms *footer*

4. Add a *Search* button that will allow searching using any of the fields in the table

4. Add a *Print Report* button that prints a report showing the list of publications available

SECTION 5.7: REPORTS

Reports have many uses. A mail-merge is a report just as a sheet of labels with names and addresses is a report – although they look very different and have a different purpose. Many reports are management tools and their purpose is to help us quickly grasp the essential elements and relationships found in raw data so we can make effective decisions.

In this section we will learn:

- ❑ An overview of reports in Access
- ❑ How to build a report using a wizard
- ❑ How to group and sort data on a report
- ❑ To customise the report
- ❑ To print and preview the report on screen

LESSON 5.7.1: OVERVIEW

Rather than opening a database and manually querying data we will often build a report to save time and make accessing the information easier. Reports are usually printed but they can be displayed on-screen, sent by e-mail or accessed via a web-page.

For a report to be effective, it has to show the right data in a logical way. If it presents the wrong data or if it presents the right data in a haphazard manner, the report may slow the decision making process or even encourage incorrect decisions.

A good starting place in the development of a report is to write out the purpose of the report in a sentence or two. This helps us focus on our primary needs, and it gives our report both a starting point and a goal. Here are some examples:

- ❑ The purpose of this report is to show monthly and year-to-date sales by sales representative, compare this year's numbers to last year, and flag representatives whose sales figures do not meet company standards.
- ❑ The purpose of this report is to show sales activity for each item in inventory, and to suggest reorder quantities based on that activity.
- ❑ The purpose of this report is to calculate bowling averages and handicaps for each member of the bowling league.

Clarifying the purpose of the report before you start is a critical step in the overall process. A report without a clear purpose is like a meeting without a clear agenda; it rambles and accomplishes little.

LESSON 5.7.2:   BUILDING A REPORT USING A WIZARD

Building a report with the wizard is similar to building a form with the wizard. Throughout this section we will be using the *Sales* database.

❑ Firstly, using the objects panel, click on *Reports*. Choose *Create a report using the wizard*.

The following dialog appears:

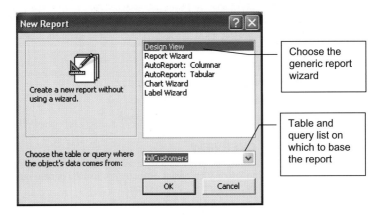

Choose the generic report wizard

Table and query list on which to base the report

Access provides several useful wizards to help us create reports ranging from label sheets to summary charts. We are going to build a report to display a list of our customers from the customers table.

❑ Choose *report wizard* and select *tblCustomers* from the table list.

Note: We can also base our report on a query by choosing a query from the list instead of a table – in this way we can select the data we wish to view by altering the query parameters before the report is run. This is one reason why prefixing query names with *qry* makes them easier to find

❑ Next choose the fields for the report.

In this case we just want a list of companies, their contacts, the county they live in and their phone and e-mail addresses. We want all fields except the individual address fields.

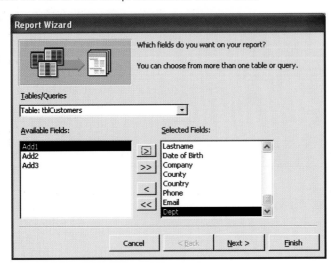

❑ Choose **Next** to advance to the next step.

Grouping report data

The grouping step allows us to group our customers together. The most logical grouping is to group all our customers who live in the same region (or county).

❑ Select **County** field and press the ⊃ button to group by **County**.

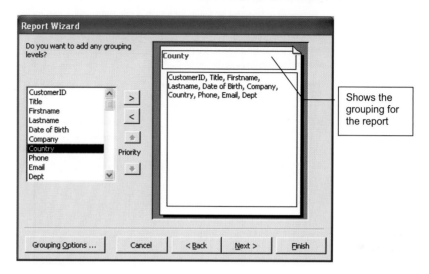

Shows the grouping for the report

❑ Now press **Next**

Sorting the report data

Our next step provides us with a means to *sort* the data on our report and gives us options for *summarising* report totals. Let's sort them alphabetically by **company**.

❑ Choose *Company* from the field drop down list

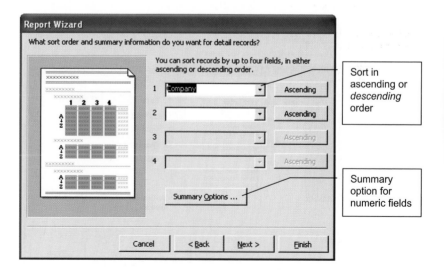

Sort in ascending or *descending* order

Summary option for numeric fields

5
Databases

Report summary totals and sub-totals

The sorting step will also allow us to create sub-totals in our report.

To add summary options:

❏ Press the **Summary Options** button

Access will show the summary options for all fields for which a summary value can be logically defined.

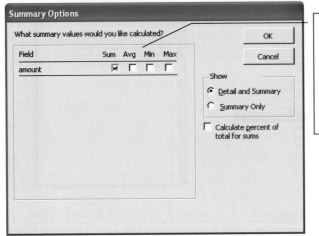

Tick for each summary type required.

We can display totals, averages, min and max values for each summary field.

The summary options allow us to view sub-totals for each group (*detail and summary*) or an overall summary (*summary only*) that will appear once at the end of the report.

❏ Press **OK** to confirm the summary options

❏ Press **Next** to advance to the next step.

Now we need to decide on the style of the report and whether it should be portrait or landscape in design.

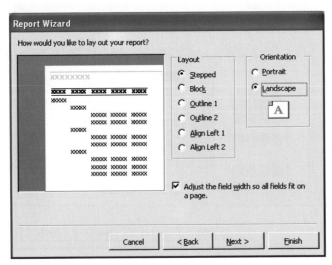

❏ Switch the report to *Landscape* mode to give the report a greater width.

❏ Click **Next**

We must now decide on a style for the reports layout.

    ❑   Choose a style for the report – *"Corporate"*

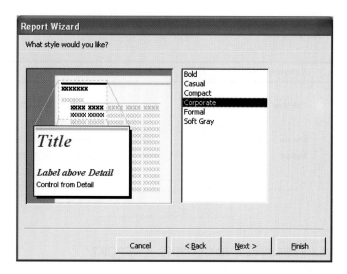

    ❑   Click **Next**.

Give the report a name call it **rptCustomers**. Now click **Finish** to preview the report.

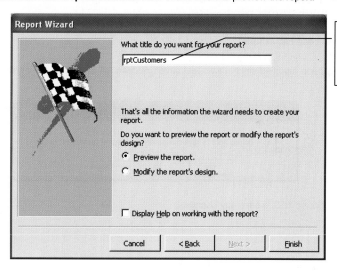

The default title (same name as the table)

The finished report should look something like this:

rptCustomers

County	Company	ID	Title	Firstname	Lastname	Phone	email
Co. Dublin							
	Café More	4	Ms.	Betty	Rubble	(01) 2347611	
Co. Wicklow							
	Bedrock	3	Ms.	Wilma	Flinstone	(01) 234556	
	Bedrock	1	Mr.	Fred	Flinstone	(01) 260002	

Records as grouped by **county**

LESSON 5.7.3: SAVING AND CLOSING A REPORT

After we have modified the layout and appearance of the report we need to save it.

To save a report

❑   Choose **File | Save** or click on the 🖫 icon

After saving we can close the report

❑   Choose **File | Close**

If the file has been modified since it was last saved Access will prompt us to save it again before it is closed.

Microsoft Office Access

⚠️ Do you want to save changes to the design of report 'rptCustomers'?

[Yes]   [No]   [Cancel]

❑   Choose **YES** to save any changes.

LESSON 5.7.4: CUSTOMISING THE REPORT

We can customize the report by opening it in *design* mode. In design mode a report is similar to a form but contains more *sections*.

Changing and adding text to a report header or footer

❑ Open the report in *Design View* by selecting the report and clicking on the  icon.

The report looks different in this mode as we only see the field names and labels not the actual raw data.

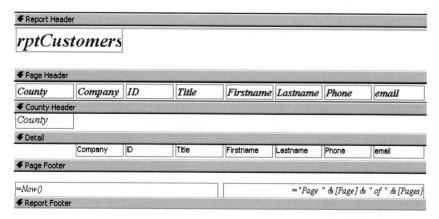

We can edit the title of the report by clicking it with the mouse and typing a new title. Type **"Customer List by County"** as the title.

To add text to a header or footer area we must use the *Label* tool on the toolbox.

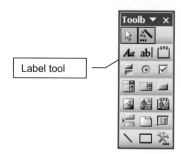

Label tool

❑ Select the label tool and click and drag the mouse in the report footer area.

❑ Release the mouse when the label is the right size and type the text into the label

Notice that this area of the footer is now white and expanded to allow for the label's height and position.

Changing the position of fields and labels

We often need to change the way the wizard positions our fields and labels in a report – to make the report easier to follow.

We can adjust the position of objects on a report by selecting them and moving them with the mouse.

❑ Click on the object and hold down the mouse button.

Handles appear around the object indicating that it is selected.

❑ Move the object to its new position and let go of the mouse button.

We have now moved the object.

LESSON 5.7.5:   DELETING A REPORT

If we wish to delete a report we must do so from the database window.

❑ Select **REPORTS** from the objects panel

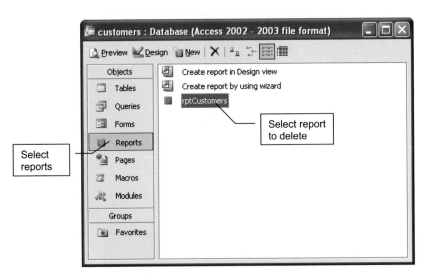

❑ Select the report to delete and press the **Delete** key

Note: Once a report has been deleted it can't be recovered.

EXERCISES TO PROVE YOU KNOW

1. Open the *Blind Date* query exercise database

    Earlier we created 13 different queries in this database.

    Create a report for the following queries:

    a) Qry1 – Save as *Rpt1*
    b) Qry2 – Save as *Rpt2*
    c) Qry10 – Save as *Rpt10*

2. Open the report *Rpt2* just created. In the design view, complete the following:

    a) In the report header, insert the title "Candidates by Gender"
    b) In the report footer, insert the text "This report was created by IACT"
    c) Format the labels so that the text is red and bold and that the background is yellow
    d) Format the control boxes so that the text is red
    e) Save and close the report.

SECTION 5.8:   PRINTING AND PAGE SETUP

We can preview our tables, forms or reports before we print them. In this section we will learn how to:

- ❑ Print and preview tables, queries, forms or reports
- ❑ Modify the page setup and adjust the page orientation
- ❑ Print a range of records from a table or a query

LESSON 5.8.1:   PRINTING AND PREVIEWING

Printing any of the objects in Access works the same way.

To preview a table, query, form or report:

- ❑ Select the table, query, form or report from the database window:
- ❑ Click on the 🔍 icon on the toolbar or choose **File | Print Preview**

This will open the object and display it in *preview* mode.

From here we can adjust the page orientation and paper size.

- ❑ To print the report choose 🖨 icon from the toolbar or choose **File | Print**.

It may be necessary to adjust the orientation of the page in order for the report to fit on the page – we will look at this next.

LESSON 5.8.2:   CHANGING PAGE ORIENTATION AND PAPER SIZE

Whilst previewing our table, query, form or report we can adjust the page orientation and size.

- ❑ To change the orientation of our page choose **File | Page setup**

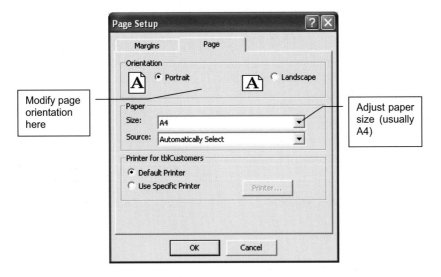

- ❑ Select the *page* tab and choose *Portrait or Landscape* and press **OK**.

This will re-orient the page layout to suit.

To change the paper size – choose the size of the paper from the **Size** drop-down list. In Europe our paper size is usually **A4** (210mm wide x 297mm tall) in America it is usually **Letter** (216mm wide x 278mm tall). Be sure to set the paper size correctly – it is often incorrectly set in Europe because the defaults used during program installation are often the American sizes. If we are printing to larger or other paper sizes we can choose these from the drop-down list.

LESSON 5.8.3: PRINT OPTIONS WITH TABLES AND QUERIES

Access lets us print the contents of a table or a query directly. We can do this when we view the records from a *table* or *query*. We can print a range of selected records, all the records or a range of pages.

To print the selected records:

❑ Open the table or query and select the records to print by dragging with the mouse.

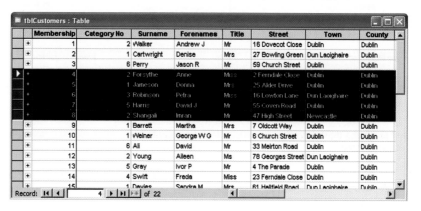

❑ Choose **File | Print**

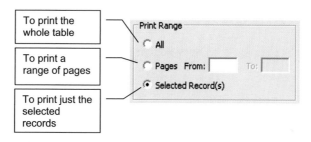

We have a number of options in the *Print Range* section of this window.

To print the whole table or query	Click the **ALL** option
To print a page or a range of pages	Choose **Pages** and enter the start and end page range into the *From* and *To* text boxes.
To print the selected records	Click the **Selected Records** option

When all the options are selected

❑ Press **OK** to print.

LESSON 5.8.4: PRINTING IN FORM LAYOUT MODE

When we view the contents of the database in Form Layout mode we have similar print options. We will often want to print just what we see on screen, or all the data the form can display.

Below we have a form showing 3 records.

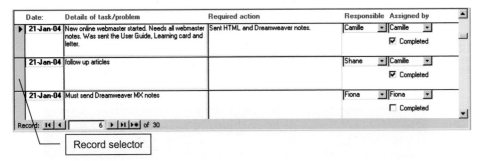

Record selector

To print just these three records – we must select the records using the record selector buttons at the side of each record.

- ❑ Choose **File | Print** menu and follow the steps outlined in the previous lesson for working with queries and tables.

LESSON 5.8.5: PRINTING REPORTS

Printing the contents of reports is similar to printing in other parts of Access.

- ❏ Firstly open or preview the report that we want to print – choose **File | Print Preview**

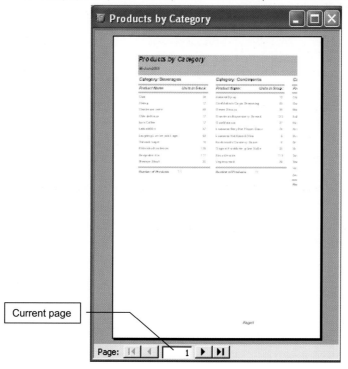

Current page

- ❏ If you are satisfied with the appearance of the report choose **File | Print**

- ❏ Specify **ALL** to print the entire report or choose **Pages** to print a range of pages.

Changing the page margins

The margins of a page determine where on a page a report or form will print. We can add or remove space from this white area of the page from the page setup dialog box.

- ❏ Choose **File | Page setup** and click on the **Margins** tab.

Enter values for the left, right, top and bottom margins.

- ❏ To save the changes the margins press **OK**.

Note: The margins specified in the page setup tab are not included on the visible area of the report when we edit it. This can lead to page overflow even though it doesn't appear like it would on screen.

EXERCISES TO PROVE YOU KNOW

1. Print the reports created in the previous section in *landscape* mode.

2. Using the *sales.mdb* or any other database print the structure of the tables in the database.

SECTION 5.9: EXAM OVERVIEW AND TIPS

In the exam for Module 5, Databases, you will be given a floppy disk which will have all the files that you will need to answer the 2 sections. Be sure to hand the disk up at the end of the exam.

There are 2 Sections in this exam. The first section can have up to 15 questions and there are 15 marks for this section. Section two is the same. All areas in the module can be tested.

Points to Note:
- Time allowed: 45 minutes
- Answer all questions in both sections:
- Marking System
  - Each section has 15 marks awarded to it – total of 30 marks

About the Sections
Section 1
Here you will be asked to design a database. Be sure that you are able to:

- Create a database
- Create tables and insert data types
- Create forms
- Enter data
- Sort data

Section 2
Here you will be asked to work on a database that already exists. Be sure that you are able to:

- Create queries
- Create Reports

All of the topics covered in this Module could be asked in the exam.

For sample examinations visit **http://www.iactonline.com/ecdl**

Module 6
PRESENTATION
GRAPHICS

The complete IT training provider

MODULE 6: PRESENTATION GRAPHICS

Apparently, the majority of us fear public speaking more than death! Perhaps one of the reasons for this is a fear of standing in front of an audience and having nothing to say - that can be pretty scary! PowerPoint is an excellent tool for creating presentations. It allows us to prepare slides and handouts that we can use when giving a presentation. And there is one thing that makes a big difference in presentations – and that's *preparation.*

The PowerPoint program has a lot in common with *Microsoft Word* – many of the buttons on the toolbar are similar and opening and closing files is exactly the same.

Before we start here are a few important things to keep in mind if delivering or preparing slides for a presentation:

Some points to remember:

- ❑ Keep the number of points on a slide small (under 7 points per slide). Slides are meant as a guide to speaking – they are not supposed pre-empt what the speaker says or require the audience to read them in detail.

- ❑ Try to make the slides visually interesting – charts, photos and clipart all help here and will help the presentation be more interesting and engaging.

- ❑ Reinforce important points with repetition and visuals

- ❑ Interact with the audience – try to get them involved in your presentation. Humour, if you feel up to it, is an excellent ice-breaker

- ❑ Have handouts if the presentation is not on a big-screen or might be hard to see

- ❑ Prepare thoroughly for your presentation – practice each slide and time your presentation so you know how long to spend on each slide.

Getting ready to present

Delivering a presentation can be daunting. Before delivering the presentation perform these final checks:

- ❑ Check the presentation's spelling (see *Spelling, Thesaurus* on page 190).

- ❑ Ensure the presentation page orientation and size are correct.

- ❑ Ensure clipart and graphics are appropriate for the target audience – leave them out if you are not sure – think of your audience.

- ❑ Make sure there are no gaps in the presentation or missing slides/data you were to return to.

- ❑ Become familiar with the presentation equipment (video projector etc.) and how it is connected, what remote control to use and how it works. Do the batteries work?

- ❑ Create a second back-up copy of the presentation on disk or CD-ROM for an emergency.

- ❑ Give yourself plenty of time before the presentation – finish preparing the presentation at least 24 hours before you are due to deliver it.

SECTION 6.1:   INTRODUCTION TO POWERPOINT

PowerPoint is a fantastic tool for creating presentations – and it is easy to learn. In this section we will learn how to:

- ❏ Start PowerPoint
- ❏ Create a presentation using the *AutoContent Wizard*
- ❏ Tour the PowerPoint screen
- ❏ View the Presentation on-screen

Let's get started.

LESSON 6.1.1:   STARTING POWERPOINT

To start PowerPoint we need to go to the **Start** menu, choose **All Programs** and choose **Microsoft Office** and click on **Microsoft Office PowerPoint 2003**:

PowerPoint will start after a few moments and the opening screen will appear.

LESSON 6.1.2: CREATING A PRESENTATION WITH A WIZARD

When PowerPoint first starts the **Getting Started** panel is visible on the right hand side of the screen. This panel allows us to:

- ❏ Create a presentation based on a wizard – this tool guesses the presentation content by topic and then lets us edit it later
- ❏ Create a presentation based on an existing template or layout
- ❏ Create a completely blank presentation

or

- ❏ Open an existing presentation

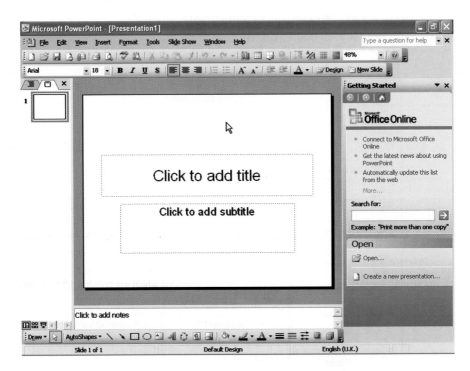

Opening and switching between presentations

To open an existing presentation:

- ❏ Click on the **Open...** option in the **Getting Started...** panel and locate the presentation to open.

To open one or more presentations choose **Open** from the **File** menu or press **Ctrl+O** and select the file you want to open. Review *Module 3 - Word Processing* (page 159) for a review of this process.

If we have several presentations opened at once it is useful to be able to switch between them. To switch between the open presentations:

- ❏ Go to the **Window** menu and click on the presentation to view

See *Lesson 3.1.7:Opening Several Documents* on page 159 for a full review of this process.

Creating a new presentation

As this is our first time in PowerPoint - let's create a new presentation.

> ❑ Click on **Create a new presentation...** on the **Getting Started** panel and the **New Presentation** panel will appear.

There are a number of ways of building our new presentation – one of the quickest is to use the *AutoContent Wizard* to quickly create an ***outline*** for the presentation.

We are going to produce a presentation of a *Marketing Plan* using the wizard:

> ❑ Click on **From AutoContent wizard...** to start creating the presentation.

The AutoContent Wizard will create several slides, which we can ***expand and adapt*** to create a detailed presentation. The slides the wizard creates depend on the content chosen for the presentation.

Once the wizard starts it has to ask us a series of questions which will help build the presentation. After each stage in the process we press **Next** to move to the next stage.

> ❑ Click **Next**

PowerPoint shows us a list of presentation categories. We're building a *Marketing Plan* so choose *Sales/Marketing* and pick *Marketing Plan* as the template. This will automatically fill in information for a typical marketing plan.

❑   Click **Next.**

Deciding on the presentation format

When we produce a presentation we may deliver the final presentation in many different ways – ranging from an *on-screen slide show*, to a *black and white printout*. The options we choose here will determine the colouring and the page size PowerPoint uses when building our presentation. The most common format is 'On-screen presentation'.

❑   Choose **On-Screen Presentation** and click **Next**

❑   The final screen requires us to enter a *title* for the presentation and any other additional information that we would like to include on each slide. Enter some appropriate details. When these are entered press **Finish**

This wizard has now created a default template for our Marketing presentation. This is just a guide – but a good start – for our presentation.

LESSON 6.1.3:   CREATING A PRESENTATION FROM SCRATCH

Rather than using the wizard to build our presentation - we can also start with a blank presentation and build the content ourselves. Let's try this out.

If PowerPoint has just opened

❑   Click on **Create New Presentation…** and then choose **Blank presentation** from the **New Presentation** panel

or

❑   Go to the **File | New** menu or press **Ctrl + N**

The **New Presentation** panel gives us the option to create a blank presentation or use the auto content wizard (which we used earlier) or build the presentation from a design template.

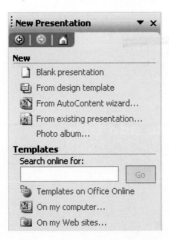

Choosing the **From design template** option displays the **Slide Design template** panel that allows us to choose a background and colour scheme for our slides.

❑   Click **From design Template**

The design template panel will open.

We can now click on the different templates to preview them.

Slide design panel

Choosing a template will create a new blank presentation with a title slide

❑   Choose the **Fireworks** template to create a new presentation that looks like this:

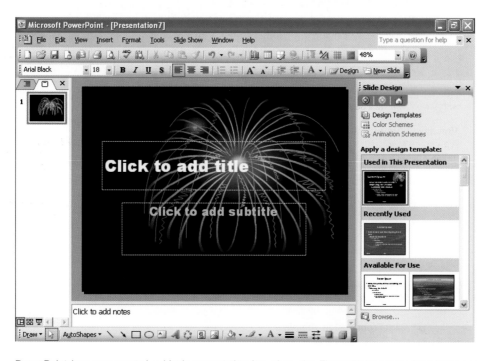

PowerPoint has now created a blank presentation based on the Fireworks template (or whichever template we used) and we can start building our presentation.

LESSON 6.1.4: TOURING POWERPOINT

Once PowerPoint has opened or created a new presentation it is in *Normal View* mode. When in Normal mode the PowerPoint window has several different sections.

Let's have a look at these:

1. *Outline* or *mini-slide* area – which shows us the textual content on each slide.
2. The *Slide* area shows us the current slide
3. The *Notes* area lets us view and edit notes for a slide

In addition PowerPoint has the regular *standard* and *formatting* toolbars and the usual *task pane* area.

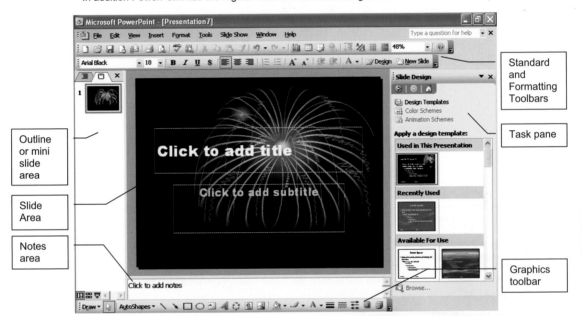

We can adjust the width and height of these different screen sections by sliding the window borders with the mouse we'll see how to do this later.

Viewing a presentation
We can quickly view our presentation by pressing **F5** or by choosing *View* **Slideshow** from the **View** menu. This will display the slide in full-screen view and we can advance through the slides by pressing the left mouse button or by pressing the space bar. Press **ESC** to return to the PowerPoint screen.

Saving a presentation
To save the presentation press **Ctrl+S**. Locate the folder to save it into and give the file a name. Refer to *Module 3 – Word processing* on page 155 for more information on saving files.

Hiding or Displaying PowerPoint's Toolbars and the Task pane
We can modify the toolbars displayed in PowerPoint by choosing

❑ **View | Toolbars** and ticking or unticking the toolbars we want to display.

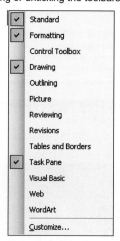

We will work mainly with the **Standard, Formatting** and **Drawing** toolbars in PowerPoint so ensure that these toolbars are visible. We will also regularly work with the **Task Pane.**

Use the **Customise** option to add and remove buttons from the toolbar by clicking and dragging icons to and from the toolbar with the mouse.

Closing a presentation
To close the presentation choose **File | Close**

If you have made changes since you last opened the presentation, PowerPoint will prompt us to save the changes before you close the presentation.

Exiting PowerPoint
To close PowerPoint choose **File | Exit**.

EXERCISES TO PROVE YOU KNOW

1. Open PowerPoint

2. Create a presentation, using the AutoContent Wizard, that will create an outline for a Project Overview presentation.

3. How many slides are in the presentation?

4. Save the presentation on to your Desktop and name it *Project.ppt*.

5. Exit PowerPoint.

SECTION 6.2:   WORKING WITH SLIDES

In the previous section we built a presentation using the AutoContent wizard. In this section we'll work in *outline* mode to build the textual content of the presentation before viewing the final result. We'll also look at how we can quickly change the look of our presentation by changing the slide template and background colours.

We'll learn how to:

❑ Switch *view modes* in PowerPoint

❑ Work with the slide outline to create a presentation

❑ Understand the relationship between slide outline and slide view

❑ Rearrange the slides in a presentation

❑ Alter a presentation's appearance by changing the slide template and slide colour scheme

LESSON 6.2.1:   SWITCHING VIEW MODES

There are several ways in PowerPoint of editing a presentation. The different modes and slide areas suit the type of work being carried out in the presentation. To switch between the different modes we use the icons at the bottom of the PowerPoint screen or choose them from the **View** menu.

We can also switch between outline and mini-slide view modes using the tabs in the left hand window.

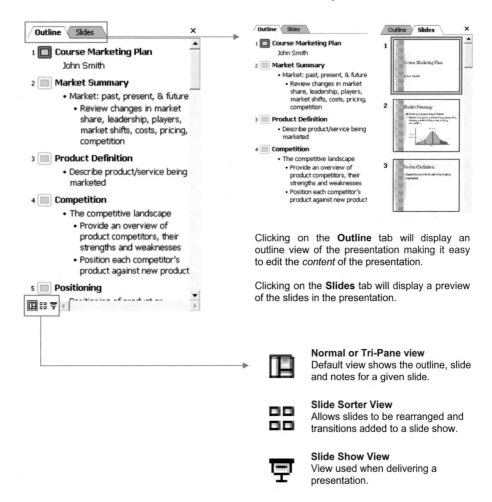

Clicking on the **Outline** tab will display an outline view of the presentation making it easy to edit the *content* of the presentation.

Clicking on the **Slides** tab will display a preview of the slides in the presentation.

Normal or Tri-Pane view
Default view shows the outline, slide and notes for a given slide.

Slide Sorter View
Allows slides to be rearranged and transitions added to a slide show.

Slide Show View
View used when delivering a presentation.

6
Presentations

LESSON 6.2.2: WORKING WITH OUTLINE VIEW

The presentation outline shows the text that is on each slide of the presentation. Working with just the outline we can very quickly edit the text and add new text or slides to a presentation.

Here is the outline view for part of our presentation showing the first 5 slides.

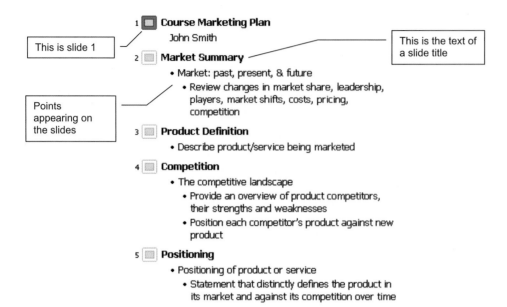

Note: It's a good idea to start a presentation in outline mode to build up the content of the slide show. Its easy to get distracted with the graphics and clipart and forget about the actual text that appears on the slides!

Adding a slide in outline mode

Adding a slide or a point from the presentation outline is easy. Let's insert a new slide in the presentation between slides 4 and 5.

❑ Position the cursor at the end of the last point of slide 4

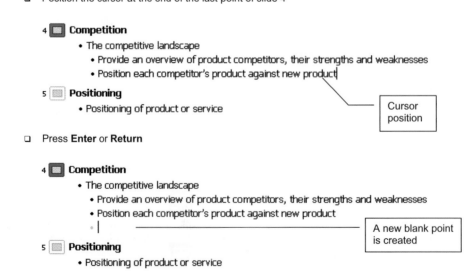

❑ Press **Enter** or **Return**

We've now added a new *point* to slide 4.

To add a new slide we must *promote* this point to a slide *heading* position.

❑ Press the 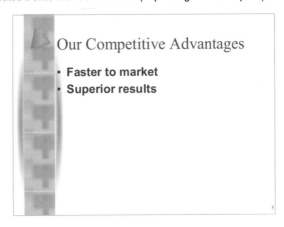 button twice or press **Shift + Tab** twice.

This will promote the point to a heading level.

4 ▨ **Competition**
- The competitive landscape
  - Provide an overview of product competitors, their strengths and weaknesses
  - Position each competitor's product against new product

5 ▨ | ————————————————————————————— | New blank slide |

6 ▨ **Positioning**
- Positioning of product or service

Notice that the old slide 5 has now become slide 6 and we can enter a new slide title.

Let's give the slide a title

❑ Type "Our Competitive advantages" and press **Enter**

❑ Press ▨ button once or press **Tab** to create a slide bullet point

❑ Type "Faster to market" and press **Enter**

❑ Type "Superior results" and press **Enter**

Our outline view will now look like this:

5 ▨ **Our Competitive Advantages**
- Faster to market
- Superior results|

We have in fact created a slide that looks like this (depending on the template):

Since we have been working in presentation outline mode – we didn't have to worry about the look of this slide and so we could focus just on the textual content as the slide was being built. Later we'll see how to change the appearance of the slides.

LESSON 6.2.3: EXPANDING AND COLLAPSING SLIDE DETAILS

Sometimes its useful to be able to expand and collapse the contents of the slides. The slide titles usually provide a *summary* of the information on the slide. We sometimes view slides in this way in order to check the logical flow of the presentation. We can then re-order slides so the presentation flows in a logical fashion or so we can delete unnecessary slides.

To expand, collapse and reorder slides we must display the *outlining* toolbar. This toolbar will appear either vertically or horizontally with the following buttons:

To view this toolbar, go to **View | Toolbars | Outlining**

❑ To view only the slide titles and hide the content of the slides click on the ↑☰ icon.

This will display just the slide headings – and can be useful if we wish create a summary of a presentation or check the logical flow of a presentation.

Above we can see a collapsed view of the first 7 slides of our presentation – showing just the slide titles. Notice the line under the headings indicates there are more point below.

To return to view the fully expanded slides:

❑ Click on the ↓☰ icon.

We can also choose to expand or collapse specific slides using the ✛ and ━ icons.

❑ To expand the current slide click on the ✛ icon.

❑ To collapse just the current slide press the ━ icon.

LESSON 6.2.4: REARRANGING SLIDES

We can re-order our slides while in the presentation outline by selecting the slide and *dragging* it to its new position.

❑   Select the slide by clicking on the *slide* icon.

Slide selection icon.

❑   Now *drag* with the mouse or click on the ⬆ and ⬇ arrows on the outlining toolbar to move the slide to its new position relative to the other slides.

New position for slide

A horizontal line will indicate where the slide will be moved to.

LESSON 6.2.5: PROMOTION AND DEMOTION

Although it might sound like something that only happens in the office - PowerPoint lets us *promote* or *demote* items in a presentation. We can *promote* or *demote* the points on a slide as we find we need to expand on points or decrease the significance of a particular point.

For example consider the following slide:

5 ▣ **Our Competitive Advantages**
      • Faster to market
      • Superior results

Let's make the point "Faster to market" a slide in its own right.

❑   Click on the text *"Faster to market"* and then press the ⬑ icon to *promote* the point.

PowerPoint now makes this point a *slide title*.

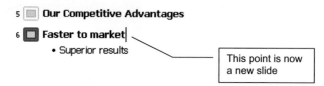

5 ▣ **Our Competitive Advantages**

6 ▣ **Faster to market**|
      • Superior results

This point is now
a new slide

The ⬒ icon is the opposite and *demotes* a slide to a point or sub-points.

Using the demotion and promotion tools allows us to quickly expand or shorten our presentation as we review our presentation.

LESSON 6.2.6: COPYING, MOVING AND DELETING ITEMS IN POWERPOINT

We can copy, move and delete text and graphics from one slide to another or from one presentation to another much as we can in all Window's applications.

In each case whether we care copying, cutting or deleting:

❑ We must first select the text or graphics to move or copy

Then depending on what we plan to do we:

❑ Press **Ctrl+C** (if we are copying) or **Ctrl+X** (if we are moving or deleting).

Then do one of the following depending on the required result:

Moving or copying text or graphics

1: To move or copy text or graphics within the presentation:

❑ Select the destination slide either by scrolling to the slide or from within slide-sorter view

❑ Press **Ctrl+V** to paste and then move the text or graphic to their correct position on the slide.

or

2: To move or copy text or graphics to a different presentation

❑ Open the destination presentation (press **Ctrl+O** and locate the file) or select the presentation from the **Window** menu if it is already open. Click on the destination slide and press **Ctrl+V**.

Deleting text or graphics

To delete text or graphics from a presentation:

❑ Select the text or graphic to delete and press the **Delete** key.

Undo and Redo

Like the other parts of Microsoft Office – PowerPoint supports **Undo** and **Redo**.

Most actions we perform in PowerPoint we can reverse by pressing **Undo** (**Ctrl + Z**) or pressing **Redo** (**Ctrl + Y**)

❑ To reverse an action press the **Undo** button or press **Ctrl+Z**.

As with Word there are several levels of *undo* available in PowerPoint depending on the amount of memory we have. Each time we press the **Undo** button the previous action is undone. Press it a few times to see what happens.

If after we have *undone* an action we wish to Redo it we simply press the **Redo** button.

LESSON 6.2.7:   WORKING IN THE NORMAL OR TRI-PANE VIEW

The Normal view is also known as the *tri-pane* view as it is split into three sections:

    1:      Outline text area
    2:      Slide preview / edit area
    3:      Notes area

In this view we have a choice of where to enter our text. We can enter it onto the slide itself, or into the outline view, or we can add slide *notes*.

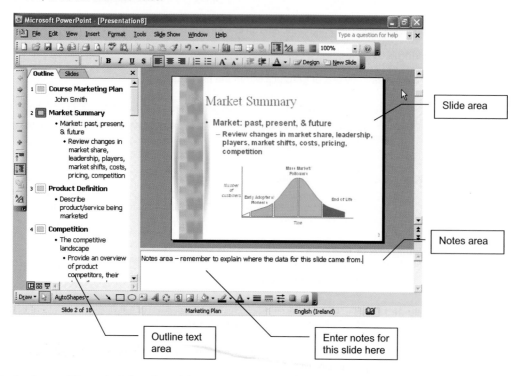

This view is one of the easiest views to work in as we get to see all of the slide information at the same time.

Editing the content on slides and notes pages
We can easily edit the content on a slide by clicking and editing the text that appears in the slide outline.

- ❑   Move to the slide that contains the content to edit – use the scroll bars or the cursor keys
- ❑   Select the text to change and type the new text

We can modify any of the text that appears on a slide in outline view. We can also edit the text directly on the slide by clicking directly into the text boxes.

Adding slide notes
Slide notes are a very useful feature in PowerPoint. They allow us to insert extra information that can be printed below each slide in our presentation. Our notes might be useful reminders to the presenter or additional reference information for the reader. To add notes to a particular slide

- ❑   Move to the desired slide by pressing the **PAGE-UP** or **PAGE-DOWN** keys or by using the scroll bar.
- ❑   Type into the notes area. We can edit existing notes the same way we would edit text in Word or any other text editor.

We will see later how we can print out the notes attached to each slide – which is useful for both the presenter and the audience.

LESSON 6.2.8:   WORKING DIRECTLY WITH A SLIDE

After we've created the outline of the presentation we can refine it and add graphics and charts to the presentation by working directly with the slide. We can maximise the slide area by resizing the outline and notes view sections of the tri-pane window and adjusting the slides magnification.

❑   Using the mouse resize the outline and notes panels to hide the outline and notes areas.

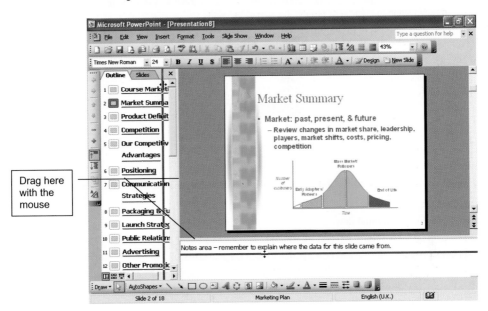

Drag here
with the
mouse

❑   Resize the note and outline panes to the bottom and left of the screen to maximise the slide area. Now we can see just one slide at a time.

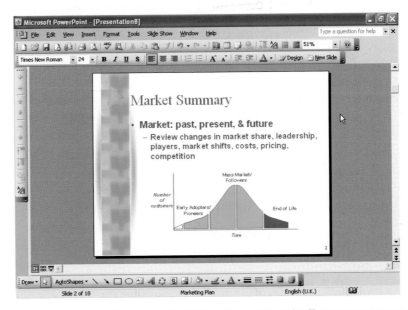

With the slide area maximised we can work with the slide exactly as it will appear on screen or when printed.

The Zoom Tool

We can adjust the magnification of our slide using the zoom or magnification tool – this will make it easier to work with the details on our slides.

To increase (or decrease) the magnification on our slide:

❑ Click on the scale drop-down arrow on the standard toolbar and choose a percentage magnification to enlarge or reduce the size of the slide.

Larger values will increase the size of the slide – smaller values will reduce the size of the slide.

Restoring normal view

To restore PowerPoint to normal view:

❑ Choose **View | Normal (Restore Panes)**

PowerPoint will resize the outline and notes panes to their original sizes.

EXERCISES TO PROVE YOU KNOW

1. Create a NEW presentation using the **"Ocean"** Design Template and recreate the following slides:

Slide 1 (Title Slide)
BRAZIL
Investment opportunities
Simpson Investment Advisors

Slide 2 (Bulleted List)
Brief History of Brazilian Economy
- Debt crisis in the 1980s
- Increased foreign borrowing
- Rising international interest rates
- Recent recovery of the economy
- Research department's report on the history of the economy

Slide 3 (Bulleted List)
Why is the Brazilian Economy Ready for Investment?
- Undervalued
- Specific stocks
- Government debt

---

2. Save as Brazil.ppt.
3. Using the Outline view, add in the following slide to the end of the presentation.

Slide 4: (Bulleted List)
Conclusion: Reasons to invest through Simpson Investment Advisors
- Rate of return on investments
- Global trading
- Highly trained professionals

---

4. Expand and collapse the details in the slides in the Outline view.
5. Move slide 4 and place it in front of slide 2 (*Brief history of…*)
6. Delete slide 3 (*Why is the Brazilian Economy…*)
7. Click on the bullet point *Global trading* on slide 4. Promote this point so that it becomes a Slide on its own with *Highly trained professionals* as a bullet point.

SECTION 6.3:   LAYING OUT SLIDES

Slides in a presentation fall into a set of categories depending on the type of information they display or contain. For example our slides might have: just text, text and a table or text and some clipart.

We can change the default layout of our slides in order to allow us to easily add additional content to the slide.

In this section we'll learn how to:

- ❑   Add a new slide to a presentation
- ❑   Alter the slide layout
- ❑   Work with organisational charts
- ❑   Add charts and graphs to our slides
- ❑   Add sound and video clips to slides
- ❑   Change the design template or colour scheme
- ❑   Add and amend transitions to our slideshow

LESSON 6.3.1:   ADDING A SLIDE TO A PRESENTATION

We can add a new slide to our presentation and determine the slide type at the same time.

To insert a new slide:

- ❑   Choose **Insert | New Slide**

The **Slide Layout** panel will appear:

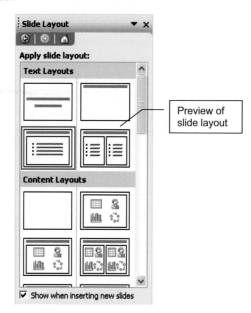

Preview of slide layout

By clicking on different layout options we can create different slide layouts. From here we can insert a new slide which contains bulleted text, a chart, table, clipart, an organisational chart or a combination of these. We can then adjust the layout after the slide is inserted.

- ❑   Click on the slide type required to change the slide layout.

PowerPoint inserts the new slide after the current slide. We can add text and graphics to the slide using the default layout as a guide.

LESSON 6.3.2: CHANGING THE SLIDE LAYOUT

The slide layout determines what items we want to appear on a slide. PowerPoint gives us many different items to choose from – including clipart, tables, charts and organisational charts all of which can help spice up a presentation.

To change the layout of a slide:

- ❏   Go to **Format | Slide layout**.

Different slide layouts

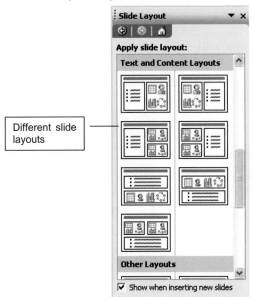

- ❏   Select the new slide layout from the **Slide Layout** panel.

The slide layout panel shows the most popular slide layout options and we will look at these next.

6

Presentations

LESSON 6.3.3: CLIPART SLIDE LAYOUT

The clipart slide layout allows us to modify a slide to include clipart items.

Let's change the layout of our slide to include some clipart.

- ❑ Reproduce the **Positioning** slide shown below.
- ❑ Change the slide layout to the clipart slide layout using the **Slide Layout** panel

Choosing this slide layout option changed this slide

..into this slide.

Positioning

- ■ **Positioning of product or service**
  - • Statement that distinctly defines the product in its market and against its competition over time
- ■ **Consumer promise**
  - • Statement summarizing the benefit of the product or service to the consumer

Positioning

- ■ Positioning of product or service
  - • Statement that distinctly defines the product in its market and against its competition over time
- ■ Consumer promise
  - • Statement summarizing the benefit of the product or service to the consumer

Double click to add clip art

We can add clipart by double-clicking here

By using the **Slide Layout** panel we can change a slide as we need to and PowerPoint does all the hard work.

Let's choose some clipart for our slide.

- ❑ **Double-click** on the clipart icon and search for the clipart called "Aligning"

- ❑ Press **OK** to insert the clipart onto the current slide.

We can now see the clipart on our slide.

LESSON 6.3.4: INSERTING CLIPART AND IMAGES

We can also insert multiple pieces of clipart onto our slides without changing the slide layout.

❑ To insert clipart without changing the slide layout choose **Insert | Picture | Clipart** or click on the clipart icon 🖻 on the toolbar.

The **Clip Art** panel will appear and we can browse through the clipart or search for the graphic we are looking for.

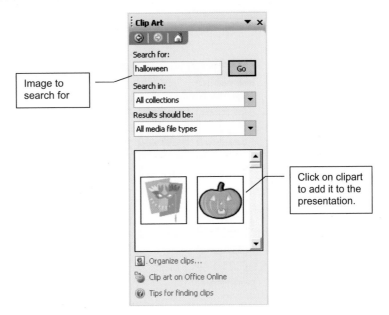

Image to search for

Click on clipart to add it to the presentation.

Once inserted the clipart will appear on the slide and we can resize and position it as required.

Moving, copying and deleting clipart images between slides
The easiest way to move or copy an image between slides is to use the clipboard.

Moving an image
Select the image to move and choose **Cut** from the **Edit** menu or press **Ctrl+X**. Navigate to the destination slide for the image and choose **Paste** from the **Edit** menu or press **Ctrl+V**.

Copying or duplicating an image
Select the image and choose **Copy** from the **Edit** menu or press **Ctrl+C**. Navigate to the destination slide for the image and choose **Paste** from the **Edit** menu or press **Ctrl+V**.

Deleting an image
Select the image to delete and choose **Cut** from the **Edit** menu or press **Delete**.

6
Presentations

LESSON 6.3.5:   THE ORGANISATIONAL CHART SLIDE LAYOUT

Adding an organisational chart to a presentation is a common requirement. The easiest way to insert one onto a slide is to insert a new slide and change the layout to one that includes an organisational chart.

We follow the same procedure we used to alter the slide layout earlier.

- ❑   Insert a new slide into the presentation
- ❑   Go to **Format | Slide layout** to display the **Slide Layout** panel

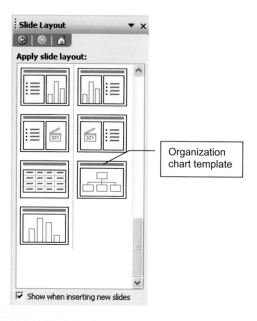

Organization chart template

- ❑   Select the organisation chart template (shown above).

When we have changed the slide layout to insert the organizational chart an icon will appear in the middle of the slide and our slide will now look like this:

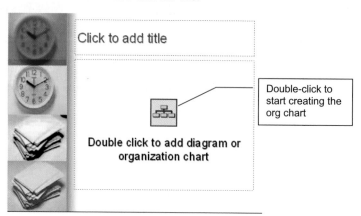

Double-click to start creating the org chart

- ❑   Double-click on the org-chart or diagram object to edit it

The Diagram Gallery window will appear allowing us to select the type of diagram we wish to insert.

❑ We are going to insert an **Organisational Chart** – so pick the first option and choose **OK**

The *Organization Chart* builder inserts a new object onto our slide along with the Organisational Chart toolbar.:

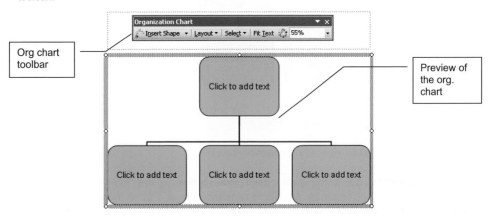

We can now build the org chart by entering the names and titles into the textboxes.

❑ Click into the first textbox and start typing – this is the root of the Organisational chart.

Let's place the *Managing Director* into the top position.

❑ Type "Managing Director" and press **Enter**

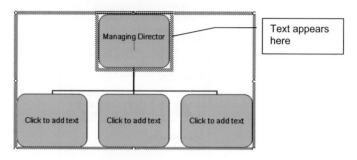

❑ Now type "**Michael Dell**" and *(World-wide)*.

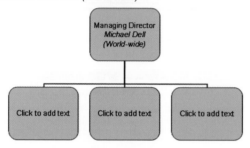

We can change the formatting in the chart in the same way we would normally format the text in our presentation from the **Format | Font** menu.

❑ Format the text we have just entered in italics.

We can proceed like this with any available textboxes that we wish to fill in – this is easy for the first 3 subordinates under the *Managing Director*. Let's add some more management – fill in the following details for the next three textboxes:

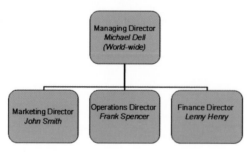

Adding managers, co-workers and subordinates to our chart

We can add additional items from the Organisational chart toolbar and the **Insert Shape** menu.

Let's add a *co-worker* to the management team.

- ❑ Click on the textbox for *Frank Spencer.*
- ❑ Select the **Co-worker** option from the **Insert Shape** menu

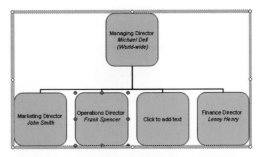

We can now add our *Sales Director* to the team:

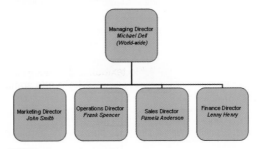

- ❑ Type **Sales Director** and press **Enter** and then type **Pamela Anderson**

We can also add *Subordinates, Assistants* and *Co-Workers* using the icons on the **Org Chart** toolbar.

6

Presentations

Changing the structure of the organisational chart

Organisational charts can become quite large – and its important to be able to change their layout or structure.

We can change the layout of the org chart using the options in the **Layout** menu found on the **Org Chart** toolbar.

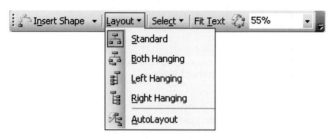

☐ Select *Managing Director* position in the Organisational chart.

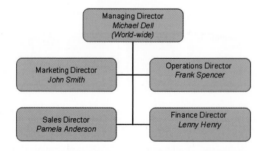

☐ Choose **Both Hanging** from the **Layout** menu

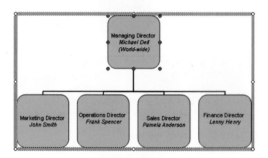

Notice that the Organisation chart layout has now changed. We can use this technique to group departments and layout the organisational chart as required.

Re-editing the organisational chart.

If we wish to make any further changes to the org chart once we've initially made it – we simply *click* on it with the mouse. The *Organisation Chart* toolbar will then reappear and we can edit the object as before.

Removing items from an organizational chart

To remove any element from the organizational chart

☐ Select the element to remove (manager, co-worker etc.) by clicking with the mouse

☐ Press the **Delete** key

LESSON 6.3.6: CHART SLIDE LAYOUT

Graphs and charts can greatly increase the visual value of a slide. We can bring charts from Excel into our PowerPoint presentations or we can create them from scratch in our presentation. To change the slide layout to include a chart – pick any with the visual of a chart like this:

This will insert the object on the slide or we can choose to insert it directly by choosing **Insert | Chart**

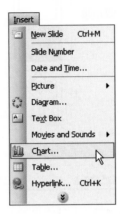

❑   Create a new slide and insert a chart onto the slide.

Charts are created in PowerPoint in much the same way as they are in Excel. We need to provide the raw data making up the chart and then we can choose a chart style. Notice when we insert the chart object into PowerPoint the menu will change to reflect the fact that we are now editing the chart.

New menu and toolbar

When we first insert the chart a mini spreadsheet called a *datasheet* will appear like:

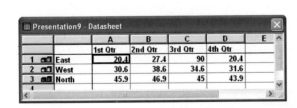

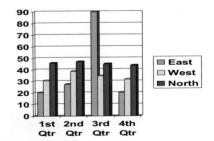

Default datasheet and sample chart in PowerPoint

We can add *rows* to the datasheet and *columns* to change the appearance of the chart

---

Changing the appearance of the chart

We can easily change the appearance and the format of the chart to suit the type and style of data that we are displaying.

❑   To change the chart type, go to the **Chart** menu and choose **Chart Type.**

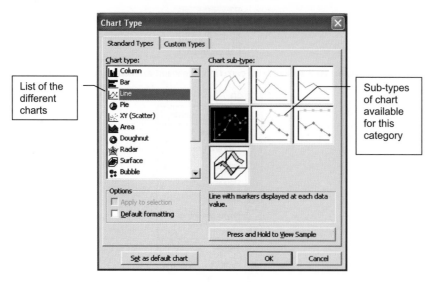

There is a long list of built in chart types to choose from. Select the chart style from the **Chart type** menu and then the **chart sub-type** from the main display window.

Pie Charts

Pie charts are very popular in presentations. Pie charts only use one data series. To create a pie chart we need to delete the un-used rows from our datasheet.

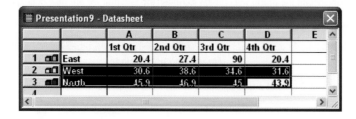

❑   Select the rows to remove (West and North) and press **Delete**

❑   Change the chart type to a *Pie Chart* by choosing **Chart Type** from the **Chart** menu.

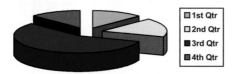

Configuring charts in PowerPoint is identical to working with charts in a *spreadsheet*. Review *Module 4 – Spreadsheets page 321* to see the additional chart features.

LESSON 6.3.7: TABLE SLIDE LAYOUT

Sometimes we'll want to layout tabular data on a slide – the Table slide layout lets us do this.

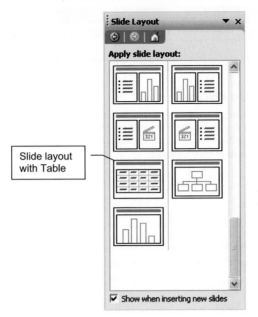

Slide layout with Table

Alternatively we can use the insert **Table** icon on the toolbar or choose **Insert | Table**.

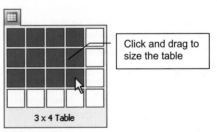

Click and drag to size the table

3 x 4 Table

❑ Choose a 4 x 3 table and PowerPoint will insert it onto the slide:

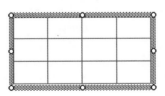

We can use the **Tab** key to move between the cells and type text into the individual cells.

	Jan	Feb	Mar
Dublin	100	200	324
Cork	120	340	450

6

Presentations

The entire table can then be stretched or resized like any other PowerPoint object. Use the **Table and Borders** toolbar to align, colour and shade the cells of the table – exactly as with *Microsoft word*.

EXERCISES TO PROVE YOU KNOW

1. Open the Brazil presentation created earlier, insert the following slide at the end of the presentation. Create the slide using a bulleted list slide:

> **Overview of Possible Investments**
> Stocks in
> - Coffee
> - Steel
> - Chemical

a) Change the slide layout so that it can hold two bulleted columns.

b) Add the following text to the right hand bulleted column.

> **Bonds**
> - Short Term
> - Long Term

2. Insert a clipart image into the first slide and resize it and place it on the lower right hand side of the slide.

3. Change the layout of slide 2 so that it can hold an image on the right hand side of the slide. Use the clipart placeholder to then insert a clipart image.

4. Insert a new slide to the end of the presentation. Make sure that the slide will contain an organisational chart.

a) Create the following organisational chart on this slide:

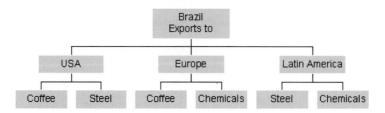

5. Open a new presentation. Create a title Slide and insert the heading *Tourism*.

a) Insert a table slide and input the following data into the table. Type in the heading *Australia Data*.

	1997	1998	1999
Tasmania	14	15	16
Queensland	200	250	300
New South Wales	200	200	200
Western Australia	100	150	160
Northern Territory	160	170	190

b) Insert another new slide and create a graph or chart of the information in the table. Create the graph so that it looks like the one below:

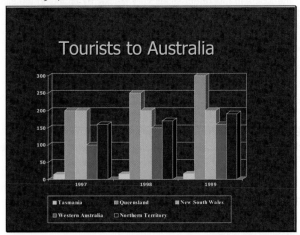

c) Change the Chart type to a column/cylinder Bar chart and change the colours of each of the data sets.

d) Save the presentation as *Tourism.ppt* and close it.

SECTION 6.4: SLIDE DESIGN AND ANIMATION

We can change the *look and feel* of our slides very quickly by changing the slide *design template* or altering the slides' colour scheme. PowerPoint ships with dozens of excellent slide design templates and we can alter the colour scheme very easily to suit our needs.

In this section we will learn how to:

- ❑ Change the slide design template
- ❑ Alter the colour scheme of our slides
- ❑ Add animation to our slides

LESSON 6.4.1: CHANGING THE SLIDE DESIGN TEMPLATE

Altering the slide design template can radically alter the appearance of our slides. Let's see how our presentation looks with a different design template.

- ❑ To change the template that the presentation is based on, go to the **Format** menu and choose **Slide Design**.

The **Slide Design** panel will appear:

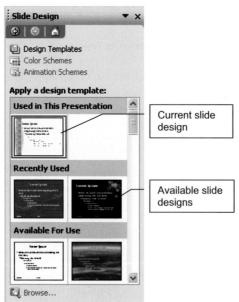

Current slide design

Available slide designs

PowerPoint displays a long list of built-in templates and as we choose different options a preview will appear to the right of the template.

❑ Choose the style called **Fireworks**

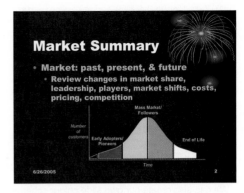

Slide before the template changed   *Slide with Fireworks template applied*

As we can see there is a huge difference in the appearance of the slides with the new template layout – but the text and graphics remain the same.

LESSON 6.4.2:   CHANGING THE SLIDE COLOUR SCHEME

Sometimes we'll like the slide template but we'll want to alter the colour scheme used on the slides.

To change the slides colours

❑ Go to the **Format** menu and choose **Slide Design**.

The Slide design panel will appear as before.

❑ Click on the **Color Schemes** option

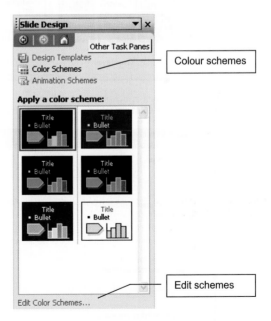

PowerPoint displays a selection of different colour schemes in the panel – and we can click on the different built-in colour schemes to apply them just as we applied the slide design templates earlier.

Changing the slide colour scheme can drastically alter the appearance of a slide. Compare the two slides below – they are based on the same design templates but using a different slide colour scheme:

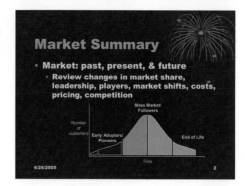

We can also create our own slide colour scheme which can conform to our corporate colours, our local teams colours or any other scheme we require.

To edit the slides colour scheme:

❑ Click the **Edit Color Scheme** link on the Slide Design panel

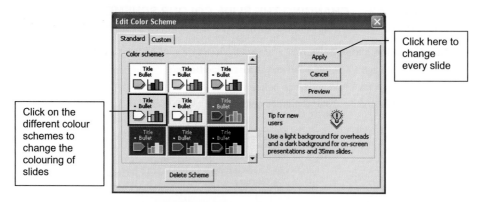

The standard tab displays the built-in schemes for our presentation which we used directly from the colour scheme panel earlier. The **Custom** tab allows us to alter the colours used in the presentation.

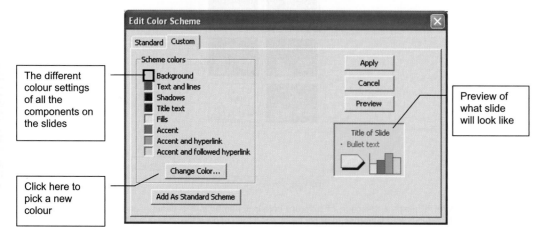

❑ Choose the item to change – in this case we'll change the *background* colour of the slides.

❑   Click on the **change colour** button to reveal a colour swatch

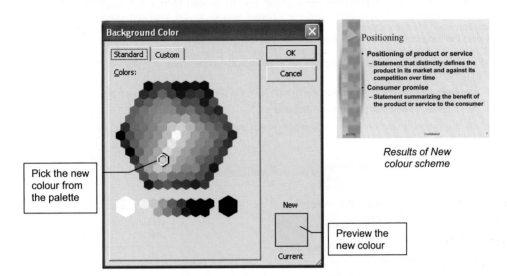

Results of New
colour scheme

Pick the new
colour from
the palette

Preview the
new colour

❑   Press **OK** to choose the colour and then click **Apply** to change the slides colour scheme.

Our slide colour scheme is changed. Pressing **Undo** will quickly reverse our changes

LESSON 6.4.3:   SLIDE ANIMATIONS

PowerPoint has a number of preset animations that can be applied to text and graphics in our presentation. These preset animations perform different effects to the text and graphics in the presentation when the slide appears. For example – if we choose the *Flying* preset –the text or graphic will fly onto the slide from the left of the screen to its final resting position.

To add a preset animation to text or a graphics we must be in slide view mode.

- ❑   Select the text or graphics with the mouse (use the **Ctrl** key to select more than one item)

- ❑   Choose **Slideshow | Animation Schemes**

By default the preset animation is **No Animation** which indicates that no animations are currently applied.

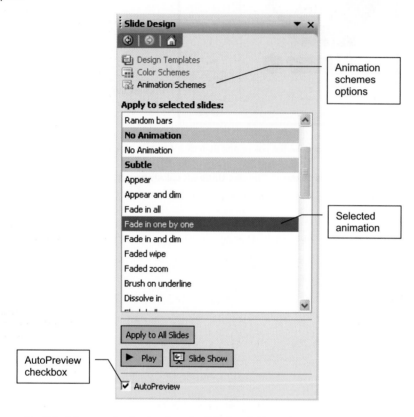

- ❑   Select the preset animation from the list of available options

Ticking the AutoPreview checkbox will show us a preview of the animation once it is selected. If it is not select click on **Play** to view the animation.

- ❑   To view the animation in the presentation press **F5** or choose **Slide Show | View Show**.

LESSON 6.4.4: CUSTOM SLIDE ANIMATIONS

As well as directly inserting sounds and movie files onto our slides – we can also add custom animations to the items on a slide. In this way we can associate a sound or an action with a particular item on a slide for dramatic effect with on-screen slide shows – for example creating a swoosh sound when some text or a graphic item appears on screen. Let's look at how we can do this.

To add a custom animation:

❑ Select the item on the slide to modify – for example we can select the title text on a slide like the one below.

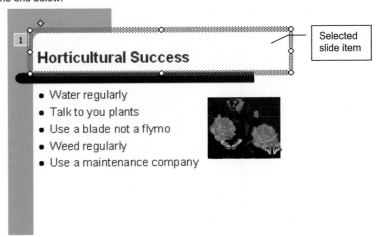

❑ Choose **Slide Show | Custom Animation**

PowerPoint will display the **Custom Animation** panel. From here we can choose to add an effect to the slide animation. Effects such as *Dissolve, Diamonds, Checkerboard etc.* can be applied individually to each item on a slide.

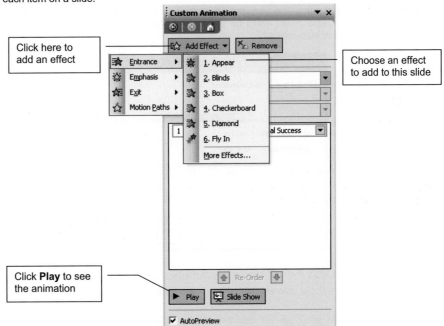

❑ Click **Play** to preview the custom animation or tick the **AutoPreview** button and the animation will automatically play when a change is made to the animation settings.

For each item on the slide that we animate – PowerPoint adds an entry into the Custom animation list. Items in the list are numbered and the numbers refer to the sequence in which a given animation will appear.

We can further refine our animation by choosing **Effect Options...** from the animation drop down list.

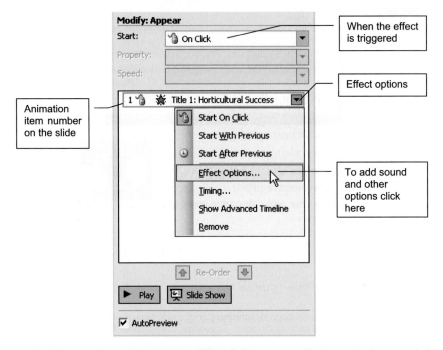

Choosing the **Effect Options...** item from the Effect Options menu will display the **Appear** window. From here we can choose a sound effect for the animation and determine what effects should be applied after the animation is completed.

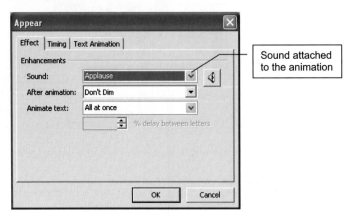

- ❏ Press **OK** to apply the animation enhancements.
- ❏ Experiment with the different settings and click **Play** to see the effect.

When we view the slide show we will see the effects including any sounds associated with the individual slides.

NOTE: Don't mix and match too many different animation effects on the same slide – as the audience will be looking at the *effect* and not the content of the slide!

EXERCISES TO PROVE YOU KNOW

1. Create a new blank presentation. Change the colour scheme of the slides to the following:

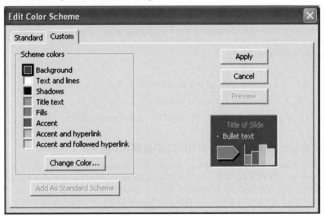

2. View this presentation in the slide show mode.

3. Apply a design template called *Capsules* to all slides. Now apply the *Fireworks* design template to all slides.

4. Insert a new slide. Change the colour scheme of this slide to *Black and White*.

5. a) Create a new slide layout with the following text and clipart graphics:

Before You Go

- Check your Passport is in date
- Pay your Credit Card bill
- Leave the car in for a service
- Leave the dog with Mum

---

b) Apply the following animation effects, in the following order:

Title Heading	Fly from Top
Bulleted text	Fly from Right, all at once, dimming to a different colour
Clipart Image	Swivel, with Camera sound

6

Presentations

SECTION 6.5:   MASTER SLIDES

When we work with the slides of a presentation – the background graphics, fonts and bullets that appear on each slide should appear consistently across the presentation. PowerPoint achieves this by creating a series of *master slides* which set the fonts, positioning and graphics for every slide.

In this section we'll learn to:

- ❑ Edit the *master slide* of our document.
- ❑ Add headers and footers to our slides
- ❑ Change the default text and bullet format on each slide

LESSON 6.5.1:   VIEWING THE SLIDE MASTERS

We need to be able to edit the master pages of a presentation in order to add graphics or text onto every page – and to ensure that those text and graphic images are in *exactly* the same place on all those pages. Slide numbers, a company logo, the date, the company name and presentation details are often included on every slide. By placing these items on the master page they are easy to move and reposition as required.

There are two master slides associated with our slide show:

1. The slide *title* master

And the

2. Slide master

Let's have a look at the *slide master.*

- ❑ Choose **View | Master | Slide Master**

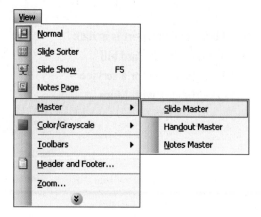

We can now see the *template layout* for our slides.

PowerPoint displays two master slides when we switch to Master Slide view.

1. Slide Master
The *Slide Master* is the slide layout that is used on all slides except the first slide in the presentation.

Modifying or changing the master slide layout, fonts and background graphics will effect all slides in the presentation except the title slide.

2. Title Master
The *Title Master* is the layout for the first slide in the presentation – the "title" slide. Modifying the appearance of the title slide effects the first slide of the presentation.

The Slide master is broken into different sections that are common to most slides.

PowerPoint's view of the *Mountain Top* PowerPoint template

The Master slide doesn't display the contents of the slide – but "placeholders" for the text and graphics that will appear on the slide. By altering the appearance of the placeholder text we can alter the appearance of the text on every slide based on the master slide.

6
Presentations

LESSON 6.5.2: ADDING A FOOTER TO SLIDES

We will now add the slide number to the bottom of each slide using the *brazil.ppt* presentation created earlier. This will help us to see how many slides we have remaining as we give the presentation.

The slide number won't appear until we make a change to the *header and footer* settings for the slide show.

❑ Choose **View | Header and Footer**.

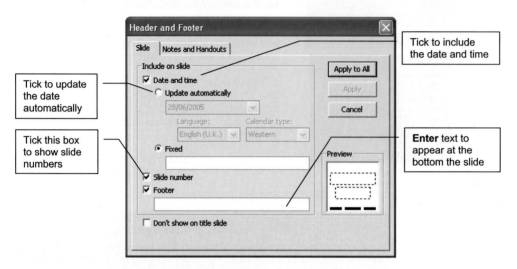

❑ To add text to the bottom of the slide type into the *footer* text box. This text can appear on the current slide or on all slides.

To make the text appear at the bottom of all slides:

❑ Click the **Apply to All** button

To make the text appear just at the bottom of the current slide

❑ Click the **Apply** button

LESSON 6.5.3:   ADDING A DATE TO SLIDES

We can add a date and a time to any text box in our presentation.

    ❑   Click inside any text box and choose **Insert | Date and Time...**

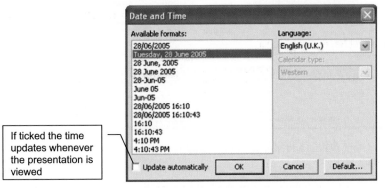

If ticked the time updates whenever the presentation is viewed

    ❑   Select the date and time format from the list of available formats

To have the date and time update automatically when we start the presentation click the *Update automatically* check box.

    ❑   Click **OK** to insert the date and time into the current text box.

LESSON 6.5.4:   CHANGING SLIDE FONT AND BULLET SETTINGS

We can alter the bullet and font style of the text appearing throughout the entire presentation by changing the settings in the main text area on our master slide. Changes made here will impact on all of the text in the presentation. Let's change the bullet style and colour.

    ❑   Place the cursor on the top level bullet in the text box.

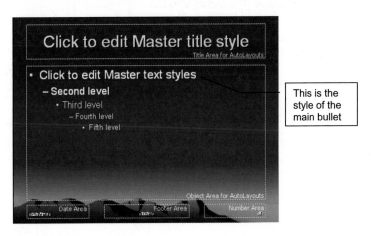

This is the style of the main bullet

    ❑   Choose **Format | Font** menu and then choose *verdana 24pt* with a text colour of *white* and then click **OK**

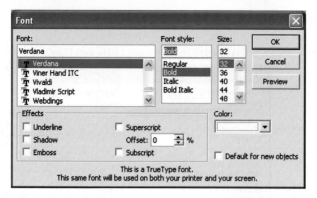

This is the standard font dialog and works in the usual way. When we press **OK** the font settings will change for text.

Let's change the bullet style. With the cursor on the first paragraph:

❑   Choose **Format | Bullets and Numbering..**

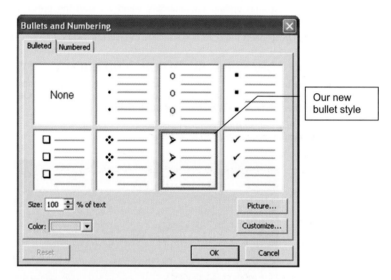

Now that the text and bullets have been changed our text format should look like this:

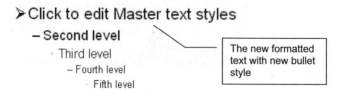

Let's return to our **Normal** view to see these changes.

❑   Choose **View | Normal**

Notice that our slides will now appear with this new font and bullet style.

Also notice the *presentation title* and *slide number* also appear on the slide.

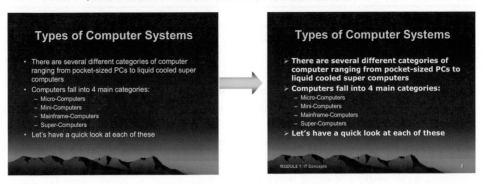

*a) Slide **before** modification of Master Slide*   *b) Slides **after** the modification of the Master Slide*

Notice the difference between slide **a** and slide **b**. The bullet and main text fonts have changed and also the presentation title and the slide number are now showing at the bottom of ALL slides in the same place.

Moving objects to the Master Slide

Sometimes after we have inserted an object such as a graphic or logo onto a slide we want it to appear on all slides. To achieve this we must move the object onto the *Master slide.*

❑   Select the object to move and press **Ctrl+X**

This moves the object onto the clipboard for temporary storage

❑   Choose **View | Master | Slide Master**

❑   Press **Ctrl**+V to paste the object onto the slide.

❑   Position the object as required and return to slide view mode.

The object will now appear on all slides.

EXERCISES TO PROVE YOU KNOW

1.   Open a new presentation and view the *Slide Master*.

 a) Move the date box so that it is positioned on the top right of the slide.

 b) Apply the following to all slides:

Date	A date that will update automatically
Slide Number	Enters the slide number automatically
Footer	Created by *Students Name* for ECDL Exam

 c) Ensure that the above is visible on all slides by adding in three blank slides to the presentation.

 d) Save the Presentation as Schools.ppt

2.   Re-open *Schools.ppt* and insert an appropriate graphic on to all slides in the presentation.

 a) Change the bullets on all slides to red boxes.

 b) Change the font of the title headings to red, 44pt and *Comic Sans*.

SECTION 6.6: CREATING SLIDE GRAPHICS AND TEXT

Presentation graphics are an important part of preparing a professional presentation. Being able to work with graphic objects is an important skill.

In this section we'll learn to

- ❑ Draw and colour lines, circles and other shapes
- ❑ Add, resize and position text boxes on a slide
- ❑ Format text in text boxes
- ❑ Place shadows and 3D effects on graphics
- ❑ Add clipart to slides
- ❑ Use *word art* for special effects with text

LESSON 6.6.1: TEXT BOXES

All text that appears on a PowerPoint slide actually lives in a textbox. Text boxes are very useful as they allow us to place text anywhere on the page – without having to use tabs or tables or any special effects.

The textbox icon  is easy to use. We simply draw a rectangular area into which we want to type:

The handles around the outside of the textbox allow us to stretch the textbox as we need to. To make the textbox taller we simply hit **Enter** to advance to a new paragraph.

- ❑ Draw a text box and enter the following text:

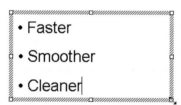

Resizing the textbox is easy – simply grab one of the corners and pull to the left or right to shrink or expand the text box horizontally. To expand the textbox vertically we must insert more paragraphs into the text box.

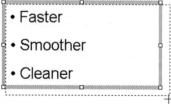

Move the text box by clicking and holding the mouse down on the border of the box and then moving the mouse to its new location.

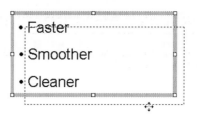

Mastering the use of textboxes can make using PowerPoint much easier.

LESSON 6.6.2:   FORMATTING TEXT IN TEXT BOXES

We can format the text on our individual slides to change the font, colour and alignment of the text. (See *Master Slides* on page 474 for details of changing font and text settings for all slides).

Changing the font style, colour and type
To change the font style used in a text frame

     ❑   Select the text to change

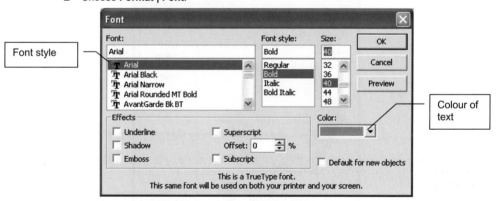

     ❑   Choose **Format | Font**.

The standard font dialog box will appear. It allows us to choose the font, size, effect and style of the text selected. We can also make the text *superscript* and *subscript* from this window.

     ❑   When the settings are correct press **OK**.

We can also make our text **BOLD,** *Italic,* underlined or **shadowed** using the formatting toolbar.

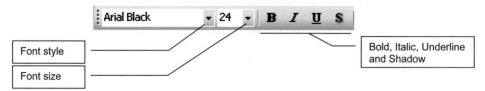

Font style
Font size

Bold, Italic, Underline
and Shadow

To turn on or off this text formatting

❑ Select the text to format and press the **BOLD,** *Italic,* underlined or **shadowed** buttons.

For example to make the text **Shadowed**

❑ Select the text and press the **S** button.

Changing the text colour

To change the colour of text in our presentation:

❑ Select the text and choose **Format | Font** or click on the down-arrow **A ▾** on the text colour icon on the drawing toolbar

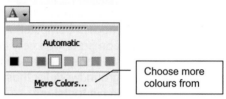

Choose more
colours from

❑ Clicking on **More Colors** will display the colour dialog box which allows us to choose any colour we wish:

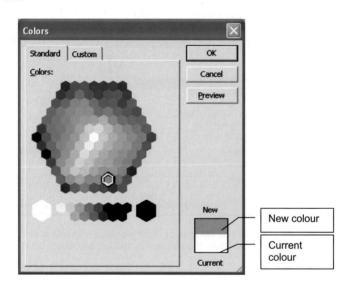

New colour

Current
colour

❑ Select a colour and press **OK** to change the text colour.

Changing sentence case

We can change the case of our text just as with word.

❑ Select the text to alter and choose **Format | Change Case**

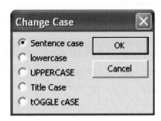

❑ Select the appropriate case style for the selected paragraph and press **OK**

Horizontal text alignment

We can change the *horizontal alignment* of text in our text frames using the formatting toolbar:

The formatting toolbar contains up to four buttons for aligning text:

Button:	Action:
≣	Left align selected paragraph.
≣	Centre selected paragraph.
≣	Right align selected paragraph.
≣	Fully justify selected paragraph[†].

These icons work in the same way as they do in Word and Excel aligning the select paragraphs along the left, right or centre of the text box.

[†] If the *Justify* icon isn't displayed we can justify the text by choosing **Format | Alignment | Justify** or add the toolbar icon to the toolbar by customising the toolbar.

Vertical Text Alignment

To change the *Vertical Alignment* of text in a text frame

- ❑ Select the text frame and choose **Format | Format Placeholder** or **Format | Text**
- ❑ Click on the **Text Box** tab.

We can now change the vertical alignment of the text by altering the text anchor point settings.

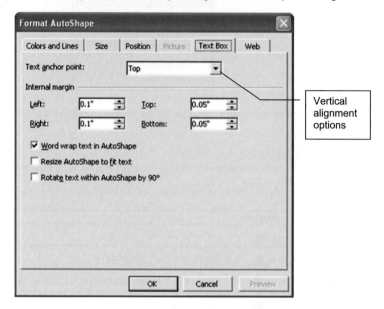

From here we can also adjust the internal margin of the text frame. This keeps the text away from the edge of the frame which can be useful if there is a border on the frame.

LESSON 6.6.3: ADJUSTING PARAGRAPH AND LINE SPACING

PowerPoint's line spacing options allows fine control over the space between lines in a paragraph as well as the space before and after a paragraph. To adjust the line-spacing in a text box:

❑ Select the text to adjust and choose **Format | Line Spacing**

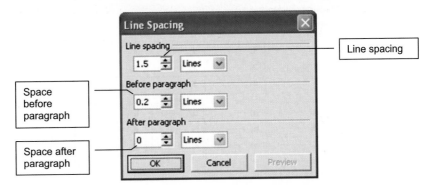

From this window we can adjust the intra-line spacing and the before and after paragraph spacing. A line space setting of 1.5 lines will leave an extra "half line" between each line in a paragraph. We can also control the spacing before and after a paragraph which allows us to accurately control the spacing above and below a paragraph.

❑ Set the line spacing to 2 lines (this will leave a blank line between every line in the paragraph)

❑ Press **OK**

Note: These options usually live in the Format | Paragraph options note the difference here with PowerPoint.

LESSON 6.6.4: BULLETS AND NUMBERING

The bullets and numbering options are normally set globally for the whole presentation and we will see how to do this later – but we can also change the bullet and number styles for our text. To choose a different bullet style:

❑ Select the text to change and choose **Format | Bullets and Numbering**

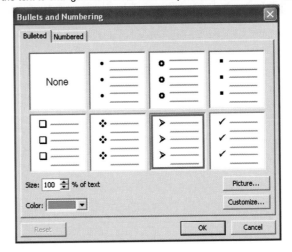

We can choose a different bullet style and adjust the size and colour of our bullets from this window.

To change the number style of our paragraph:

❑ Select the text to change and choose **Bullets and Numbering** from the **Format** menu and click on the **Numbered** tab.

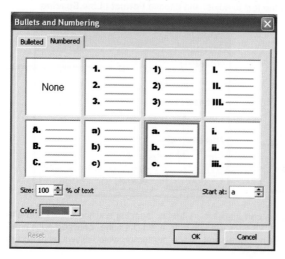

We can change the style of numbering used e.g. **1, 2, 3** or **a, b, c** and also set the starting number for our slide. This is useful if we have to split our points across a number of slides.

LESSON 6.6.5:   THE GRAPHICS TOOLBAR

To work with the graphics toolbar we will need to be in *normal view* mode. To switch to *normal* view,

❑ Go to the **View** menu and choose **Normal**.

All of the *Microsoft Office* applications support a drawing toolbar that allows us to build and work with graphic objects. This toolbar is normally located at the bottom of the screen. If the toolbar is closed, we can open it by going to the **View | Toolbars** menu and choosing **Drawing**.

Let's have a look at the tools it provides

The first tools we've got to learn are the *line, arrow, box* and *circle* tools.

LESSON 6.6.6:   DRAWING BOXES, LINES, CIRCLES AND SQUARES

To draw a line on a slide

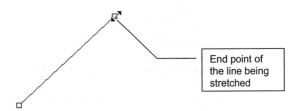

- ❏   Select the *line* tool and click and drag with the mouse.

End point of
the line being
stretched

Notice as we drag with the mouse the mouse pointer changes to a *two-way* arrow.

We can change the angle the line is at by clicking the end point and moving the mouse. As we move the mouse the original line will stay in place until we release the button.

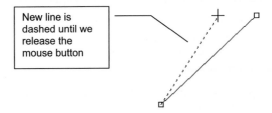

New line is
dashed until we
release the
mouse button

Once we release the mouse button the line is drawn. We can reposition the line at any time by reselecting the end of the line and moving it as before.

We can draw a series of straight lines using this tool to draw simple shapes like this house:

Drawing arrow heads

Use the tool to draw arrows to point at areas on graphs or to highlight points in a presentation.

To change the line end points use the icon on the drawing toolbar.

Line style and thickness

We can change the thickness ▬, style ▦ and the endpoints ⇄ of our lines using these tools.

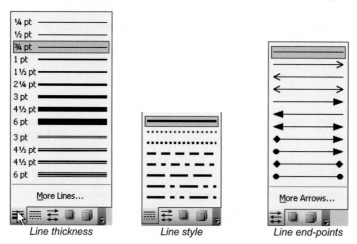

| Line thickness | Line style | Line end-points |

Once the line is selected we can change all its settings by clicking on the option with the mouse.

Here are some sample line styles:

Drawing free form lines

We can use the *scribble* tool to draw free-form lines on a slide.

Scribble tool

Select the tool and then hold down the mouse button whilst moving the mouse on the slide. As the mouse is moved a free-form line can be drawn.

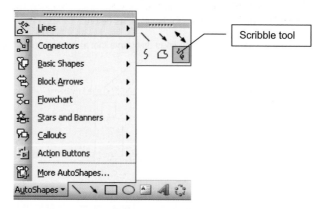

Drawing boxes and circles

The ☐ and ◯ tools let us draw rectangular and circular shapes.

- ❑ First select the tool from the toolbar then click and drag with the mouse to draw the required shape:

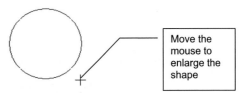

Move the mouse to enlarge the shape

The mouse will change to a cross hair as the shape is drawn.

LESSON 6.6.7:   RESIZING AND MOVING OBJECTS

Circles and other shapes can all be resized by clicking on their drag handle and pulling outwards from the centre of the shape to enlarge it or moving in towards the centre of the shape to shrink it.

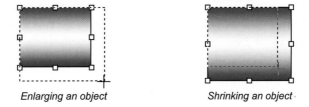

Enlarging an object   *Shrinking an object*

Retaining the objects size proportions when resizing

Hold down the **Shift** key to constrain the proportions of the shape to make a perfect circle or square and to avoid stretching images more in one direction than another.

NOTE: when resizing a photograph it is very important to retain the proportions exactly – otherwise we are likely to create fat or skinny objects in our presentations!

Moving objects and images

We can move an object within a slide by clicking and holding the mouse button and then dragging the object to a new location.

Notice that the mouse changes to a 4 way arrow and an outline box shows where the object will move to.

6
Presentations

LESSON 6.6.8:   ROTATING AND FLIPPING OBJECTS

Sometimes we'll want to rotate an object on our slide – either text or a graphic image. We can use the *rotate* tool to do this:

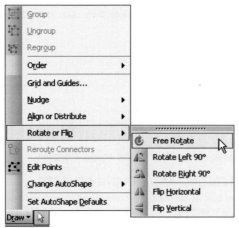

- ❑   Select the shape and then choose **Draw | Rotate or Flip | Free Rotate**

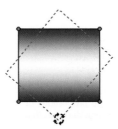

- ❑   Click and hold one of the green edges on the shape and move the mouse. The shape will rotate around the selected edge (or *node*). Release the mouse when the required angle is reached.

Flipping objects

Sometimes it is useful to get the mirror image of an object.

- ❑   Firstly select the shape or object

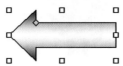

- ❑   Next choose **Flip horizontal** or **Flip vertical** from the **Draw | Rotate or Flip** menu.

Depending on the option chosen we'll create a mirror image of the shape.

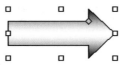

The object created is an *exact* mirror image.

LESSON 6.6.9:   COLOUR SCHEMES

Changing the border or outline colour

We can change the line colour of any shape using the *paintbrush* icon .

> ❑   Select the line and then click the arrow next to the paintbrush tool.

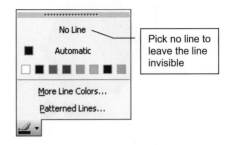

> ❑   Select a colour for the line.

A useful option to note is the *no line* option, which means no outline will be drawn on the shape. Notice the difference with these two circles – one has an outline and the other doesn't – this is achieved using the *no line* option.

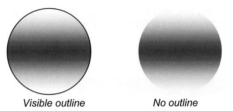

Visible outline   No outline

Filling or colouring shapes

If the shape is closed it can be filled with the currently selected *fill colour*. This can be seen from the

icon on the toolbar. Many of the special effects created on a slide master are created with special fill settings – so it's worth getting to know how to get the most from the fill palette.

> ❑   To change the colour of a shape select it and choose a new colour from the Fill pop up palette.

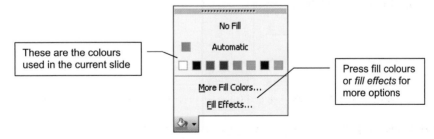

The shape should change colour immediately. PowerPoint gives us access to the small set of colours that are already in use on the slide – but we can pick a different colour.

❏ Click on the **More Fill Colors …** option to show the full colour swatch.

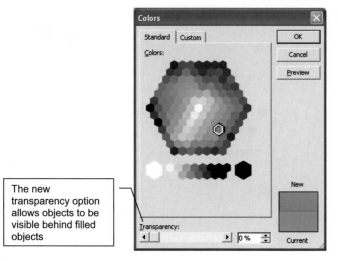

The new transparency option allows objects to be visible behind filled objects

Advanced Fill Effects

Also in the *Fill Effects* dialog box, we can create a *blend* of colours and use special textures to fill the shape. Choose **Fill Effects** and the **Fill Effects** window will appear:

The first tab displays a *gradient* fill – which is a blend between 1 or more colours to create a graduated fill.

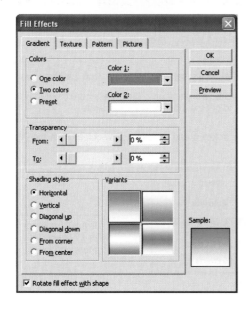

This style is very effective if used as a background for a slide or side panel:

Technology

for

tomorrow

The Gradient fill blends colours

The second tab is the texture tab and it displays a collection of different real-world textures such as wood and marble, which can be used to fill shapes.

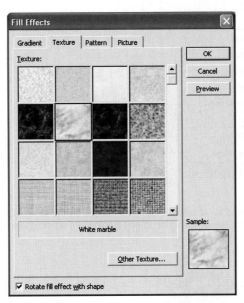

This textured fill can give a completely different style to a slide show

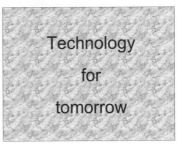

Textured fills give realistic background textures such as marble and wood

The pattern and picture tabs let us use a patterned fill for shapes or to fill a shape with an image.

LESSON 6.6.10: AUTOSHAPES

Microsoft ship a range of useful shapes, which can be used for drawing or highlighting areas on a slide. The auto shapes icon on the drawing toolbar displays several categories of shape we can use.

The shapes are easy to draw – they just need to be selected and then placed on the slide as required. Here is an example of the *rectangular callout* auto shape used to add a voice to a clipart character:

The auto shapes are semi-smart and allow us to move parts of the shape so that it will behave correctly. In the case of the callout above we can drag the *yellow* dot to reposition the start of the speech bubble.

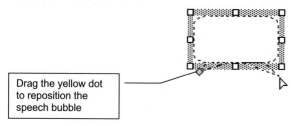

Drag the yellow dot to reposition the speech bubble

The *block arrow* auto shapes are useful for creating simple process flows on our slides. When we fill them with interesting fill styles they look very impressive.

| Marketing | Sales leads | Sales |

There are many different autoshapes to choose from that allow us to create many different types of drawings in our presentations. Experiment with the autoshapes to become familiar with the options.

LESSON 6.6.11: ADDING SHADOWS

We can add depth to our slide objects using the shadow tool . Let's try this with a rectangle.

❑   Draw a green rectangle like the one below.

❑   Make sure the rectangle is selected.

❑   Click on the shadow tool and a whole host of options will appear:

Pick one of the shadow options and view the results.

Shadow added to block

The shadow settings Toolbar allows us to change the colour of the shadow and nudge the shadow in different directions.

Nudge shadow

Shadow colour

Note: Don't mix and match too many different shadows on the same slide or even in the same presentation. Shadows should appear the same direction and be of the same colour in order for the presentation to look consistent.

6

Presentations

LESSON 6.6.12: ADDING A 3D EFFECT

PowerPoint supports a clever tool to help give depth to our graphic drawings.

- ❑ Draw a new square – or select an existing one. Handles will appear around the shape when it is selected like this:

- ❑ Select the 3D tool

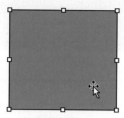

Choose a style for the 3D effect. Here are some of the results with the different settings for our cube. This tool can be an excellent way of building shapes and graphs for our presentations – although it takes time.

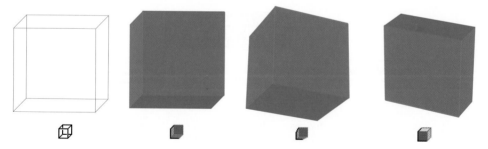

Results of different 3D modes on our original square

Changing 3D Settings

Pressing the [3-D Settings...] option displays the 3D settings toolbar. This allows us to change the lighting and rotation of the 3D object once we've drawn it.

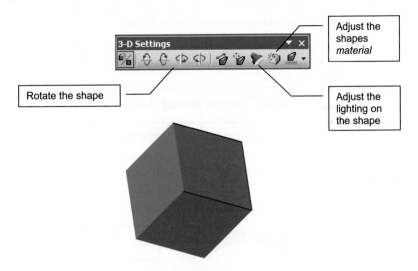

Adjust the shapes *material*

Rotate the shape

Adjust the lighting on the shape

Result of adjusting our "Green, Metal cube"

Select the 3D object and use the rotate, lighting and material options to alter the shapes appearance.

LESSON 6.6.13: WORDART

Sometimes we'll want to add some exotic text to our page – perhaps on the title slide or as a special headline. This is where *word art* is very useful.

❑ To bring up the Word Art dialog box press on the  icon.

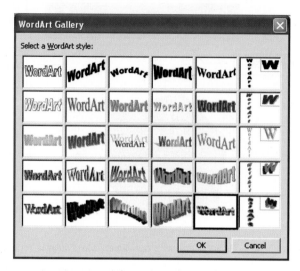

We can see a whole range of different text styles to choose from.

❑ Select one of the styles and click **OK**.

We now need to enter the text we want to appear in this style. We can set the font style, the size and whether the font is bold or italic from this dialog box.

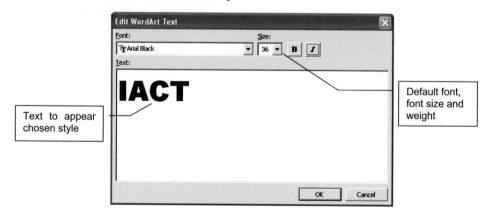

Text to appear chosen style

Default font, font size and weight

Usually one or two lines of text are more than sufficient in this style.

The resulting word art is a graphic that can be stretched and re-sized as required.

www.iactonline.com

Adjusting word art settings.
When the word art graphic is selected we can adjust the text and its settings from the word art toolbar.

We can rotate the text using the 🔄 tool that we used earlier.

- ❑ Select the word art text and then use the rotate tool 🔄 to rotate the graphic

Changing the style of WordArt
After we've created our design – we can change both the text and the style of the text from the word art

toolbar. To change the design of the text click on the *word art gallery icon* 🔲 to edit the style of the word art.

We can change to any of a wide range of different styles.

Different word art options make a big difference to the appearance of text.

LESSON 6.6.14: ADDING MOVIES AND SOUNDS

Video and sound clips can add a lot to a presentation. PowerPoint comes with a range of built in clips that can be useful in spicing up a presentation – or we can also search on the web for suitable files.

❏ Build this slide either in *outline* mode or directly in slide view mode use the design template called "*capsules*"

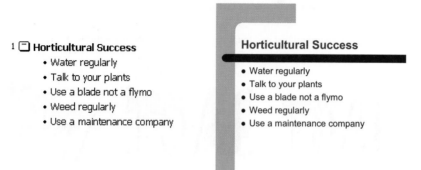

1 ☐ **Horticultural Success**
- Water regularly
- Talk to your plants
- Use a blade not a flymo
- Weed regularly
- Use a maintenance company

We are going to add a movie clip to this slide.

❏ Choose the clipart 🖼 icon from the drawing toolbar and the Clip Art panel will appear.

❏ Select the *Movies* as the media type to view

Type ***Butterfly*** to find all movies that relate to butterfly in the clipart gallery.

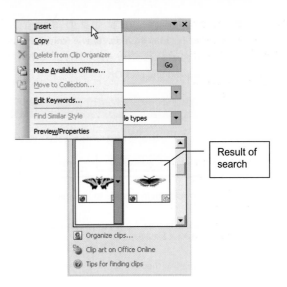

Result of search

□ Select the butterfly and then click the **Insert** button to insert the butterfly into the presentation.

We can reposition the movie clip on the page just like a piece of clipart.

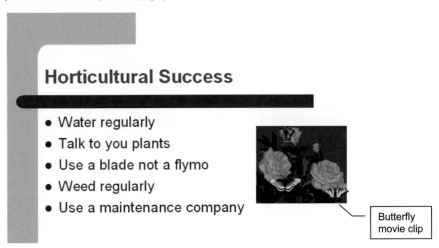

Butterfly movie clip

□ When we view the slide show we'll be able to see the animations in action. Press **F5** to view the presentation and watch the animation.

PowerPoint supports a number of different movie formats including: *animated GIFs, AVI files, and Apple .MOV files*. If we have a digital video camera or another source for creating video files we can insert these files directly.

6

Presentations

To insert a movie into our presentation:

❑   Go to **Insert | Movies and Sounds | Movie from file**

Movie files usually have an extension such as .AVI, .MPG or .MOV

❑   Locate the file to insert and click **OK**

PowerPoint will ask us if we would like the movie to automatically play when the presentation runs.

❑   Click **Automatically** to play the movie when the slide first appears – or **When Clicked** to play the movie when it is clicked.

We can scale a movie – but making them larger than their original size will cause them to look *pixilated* or *grainy*.

We can insert sound files in exactly the same way.

❑   Go to **Insert | Movies and Sounds | Sound from file**

PowerPoint will ask us if we want the file to play automatically when the slide runs the same as when the Movie was inserted. Choose **Automatically** to play the sound when the slide appears.

When a sound is inserted onto a slide a small sound file icon will appear.

If we have chosen to have the sound play only when the icon is clicked we can place it discretely on the slide. We can also reduce the size of the icon so that it is no longer visible or hide it behind another object on the page.

LESSON 6.6.15: IMPORTING DATA ONTO A SLIDE

It is often useful to bring data from a *text file* or a *spreadsheet* into our presentation. The easiest way to do this is to *copy* the information from the source program directly into the presentation. To do this we use the clipboard as our transport mechanism.

❑ Open the application to import from (e.g. *Notepad*) and copy the text to be imported (highlight it and press **Ctrl+C**).

❑ Switch back to the PowerPoint presentation and locate the slide onto which the text is to be imported. Press **Ctrl+V** to paste it into the slide.

Alternatively we can insert other objects into our presentation directly. To insert any object into our presentation:

❑ Choose **Object** from the **Insert** menu.

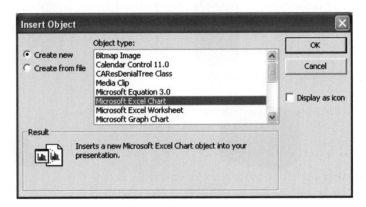

❑ To insert a blank spreadsheet object choose *Microsoft Excel Worksheet* and click **OK**.

or

❑ To import an existing spreadsheet choose **Create from File** and browse to locate the spreadsheet to import.

This technique works with all of the office applications.

EXERCISES TO PROVE YOU KNOW

1. Draw the following shapes onto a slide in a new presentation

2. Rotate the line and the rectangle by 60 degrees.

3. Draw the following using the *AutoShapes* toolbar.

4. Reproduce the following 3D shapes

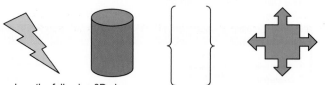

5. Using *WordArt* create the following on a new slide:

IACT ECDL

SECTION 6.7: ARRANGING AND GROUPING OBJECTS

When preparing a presentation or creating a document containing graphics one of the biggest contributors to the *professionalism* of the end result is the alignment and distribution of the shapes on the page – surprisingly this is often overlooked. Also we will find that when we work with many different objects we'll have to learn how to group and ungroup these objects in order to have them work as one.

In this section we will learn how to:

- ❑ Align and distribute shapes or objects on a slide
- ❑ Group and ungroup objects
- ❑ Dismantle and reassemble clipart graphics

LESSON 6.7.1: ALIGNING SHAPES

Look at the following slide. It contains four bulleted paragraphs that were drawn in separate text boxes. They were aligned by hand and although the effect has been amplified here – on a smaller scale the result is still very noticeable.

Antiques all around us

- ◆ Clocks
  - ◆ Tables
    - ◆ Desks
- ◆ Curtains

Items should line up *exactly* along this line

Aligning textboxes, clipart and other shapes is best done using the **Alignment** options in the **Draw** menu - as we cannot trust our 'eye' when aligning shapes.

6

Presentations

To align a number of shapes we have to first *select* them. We can select more than one object by holding down the **Shift** key and clicking with the mouse, on each object individually.

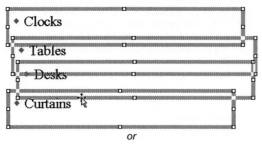

or

❑ Select the text boxes by clicking and dragging with the mouse over the objects creating a *marquee*

The selected objects have their *resize* handles how visible along with a fuzzy border. We want to align these objects along their *left* edges.

❑ Choose **Align or Distribute** from the **Draw** menu on the drawing toolbar.

Notice the Align Left icon:
It shows all the shapes aligned along their left hand side.

❑ Select Align Left from this menu

Once aligned the objects will look like this:

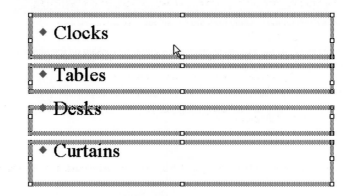

These shapes are now all aligned properly along their left edges.

We can align objects along any edge from left to right or from top to bottom with the different options available in the **Draw | Align or Distribute** menu.

The slide will look much better immediately – but there is one more step we can take to improve the layout – standardising the vertical spacing of the textboxes which we will look at next.

LESSON 6.7.2:   DISTRIBUTING OBJECTS

We distribute objects vertically and horizontally to balance the space between them. We want to distribute these textbox shapes evenly from top to bottom.

❑   Firstly select all the shapes to distribute – either by clicking on the shape and holding down the **Shift** key or using the *marquee* select technique we saw earlier.

Now choose **Distribute Vertically** from the **Draw | Alignment or Distribute** menu.

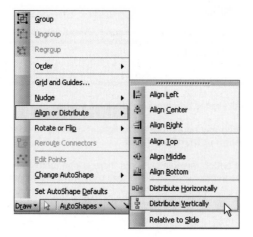

PowerPoint has now equalised the space between all the textboxes on the slide.

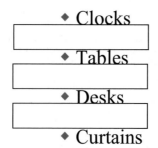

The textboxes are now all equally spaced vertically

Use this technique to ensure objects are properly spaced.

LESSON 6.7.3: GROUPING AND UNGROUPING OBJECTS

When our graphics consist of many different parts – it is particularly useful to be able to *group* and *ungroup* them. When an object is grouped together it moves, scales and rotates as one object. The images in our clipart gallery for example are mainly just a collection of grouped shapes.

Let's ungroup a piece of clipart and see how it is composed – and then reassemble it.

Choose some clipart – we'll use the *lighthouse* from the *buildings* category.

❑   Now select the clipart object and choose **Ungroup** from the **Draw** menu.

As this is a piece of clipart PowerPoint asks us if we want it to convert to a drawing:

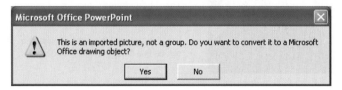

❑   Click **Yes**. Now choose **Ungroup** from the **Draw** menu again.

Clipart prior to ungrouping   *The clipart image showing resize handles for all its composite images.*

To work with this clipart image in all its individual parts would be very difficult and it would be very easy for the image to get distorted. However we *can* now change the individual components of this clipart image – removing, re-colouring or resizing them as we wish.

Let's make a change to this image – we'll remove the *clouds* and the *rock face* that the *lighthouse* sits on and then regroup the image.

6
Presentations

- Firstly – deselect the image by clicking somewhere else on the slide. The sizing handles will disappear.

- Now select the *cloud* graphic image.

Boundaries of the cloud

When we select the cloud image the boundaries of the cloud become visible.

The boundaries are a *bounding box* reaching to the extents of the shape.

We can move the cloud with the mouse, resize the cloud, rotate it or delete it.

- Press **Delete** to delete the cloud.

With the cloud removed we can see the shadow beneath it.

We need to *delete* the shadow as well.

- Select the shadow and press **Delete.**

Repeat this for the rock face.

This should leave us with an image something like this:

The lighthouse now looks like it is floating in the sky!

However we can fix this by adjusting the height of the blue rectangle, which is behind the lighthouse.

LESSON 6.7.4: GROUPING OR RE-GROUPING A SET OF SHAPES

Now that we've finished editing the clipart image – we should regroup it in order to make it easier to move about and to protect it from further changes.

To regroup the image we've got to select all the shapes that make it up.

❑ Use the *marquee* select technique to select all of the shapes (there too many small shapes to select individually – also notice some of the shapes are *behind* other shapes and these may not be selected otherwise).

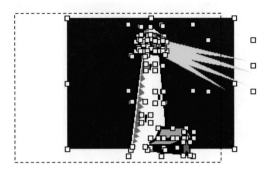

❑ Choose **Group** from the **Draw** menu.

The shape is now grouped and will behave like our original clipart image.

LESSON 6.7.5: CHANGING THE Z-ORDER OF AN OBJECT

When we place an object onto a slide in our presentation, it is rather like placing a piece of paper onto a desk. The next time we add a item to the same slide it must go either on top of or behind the objects which are already there.

If we look at the clipart image we ungrouped earlier we can see it is made up of a number of overlapping shapes. If the order of these shapes is changed – we'll end up with a different image. The example below shows the clouds in front the lighthouse, behind the sky and behind the lighthouse but in front of the sky – 3 very different images.

Clouds in front of lighthouse   *Clouds behind sky (hidden)*   *Clouds behind lighthouse in front of sky*

This happens with all objects we place on our slides – charts, organisational charts, text boxes, graphics, lines and clipart.

The z-order refers to the position *in front of* or *behind* a particular shape or group of shapes.

To change the z-order of an object:

    ❑ Select the object (text box, clipart, chart etc.)

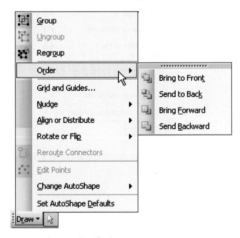

    ❑ From the **Draw** menu choose the **Order** menu

We can change or swap the relative position of the selected shape using the four options provided.

Bring to Front	Bring the current object in front of all other objects
Send to Back	Send current object behind all other objects
Bring forward	Bring current object forward one layer
Send backward	Send current object back one layer

Experiment with these options to become familiar with them.

EXERCISES TO PROVE YOU KNOW

1. Locate and insert the clipart graphic seen below. Use *ungroup* to change the clipart image from **a** to **b**. Re-group the final graphic.

a.

b.

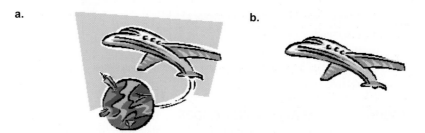

2. Draw three identical circles and a line and align them horizontally like this:

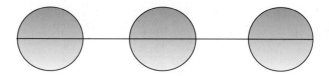

3. Draw 8 boxes and 2 lines and arrange them so that space between them is equal like this. Make every odd box align to the top line and every even box align to the bottom line.

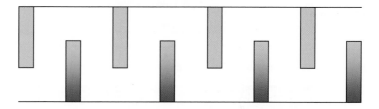

6
Presentations

SECTION 6.8:   POLISHING OUR SLIDES

In this section we'll learn to add special effects to our slides and add notes to our slide handouts. We'll learn to:

- ❏ Work in *slide sorter view* to rearrange slides
- ❏ Add transitions to a slide
- ❏ Hide slides from a presentation
- ❏ View a slide show and annotate and navigate through slides
- ❏ Add notes to a presentation

LESSON 6.8.1:   REARRANGING SLIDES

This easiest way to rearrange our slides is from slide-sorter view. So let's first switch to *slide sorter* view choose – **View | Slide Sorter** or click on the slide sorter icon at the bottom of the PowerPoint window

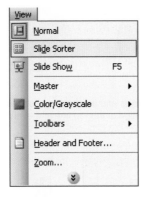

PowerPoint shows miniatures of all the slides in the presentation:

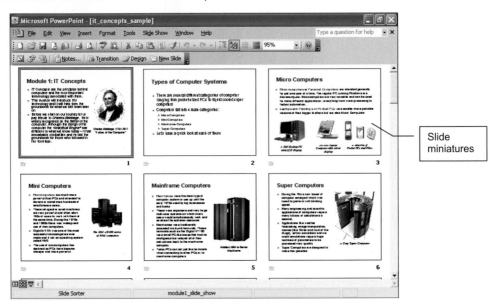

Slide miniatures

Moving and Duplicating Slides

We can change the order of the slides whilst in slide sorter view by dragging the slide to a new location. The mouse will change to a ⬚ symbol indicating that the slide is being moved. Alternatively we can use the *cut* and *paste* tools to move a slide within a presentation. Select the slide and press **Ctrl+X** and then click in the new location for the slide and press **Ctrl+V**.

We can also duplicate the slide in the same way by selecting the slide and pressing **Ctrl+C** and then clicking in the new location for the slide and pressing **Ctrl+V**.

Moving or copying the slide to another presentation

To move or copy the slide to another presentation:

- ❑ Select the slide and press **Ctrl+C** (if copying the slide) or **Ctrl+X** (if moving the slide).
- ❑ Choose the presentation from the **Window** menu or open the presentation by pressing **Ctrl+O** and locating the file in the usual way.
- ❑ Switch the presentation to *Slide Sorter* view and press **Ctrl+V** to paste the slide.

LESSON 6.8.2:   DELETING SLIDES

We can quickly delete a slide or a set of slides from slide-sorter view:

- ❑ Select the slide or slides using the mouse. Hold the **Ctrl** key to select more than one slide.
- ❑ Press **Delete** to delete the slides.

PowerPoint will delete the slides.

LESSON 6.8.3:   HIDING AND UN-HIDING SLIDES

We can hide a slide by pressing the ⬚ icon. This will not delete the slide but hide it so it won't appear when being viewed in slide-show mode.

When a slide is hidden it shows the slide number with a line through it:

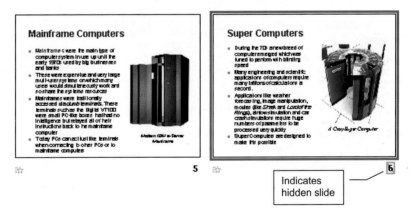

- ❑ To un-hide the slide simply press the ⬚ button again.

LESSON 6.8.4:   SLIDE TRANSITIONS

When we view a slide show on-screen we can add slide *transitions* which change the way individual slides appear. For example – we could have our slides *fading* in on top of each other or *sliding* from left to right. The easiest way to add transitions to a slide is from *Slide Sorter View* – so switch into Slide Sorter view if PowerPoint is not already in this mode.

Let's try this out.

❑   Select the first 3 slides of the **it_concepts_sample.ppt** presentation. We use the mouse to select the slides. Click on the slide whilst holding down the **Ctrl** key – when a slide is clicked for the first time it becomes selected – when we click it again it is de-selected.

❑   Next we press the Transition button.

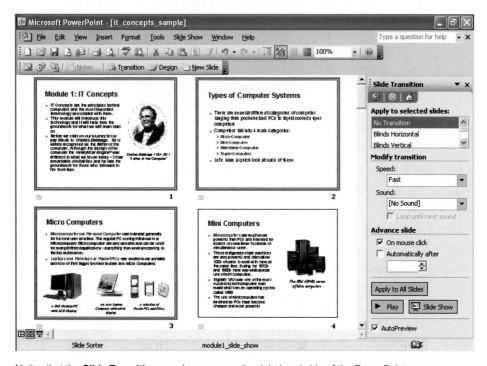

Notice that the **Slide Transition** panel appears on the right hand side of the PowerPoint screen.

Now we can assign a *transition* to the slides.

❑ Select the transition *Checkerboard Across* from the list of transitions.

We can put as many different transitions onto separate slides as we need. PowerPoint will preview the slide transitions so we can see what it looks like when applied.

We can also specify a speed for the transition and a sound that will be played when the transition starts.

❑ Specify *Slow* as the speed and leave the sound option as **[No Sound]**

Note: It is best not to mix too many transition effects in the one presentation – as these can become distracting.

LESSON 6.8.5: VIEWING THE SLIDE SHOW

In order to view the transitions and the slide show on screen we need to *view the show*.

❑   To view the slide show choose **Slide show | View show** or press **F5**

PowerPoint will now display the slides in full screen mode.

We can also start the show at a particular slide

❑   Choose **Slide show | Setup show**

The following options are then available:

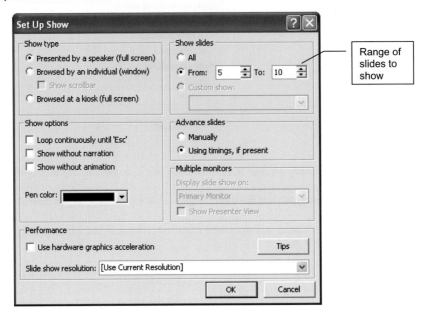

❑   Specify the starting and end slide and press **OK** (the slide show starts on slide 5 and finishes slide 10 in the above dialog).

When we view the presentation it will now start at slide 5 and finish at slide 10.

Whilst in slide show mode:

❑   Pressing the **space** bar, **page down**, or using the **mouse button** will advance the slide show.

❑   Pressing **ESC** will abort the show

❑   Using the **page up** button will return to the previous slide.

LESSON 6.8.6:   ANNOTATING AND NAVIGATING SLIDES

When the slideshow starts we'll notice at the bottom left of the slide there are four feint icons that we didn't put there. They look like this:

These icons allow us to navigate through our presentation and make annotations on the slide during the presentation.

The left and right-pointing arrows allow us to move forwards and backwards a slide at a time. This is the same as using the **Page Up** and **Page Down** keys during the presentation but can be useful if we are using a remote mouse and need to move forwards or backwards through the presentation.

The **Slide Show GO** menu can be displayed by clicking on the  icon.

This menu contains options to allow us to directly navigate to a particular slide in the presentation as well as options to blank the screen and change the pen style.

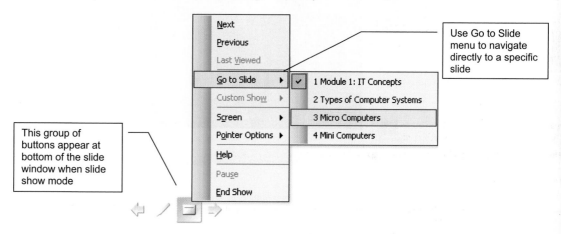

The slide navigator shows a complete list of all the slides and is very handy for quickly moving to that slide.

The **Pen** icon allows us to annotate the slides as we view them or highlight areas on the slide using the mouse like a pen. It can be handy to circle a key point or draw an arrow between items on a slide. If we work with a touch tablet we can even write on the slide!

When we click on the pen tool we can choose the type of pen we want to work with as well as the ink colour.

We can annotate slides whilst in slide view mode

Annotations are usually discarded once the presentation is ended but we can choose to save our annotations and they will be visible the next time the presentation is run.

Spell checking the presentation

Before delivering the presentation, it is crucial to run the spell check application. This tool works the same way as it does in Word and Excel.

❑ Press **F7** to start the spell checker.

Review *Module 3 – Word processing page 190* for additional information on spell checking.

LESSON 6.8.7: ADDING NOTES TO SLIDES

When delivering a presentation we'll often have additional information that won't appear on a slide. Since our slides are usually for guidance we won't have every detail at hand. PowerPoint provides a way of adding some additional information to a slide – without including it on the slide itself. That way if we want we can put special notes against the slide for our own use as we deliver a presentation or we can include extra information when we print out the slides that may be of use to our audience.

To add notes to our page we type into the notes section of the slide – or use the **Notes Page** view. To switch to **Notes Page** view:

❑   Choose **View | Notes Page**

A screen like this will appear that shows a preview of the slide and a text box beneath it. This is the *Notes Page* view and these pages are normally printed A4 portrait in size.

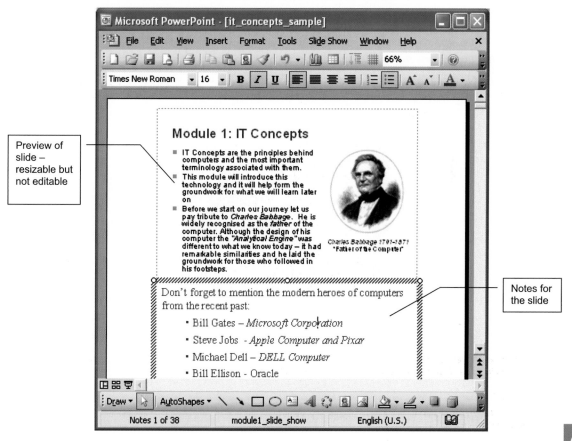

We can add any text we like to the notes page text box. There is a separate notes page for every slide.

When we look at PowerPoint's print options we will learn how to print the notes pages as handouts for our presentation.

EXERCISES TO PROVE YOU KNOW

1. Open the *Brazil.ppt* created earlier. Using the slide sorter view, hide slides 3 and 4.

2. View the presentation to ensure that the slides are hidden.

3. Unhide slide number 3.

4. Go to slide 2 and add the following to the *notes* for that slide:

   > **Remember to get up and walk around at this point. Leave the slide on view on screen and ask questions.**

5. In slide sorter view, add the transition effect *Cover Down* to all slides in the presentation Brazil. Add the transition effect *Cover Up* to the first slide only.

6. Check the spelling of the presentation.

7. Run the slide show from slide number 1. From slide 1 navigate directly to slide 4. Turn on the pen, change the colour of the pen to red and draw a red line under the title.

8. End the slide show without continuing to the other slides.

SECTION 6.9: PRINTING AND PUBLISHING

PowerPoint has many ways of printing and publishing our presentation depending on our audience and their requirements.

In this section we will:

- ❏ Learn about the different print options available in PowerPoint
- ❏ Publish our presentation to a web site
- ❏ Use PowerPoint's help system

LESSON 6.9.1: PRINTING A PRESENTATION

Printing a presentation is easy – once we are familiar with the options.

PowerPoint lets us print:

- ❏ Slides
- ❏ Note pages (slides with the notes attached)
- ❏ Handout pages (multiple slides per page)
- ❏ The Slide outline

Choose **Print** from the **File** menu to bring up the print dialog box:

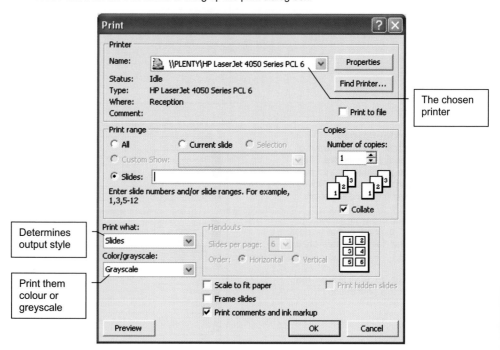

The options available here are very similar to the standard print dialog box but they also allow us to choose the style of the item we want to print.

Overleaf we can see the results of printing with these different output style options.

Printing – Single Slides

When we choose to print just the slide either in black and white or full colour a complete copy of the slide and its contents will be printed taking as much room as possible on the page itself.

This style of printing is best printed in *landscape* mode to avoid lots of blank space on the page. Notice the printer can rarely print to the very edge of the paper.

Sample printed A4 landscape black and white slide

Printing - Note pages

Notes pages include the slide at the top of the page and notes associated with that slide at the bottom.

This style of printout can be used to allow the reader of the presentation to add additional information to each slide – or to allow the presenter to include extra notes for themselves or their audience.

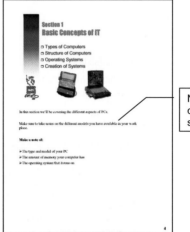

Notes view of same slide on an A4 page

Printing - Handout pages

This is the most common way of handing out long presentations. The slides are quite readable at this size and viewers don't have to keep flicking the page each time the slide changes.

This suits presenters who go through many slides in a short period – not those who speak for 60minutes on a single slide.

We can print up to 9 slides on the same page with this print option.

Handout pages showing 3 slides per page

Printing- Slide outline

Choosing to print the slide outline will print the textual content of each slide – which can be useful for the presenter as a summary of the presentation.

Slide outline view

Slide orientation and output format

We can change the slide orientation and output format.

❑ Choose **File | Page Setup**.

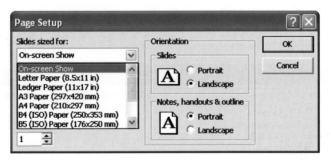

From here we can change slides from portrait to landscape orientation and change the slide sizes to suit different paper and output formats for example 35mm slides, overheads or on-screen slide shows.

6
Presentations

LESSON 6.9.2: PUBLISHING A PRESENTATION TO THE WEB

It is now becoming popular to publish a presentation to the web to allow the broadcasting and archiving of presentations.

PowerPoint has a wizard that makes this straightforward.

❑ To save a presentation for web access, choose **Save as Web Page** from the **File** menu.

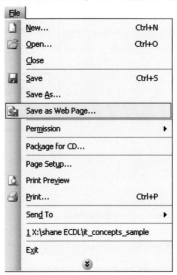

PowerPoint shows us a *save dialog* where it asks us to specify the location for all the published files. PowerPoint will need to create many separate files in order to publish the presentation.

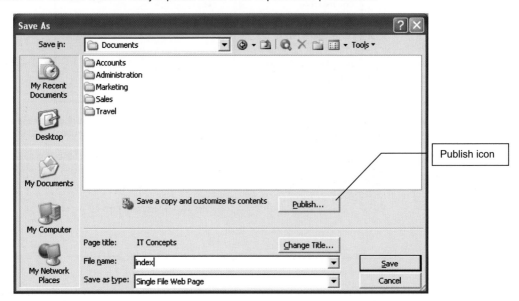

We can change the settings that *PowerPoint* uses to publish the web site by clicking the *publish* icon.

❑ Click on the **Publish** button.

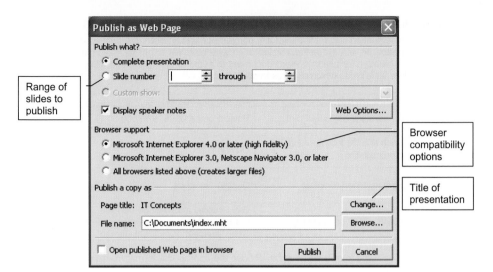

We can now change the publishing settings. We can publish part of a presentation by specifying a range of slides to include and specify the browser options for publishing. Once the settings are correct:

❑   Choose **Publish** to publish the presentation as a web site.

After a few moments the web pages are created. To view the pages – open them in the *Internet Explorer* and they should be laid out something like this:

Preview of the presentation in Internet Explorer

We can now view the presentation from wherever the published files are available – if we published to our *intranet* everyone within our company will be able to view the presentation – if we published to a public web site – everyone on the *web* will be able to see it!

LESSON 6.9.3:   SAVING POWERPOINT INTO ALTERNATIVE FILE FORMATS

There are many situations where it is useful to convert our presentation into a different format for use in another application or with an earlier version of PowerPoint. We might for example want to save the text of our presentation for use in a Word document to avoid re-typing the text. PowerPoint supports a variety of different file types which allow us to do this.

Format to save in	Option to choose
Earlier versions of PowerPoint	PowerPoint 4.0, 95, 97-2000
As a *rich text file* for importing into word-processors	Outline/RTF
As a presentation template	Design Template
As a .GIF, .PNG or .BMP files	GIF Graphic Interchange Format PNG Portable Network Graphics Format BMP Device Independent Bitmap

When we choose **Save** from the **File** menu choose the appropriate format from the *save as type* drop down list.

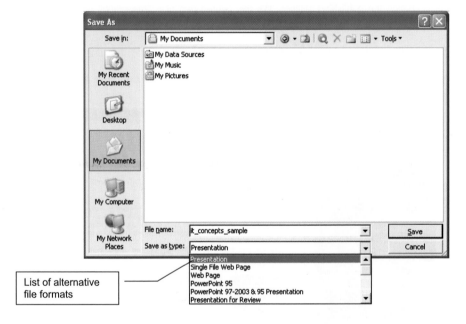

List of alternative
file formats

When we press **Save** PowerPoint will save the file in the new format requested.

LESSON 6.9.4: CHANGING POWERPOINT'S DEFAULTS

We can change the defaults that PowerPoint uses when saving files. These defaults include the default directory that our presentation is saved to and the default directory used when PowerPoint tries to open a presentation. We can also change the default username assigned to the presentation – useful when trying to identify who originally created the presentation and when sharing presentations.

To change these defaults

  ❑ Choose **Tools | Options** and click on the **Save** tab

  ❑ Change the location files are opened or saved from by changing the *default file location*

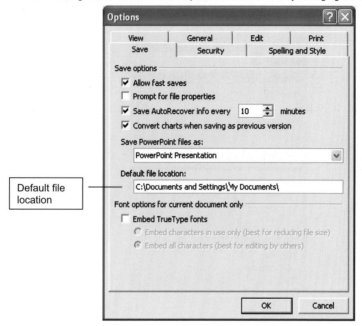

To change the default **Username**

  ❑ Click on the **General** tab and fill in the *User Information*

  ❑ When these settings are correct press **OK**

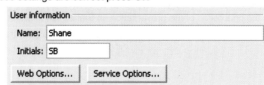

LESSON 6.9.6: USING THE HELP TOOL

One of the most useful facilities offered by Windows is its *Help* utility. Most Windows products come with excellent help facilities usually containing as much if not more information than the accompanying reference guides. The help system uses a technique called "hypertext" to access information relating to a particular topic. This system allows the reader to follow a *thread* through the help database, constantly looking up and referring to related information.

LESSON 6.9.7: USING THE HELP FUNCTION

Help can be started in PowerPoint by pressing **F1** or choosing **Microsoft PowerPoint Help** from the **Help** menu.

This will display the Microsoft PowerPoint help panel:

We can search for help on any feature in PowerPoint – including all the formulae and functions. The help feature in *Microsoft PowerPoint* works exactly the same as it does in *Microsoft Word*. Review Using Help on *page 257.*

EXERCISES TO PROVE YOU KNOW

1. Open the *Brazil.ppt* presentation created earlier and print it in the following ways:

   a) Print the presentation one slide per page in pure *black and white* with framed slides

   b) Print slides 1 and 3 only, one slide per page

   c) Print the notes pages for all slides in the presentation

   d) Print handouts with 3 per page and 6 per page

2. Change the orientation of the presentation so that all slides are seen in portrait.

3. Publish the presentation to the web, save it as *web1.htm*. View this in a browser.

SECTION 6.10:   EXAM OVERVIEW AND TIPS

In the exam for *Module 6, Presentations*, you will be given a floppy disk which will have all the files that you will need to answer the 2 sections. Be sure to hand the disk up at the end of the exam.

There are 2 sections in the presentations module. The first section has 15 questions and is worth 15 marks. Section 2 is the same. All areas in the module can be tested.

Points to Note:

- Time allowed: 45 minutes
- Answer both sections
- Marking System
    - Each section has 15 marks awarded to it – total of 30 marks.

About the Sections
Section 1
Here you will be asked to start on a blank new presentation. Be sure that you are able to:

- Insert slides
- Format slide layout
- Insert text
- Format bullets
- Insert images and resize/move images
- Insert Org Charts
- Insert tables
- Insert graphs
- Headers and Footers
- Print slide settings

Section 2
Here you will be asked to work with a presentation that already exists. Be sure that you are able to:

- Delete slides
- Move slides
- Edit slides
- Change slide layout
- Change Headers and Footers

All of the topics covered in this Module could be asked in the exam.

For sample examinations visit **http://www.iactonline.com/ecdl**

Module 7
INFORMATION
& COMMUNICATION

iact

The complete IT training provider

MODULE 7: INFORMATION AND COMMUNICATION

The *World Wide Web* – WWW officially came into being in 1991, thanks to developer *Tim Berners-Lee* and others at the *Conseil Européenne pour la Recherche Nucléaire* (CERN). The CERN team created the protocol based on hypertext that makes it possible to connect content on the Web with hyperlinks. Berners-Lee now directs the *World Wide Web Consortium* (W3C), a group of industry and university representatives that oversees the standards of Web technology.

Tim Berners-Lee
one of founders of
WWW

The web is one of the most widely used and important parts of the Internet. It is possible to find out just about anything from the huge repositories of data that live and can be accessed through a web browser.

We can buy practically anything on the web and shop around to get a good deal. Music companies, film and game studios are starting to distribute their music, films and games via the web. Before long broadband (or high-speed) Internet connectivity will mean we will all have TV quality movies on demand through the Internet from anywhere in the world. We may think that we use the web and the Internet extensively at the moment – but within a few years we won't know what we did without it.

E-mail is still the main application of the Internet. It has subtly invaded the way we work and replaced traditional post and courier delivered messages. It allows us a way of contacting people as they travel, sending messages, photographs even movies and sounds anywhere in the world. E-mail knows no borders and can travel thousands of miles in seconds carrying with it our messages, presentations and other attachments. E-mail is also remarkably cheap – with the costs of sending a message once the equipment is purchased a tiny fraction of traditional mailing costs.

We have become so reliant on e-mail that some of us can't leave our desks without it! Mobile hand-held computers can now pick up our e-mail messages while we are on the move, or transfer them via text messages to our mobile phones. Web-based e-mail systems like *Hotmail* allow us to retrieve our mail from anywhere we can get Internet access – no matter where we are or what type of PC we are using.

Every age group has adopted e-mail as a reliable way of communicating. There is even a subtle language of abbreviations and shortcuts that pervade the messages we receive. Who knows what our messages will look like in a couple of years time.

In this module we'll learn about the Internet and its history and how to send and receive e-mail messages from our computers.

SECTION 7.1:   THE INTERNET AND WWW

In this section we will learn

- ❏ A brief History of the Internet and the WWW
- ❏ How to connect to the Internet
- ❏ How to navigate with a web browser and follow links
- ❏ How to open a specific web site
- ❏ How to use the browser *history*

LESSON 7.1.1:   BRIEF HISTORY OF THE INTERNET

The *U.S. Department of Defence* laid the foundation of the Internet roughly 30 years ago with a network called *ARPANET*. Most of us didn't get to use the Internet much until after the development of the **World Wide Web** in the early 1990s and in fact as recently as June 1993, there were only 130 Web sites in the whole world! Now there are millions.

In 1957, the U.S. government formed the *Advanced Research Projects Agency* (ARPA), a segment of the *Department of Defence* and charged it with ensuring U.S. leadership in science and technology with military applications. In 1969, ARPA established ARPANET, the forerunner of the Internet.

Research and education
ARPANET was a network that connected computers at the *University of California at Los Angeles*, the *University of California at Santa Barbara*, *Stanford Research Institute*, and the *University of Utah*. Within a couple of years, several other educational and research institutions joined the network.

In response to the threat of nuclear attack, ARPANET was designed to allow continued communication if one or more sites were destroyed. Unlike today, when millions of people have access to the Internet from home, work, or their public library, ARPANET served only computer professionals, engineers, and scientists who knew their way around its complex workings.

Evolution
Throughout the 1970s, developers created the protocols used to transfer information over the Internet. By the early 1980s, Usenet newsgroups and electronic mail had been born. Most users were affiliated with universities, although libraries had also begun to connect their catalogues to the Internet. During the late 1980s, developers created indices, such as *Archie* and the *Wide Area Information Server* (WAIS), to keep track of the information on the Internet – these were the forerunners to the modern search engines. To give users a friendly, easy-to-use interface to work with, the University of Minnesota created its Gopher, a simple menu system for accessing files, in 1991.

Early on, the Internet was limited to non-commercial uses because its backbone was provided largely by the *National Science Foundation*, *NSA*, and the *U.S. Department of Energy* whose funding came from the US Government. But as independent networks began to spring up, users could access commercial Web sites without using the government-funded network. By the end of 1992, the first commercial online service provider, *Delphi*, offered full Internet access to its subscribers, and several other providers followed.

In June 1993, the Web boasted just 130 sites. By a year later, the number had risen to nearly 3,000. In April 1998, there were more than 2.2 million sites on the Web today there are millions more.

No one authority controls the *World Wide Web*. Today's Web site authoring tools allow virtually anyone who has access to a computer and the Internet to post to a Web site and contribute to the definition of what this medium is and what it can do. However The *World Wide Web Consortium* oversees the development of Web technology and provides guidelines for future developments.

The Browser Wars

There was strong competitive rivalry between *Microsoft* and *Netscape* with the creation of commercial tools to browse the web. This battle ultimately lead to an anti-trust lawsuit against *Microsoft*. The battle now appears to have ended – however the race to bring ever more powerful features, security and flexibility to the browsers has lead to fantastic improvements in technology in a very short space of time.

Jim Clarke
Founder of Netscape

Bill Gates[†]
CEO and Founder of Microsoft

Netscape®

Both Netscape Navigator and Internet Explorer offer very similar features – for users familiar with *Microsoft* products such as *Word* and *Excel* – *Internet Explorer* is probably more familiar. However *Netscape Navigator* does provide a pleasant alternative and some unique features. Both camps have their avid supporters who will never switch – but for the rest of us it doesn't make too much difference so long as we can browse the web.

The web itself is an excellent source of information on its history – check out:

http://dir.yahoo.com/Computers_and_Internet/History/

or do a search for "History of the Internet" on the search engine **www.google.com**

The Internet and the world-wide-web

It is important to be able to distinguish between the *Internet* and the *World Wide Web*.

The **Internet** is the *physical network* of millions of computers around the world. The Internet supports many different uses – including e-mail and the world-wide-web.

The **World Wide Web** (www) consists of *millions of web pages* located across this network of computers that can be accessed through a web browser.

[†] Bill Gates is the World's richest man but also the World's greatest ever philanthropist donating hundreds of *millions* of dollars to charities particularly those in Africa.

LESSON 7.1.2: CONNECTING TO THE INTERNET

If this is the first time our computer has connected to the Internet we need to configure its Internet connection settings. Most of us connect to the Internet via some form of *modem* but many businesses connect via their LAN.

The Internet configuration process may have been completed automatically by the installation software provided by the **ISP** (*Internet service provider*) or a company's IT department. If Windows determines that it cannot connect to the Internet it will start the **New Connection Wizard** which will walk us through the process.

The wizard starts like this:

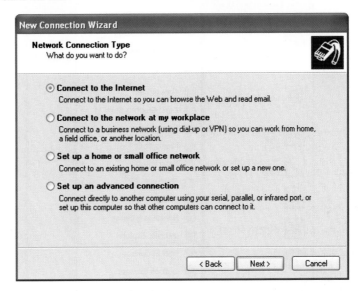

The wizard is pretty automatic – but we have to answer a couple of questions in order to sign up.

To gain Internet access our ISP provides a *username* and a *password*. When we dialup we are connecting directly to this ISP. The ISP then routes our requests for web pages around the world sending them back once they are retrieved.

Once connected to the Internet we can start browsing web pages, sending e-mails, video conferencing, make long distance phones calls and much more. Let's get started.

LESSON 7.1.3:   OPENING A WEB BROWSER

To start surfing the web – we must first open up a web *browser.* Let's open up the *Internet Explorer* web browser:

❑   Go to the **Start** menu and choose **All Programs** and click on **Internet Explorer**.

Similarly to start *Netscape Navigator* or any other browser application locate its icon and click on it.

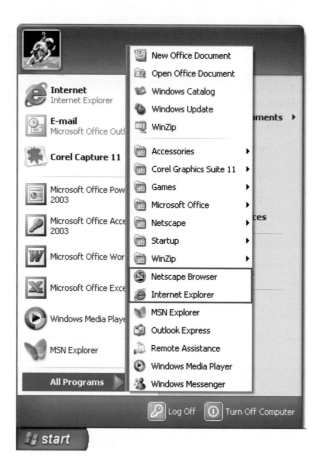

Alternatively locate either of these icons on the Desktop and double-click on them.

After a few moments the browser window will appear – and the default *Home* page should load.

LESSON 7.1.4:   WEB BROWSERS

In order to view the Internet we need a browser. There are two main browsers – *Internet Explorer* (from Microsoft) and *Netscape Navigator* (from Netscape). These are often referred to just as *Explorer* and *Navigator*. Web sites should look much the same in either browser – and both support similar features. Here is the IACT site opened in both Explorer and Navigator.

Navigator's default toolbar

The current URL or web address

http://www.iactonline.com open in *Netscape Navigator*

Explorer's default toolbar

The current URL or web address

The same page open in *Internet Explorer*

Touring the Browser

Let's have a look at the browser's features and at how they work.

The most important parts of the browser are:

- ❑ The page area where the web page will be displayed
- ❑ The toolbar and menu bar for controlling the program
- ❑ The address bar indicating which web page or web site we are viewing

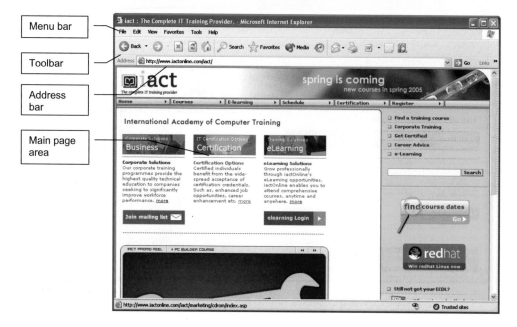

To open or close these toolbars:

- ❑ Go to the **View | Toolbars** menu and ensure that the *standard toolbar* and the *Address Bar* are open.

Getting Help

The browser's **Help** menu contains information on common issues with browsing the web and configuring the browser.

- ❑ To start help press **F1**.

The help tool works the same as in the Office applications - refer to page 257 for information on using Help.

Closing the browser

To close the browser:

- ❑ Choose **Close** from the **File** menu.

Explorer's Toolbar buttons

The buttons on the *Internet Explorer* toolbar are fairly intuitive – especially with the text showing. Think of these buttons as allowing us to browse the pages of books in a huge library. Explorer's toolbar usually looks like this:

Here is an overview of what each button does:

The **Back** button makes the browser return to the previous page (if there was one). This is like switching to the previous page of a book.

Once you've returned to a previous page we can move forward again using the **Forward** button.

Press the **Stop** button to abort the downloading of a web page. When the browser is busy and the stop button is available it will be coloured RED.

Refresh the page if the contents are out of date or if it didn't finish downloading (either through some interference or through a bad connection).

The **Home** page is the start-up page we first see when we connect to the Internet. We can set the start-up home page to be any page we regularly visit. ISPs usually set this to default to their own home pages.

Use the **Search** icon to start up Microsoft's search tool. This allows us to search the web for items, solutions and people. We'll look at how to best use this later.

The **Favourites** icon brings up shortcuts to regularly visited websites. Once configured correctly this can make visiting our *favourite* site quicker and more convenient.

The Media icon brings up the Windows Media player to allow us to play music and videos available on the Internet or on our computer.

The **History** icon displays the most recently visited pages during the last few hours, days or even weeks depending on its configuration.

The **Mail** icon will start up our e-mail programme and allow us to send and receive e-mail messages.

The **Print** icon will print the contents of the current web page.

The **Edit** icon allows us to import the current webpage into Microsoft Word or another Web page editing tool for editing or updating.

The **Discuss** button opens a discussions toolbar in Internet Explorer that will allow you to discuss the topic in question with other interested users (if supported by the website).

The **Research** button opens the *Research Panel* to allows us to search reference books and the Internet for items of interest.

LESSON 7.1.5: THE ADDRESS BAR AND URLS

The web is made up of millions of inter-connected web sites. Each web site has a default *home page* – which is the page we see first when we visit a web site.

We can open a web page directly once we know the *Web Address* or *location* of the page. The web address is given by a **URL** – a *Uniform Resource Locator* - a reference that tells the computer how to access the page from any computer connected to the Internet.

A webpage's address is located below the main toolbar. If the address bar is not showing we can turn it on as follows:

    ❑   Choose **View | Toolbars** and check that the *Address Bar* option is ticked.

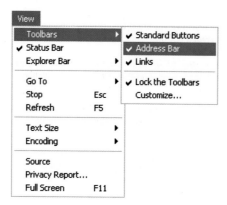

The address toolbar looks like this:

URLs – Uniform Resource Locators
The location of a web page will usually start with **http://** however we can usually omit it. HTTP stands for *HyperText Transfer Protocol*.

So the location or URL (*Uniform Resource Locator*) for **google** is:

                http://www.google.co.uk

but

                www.google.co.uk

will also work.

The structure of a web address

A web address or URL consists of 3 parts.

Part 1: http://www	Nearly all web sites will start with **http://www** indicating that it is a web address. The **http://** can usually be omitted.
Part 2: *Domain Name*	The web sites domain is usually the company or product name. For example Virgin Airlines use **VIRGIN** as their domain. BBC use **BBC** and so on. Most companies will try to use the most obvious domain name for their web site or product. Good domains are usually short and don't contain unusual characters such as hyphens.
Part 3: *Suffix or global domain*	The suffix usually indicates the type of organisation or web site using the address (e.g. *Government* or *Academic*) or it may indicate the country hosting the web site or both. The suffix **.GOV** represents government agencies in the US. The suffix **.CO.UK** indicates companies in the UK. The suffix **.IE** indicates limited companies based in Ireland. For a complete list of top level domains visit **http://www.iana.org/cctld/cctld-whois.htm** The most common and sought after suffix is **.COM** (commercial) which originated on American sites but is the first suffix to try for any domain. **.COM** domains usually represent international companies. Recent additions which are becoming popular include **.INFO**, **.TV** and **.BIZ**

Here are some more web addresses that may be of interest:

www.microsoft.com	*Microsoft's Homepage – an enormous website with huge amounts of useful resources for your PC.*
www.cnn.com	*CNNs Homepage – check up the World news and watch video clips on the excellent site.*
www.nasdaq.com	*Nasdaq's Homepage – check the value of stocks and shares on the Nasdaq market.*
www.virgin.net	*Virgin's Home Page*
www.cam.ac.uk	*Cambridge University's Homepage*
www.whitehouse.gov	*The White House – the official site for the President of the United States.*
www.crystalmedia.ie	*Crystal media's home page – converting multiple formats including VHS and cine to DVD*
www.iplanit.tv	*IPLANIT develop professional web sites for businesses and provide hosting*
www.iactonline.com	*IACT's classroom and online training site – details of all our courses as well as access to our e-Learning system.*

LESSON 7.1.6:   OPENING A WEB PAGE URL DIRECTLY

To open a web page directly we type its web address or URL directly into the address bar. Let's have a look at the Nasdaq homepage:

- ❑   Click into the *address* toolbar
- ❑   Type **http://www.nasdaq.com** into the text box and click **Go** or press **Enter**

Internet Explorer will now attempt to establish a link to the site location and open the page.

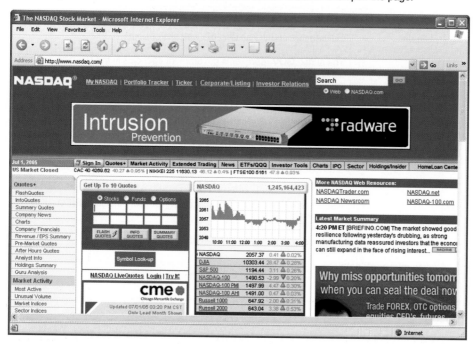

The Nasdaq home page opened in the browser

Recall that the web site address is often called a **URL** – (short for *Uniform Resource Locator*)

After a few seconds the homepage for *NASDAQ.COM* should appear and look something like the page above.

LESSON 7.1.7: SETTING OUR DEFAULT HOME PAGE

A default home page is the page that our web browser will open up automatically at start-up and when

we press the Home button 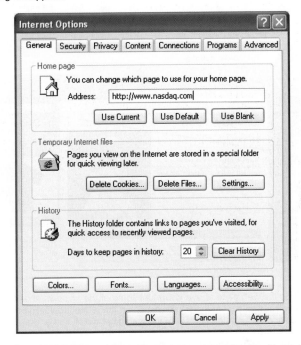 on the standard toolbar.

To set the default home page

      ❑   Choose **Tools | Internet Options**.

The following dialog will appear:

From here we can change the address of the home page to any valid web address. This page will then appear whenever the home icon is clicked and when we first connect to the Internet.

Press **Use Current** to set the current web page as the *default* home page.

LESSON 7.1.8: NAVIGATING THE WEB

Web browsers provide a revolutionary way to view information. Using a technology called *Hypertext*[†] web pages can be browsed or navigated using just the mouse. Web pages are linked together by *hyperlinks* – clickable text or graphic areas that lead to related pages. Hyperlinks are links to related topics within a web site or on a completely different web site. Hyperlinks usually consist of underlined text or graphic images.

Here some examples of hyperlinks on the Wimbledon home page **http://www.wimbledon.org**

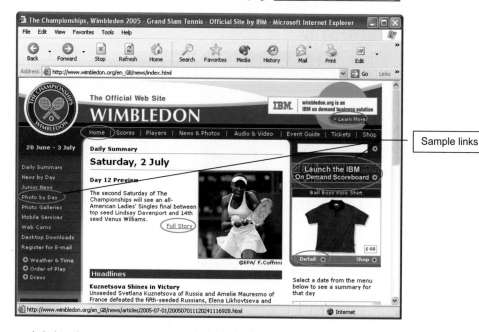

The areas circled on the web page above show just some of the *Hyperlinks* on this web page. Clicking any of these links will navigate us to more information on the related topic. Hyperlinks can be images or text – and it is usually clear from the context of the web page which text or graphics are 'clickable'.

By hovering with the mouse over a text or graphic area the mouse pointer will change to a *hand* symbol if the text or graphic is a link:

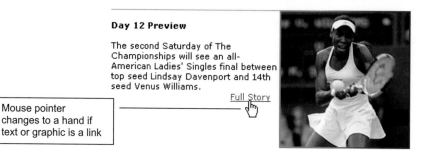

Visit the www.wimbledon.org website and follow some of the links from the home page.

When we click on a link our browser will follow the link and open up the linked page in the browser. Press the **Back** button to return to the previous page.

[†] The term *"hypertext"* was coined by *Ted Nelson* in 1965 but credit for the invention of the "Hypertext Markup Language" (HTML) on which the web is based goes to *Tim Berners-Lee*.

LESSON 7.1.9:   OPENING A LINK IN A NEW WINDOW

Sometimes we will want to keep our current window whilst we follow a link in another window (Netscape Navigator conveniently lets us open a new "tab" with the same results).

To open a new window and follow a hyperlink:

❑   Right-click on the hyperlink to display a pop up menu

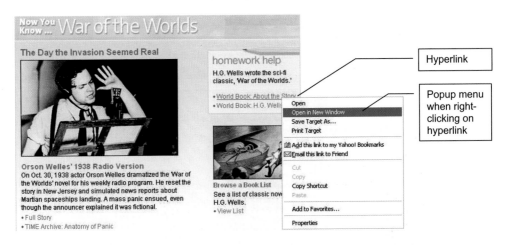

❑   Click **Open in New Window** to follow the link in a new window.

Internet Explorer will open the link in a new window and leave the current window open.

We can also copy the current web page in a new window:

❑   Choose **File | New | Window** or press **Ctrl+N.**

A new browser window will open with the current web page in it.

LESSON 7.1.11: NAVIGATING WITH THE BROWSER

As we navigate the web our web browser keeps track of the pages that we visit. This way if we found an interesting site and surfed to a new location we can always find our way back.

Internet Explorer has several ways to help us return to previously visited web pages. Let's look at the most common first.

Navigating with the Address bar
To display the list of previously visited web pages:

❑   Click on the down arrow on the browser address bar.

Internet Explorer shows a list of the most recently visited web pages and we can quickly navigate to any of these pages by choosing the website address from the list.

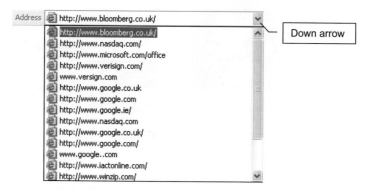

Navigating with the Back and Forward buttons
To move to the previous webpage that we had visited:

❑   Use the **Back** button on the browser toolbar. Each time we press the back button the browser returns to the previous page.

❑   Use the **Forward** icons to move forwards and backwards through the links.

Pressing the down arrow next to the Forward or Back buttons reveals the full *back* or *forward* history. We can jump directly to a web page by choosing an item from the list.

Navigating with the History Panel

Internet Explorer keeps a track of all the web pages we visit in the browser's history. We can use the browser's History panel to navigate to any webpages that we have visited.

To display the history panel:

❏ Press the 🧭 History button on the tool bar

The history panel will open in the browser showing recently visited web pages.

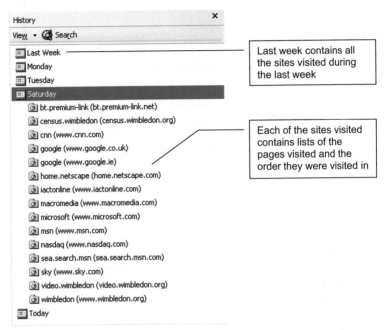

Last week contains all the sites visited during the last week

Each of the sites visited contains lists of the pages visited and the order they were visited in

The contents of the history panel are dependent on the sites that have been visited by the user over the last number of days and weeks.

By clicking on the page in the history panel we can go straight to the page in the browser. The history of all the sites or web pages that we visit is automatically created by the browser.

LESSON 7.1.12: CONFIGURING BROWSER HISTORY

The default browser history lasts for 20 days. To clear the history, shorten it or lengthen it:

    ❑   Go to the **Tools** menu and choose **Internet Options**.

We can change the number of days the browser holds in its history by changing the "Days to keep pages in history" property.

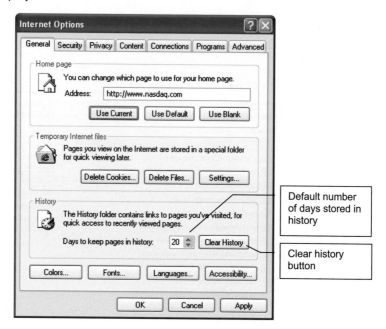

To clear the history and erase the details of all visited pages:

    ❑   Click on the **Clear History** button.

LESSON 7.1.13: PRINTING AND PREVIEWING A WEB PAGE

Just as with our other applications – we will often find that we wish to print the contents of a web page to keep as reference or as a receipt (in the case of airline tickets and other purchases). Printing a web page is very similar to printing from any other application in Windows – but due to the nature of the design of web pages we have some additional options.

To print a web page:

❑ Open the page to print and press **Ctrl + P** or choose **File | Print**

The options for adjusting page margins and printing a range of pages or the current page are identical to other applications. Review *Lesson 2.5.4:Page setup and Printing* on *page 135* for more details.

Printing pages made up of *frames*

Some web pages are made up of separate frames of information. We can usually identify these types of web pages as they may have a scrolling area in more than one part of the screen when we make the browser window smaller. With these types of web pages we can use the settings in the *options* tab to determine how we would like the web page printed:

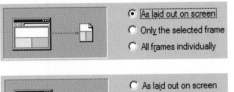

This setting will print the web page exactly as displayed on screen. Occasionally this can make the printout difficult to read with large blank areas.

To print just one frame – select some text or a graphic in the frame and choose this option.

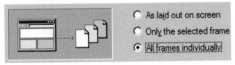

To print each frame individually on separate pages choose this option.

Previewing a web page

To preview a web page before it is printed:

❑ Choose **File | Print Preview**

From here we can adjust print settings directly or return to **Page setup** mode and adjust them from there.

Adjusting web page margins

We can adjust the margins of our web pages from the **Page setup** window.

❑ Choose **File | Page Setup**

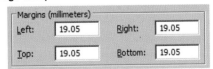

❑ Enter the values for the top, bottom, left and right margins and press **OK.**

To review other print options see *Page setup and Printing* on *page 135*.

LESSON 7.1.14: BROWSER VIEW OPTIONS

Hiding or showing web images

Some web pages are made up of many images which may take quite some time to download. To speed up our web page browsing – if it is just the text on the page that we want - we can choose to avoid this delay by turning off the web page images. Our web browser then just shows us the text on each web page and uses a marker for where the images would appear.

To turn *on* or *off* the images:

      ❑   Go to **Tools | Internet Options**

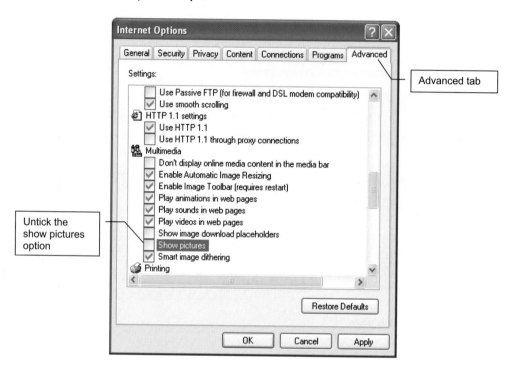

      ❑   Choose the **Advanced** tab and turn off the *show pictures* option.

In this option there are other **Display Modes** that we can turn on and off. This list is worth reading through to see the options available.

Hiding or showing Explorer's toolbars

Like most modern applications we can modify the **Internet Explorer** toolbar display – adding or removing buttons as required. To customise the toolbar:

❑ Choose **View | Toolbars | Customise...** or right-click on the toolbar area and choose **Customize...**

Internet Explorer brings up the following window, which allows us to add and remove buttons from the toolbar.

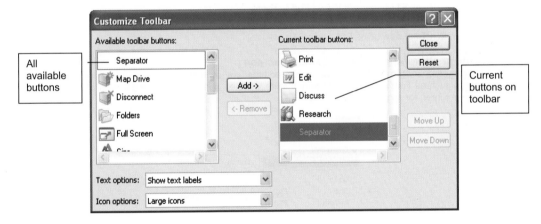

❑ Select toolbar buttons from the left hand window and click on the ⌐Add -> ⌐ button to add them to the toolbar.

❑ Select toolbar buttons from the right-hand window and then click on the ⌐<- Remove⌐ button to remove a button from the current toolbar.

We can use the **Text Options** combo box to show or hide text labels under or beside each of our toolbar buttons.

We can use the **Icon Options** button to increase or decrease the size of the icons on the toolbar.

Increasing the text font size in the browser

We can enlarge the font size on our web pages by setting the **Text Size** from the **View** menu.

This is a useful way of enlarging the text on all sites that we browse.

Working in Full Screen Mode

A useful technique for browsing large web sites is to switch the browser into **Full Screen** mode. In this mode the browser maximises the use of the screen. To put the browser into full screen mode:

> ❏   Press **F11** or choose **View | Full Screen**.

To return to normal view press **F11** again.

Hiding or showing parts of the Explorer screen

We can use options in the **Explorer Bar** menu to hide or show features that we commonly use. These features such as *Favourites* or the *History* feature will then appear in the sidebar area of our Internet Explorer screen for easy access.

Turn on and off the different Explorer bar areas using these options.

LESSON 7.1.15: SAVING AND RE-OPENING A WEBPAGE

Sometimes when we visit a web page we will want to save the contents to use again later. Internet Explorer lets us save a webpage onto our local PC – and then view it again while offline.

To save a web page:

❑ Navigate to the page we wish to save

❑ Choose **File | Save**.

Internet Explorer lets us save a web page in a number of different formats – depending on what we plan to do with the web page. The options are available from a drop-down list:

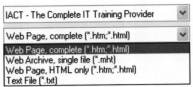

This table outlines what each option means and when we might use that option.

Web page, complete (*.htm, *.html)	Saving with this option will save the web page and all the images on the page into a sub-folder. If we want to save all the graphics on a web page as well as the text this is the option to choose.
Web Archive, single file (*.mht)	Saving with this option conveniently creates a single file that represents everything on the current web page. This avoids creating lots of separate files for one page.
Web Page .HTML only (*.htm, *.html)	This saves just the HTML that makes up the web page. We might do this if we didn't care for the graphics or wanted to view the HTML.
Text File (*.txt)	This saves just the text on the web page in a plain text format which can be viewed in Notepad or Word. If we want to remove any formatting from the web page this is the option to use.

❑ Choose the most appropriate option (probably **.HTM** or **.MHT**) and press **Save**

The saved page can then be viewed from within a browser whenever required:

To open a previously saved page in our browser:

❑ Choose **File | Open** and press **Browse** to locate the web page to open.

❑ When the file is located press **OK**.

Internet Explorer will display the saved page in the browser window.

LESSON 7.1.16: COPYING TEXT, GRAPHICS AND LINKS FROM A WEB PAGE

Sometimes we will just want to copy part of a web page without saving the entire page. We can do this using the clipboard.

To copy text, graphics or a URL from a page:

- ❏ Select the text, graphics or the URL to copy

The text and graphics will remain highlighted

- ❏ Right-click on the selected area and choose **Copy**

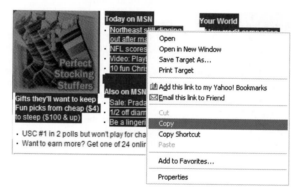

Once on the clipboard the contents can be pasted into a Word document, an Excel Spreadsheet or a PowerPoint presentation in the same way.

We'll paste into Word.

- ❏ Open *Microsoft Word* and place the cursor on a blank line

- ❏ Choose **Edit | Paste,** press **Ctrl + V** or choose paste 🖻 from the standard toolbar.

The text and graphics will then appear in Word with most of the formatting intact.

EXERCISES TO PROVE YOU KNOW

1. Draw a time-line showing the evolution of the Internet and the world wide web.

2. Open the URL www.iactonline.com and save the home page to the Desktop.

3. Open the URL www.nasdaq.com and copy the home page into a new Word document.

4. What do the following domain suffixes represent:

   a) **.COM** b) **.GOV** c) **.CO.UK** d) **.IE** e) **.NET**

5. Set www.iactonline.com as the default home page in the browser.

6. What do each of these icons on the Explorer toolbar do?

SECTION 7.2:   WEBPAGE BOOKMARKS

As we browse the web we'll come across many different web sites. We might wish to return to these sites or sometimes to a particular page in the site in the future.

Rather than writing down the URL (which is sometimes very long and therefore error-prone) Explorer provides us with a way of recording the sites we've visited and filing them under an appropriate category so that we can return quickly later on.

Explorer lets us do this using *Favourites*. Favourites are also known as *Bookmarks*.

In this section we will learn how to:

- ❑   View the bookmarks in our browser
- ❑   Create a new bookmark for a web page
- ❑   Organise our bookmarks into folders

LESSON 7.2.1:   VIEWING OUR BOOKMARKS

When we install Explorer it creates some default links to commonly visited sites.

- ❑   To view the links click on the Favorites button. This will display a new panel at the side of the browser.

Favourites are usually organised into folders which in turn contain additional links to other web pages. So we know when we are searching for a particular page we can start by looking in the right folder.

We can create, rename and update these bookmark folders easily – much as we created folders for our documents and spreadsheets earlier.

LESSON 7.2.2:   CREATING A BOOKMARK

To create a bookmark we must first open the web page we wish to bookmark in the browser.   Let's bookmark http://www.cnn.com

- ❑   Go to this web site by typing in the following URL:

- ❑   Press **Enter** and the CNN site appears in the browser window.
- ❑   Click on the *Favourites* button on the standard toolbar.
- ❑   Now click on the 🔖 Add... button to add it to the list of favourites.

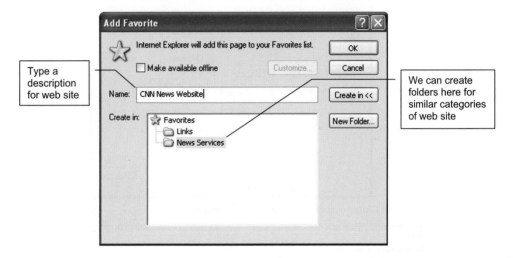

- ❑   Type a description for the site into the *Name* text box – type "CNN News Website".

This doesn't have to be the name of the site – but it should help you remember what the site is about.

- ❑   Press **OK**

The new site will now appear in our list of favourites.

Displaying a bookmarked web page

We can now quickly return to the *CNN* page by clicking on our link in favourites.

LESSON 7.2.3: GROUPING OUR BOOKMARKS

As we visit more sites and create more bookmarks we need a way to categorise and organise them in an easy to follow manner. We do this in a similar way to the way we create folders and sub-folders in Windows. Review Section 2 on *File Management* to gain more information on the principles involved.

❑ To organise the favourites click on the 🗂 Organize... button or choose *Organize* from the *Favourites* menu.

Let's create a new category for our links called "News Services"

❑ Click on **Create Folder** and type "News Services" into the folder icon when it appears

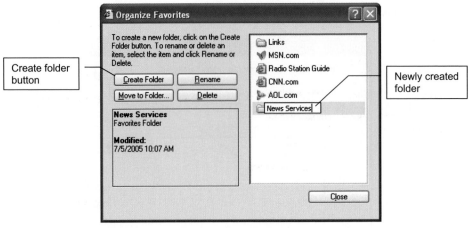

❑ Press **Close** to close the Organize Favourites window.

We can create as many categories as we need – we can even create sub-categories.

Moving a Link to a Folder
Once the folder has been created we can move our *CNN News Website* link into the folder.

❑ Click on Organize 🗂 Organize... if the *Organize Favourites* Window is not open.

❑ Select the *CNN News Website* link and press the **Move to Folder** button

A new window appears showing the current folders or categories of links

❑ Select the *News Services* folder and click **OK**

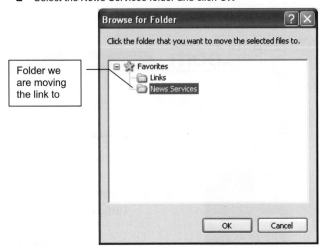

Our link has now moved inside the News Services folder.

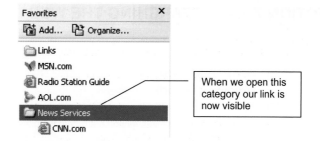

When we open this category our link is now visible

We can create as many links and categories as we need to keep tabs on the websites we regularly visit or found of interest.

Deleting a bookmark
To delete a bookmark

❑   Click on the [Organize...] button or choose **Organize** from the **Favourites** menu.

❑   Select the bookmark and press **Delete**

The bookmark is now deleted.

EXERCISES TO PROVE YOU KNOW

1.   Visit www.microsoft.com and www.ibm.com to create a bookmark for each URL

2.   Create a bookmark folder called *Industry Giants* and place the Microsoft and IBM bookmarks into the folder.

3.   Visit the IBM website by going to the IBM bookmark.

4.   Visit **www.cnn.com** and **http://www.sky.com/skynews/** and bookmark both websites.

5.   Create a bookmark folder called *News* and place the CNN and Sky websites into the News folder.

6.   Delete the *Industry Giants* bookmark folder

SECTION 7.3: SEARCHING THE WEB

In this section we will learn to:

- Search for web pages
- Search for photographs and images
- Search for a friend or business contact
- Search for a map to find a monument or famous place
- Learn about dedicated search engines
- Use a *search engine* to look for information

LESSON 7.3.1: SEARCHING WITH THE BROWSER

Microsoft includes a search icon on the toolbar 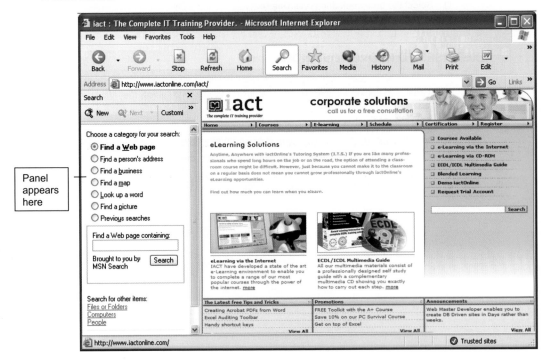 Search which causes a search panel to appear in the browser window.

Panel appears here

This is a convenient way of quickly searching the Internet and it allows us to search for:

- Web pages
- People
- Businesses
- Maps
- Words and Pictures

Let's try this out.

❑   Click on the search icon

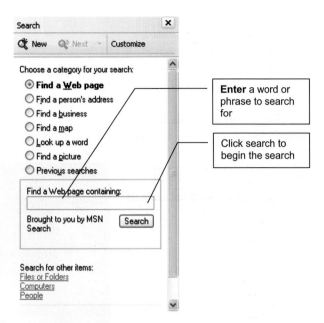

Let's suppose we are interested in photographs or information about the movie "The Matrix"

❑   Type "The Matrix" into the text box and press **Enter** or click **Search**

After a couple of seconds a screen like will appear showing matches for our search. This list is ranked based on finding the most likely page to meet our search.

The first link is to page called **The Matrix – Official Site** - this looks promising...

Note: Search engine results will change constantly – if you try out this search now you may experience different results.

Viewing the results of the search

❑   To visit the site just click on the link.

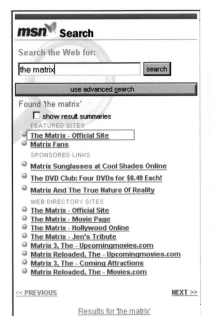

The site located with the search tool was the official matrix site from Warner brothers – we're not always this lucky though!

There are many other links, in fact our search could have turned up thousands of links – to web sites ranging from fan clubs to companies selling the DVD.

Note: The more specific we can be about the information we are looking for the better our search results will be.

Once we have finished searching we can close the search panel and use our browser normally.

LESSON 7.3.2: SEARCHING FOR A PERSON

When we move about it's easy to lose track of people. Friends from old neighbourhoods, schoolmates even distant relations in far off countries sometimes need to be tracked down!

There are search engines to help locate people by location, by their e-mail address or just by their name. The **Yahoo** search engine has a powerful tool to search by name, e-mail and even phone number. The US have the best facilities for helping us search for individuals as most of their phone directories are available online.

Let's see if we can locate someone using the website http://people.yahoo.com

❑ Open the site by pointing the browser to **people.yahoo.com**

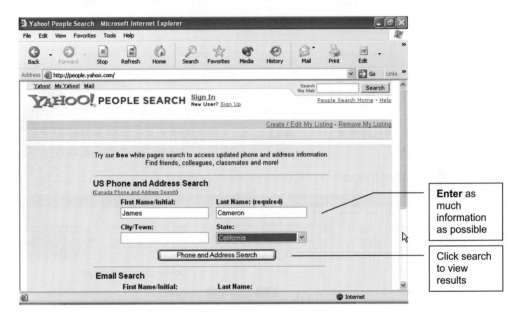

❑ Enter as much information as is known about the person being searched for and click on the **Phone and Address Search** button.

After a couple of seconds the following page will appear:

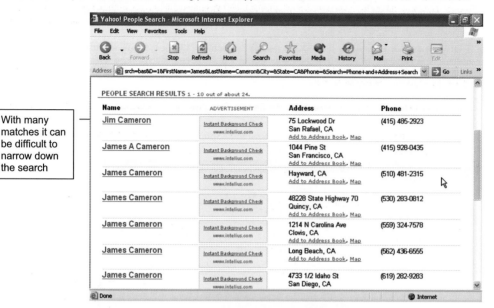

With many matches it can be difficult to narrow down the search

In the UK http://www.192.com is a good location to search for people

The Following Websites are also worth checking out:

- ❑ **www.missing-you.net**
- ❑ **www.bt.co.uk/phonenetuk/**

And there are many other search engines to try.

Remember just as we might be trying to find someone – so too someone might be trying to find us. If we register with the search engines we will make their job easier. All of the search engines have a login option to allow us to register with them and include our details – that way someone looking for us on this service will be able to find us.

Searching for a landmark

When travelling or visiting a foreign country – what could be more convenient than an easy way of getting a map to a famous landmark?

We can search for a *map* using the Microsoft search tool. Let's search for a map leading us to the *Eiffel Tower*.

❑ Click **find a map** and choose **Place or landmark** from list of things to search for

❑ Type **Eiffel Tower** and press **Enter**

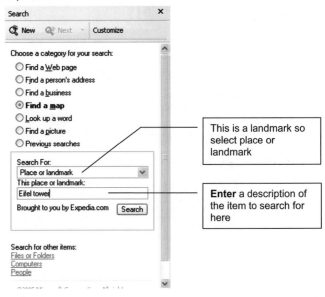

This search returns the *Expedia* web site showing a map of Paris and the location of the Eiffel tower!

Results of the search:

LESSON 7.3.3:   WORKING WITH THE ALTA VISTA SEARCH ENGINE

Let's suppose we want to search for information on the paint package **Corel DRAW!** using the *AltaVista* search engine.

- ❑ Firstly open the browser at *Alta Vista's* home page by pointing the browser to **www.altavista.com**
- ❑ Type **Corel Draw Training** into the search box.
- ❑ Now press the **FIND** button.

After a couple of seconds a page like the following will appear:

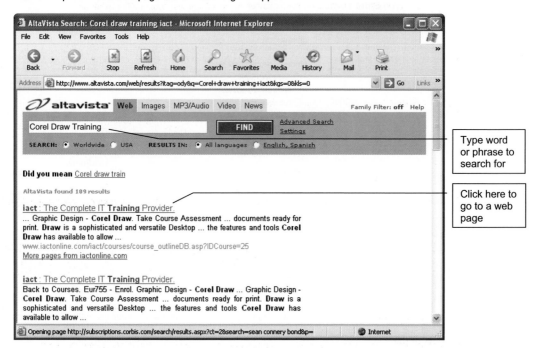

A list of sites with related information on them will be displayed. Depending on how specific our search was we may get some sites with very little information on them. In our case we now have a list of places we can visit to try and find out more about our *Corel DRAW!* package.

- ❑ To move to a particular site simply press on any of the hypertext links (underlined in blue).

LESSON 7.3.4:   COMBINING SEARCH CRITERIA

In *Module 5 – Databases* (page 397), we introduced *George Boole* and his logical operators. We can use these same operators with search engines to help narrow down the list of matches for our search and attain more accurate results.

Most search engines support these logical operators and they allow us to write more complex queries for the search engine database. The following syntax is understood by most search engines automatically or under their *advanced* search option.

+	This operator means **AND** so the word must be included in the list of returned sites for a successful match.
-	This operator means **NOT** so the word or phrase must not appear in matching sites.

For example entering **+Python –Monty** as the search criteria will require the search engine to display all sites about *pythons* but omit those contain the word *Monty* (from the TV series). For example the default search for **Python** on Alta vista:

Resulted in 43,975 matches.

By using logical operators to more specifically match sites and remove those relating to "Monty Python"

Resulted in 28,785 matches.

By further specifying that the word 'Snake' must appear in the results the list is further reduced.

Resulted in 3,211 matches.

By combining these logical operators in our search we can more precisely define what we are looking for and get better results from our search.

LESSON 7.3.5: WORKING WITH THE GOOGLE SEARCH ENGINE

Google is by far the most popular search engine today. We can use it to search for answers to common questions as well as images, news and much more. It is tremendously powerful but still very easy to use.

Let's use **Google** to find a photograph. We're going to try to find a picture of *Sean Connery* as *James Bond 007.*

- ❑ From the browser open the URL **www.google.com** and click on the *images* category
- ❑ Type "Sean Connery Bond" and press **Enter** or click on **Search**

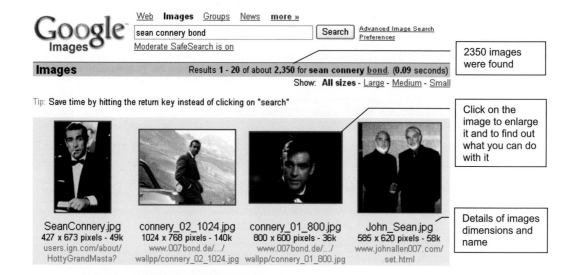

In usually less than a second a new page will appear with images matching our description. We can enlarge or zoom in on the images by clicking on them.

This search found 2,350 images on the Internet for "Sean Connery Bond" and displays the most relevant images first.

Images on the web are seldom free. However they can often be e-mailed and used for personal use without a charge.

Other search engines

There are many dedicated search engines with specific uses. Although Microsoft's built-in search feature is convenient it is important not to forget these other tools. The Internet is enormous and to help us find our way around - search engines index sites and attempt to measure the relevance of a site by looking for *keywords*.

To successfully search the web we must refine our search and use the best keywords and search engines we can find. Remember a search engine is just a tool to let us explore databases containing the text and links from hundreds of millions of web pages.

Other Search Engines

There are thousands of different search engines to choose from – including many specialist sites. For general web browsing here is a list of the most important search engines:

The main search engines		What they do best
Google	(www.google.com)	Very good easy to use general search engine
Yahoo	(www.yahoo.com)	The most detailed web directory, a good choice for exploring a subject and the web
Alta Vista	(www.altavista.com)	Great at obscure facts and phrases
Excite	(www.excite.com)	Current news articles and travel information
HotBot	(www.hotbot.com)	Search for multimedia files and locate websites by location
Lycos	(www.lycos.com)	Good web site reviews, good multimedia searching

Here are a few tips for successful web searches:

- ❏ Pick the right search engine
- ❏ Choose unique keywords:
- ❏ *"Monet AND Renoir"* is better than *"impressionists AND painters"*
- ❏ Type in lower case
- ❏ Consider the source of the information
- ❏ Once you have located your site add it to your list of favourites

EXERCISES TO PROVE YOU KNOW

1. Use the Google search engine to lookup information on the following topics:
    a) Water purification
    b) Making beer
    c) Saturn
    d) Jaguar XJ8
    e) Your company, college or school

2. Find a picture of the following people on the web and copy the image into a Word document:
    a) Sean Connery
    b) Robert Dinero
    c) Michelle Pfeiffer
    d) Britney Spears

3. Find a map of Dublin, Ireland and locate St. Stephen's Green south.

4. Visit www.microsoft.com and using the built-in search engine – search for *PowerPoint Templates and graphics*

SECTION 7.4:   DOWNLOADING FILES

The web contains millions of resources that can be invaluable. These include documents, tools, utilities and other software programs that can be accessed from web pages or directly via FTP[†] (File Transfer Protocol) sites.

Many features on websites require access to *plugins* or *applets* that allow additional features not built into the browser to work (*Flash* is one of the most widely used plugins). In order to access these plugins and in order to get the most from browsing the web we need to be able to download files from the Internet.

In this section we will look at:

- ❑   Downloading a file
- ❑   Installing a downloaded program file

LESSON 7.4.1:   DOWNLOADING FILES

Downloading (or saving) a file from the Internet is very easy – we might even have already done it by accident! Sometimes when we click on a link in a web page – *Internet Explorer* will ask us what we would like to do with the file – *open it or save it*? If we choose to *Save* the file we are in fact *downloading it*. Depending on the size of a file it could take a couple of seconds or several hours to download.

Downloading text, image, sound, video or PDF files
We will download a file from the IACT website.

- ❑   Go to the URL **www.iactonline.com/ecdl/trial_exams**

A web page with links to other files appears:

- ❑   Right-click on one of the **Download Files** links and choose **Save Target As...**

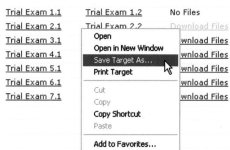

- ❑   Choose a location to save the file to and give it an appropriate name and press **Save**

After a few seconds the file will be downloaded and saved to the location specified. We can repeat the exact same steps to download any other type of file on the web.

We can download an image file, a sound file, a video file, an Adobe Acrobat PDF file, or a program file in the same way. Be careful where you source files to download however. Not all sources on the Internet are legitimate and be aware that downloading files might put you at risk of installing a Virus or breaking copyright law.

Here are some good locations to look for sample files to download:

For **MP3** sound files	www.apple.com/itunes
For sample **Video** files and movie clips	www.windowsmedia.com
For Acrobat reader and **PDF** files	www.adobe.com
For **images** and graphics	www.corbis.com

[†] *FTP sites are like remote directories where companies and individuals copy and download files. When we create web sites we usually use the FTP protocol to transfer our local web pages onto the remote web server computer.*

LESSON 7.4.2:   DOWNLOADING A PROGRAM FILE

We are going to download a file that lets us view video in our browser. This particular program is from the company **Real Networks** whose web site is ***www.real.com***

Usually when we try to access files that need a plugin, a message will appear requesting that we download it, or a message will appear asking us to save the file.

The *real player* is one such plugin that gives us access to streaming media files like radio, music, video and other movies.

Let's have a look at the site **http://www.real.com**. *Real.com* have regular show cases and include live broadcasts from programs such as **Big Brother** and **MTV**. To view these broadcasts though we need the *real player* plugin. The *realplayer* is a tool to allow us to view streaming media files. This player comes in different flavours – the most exotic costs about $19.99 but there are free ones we can use too.

When we try to connect to the site and view one of the media files – unless we have the *plugin* to view the files nothing will happen.

Therefore, we will need to download and install this player. Currently visiting **http://www.real.com** and following the **download** links will lead us to a page something like this:

Filling in an online form
In order to be able to download the software – **Real Networks** require us to register with them as users of the product. Web pages that request information from us are called *Interactive forms*. To buy anything online and use any of a web-pages' interactive features we usually need to fill in a form.

Fill out this form to download free RealPlayer

E-mail: fred.flinstone@hotmail.com

Country: Ireland

1. Windows 2000

2. English

3. 56 kbps modem

4. **Step-up to** <u>SPINNER</u> **reliability and start enjoying pure digital music streaming over the Internet today!** Listen to 140+ exclusive non-stop channels and instantly match your mood. Rock, Jazz, Classical, World.

☐ Bundle SPINNER with my free RealPlayer. (Available with English only) *Spinner activation is FREE and easy. Windows only.*

Spinner comes with RealPlayer 8 Basic Complete Download, which also includes RealJukebox and RealDownload.

5. ☑ Notify me of important news about RealNetworks consumer products and special offers. (Note: GoldPass Subscribers will receive e-mail notices about GoldPass services even if this box is not checked.)

Download FREE RealPlayer Basic

Privacy guarantee: We will not sell, rent or give away your e-mail address or personal information without your consent.

Fill in the details requested and press the **Download Free RealPlayer Basic** button.

Sometimes we are asked where we wish to download the file from. Pick the closest location to you – this will normally be the fastest place to download from.

When the player starts to download we will be requested for a location to save the file.

It's a good idea to create a folder to save our downloads to – that way we can find them the next time we need them.

We are going to save our *RealPlayer* program into the **c:\downloads** directory.

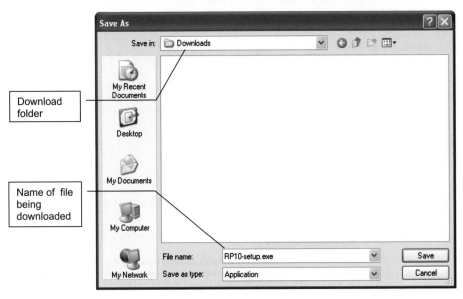

Download folder

Name of file being downloaded

❏ Click **Save** to download the file into this folder.

Plugins tend to be large so expect to wait for the download to complete. As it is downloading we should see the following screen:

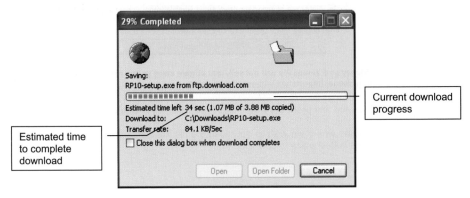

Estimated time to complete download

Current download progress

We can continue to browse the web as the file is downloading – but this may slow the download process.

LESSON 7.4.3:   INSTALLING A DOWNLOADED FILE

Once a program file has downloaded, we need to install it. To do this we run the downloaded program.

In our case we are going to run the file just downloaded to the **c:\downloads** folder.

❑   Go to the **Start** menu and choose **Run**

❑   Click browse and locate the **c:\download\rp10-setup.exe** file just downloaded
❑   Now click **OK** and follow the instructions onscreen.

If everything went smoothly we'll now have access to our streaming video and sound files.

Other plugins
There are many useful plugins to install to get the most from the web – some of these plugins may already be installed on your PC. However, you may find the following are very useful:

❑   *Adobe Acrobat Reader* – available from www.adobe.com
❑   *Macromedia Flash Player* – available from www.macromedia.com
❑   *Macromedia Shockwave Player* – available from www.macromedia.com
❑   *Real Player* – available from www.real.com
❑   *Microsoft Media Player* – (if not on your PC) from www.windowsmedia.com

Note: Be careful downloading plugins from sources other than trusted software manufacturers (the likes of *Microsoft, Adobe, Macromedia* etc.) as they are an easy way to contract a Virus.

EXERCISES TO PROVE YOU KNOW

1.   Visit the following sites and follow the links to download the corresponding files:

www.real.com   Free real player plugin

www.adobe.com   Free acrobat reader

www.winZip.com   Trial version of WinZip

www.macromedia.com   Trial version of Macromedia Flash

2.   Install the WinZip utility and check it works ok.

SECTION 7.5: SECURITY

When we access information from the Internet or send and receive e-mail messages we are doing so over a public shared network. It is possible that our actions on a site could be monitored and information sent from our computer to a remote computer could be spied on illegally. Most of the time this probably doesn't matter too much – but sometimes – particularly when carrying out financial transactions or accessing sensitive information it can be very important.

In order to help combat this problem programmers have developed ways to help secure the Internet. In this section we will look at the techniques that are used to help make our online transactions safe.

LESSON 7.5.1: PROTECTED WEBSITES

Usually when we visit a web site we are able to browse throughout the site without restriction. Companies can often use their websites to help distribute information to staff, partners and distributors in a more controlled way – so that the information does not get into the public domain. Sites that provide services that allow us to upload and record sensitive information also require a way of restricting access and protecting our information.

Protected websites usually require a *username* and a *password* to login.

On Microsoft's sites and those using Microsoft technology we will often see a *Sign In* button. On other sites there may be an option for a member to login.

When we click on the *Sign In* button we are taken to a secure section of the site where we can enter a username and password to allow us to access our private section of the site.

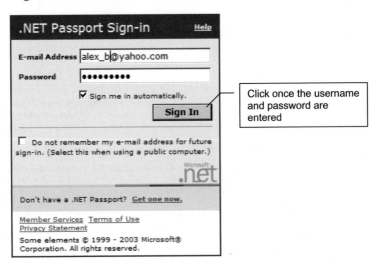

When we send passwords, credit card details and other sensitive information over the web we should do so over a *secure* connection. It is the responsibility of the web site owner to ensure the security is available – but it is our responsibility to check that it is present.

Encryption

Secure connections *encrypt* the information sent and received between our computer and the web server we are connected to. *Encryption* is a technique for encoding data in a way that should only be readable by those with the correct *key*. Different levels of encryption exist – 56bit encryption is the weakest – with 1024bit being viewed as very secure. When secure information is being sent we should see a small lock symbol 🔒 in the status bar of the browser – this indicates that the information sent from our computer is encrypted and is being sent securely over the Internet.

Double-clicking on the lock will identify the authentication and security details of the site we are sending information to:

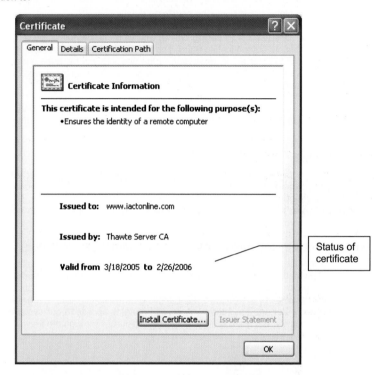

Status of certificate

The presence of the security symbol and the corresponding digital certificate helps us verify that the site is secure and run by a legal company. Be aware that there are fraudulent websites that will try to capture credit card and other details from you by deception. Hundreds of millions of pounds, euro and dollars are lost this way each year.

Digital Certificates

The security lock symbol 🔒 in the Explorer status bar indicates that there is a *digital certificate* associated with the site we are visiting and that the information sent and received to this part of the site is secure. A digital certificate is issued to companies or individuals to help verify who they are. Several companies can issue digital certificates – *Verisign* and *Thawte* are two of the most well known. It is the certificate issuers' responsibility to verify who is operating and running a site – both *Verisign* and *Thawte* check the legal status of companies and their right to use a particular domain name. This gives us the confidence to continue with our transaction – sending credit card details or other personal information over the Internet.

IMPORTANT NOTE: Sites using the *Verisign* or *Thawte* certificates usually show the following symbols somewhere on their site:

These symbols alone however **DO NOT** indicate any authentication! You must double-click on the **lock symbol** 🔒 in the status bar to verify the certificate details.

Any e-commerce sites (web sites selling online) and web sites requiring protected access will usually have a digital certificate authenticating them. The digital certificate and security symbol will only appear when we are about to enter a secure section of the site – this is because encrypting data to send on the Internet is quite slow – to have every page in a web site encrypted would slow our web access down quite considerably – and it is unnecessary.

Clicking on the *Issuer Statement* will show us who provided the certificate. *Verisign* and *Thawte* are two well known and respected providers of certificates – but there are others. **If in doubt check it out.**

LESSON 7.5.2: SECURITY AND DOWNLOADED FILES

We saw earlier in *Lesson 1.9.3:Computer Viruses* on *page* 55 that computer Viruses pose a real risk to our computer systems. E-mails containing attachments and files downloaded from the Internet are one of the most common ways our computers become infected with Viruses. Make sure any files that are downloaded to the PC are from legitimate sites and run a Virus scan on any downloaded files or attachments received by e-mail.

LESSON 7.5.3: SECURITY AND OUR COMPUTER SYSTEMS

When our computer is connected to the Internet – when we are sending e-mails or browsing the web – our computer systems are vulnerable to attack from hackers and Viruses. Information can flow into and out of our computer system over the Internet. To prevent illegal access of protected information on our network or damage to our systems we must install a *firewall*. A firewall is software or hardware placed between our computer and the Internet. A firewall restricts access to our systems by only allowing for controlled connectivity. We grant specific access to resources through the firewall.

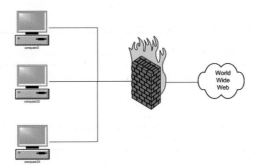

Conceptual view of a firewall. Firewalls are usually fast PCs or network routers.

IT departments in large companies may manage their own firewalls and restrict access to a range of sites and services from within the company or for specified users or machines.

Symantec (www.symantec.com) and others sell personal firewall software which we can install on our home PCs to help secure them from attack.

LESSON 7.5.4: COOKIES AND THE WEB CACHE

As we browse the web we will find that we frequently revisit the same web sites and we are often asked to enter personal information. In order to help recognise us the next time we return web designers sometimes write a small text file called a "cookie" to our computers hard disk when we visit their web site (rather like Chinese fortune cookies). The main purpose of cookies is to identify users and their preferences so that the next time we go to the same Web site, our browser will send the cookie to the Web server. So, for example, instead of seeing just a general welcome page you might see a welcome page with your name on it.

To delete the cookies stored on our computer:

❑ **Tools | Internet Options** and click **Delete Cookies**

As we visit different web pages – our browser *caches* these pages onto the computers hard disk. By caching or storing the pages the pages will load more quickly the next time we visit the page. To clear our web page cache of temporary files:

❑ **Tools | Internet Options** and click **Delete Files**

This will remove all temporary Internet files from our computer.

EXERCISES TO PROVE YOU KNOW

1. Encryption is a way of:

    a) Reducing the space taken up by attachments.

    b) Encoding a message or an attachment to protect it from unauthorised access.

    c) Encoding messages sent between non-Windows based PCs

    d) Protecting software copyright on downloaded software.

2. What do logos like these on a site mean?

    a) The site is secure and safe and we can enter our Visa cards without issue
    b) The site *promises* to be safe and secure but the images mean nothing
    c) The site claims to have an association with the above companies
    d) The site is using encryption keys provided from the above companies but we must verify the authenticity by using the lock symbol.

3. What does the 🔒 symbol represent when displayed in the status bar of a browser?

    a) We are prohibited from part of this site.
    b) The site is secure and a certificate is available.
    c) Key required to visit this site.
    d) Unauthorised access of this site will be recorded.

4. What is a *Firewall?*

    a) Software or hardware that protects PCs and equipment from unauthorised access
    b) A fireproof box which protects PC hardware and software in the event of a fire
    c) A fire-resistant wall used when constructing IT facilities
    d) Virus checking software

5. Why do some websites require a username and password to access some of their content?

SECTION 7.6:   E-MAIL

E-Mail is one of the Internet's most successful applications. Today more e-mail is sent each day than is delivered by conventional post or faxes combined. E-mail allows us to quickly and easily send a message to anyone with an e-mail address – or to lots of them at the same time. We can include any file with the message – including photographs, documents, spreadsheets, video and sound files. E-mail messages will also usually be delivered in a few seconds depending on the connection speed and the size of the message. To round it all off - the cost of delivering e-mail messages is practically nothing!

In this section we will learn how to send and manage our e-mail messages using *Microsoft Outlook* but the principles learned here will work with most if not all e-mail applications – including *Outlook Express*, *Eudora*, *Lotus Notes* and other e-mail applications.

In this section we will learn:

- ❏   How to start Outlook
- ❏   How to send an e-mail message
- ❏   How to reply to an e-mail message

LESSON 7.6.1:   STARTING OUTLOOK

To start Outlook we need to go to the **Start** menu, choose **All Programs** and choose **Microsoft Office** and click on **Microsoft Office Outlook 2003**:

Outlook will start after a few moments and the opening screen will appear. Outlook is a powerful e-mail package. This is the application that we need to open in order to see our received e-mails and to send e-mails. It can also keep our contacts information (like an address book) and act as a diary.

The *Outlook* window is broken into two main sections:

1. The **side panel** shows our e-mail folders and shortcuts. These contain a history of the messages we've sent and messages we have received.

2. The **main window** shows the contents of the folders (similar to the Windows Explorer window) and allows us to select or view a particular message.

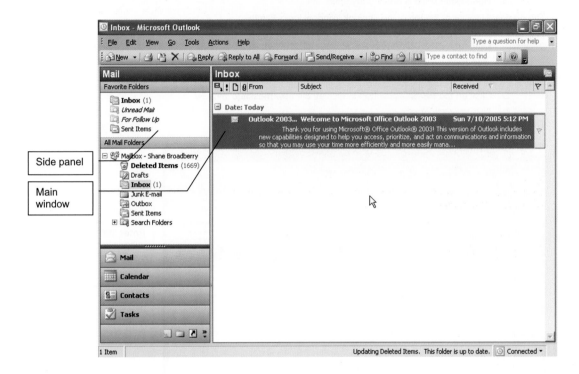

Getting Help

Outlook contains excellent help on configuring and setting up the e-mail application. To view help for Microsoft Outlook:

❑ Press **F1** from within the application or choose **Help** from the main menu

Review page 257 onwards on using the *Help* tool.

Closing Outlook

To close the mail application:

❑ Click **File | Exit.**

LESSON 7.6.2:   SENDING AN E-MAIL MESSAGE

Sending an e-mail is not unlike sending a traditional letter. To send a letter we must know the address of the recipient of the letter. Similarly to send an e-mail we need to know the *e-mail* address of the recipient. Once we know the e-mail address sending the message is easy.

To send an e-mail message:

    ❑   Open *Outlook* if it is not already open

The standard toolbar at the top of the Outlook Window looks like this:

To send a new e-mail message:

    ❑   Click on the ![New] button to display the new message window.

The new message window will appear:

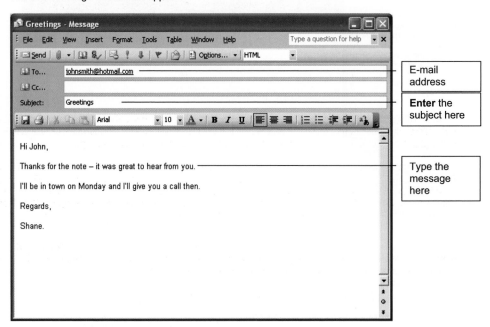

The new message window has a number of fields that need to be completed.

    ❑   We enter the *e-mail address* into the **TO:** text field. If there is more than one person to send the message to separate the e-mail address with a semicolon **;**

    ❑   We enter a *description* of the message into the **Subject:** text box - this helps identify the message when it arrives at the other end

    ❑   We type the text of the message into the main text window

If we make a mistake and need to edit the text – we can use the cursor keys and the **Delete** key to amend or Delete the text in the message.

Sending the e-mail message

    ❑   When the message is complete press on the **send** icon ![Send] and the e-mail will move into the **Outbox** on its way to the recipient.

LESSON 7.6.3: TRANSFERRING AND RETRIEVING E-MAIL

When we prepare our message and hit **Send** it first moves to the **Outbox**. The message will stay here **on our computer** until it gets transferred to a *post-office* where it will be forwarded to the intended recipients. Transferring the mail is a vital part of sending the e-mail – just like posting a letter into a post-box.

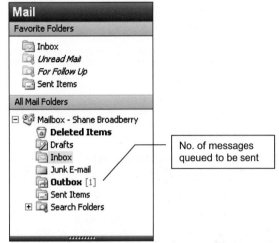

The screen above shows there is *one* e-mail awaiting delivery to the *post office* or *mail server*. If we are not permanently connected to the Internet we can prepare multiple messages *offline* (when we are not connected to the Internet) to save phone charges and then transmit them all in one go.

Many dial-up Internet users will check and send messages at specified times each day – this is usually first thing in the morning, at lunch time and last thing in the evening. If using a dial-up connection it can be difficult to connect to check our mail at these times - as everyone else is doing the same thing! We should try to vary the times of our connection if we have difficulty retrieving our messages. This does not usually apply in companies or with broadband connections.

When we click the ⬚ Send/Receive ▾ button *Outlook* attempts to deliver our messages and at the same time check to see if we have any new messages waiting for download. Our message will move from the **Outbox** to the **Sent** items folder once the e-mail has been sent.

The system will connect to the Internet if it is not already connected.

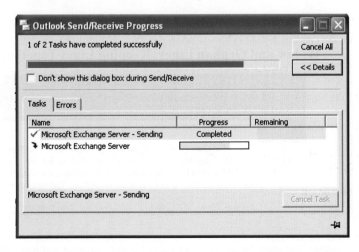

We can tick the **Don't show this dialog box during Send/Receive** check box to hide this window when Outlook is checking and sending our messages.

LESSON 7.6.4: TEXT IN OUR E-MAIL MESSAGES

Traditional e-mail messages were purely text. Now we can send rich formatted e-mails and most e-mail packages can read them. Use the formatting toolbar to change the font, colour and style of the message.

We can even insert images inline with our text like we would do in Microsoft Word.

This toolbar is the same as that seen in Module 3 – Word Processing and works in the same way. Refer to *Error! Reference source not found.Error! Reference source not found.* on page **Error! Bookmark not defined.** for more information.

Checking the spelling of our e-mail

As usual whenever we write any text on our computers it is a good idea to spell check the text before sending or printing it. The spelling checker tool in Outlook works the same way as with Word and Excel and the other Office applications.

To **Spell Check** the message prior to sending it:

❑ Press **F7** or choose **Tools | Spelling and Grammar…**

Refer to page 190 to review using the spelling checker.

Copying and Moving text within a message

We can copy or move text within a message or to another message using the clipboard. This can be useful if we are using part of a previous e-mail in a new message. To move or copy the text:

❑ Select the text with the mouse and press **Ctrl+X** (if moving the text) or **Ctrl+C** (if copying the text).

❑ Click in the new location for the text and press **Ctrl+V**.

Copying text from another application

Sometimes its handy to bring text or other items from another program into our e-mail message. This is very straightforward.

❑ Open the application to copy from (we'll use *Microsoft Word* – but the same technique will work with most applications).

❑ Select the text to copy or cut from Word and press **Ctrl+X** (to cut) or **Ctrl+C** (to copy it).

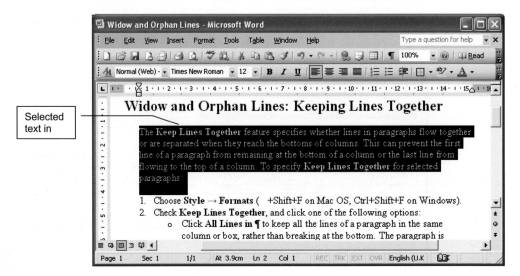

❑ Now switch back to the e-mail message (press **Alt+Tab** or click on the icon on the Taskbar) and place the cursor where the text is to be inserted and press **Ctrl+V** to paste the text into the message.

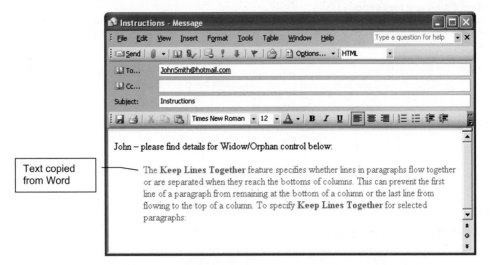

Text copied from Word

This technique works between most applications.

LESSON 7.6.5: VALID E-MAIL ADDRESSES

To send an e-mail to someone we must know their e-mail address and reproduce it accurately. Unlike the traditional postal service mistakes won't be corrected by a friendly postman who knows 'what we meant' – the message won't be delivered – it will be 'bounced'.

E-mail addresses usually look like this:

name@domain.extension

For example:

george.bush@whitehouse.gov

britney.spears@compuserve.com

These are all examples of valid e-mail addresses (although fictitious in this case). Sometimes e-mail addresses bare no resemblance to the person's name:

123349939493@hotmail.com

This is also a valid e-mail address although we have no idea who is behind it.

Note: Usually e-mail addresses don't contain spaces. They do often contain underscore characters like '_' like **fred_flinstone@hotmail.com**

Copying someone on a message

To send a copy of an e-mail to others, we can put their e-mail address into the **CC** area of the message. They will then receive a copy of the message as well as the people in the **TO** box. By placing an e-mail address in the **CC** part of the e-mail header the recipient of the message will be able to see who was copied on the message. We might copy a colleague out of courtesy or for informational purposes.

If we do not wish the recipient of the message to see who else was copied on the message we can use the **Bcc** field.

Blind Copying a message

Bcc is a *blind carbon copy* – here we can send copies of the e-mail to others, however, no one else can see that others have been sent copies. This is a good way of keeping e-mail addresses out of view.

To open the **Bcc** text box:

❑ Click on the **Options** drop down menu and ensure the **Bcc** option is ticked

We will now see an extra text field in our message header area - **Bcc**

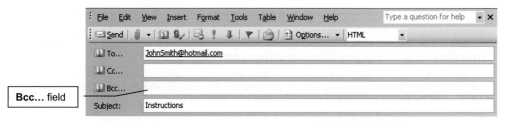

Bcc... field

Type the e-mail address of the recipient into the **Bcc** box to blind copy extra recipients.

Changing the priority of an e-mail message

Once we are ready to send our e-mail, we can change the priority settings of our e-mail. Changing the priority of a message can help the recipient of the message identify more important messages. For example if we are sending around a review of a new movie just released – we might choose to make this a **Low Priority** message. A security warning about a new Virus threat however would be marked as **High Priority**.

To modify the priority of an e-mail message:

❑ To mark a message as **High Priority** press the button.

❑ To mark a message as **Low Priority** press the button.

To leave the priority settings as **Normal** depress the **High Priority** or **Low Priority** buttons.

LESSON 7.6.6: OPENING AND CLOSING E-MAILS

Incoming messages will appear in our **Inbox** and the number of new messages will be shown by a number in brackets – in this case there is one new message.

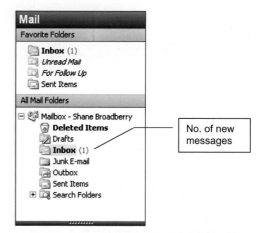

No. of new messages

To view the message select the **Inbox** folder. This will display all messages received in a list showing who they came from, the subject of the message and the date the message was received.

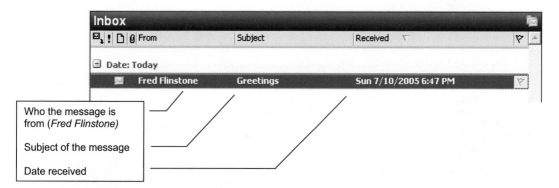

Who the message is from (*Fred Flinstone*)

Subject of the message

Date received

Selecting the **Inbox** displays a list of all messages received. New messages usually display in **bold** to help them stand out.

❑ Select the message(s) to view by clicking on them or open them by **double-clicking** with the mouse.

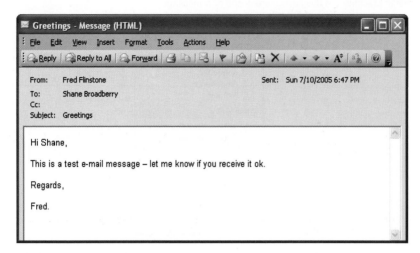

This message is from *Fred Flinstone*.

❑ Close the message once it has been read.

Switching between open messages

If we have a number of messages open we may need to switch between them. Open messages will appear as items on the Taskbar within the *Microsoft Office Outlook* group.

To return to an open message

❑ Click on the Microsoft Outlook icon on the toolbar and select the message to view.

A pop up menu will show all of the currently open message windows.

❑ Select the message to switch to by selecting it with the mouse.

Closing an e-mail message

To close the message after we have displayed it:

❑ Press the close button ⊠ in the top right hand corner of the message Window.

Outlook still has a copy of the message and we can reopen it again whenever we need to view it.

Marking e-mails as read/unread

Sometimes we will want to mark messages as read or unread from our inbox. This helps the messages standout.

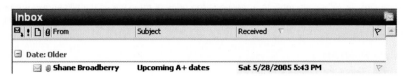

The message above is **Unread** - Outlook usually displays unread messages in **Bold** with a ✉ symbol beside the message.

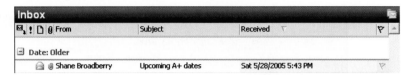

The message above is **Read** – Outlook usually displays read messages in normal text with a 📭 symbol beside the message.

To mark a message as read or unread:

❑ Select the message and choose **Edit | Mark as Unread** or **Edit | Mark as read**

LESSON 7.6.7: DELETING AN E-MAIL MESSAGE

To Delete a message click on the e-mail in the inbox or other folder.

❑ Click on the **Delete** icon on the toolbar or press the **Delete** button on the keyboard.

This will send the e-mail to the **Deleted Items** folder.

Recovering a message from the Deleted Items folder

If the **Deleted Items** folder hasn't been emptied we can recover messages from it.

To recover a message after it has been deleted:

❑ Click on the **Deleted Items** folder:

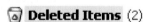

❑ Select the message to recover or "un-delete" and drag it into the **Inbox**.

The message is now recovered and won't be deleted if the Recycle Bin is emptied.

Emptying the Deleted Items folder

To permanently delete a message we have to empty the **Deleted Items** folder.

To empty the Deleted Items folder:

❑ Choose **Tools | Empty 'Deleted Items' Folder**

This will permanently delete all messages that have been deleted – and we should usually do this once the folder contains more than a few hundred deleted messages to recover disk space.

LESSON 7.6.8: REPLYING TO AN E-MAIL

Usually when we receive a message we will want to reply to it. Rather than creating a new e-mail and entering the e-mail addresses of those who sent the message by hand we can choose to *reply* to the message directly. When we reply to a message the original message is usually shown in the text area so that we can make comments on specific items in the e-mail and the address fields are automatically filled in.

To reply to a message:

- ❑ Select the message to reply to.

- ❑ Click on the **Reply** button 🔁 **Reply**

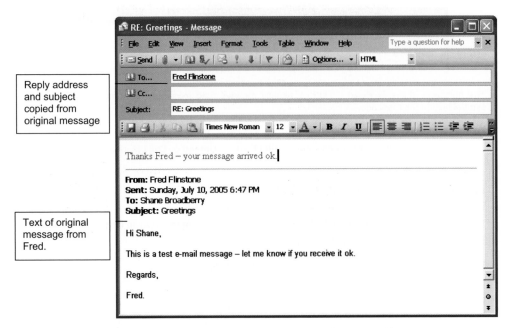

Reply address and subject copied from original message

Text of original message from Fred.

It is often useful to have the original text of the message in the reply so that we can comment on specific questions without having to remember everything in the original message. It also means we can send e-mails with very little text. Very often we will receive e-mails which say **YES** or **OK** with no reference to what is being agreed! That's because the original message was included in the message or the sender assumes that we know the context in which the reply is sent.

Notice that the **Subject** line is prefixed with **RE:** indicating that the e-mail is a reply to the message.

Reply to All

When we receive an e-mail, it may have been 'copied' to a number of other people – perhaps other friends, managers or those mentioned in the e-mail. We will know if it has been copied to others if the **CC** box has e-mail addresses in it (we won't know if the **BCC** option was used).

When we reply to a message with e-mail addresses in the **CC** field, we may wish to reply not only to the sender of the e-mail, but also to all those that were copied originally on the message. This is called ***Reply to All***.

To reply to a message and send a copy to all those on the original e-mail list:

- ❑ Click on **Reply to All** icon 🔁 **Reply to All** on the message toolbar.

Outlook will then prepare a reply e-mail as before – but include all the names in the **CC** field box.

- ❑ Enter the reply to the message and press **Send**.

Replying without the original message

As we saw earlier, when we reply to an e-mail the original text is usually included in our reply. If we do not want to send the original text in our reply we can simply delete it before sending the message. If however we find that we are deleting the original message all the time – we can turn off the auto insertion of the original message in the reply by modifying one of Outlook's settings.

To turn off the auto-inclusion of the original message in a reply:

- ❑   Select **Tools | Options** and click on the **Preferences** tab
- ❑   Click on the **E-mail Options** button to display the following window:

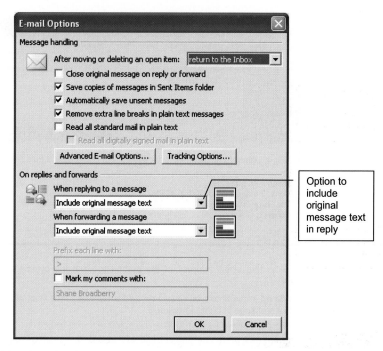

Option to include original message text in reply

Outlook lets us determine what happens to a message when we are replying to a message or forwarding a message.

- ❑   Choose **Do not include original message** from the list of options and press **OK**

Now whenever we reply to a message the original message will no longer appear. We can reverse this action at any time.

LESSON 7.6.9: FORWARDING AN E-MAIL

Sometimes we receive an e-mail intended for someone else or an e-mail we feel other people might be interested in – perhaps it's a special offer, a joke, a CV or some other news item we wish to pass on.

In these cases we *Forward* the original message onto the new recipients. Forwarding a message is very like *Replying* to a message except we specify a different destination for the message.

❑ Select the message to forward from the **Inbox**

❑ Press the **Forward** 🔁 Forward button and the mail *send* window appears

Type in the e-mail address of person that we are forwarding to

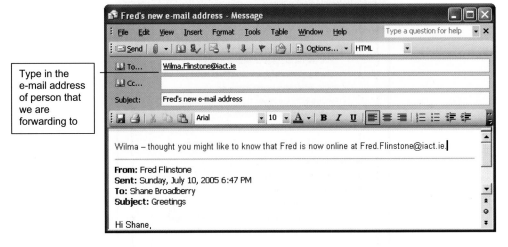

❑ Now enter the e-mail address of the person to send the message (we are sending it to *Wilma*)

❑ Press **Send** immediately or add some additional text to the message – perhaps explaining why this message is being forwarded.

Some e-mail programs will prefix the subject line of forwarded messages with **FW:** to help identify them.

LESSON 7.6.10: PREVIEWING AND PRINTING AN E-MAIL MESSAGE

Sometimes we will want to print an e-mail message – for example if booking airline flights – we often use a copy of the e-mail as a 'ticket'.

Not all e-mail applications will allow us to preview a message before we print it. *Microsoft Outlook* will allow us to preview a message. If the e-mail application supports a preview option - we should preview the message before it is printed to ensure the layout is as desired.

❑   Select the message to preview and choose **File | Print Preview**

A preview window will appear allowing us to view the message as it will be printed.

From here we can check the page setup and layout is correct prior to printing the e-mail.

❑   We can print directly from the Preview window by pressing

This will display the print dialog box.

Printing an e-mail message

We will often print an e-mail or part of an e-mail to keep as a permanent record.

❏ To print an e-mail first select it or open it from **Inbox**

To print just a selection of the message – select the part of the message you want to print.

❏ Choose **File | Print**

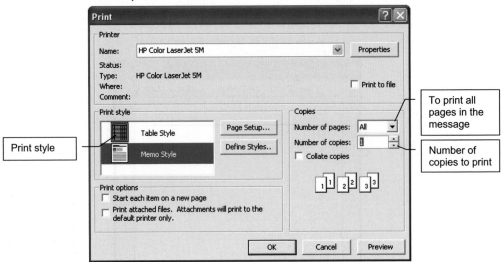

Select a print style for the e-mail. The built in styles are 'Table Style' and 'Memo Style'.

❏ To print more than one copy of the message modify the number of copies text box.

When the print settings are confirmed:

❏ Press **OK** to print the message.

LESSON 7.6.11: CUSTOMISING OUTLOOK'S TOOLBARS

We can customise Outlook's toolbars by adding or removing buttons as required. This works the same way as with other Microsoft Office applications – like Word and Excel.

    ❑   To customise the toolbar **right-click** in the toolbar area and click on **Customize** or choose **View | Toolbars | Customize**

Outlook opens the **Customize** window, which allows us to add and remove buttons from the toolbar:

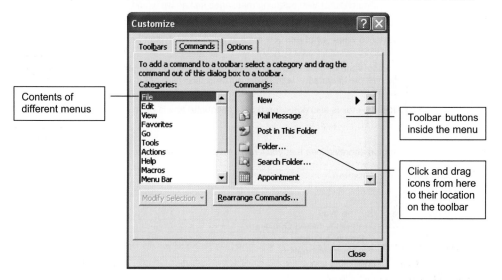

Contents of different menus

Toolbar buttons inside the menu

Click and drag icons from here to their location on the toolbar

    ❑   We can now drag toolbar icons from the right-hand window onto the toolbar area.

The mouse pointer changes shape to indicate where the new toolbar icon will appear as we move the mouse over the toolbar.

Position for new icon

    ❑   Release the mouse button to insert the new command button onto the toolbar.

    ❑   To remove a button from the toolbar – follow the same procedure – but in reverse – dragging *from the toolbar* and dropping the icon into the main window.

When we have finished editing the icons close the customise window.

LESSON 7.6.12: NETWORK ETIQUETTE OR NETIQUETTE

Network etiquette refers to the "unwritten" rules of e-mail and general use of the net. New users of e-mail often fall foul of these rules and risk being "flamed" (yelled at in text) by less tolerant users.

Here are some things to keep in mind when sending a message:

- ❑ E-mail messages should have an appropriate subject title to help users follow conversations.

- ❑ Use a spelling checker with outgoing messages just as we would with a written letter.

- ❑ Avoid unnecessarily short responses in e-mail messages as this can be viewed offensive

- ❑ Use sentence case (what you are reading now) when typing an e-mail message. Text in UPPER CASE is considered SHOUTING.

- ❑ When using Internet chat rooms or news groups keep messages on topic –no questions off topic will be tolerated – with those abusing the rules often being flamed by the sites moderator.

- ❑ Unsolicited e-mail is also considered poor netiquette and is often referred to as SPAM.

Abbreviations
Here are a few common abbreviations that you'll meet on your e-mail travels.

Abbreviation	Meaning
BFN	Bye For Now
L8R	Later
BTW	By The Way
FAQ	Frequently Asked Questions
FOAF	Friend of a Friend
FYI	For Your Information
IMO	In My Opinion
LOL	Laughing Out Loud
WRT	With Respect To

Some *Smiley Faces* (turn your head sideways to view these!)

:-)	…regular smiley
$-)	...yuppie smiley
%-)	...user has been staring at a green screen for 15 hours straight
%-6	...user is brain-dead
&-I	...that made me cry
'-)	...winking smiley
(-:	...left hand smiley
8-)	...smiley with glasses
;-(	…sad smiley
:-D	…laugh
	..there are many more!

EXERCISES TO PROVE YOU KNOW

1. Start Outlook or another e-mail application.

2. Send the following message to practice@iactonline.com

   Subject: ECDL Test Message

   Hi,

   This is a short message to test out the e-mail on my computer.

   This is the last module of the ECDL.

   Thanks,

   Your name.

3. Open the *Christmas.doc* file created in Module 3 and copy the first paragraph from Word into a new mail message. Send the message to practice@iactonline.com with the subject line: *ECDL copy and paste*.

4. Which of the of following look like *invalid* e-mail addresses? Why?

   a) Fred!flintstone.com

   b) Fred.Flinstone@hotemail.com

   c) Fred_Flinstone@hotmail.com.co.uk

   d) Fred_Flinstone@hotmail.com

   e) Fred Flinstone @ hotmail.com

5. What is the difference between **CC** and **BCC** when copying a message to someone?

6. Which of the following statements is **TRUE**:

   a) Once mail has entered the **OUTBOX** it has been delivered successfully

   b) Typing our e-mail message in upper case is considered *shouting*.

   c) Formatting the text of a message does not guarantee it will appear the same way for the recipient

   d) The Windows Recycle Bin and our mailbox Recycle Bin are the same

   e) After we have sent a message – switching our PC off will stop the message being sent.

7. What do the following abbreviations found in e-mail messages stand for:

   a) BFN

   b) L8R

   c) ;-)

   d) BTW

SECTION 7.7:   ATTACHMENTS

Very often we'll find we want to send a file or some document with our e-mail message. This is extremely useful and can save considerable costs with courier and postal charges.

Here are just some reasons we might want to send an attachment:

- ❑   Send photographs to friends, colleagues, newspapers
- ❑   Send charts and graphs by e-mail
- ❑   Sending documents – letters, legal contracts etc.
- ❑   Sending presentations by e-mail
- ❑   Sending information about products, services provided by a company
- ❑   Sending an advertisement by e-mail
- ❑   Send programs and bug fixes by e-mail

Being able to send and receive attachments is an important part of using our e-mail program to its maximum benefit.

In this section we will learn how to:

- ❑   Send an attachment with a message
- ❑   How to open and save an attachment sent with a message
- ❑   Understand the risks associated with opening attachments

LESSON 7.7.1:   SENDING AN ATTACHMENT WITH A MESSAGE

We can attach any type of file to an e-mail message – and when the message is sent the *attachment* will get sent as well. We could for example attach several photographs to an e-mail message or a couple of Word documents to a message and the recipient will be able to view the images or edit or print the Word document when the e-mail arrives.

Adding an attachment to a message does have some drawbacks however. Attachments can be quite large – so for example sending a photo, a movie clip or a sound file by e-mail can take a very long time possibly tying up our network or phone line for many hours at a time.

It is advisable not to send unnecessary attachments and only to send files that are more efficient to distribute in this way. Even if our mailbox can handle it – sometimes our intended recipient can't. Some large corporations have even prohibited e-mails beyond a certain size to stop their systems crashing. In these cases our e-mail may bounce and cause us more trouble!

Let's attach a Word document to an e-mail:

❑ Create a new mail message and enter Barney's e-mail address into the **To** box.

Attachment button

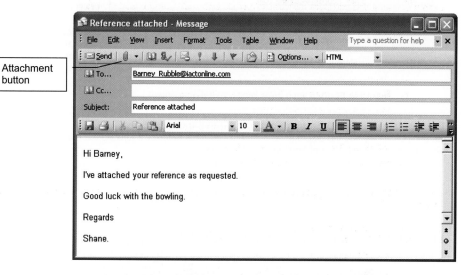

❑ Click on the attachment icon 📎 ▾ and the **Insert File** dialog box will appear.

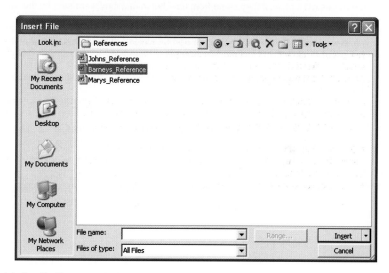

We are going to pick the file **Barneys_Reference.doc** but we could choose any file or file type to attach.

❑ Select the file **Barneys_Reference** and click **Insert**

Outlook will display a new field called *Attach* and show our attached file.

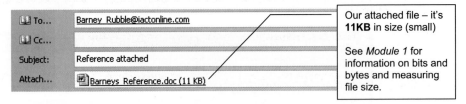

📖 To...	Barney_Rubble@iactonline.com
📖 Cc...	
Subject:	Reference attached
Attach...	📄 Barneys_Reference.doc (11 KB)

Our attached file – it's **11KB** in size (small)

See *Module 1* for information on bits and bytes and measuring file size.

❑ Now click **Send** to send the e-mail with the attachment

Deleting an attachment from an outgoing message

Sometimes we will want to delete an attachment - perhaps before we forward the message to someone else. To delete the attachment from an outgoing message:

❑ Click on the attachment and press **Delete**

❑ Press **Send** to send the e-mail without the attachment.

LESSON 7.7.2: SECURITY AND ATTACHMENTS

E-Mail attachments cause one of the biggest headaches for the security of our PCs. The nature of an attachment means that we can send and receive any type of file – including unfortunately software Viruses and worms. Viruses will often hijack our e-mail systems to send bogus messages from a users e-mail account – attaching a file that tries to infect a colleague or friends computer. These e-mail messages will look as if they came from us – but in fact they were sent by the Virus.

We should <u>**NEVER**</u> open an attachment sent from someone we do not know without taking precautions - and we should be very suspicious of normal looking e-mails arriving from friends or colleagues that seem 'out of context' but include attachments.

One of the biggest plagues of the Internet are Viruses and these spread primarily through attachments in e-mail.

IF IN DOUBT DON'T OPEN IT!

It is most likely that attachments that have a **.EXE** a **.BAT** a **.VBS** or a **.JS** file extension are in fact Viruses. Saving these attachments onto our PCs or worse – running the attachments – will infect our computer system.

Virus Protection Software cannot keep up with the number of new Viruses evolving so we must be on our guard. Remember a Virus may not appear to damage our machine immediately and it may strike at a later date destroying everything on our machine and everyone else's.

LESSON 7.7.3: OPENING, VIEWING AND SAVING ATTACHMENTS

When we receive a message that contains an attachment a small paperclip 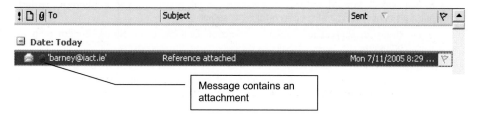 will appear next to the message in our inbox.

Message contains an attachment

Viewing and saving an attachment:

We can view and save an attachment by opening the e-mail message.

- ❏ Open the message with the attachment by *double-clicking* on it

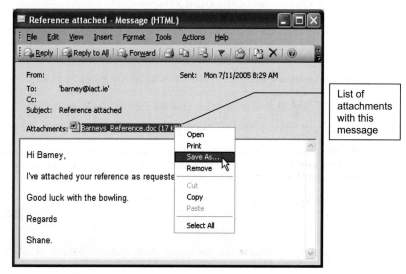

List of attachments with this message

- ❏ The attachment(s) will show in the attachment list. Right-clicking on the attachment gives options to **Open**, **Save**, **Print** the attachment.

- ❏ Choose **Open** to open the attachment straight away or **Save As…** to store it for use later.

EXERCISES TO PROVE YOU KNOW

1. Send a new mail message to practice@iactonline.com with a copy of the Brazil.ppt presentation created earlier. Give the message an appropriate subject.

2. Go to the **Sent Items** folder and open the message sent to practice@iactonline.com. Save the attachment to the Desktop as "sent_presentation"

3. Which of following file types when sent as attachments are suspicious and might contain a Virus?

   a. .VBS

   b. .BAT

   c. .EXE

   d. .MDB

   e. .JS

7
Internet & E-Mail

SECTION 7.8:   WEB BASED E-MAIL

An e-mail program is a tool for sending and receiving messages and files over the Internet. We've seen how to use Outlook to send and receive messages in the previous sections. There are in fact two different ways of accessing and sending e-mail messages:

- ❑ Using an application – such as Microsoft Outlook, Lotus Notes, Eudora or a similar program.

or

- ❑ Using a web-based e-mail application – of which there are many.

In this section we will look at:

- ❑ Creating a Web based e-mail account with *Hotmail*
- ❑ Reading and sending an e-mail messages from Hotmail

LESSON 7.8.1:   SETTING UP A WEB-BASED E-MAIL ACCOUNT

If we travel a lot or don't have access to a PC all the time – web based e-mail is the ideal solution for sending and receiving e-mail messages from any PC. Web based e-mail systems such as HOTMAIL, Yahoo Mail and some corporate e-mail systems allow us to connect to our e-mail using a web browser like *Internet Explorer*.

We can setup a free e-mail account on Hotmail by visiting www.hotmail.com

- ❑ Open Internet Explorer and type the address www.hotmail.com
- ❑ To create a new hotmail account click on the *New Account Sign-up* tab and fill in all the details.

There are millions of individual and dormant users on hotmail – so many existing e-mail addresses have long since been used up. Hotmail will try to provide an e-mail address similar to that requested – but quite often it will include numbers to help distinguish it from other others.

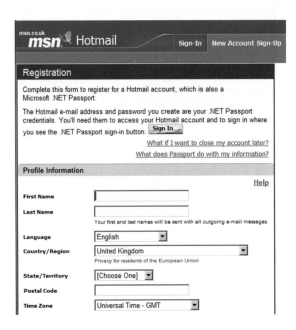

- ❑ Fill in the form as requested and read and agree to the terms and conditions.
- ❑ Take a careful note of the *username* and *password* as we will need these each time we want to view or send an e-mail message.

Once we have set up our **Hotmail** account – we can login from any PC with Internet access. It doesn't have to be the machine that was used to set up the account. This is very important as it means if we can gain access to the Internet we can check and send e-mail messages using our Hotmail account.

LESSON 7.8.2:   TOURING HOTMAIL

We can send an e-mail from Hotmail as soon as we have setup our account.

- ❑   Open *Internet Explorer* and go to www.hotmail.com

- ❑   Login to the hotmail account using the username and password created earlier by clicking on the **Sign In** .net button.

- ❑   When logged in click on the **Mail** tab

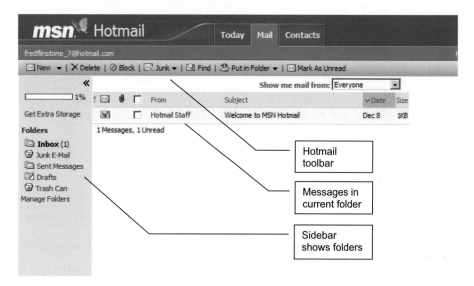

The side-bar shows us our folders – the **Inbox** will contain all our new messages. The default is the **Inbox**. We can switch folders by clicking on the folder name. The **Hotmail Toolbar** lets us send new messages, delete messages or search for a message.

LESSON 7.8.3: SENDING AN E-MAIL WITH HOTMAIL

❏ To send an e-mail from Hotmail click on the **New** button on the **Mail** toolbar

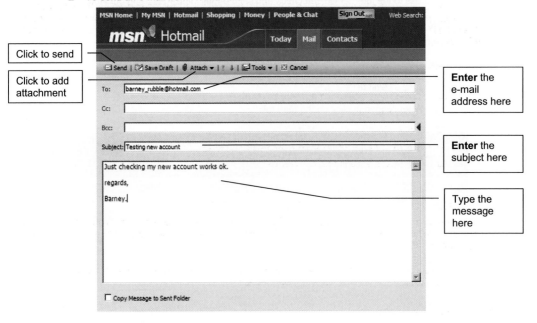

Click to send

Click to add attachment

Enter the e-mail address here

Enter the subject here

Type the message here

❏ Fill in all the required fields including the *To, Subject* and *Text* fields and press **Send**

This screen is very like the **Send message** window in Outlook – with the links and buttons performing the same tasks. In fact most of what we can do in Outlook we can do with our online Hotmail account. Hotmail does limit the size of messages that we can send and receive – there are options that can be bought to increase the size of files that can be received and sent from a Hotmail account – but most of the time these won't be necessary.

LESSON 7.8.4: VIEWING A MESSAGE

To view a message:

❏ Click on the name of the person who sent the message

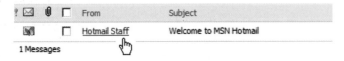

Hotmail will display the text in the message on a new page.

EXERCISES TO PROVE YOU KNOW

1. Visit www.hotmail.com and create a new *Hotmail* account.

2. Send a message to your regular e-mail address from your hotmail account. Check the message arrives ok.

3. Reply to the message from your regular e-mail address to your new Hotmail account.

4. Send a message with an attachment to your Hotmail account. Are there any restrictions on the size of attachments you can receive in your Hotmail account? What implications might this have?

SECTION 7.9:   ORGANISING E-MAILS AND CONTACTS

Once we have an e-mail account set up – it's hard to remember how we survived without it. Most e-mail users receive at least a couple of messages every day by e-mail – some receive hundreds or even thousands! It is important to manage our mail in order to be able to make the most of our e-mail application. Sorting, filing, deleting and organising our mailbox helps us do this.

In this section we will learn:

- ❏   How to filter and sort messages in our Inbox
- ❏   How to flag messages
- ❏   How to file our e-mails into folders
- ❏   How to use an address book to organise contacts
- ❏   How to add a signature to an e-mail

LESSON 7.9.1:   SORTING ITEMS IN THE INBOX

It is often useful to re-organise the items in our Inbox in order to group related messages or messages from the same person. By sorting the items by sender, date or subject we can help group related messages.

We can sort items in our Inbox or other e-mail folders by clicking on the field headings at the top of the window. By clicking on the different headings we can sort by:

- ❏   Name (from field)
- ❏   Subject (subject field)
- ❏   Date (received field)
- ❏   Attachment
- ❏   Flag

and

- ❏   Priority

Simply click on the grey field heading to sort by that field.

We can also sort in *Ascending* or *Descending* order. Clicking again on the same grey field heading re-orders the list in the opposite sort order.

Click here to sort by *subject*

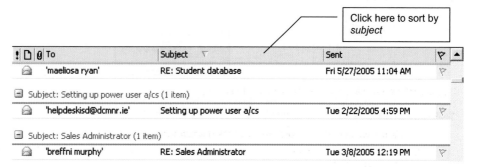

7
Internet & E-Mail

LESSON 7.9.2:   MODIFYING INBOX HEADINGS OR FIELDS

We can add or remove the headings from our Inbox.

❑ Right-click on the heading column and click on **Field Chooser**

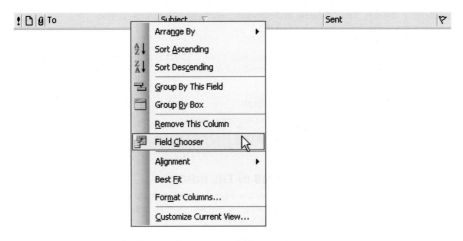

Outlook displays all the fields that are available for our messages.

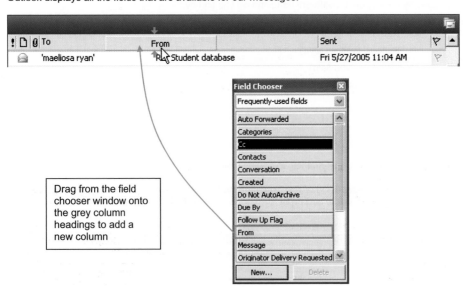

Drag from the field chooser window onto the grey column headings to add a new column

❑ Drag from the field chooser list onto the field headings to add columns to our headings

To remove a column:

❑ Drag from the field headings into the field chooser window

LESSON 7.9.4:   FLAGGING E-MAILS

We can flag our e-mails so that they stand out from others in our inbox. Outlook will put a small flag beside the message. This is useful if we want to mark it to return to later. There are a number of different types of flags.

To flag a message:

❏   Select the message from the **Inbox**

❏   Press the right-mouse button and choose from the **Follow Up** sub-menu or select **Action | Follow up** from the main menu and the select the flag to use.

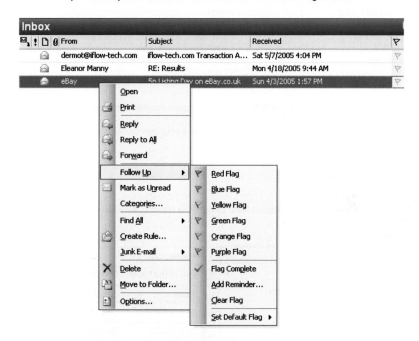

Outlook places the flag next to the message in the flag column.

We can modify or update the flag at anytime in the same way.

A tick will indicate whether the message is currently flagged. We can sort our messages to group all flagged messages together. Simply click on the flag icon on the toolbar to sort by flagged messages.

LESSON 7.9.8: CREATING FOLDERS FOR E-MAIL MESSAGES

Over time we will acquire a very long list of e-mail messages and it can become difficult to view them in a single list. Outlook gives us a way to help organise and file messages so that we don't get swamped. This system is like working with folders in Windows Explorer – so it should seem familiar.

The first thing we need to do in order to start filing our e-mails is to decide on the categories of e-mail we receive.

Let's suppose we want to organise our e-mails as follows:

Marketing Project	-	Everything to do with the marketing
Advertising	-	Information on advertising opportunities
Travel	-	Special holiday information and offers
Training	-	Training deals and upcoming courses
CVs	-	CVs applying for positions
Boss	-	Urgent E-mails sent by the boss
Colleagues	-	Other e-mails relating to work
Personal	-	All personal e-mails from friends

All we need to do is create a folder for each of these topics and file our messages when they arrive.

Outlook will even allow us to create a rule[†] to place it into the correct folder automatically when the message arrives!

Creating e-mail folders
To create a folder in our inbox:

❑   From the **File** menu choose **New | Folder** or press **Ctrl+Shift+E**

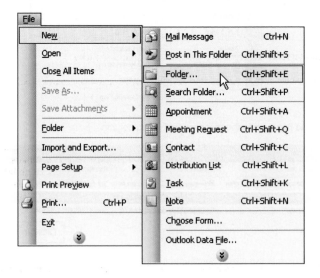

[†] *Outlook's rules are not covered in the ECDL – but IACT provide advanced training on Outlook and all of the other Office Applications – visit www.iactonline.com for more information.*

The following window will appear asking for the name of the folder to create:

We can create folders for any categories of e-mail we choose.

- ❏ Type the name of the folder to create and press **OK**

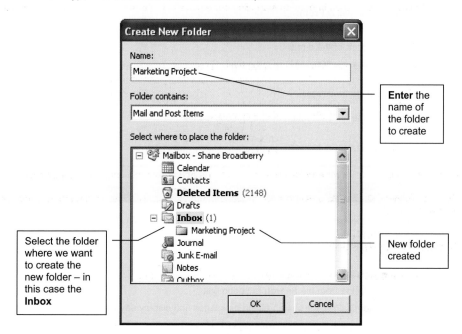

Enter the name of the folder to create

Select the folder where we want to create the new folder – in this case the **Inbox**

New folder created

We can also create sub-folders within a given folder in the same way.

Here is what our **Inbox** now looks like after we've created these extra categories.

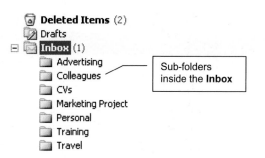

Sub-folders inside the **Inbox**

We can now categorise the e-mails in our **Inbox** and move them into their appropriate folders.

Moving e-mails between folders
To move an e-mail from the **Inbox** into its appropriate sub-folder:

- ❏ Select the e-mail message and keep the left mouse button pressed.
- ❏ Now drag the e-mail message onto the folder you wish to place it in.

The message is now moved into the appropriate sub-folder.

LESSON 7.9.9: SEARCHING FOR AN E-MAIL

Outlook provides us with a search tool for finding or searching for e-mails – useful if we are trying to find all e-mails relating to a specific topic for example.

Outlook allows us to search by:

- ❑ Who the e-mail is **From:**
- ❑ Who the e-mail is **To:**
- ❑ The **Subject:** of the e-mail
- ❑ Keywords in the **Message:** of the e-mail

To search the text of our messages:

- ❑ Click on the 🔍 **Find** button on the Outlook toolbar

Outlook will display the search toolbar:

Here we can specify the text we wish to **Look for** and where we wish to find it (**Search In**).

To search for e-mails containing the word "holiday"

- ❑ Type "holiday" into the **Look for:** field
- ❑ Choose **Inbox** from the **Search In** option box

When we press **Enter** Outlook will search all the messages and display any messages that contain the word Holiday.

If we want to have more control over how our search is carried out – we can use **Advanced Find…**

- ❑ Click on the **Options** box and choose **Advanced Find…**

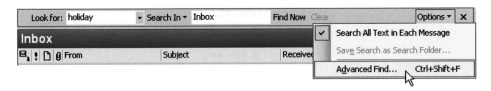

Outlook will display a new search dialog box.

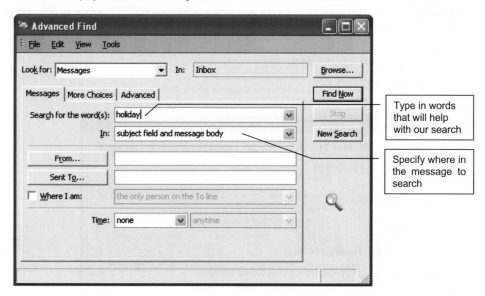

We can also search for e-mails under date and whether or not the e-mail has an attachment.

❑ Type the word or phrase to search for and specify where in the message we should look for a match (for example – we might choose to search just the *subject* line of a message – and this would be much quicker than searching all of the text of every message).

❑ Press **Enter** or press **Find Now**

Depending on how many messages there are – Outlook will return in a few moments with a list of matching messages.

LESSON 7.9.10: SIGNATURES

At the end of an e-mail we usually sign our name. Sometimes we include company details such as phone numbers, faxes and addresses. We can create a *signature* to make this process easier and more consistent and we can ask that the signature be included on all new messages that we send.

Creating a signature is straightforward.

❑ Go to the **Tools** menu and choose **Options** and select the **Mail Format** tab.

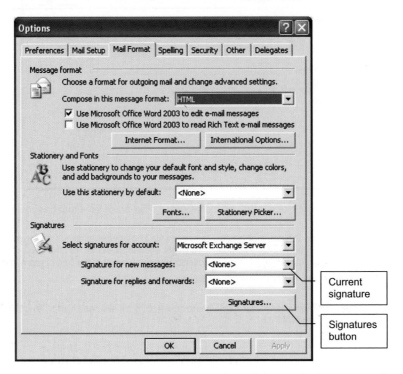

The bottom section of this window relates to the signatures that will be attached to our e-mails. Currently the signature is set to **<None>**.

❑ Click on the **Signatures** button to modify or create a new signature and then press the **New...** button

The create signature Window will then appear:

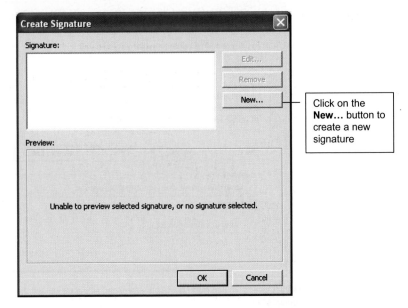

Click on the **New...** button to create a new signature

When we press **New**, Outlook starts the *Signature Wizard* that guides us through the steps to create a new signature.

❑ The first step is to give the signature a *name*. We might have a work and a home signature for example. Let's create one called **Work.**

❑ Type "Work" into the name box and press **Next**

The next step is to create the signature. The signature can be pretty much any type of text or graphic and text combination we desire – but remember that the signature will usually be attached to every e-mail that we send and large signatures will slow down our messages.

❑ Create the text and graphics for the signature in the *Signature* text box. We can use the **Font...** and **Paragraph...** options to change the colour and typeface used for our signature.

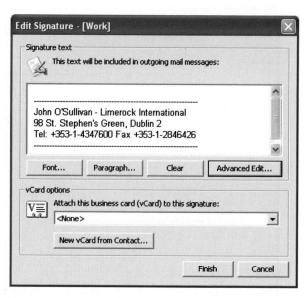

The **Advanced Edit...** option will launch Microsoft Word and allow us to use all of the features of Word when creating our signature.

❑ Click **Finish** when the signature is complete to return to the **Create Signature** window.

We can setup several signatures – for work or personal use. Click **New** and keep adding signatures as required. We can also create signatures that include graphics and special format characters, but these may not always work when sent to different e-mail system users - so are probably best avoided.

LESSON 7.9.11: ADDING A SIGNATURE TO AN E-MAIL MESSAGE

Once a signature has been created it can be inserted automatically each time we create or forward a message from Outlook.

❑   Return to the **Tools | Options** dialog box and select the **Mail Format** tab.

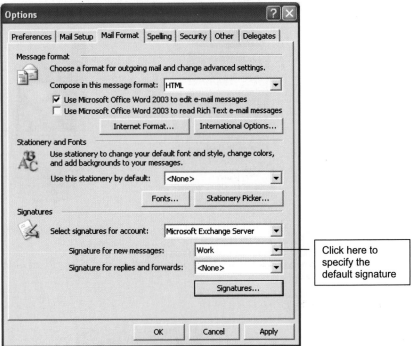

Click here to specify the default signature

❑   Choose the signature from the **Signature for new messages:** drop down list and identify the signature to use

If we are unsure of what the signature looks like – we can view it by clicking again on the **Signatures...** button.

It's a good idea to omit the signature on replies and forwards – which is the default setting.

Now whenever a new message is created our new signature will automatically appear in the message.

LESSON 7.9.12: CONTACTS AND THE ADDRESS BOOK

Outlook includes a powerful tool for keeping track of our contacts. The contacts tool lets us record e-mail addresses but also other important details such as their postal address, phone numbers and other personal details (including photographs).

Users of handheld devices and mobile phones like the *Compaq iPAQ*® and the *Treo*®*600 palm phone* can synchronise their contacts with Outlook – making it fast and easy to carry contacts on the move. This makes the contacts feature very useful and even more worthwhile setting up.

HP iPAQ® *5100 pocket PC*

Palm powered Treo 600

Creating a new contact in our address book
To create a new contact:

      ❑ Click on the **Contacts** button

The screen view will change to show the current contacts in Outlook.

The contact information window looks like this:

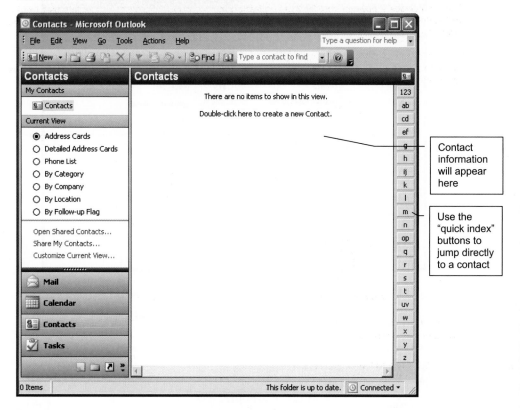

Contact information will appear here

Use the "quick index" buttons to jump directly to a contact

To create a new contact:

❑ Press the ⬛New button.

The new contact window will appear. This is where we can enter all the details for our contact.

Let's add the details for a fictitious contact who's details are as follows:

John O'Sullivan
Director
Limerock International

E-Mail: john@iact.ie
Phone: +353-1-4347600

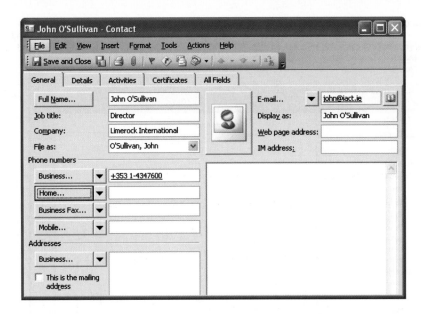

❑ Fill in the details we know about John into the text boxes provided.

❑ When all of the settings are correct press the 🔲 Save and Close button.

The contact information will now be saved and John's details should appear in our contacts list:

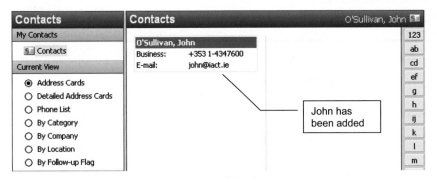

When we next send an e-mail to *John* we can now use the address book and locate John's information directly.

Working with the address book

The address book contains our contacts and we can view the address book when we are sending an e-mail by clicking on the icons next to the address fields – the **To... Cc...** or **Bcc..** fields to find an e-mail address.

Click here to open the Address Book

When we click on the contacts icon the contacts window will appear.

❑ Ensure that the **Show Names for the:** list box has the *Contacts* option selected.

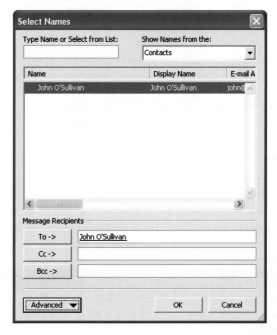

We should see the contact information for *John O'Sullivan* in the list.

❑ Clicking on the **To ->** or **Cc ->** buttons will copy the e-mail address from John's contact details.

❑ When all the contact information has been selected – press the **OK** button to return to the e-mail message.

John's name is now in the **To...** box but outlook knows the correct e-mail address to use for John. Double-clicking on *John's* name will re-display his contact details.

LESSON 7.9.13: CREATING A DISTRIBUTION LIST

A *distribution list* allows us to gather a group of e-mail addresses under one heading. This is useful for mailing groups of colleagues with the same e-mail message. Distribution lists allow a single name to refer to a number of individuals. This can be useful when messages are regularly sent to the same group of people – e.g. with Newsletters, Price list changes etc.

To create a distribution list or e-mail group:

- ❑ Create or add contact details for each person in the group as individual contacts
- ❑ Click on the drop-down arrow beside the **New** button.

A menu will appear with a list of options.

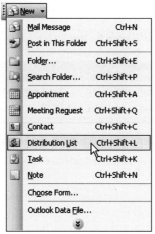

- ❑ Choose **Distribution List** from the list of options.

A new window will open.

- ❑ Type a name for the distribution list – e.g. **"Sports committee members"**
- ❑ Select the contacts that will form part of our distribution list by clicking on the **Select members** button.

- ❑ Click **Save and Close** to save the new distribution list.

Sending a message to a distribution list
Sending a message to a distribution list is the same as sending a regular e-mail message.

- ❑ Prepare the message as normal (see *Lesson 7.6.2:Sending an e-mail message on page 582*)

- ❑ Type the name of the distribution list into the **To...**, **Cc...**, or **Bcc...**

Name	Display Name	E-mail Address
John O'Sullivan	John O'Sullivan	john@iact.ie
Sports committee members	Sports committee members	

- ❑ Press **Send**

Everyone on the distribution list will receive a copy of the message.

Note: Be extra careful when using distribution lists – an error in the message will be sent to all of the people on the list at the same time.

LESSON 7.9.14: ADDING CONTACTS FROM INCOMING E-MAILS

We will often receive an e-mail from friends and colleagues and want to keep their e-mail addresses for reuse later. Outlook has a fast and easy way for us to do this once the message has been opened.

We can add an address to our contacts list from an incoming e-mail message.

- ❑ Open the message and press the **Right** mouse button on the senders name:

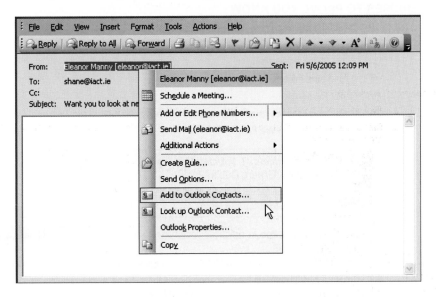

- ❑ Choose **Add to Outlook Contacts...** to add the sender to our contacts database.

Whenever we next send a message – this contacts details will be available in our list of contacts.

LESSON 7.9.15: DELETING A CONTACT FROM AN ADDRESS BOOK

To delete a contact from our address list:

- ❑ Open the contacts list by pressing **Ctrl+Shift+B** or choosing **Address Book** from the **Tools** menu.

- ❑ Select the address to delete with the mouse and press the **Delete** key.

Outlook will ask us to confirm that this contact is to be permanently deleted.

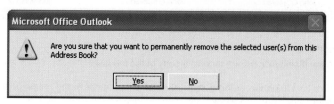

- ❑ Press **YES** to confirm the deletion.

EXERCISES TO PROVE YOU KNOW

1. Create the following new folders inside the **inbox**
   a) Marketing
   b) Sales promotions
   c) Junk mail
   d) Personal

2. Move the messages received from your Hotmail account into the *Personal* folder.

3. Create a signature like this:

   ```
   ------------------------------------------------------------
   ```
   IACT – *The Complete IT Training Provider*
   98 St. Stephen's Green, Dublin 2.
   E-mail: info@iactonline.com
   Web: www.iactonline.com
   ```
   ------------------------------------------------------------
   ```

4. Send a new message to practice@iactonline.com and add the new signature to the end of the message.

5. Create a new contact from the Hotmail message you sent to your account earlier

6. Create a distribution list for your friends or family. Send a message to the distribution list telling them your new Hotmail e-mail address.

SECTION 7.10: SECURITY AND E-MAILS

E-mail has become an integral part of our lives. E-mail messages have taken the place of faxes and traditional *snail-mail* for most of our correspondence. Knowing how to deal with unwanted mail messages and securely sending and receiving messages is an important part of using e-mail.

In this section we will look at:

- ❑ Dealing with unsolicited mail
- ❑ Digital signatures

LESSON 7.10.1: UNSOLICITED MAIL – SPAM

An e-mail address is much like a postal address. Every day most of us receive unsolicited post from advertisers and companies seeking to sell us something or let us know about their latest offers.

Most of us don't mind receiving this type of post as it is relatively unobtrusive and occasionally we receive something of interest. Since sending material by post has a definite cost – usually the marketer has done some research to assess that the product might be of interest to you.

We can also receive unsolicited material by e-mail and this is commonly referred to as SPAM. Filling in an online form with your e-mail address or giving your e-mail address to a company or individual can mean that the company or individual use your e-mail address to send you e-mail. If your e-mail address appears on a website software exists to try and harvest your e-mail address from the website and use if for marketing purposes.

Because the cost of sending hundreds of thousands of e-mails is practically free – often once your name is added to an address list you can become hounded by companies using your e-mail address to sell you everything from software to viagra. For this reason it is important that you only give your e-mail address to companies or individuals who you trust. Placing your e-mail address as a contact on a web site is a bad idea. Instead use generic e-mail address like info@iactonline.com this makes it easier to filter genuine e-mail from spam.

Viruses and SPAM

Unfortunately many of us become infected by Viruses - usually by e-mail (see *Section 2.7:Viruses* on *page* 142). Once infected Viruses try to spread to infect as many computers as they can. Often computers infected with a Virus will try to send an infected e-mail (or many e-mails) to all the individuals in an address book. These e-mails might look as if they originated from your computer or from the company that is infected. This can compound the problem of SPAM – as legitimate companies end up sending thousands of unintentional e-mails as a result of Virus infections completely unaware that they have done so until it is too late.

Protection against unsolicited e-mail

The best way we can protect ourselves from unsolicited e-mail is by keeping our e-mail address private. However there are a few steps we can take to help reduce the amount of spam we receive.

Outlook allows us to mark a message as unwanted so that all future e-mails from the same sender are treated the same way:

❑ Select the message

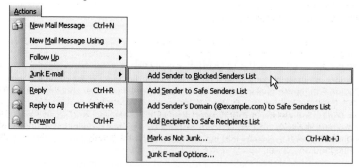

❑ Choose **Actions | Junk E-mail | Add Sender to Blocked Senders List**

Outlook will now block all messages from this sender sent in the future.

❑ To view or modify the list of blocked senders choose **Actions | Junk E-mail | Junk E-mail Options...** and choose the **Blocked Senders** tab.

There are many software products available and in development that will help reduce spam – by scanning messages for certain keywords and looking for images in our messages. These can help but none are 100% accurate – so genuine e-mails can end up getting filtered by the software.

Don't divulge private e-mail addresses to public databases or use them in advertisements. If you must give out an e-mail use a special e-mail address that you will use just for general information (like a *Hotmail* account). If you are receiving hundreds or thousands of unwanted messages a day and there is no way to un-subscribe from these services – consider changing your e-mail address – it will cause some one-off inconvenience but in the long term it will save you time.

LESSON 7.10.2: AUTHENTICATING E-MAIL - DIGITAL SIGNATURES

When we receive a letter in the post – it is usually signed by the author. The signature authenticates the letter and assures us that it was sent by the person who claimed to send it.

Digital signatures are a way of doing the same thing with an e-mail message. We can use digital signatures as a way of identifying ourselves and securing the messages that we send. As more people send confidential information by e-mail, it is increasingly important to be sure that documents sent in e-mail are not forged, and to be certain that messages we send cannot be intercepted and read by anyone other than our intended recipient.

It is very rare currently for e-mail messages to form part of a legal contract – unless they are first printed out and manually signed by the author. This is mainly because it is difficult to prove that the origin of an e-mail is tied to a particular person or entity and that the e-mail hasn't been interfered with.

If we apply for a mortgage through a web site for example we will still have to sign the documents by hand before the bank will hand over any money – we can't send an e-mail confirming our identity. As the use of digital signatures becomes more widespread and the security of our computer systems improves we are likely to see an increase in the use of the web and e-mail for legal and financial transactions that currently require our signature. This should greatly simplify the way these forms are currently designed and speed up the whole application process.

To find out more about digital signatures search for *digital IDs* in Microsoft *Outlook* Help.

Encryption - protecting the information in a message

Digital signatures in conjunction with a private and public key can also be used to encode or encrypt the information in an e-mail message so that nobody but the intended recipient can read it. Visit www.verisign.com or www.thawte.com to learn more about acquiring a public and private key.

EXERCISES TO PROVE YOU KNOW

1. Visit www.google.com and look up information on the origin of the word SPAM.

2. If you have received an unwanted message and still have it – add it to your list of blocked senders.

3. Visit www.thawte.com and read about and request a digital signature for your e-mail messages.

SECTION 7.11:   EXAM OVERVIEW AND TIPS

In the exam for *Module 7, Information and communication*, you will be given a disk. The disk will only have one file on it – ***answerfile.doc***. The answerfile is a Word document that you will type the answers into. It looks like this:

Candidate Identification :_____

Question No.	Response
1.	
2.	

You will need to be able to locate this *answerfile.doc* on the floppy disk, open it and type into it. It is important that you remember to save this file as you go and at the end of the exam.

There are 2 sections in this module. The first section has 15 questions and is worth 15 marks. Section 2 is the same. All areas in the module can be tested.

POINTS TO NOTE:
- Time allowed: 45 minutes
- Answer both sections:
- Marking System
  - Each section has 15 marks awarded to it – total of 30 marks.

About the Sections:
Section 1
Here you will be tested on the Internet. Topics Checklist:
- Open a browser
- Open a website
- Navigate hyperlinks
- Copy information from the web page to a Word document
- Search Engines

Section 2
Here you will be tested on E-mail. Topics Checklist:
- Open E-mail
- Send E-mail
- Reply to E-mail
- Forward E-mail
- Attach a file
- Print E-mail messages

All of the topics covered in this Module could be asked in the exam.

For sample examinations visit http://www.iactonline.com/ecdl

INDEX

3

3D Effect · 496

A

Absolute References · 306
Access · 19, 90, 136, 349
Acer tablet PC · 3
Address Book · 616
ADSL · 43
AIBO · 47
Aligning · 505
Alta Vista · 571
Analogue · 42
AND truth table · 397
Animation · 471
Annotating slides · 519
Apple · 28
Apple Lisa · 64
Apple Mac · 64
Apple Macintosh · 28, 63, 64
Applications software · 27
ARPANET · 535
Arrow keys · 163
Arrows · 487
ATMs · 34
Attachments · 598
AutoFill · 302
Automating · 411
Automation · 46
Autonumber · 367
AutoShapes · 494
AutoSum · 296
AutoText · 216
Average() · 297

B

Backspace key · 164
Backups · 53
Banking · 34
Bar Chart · 323
BCC · 586
BFN · 596
Biometrics · 53
BITS · 24
BMP file format · 90
Bond *James* · 570
Bookmarks · 558, 560
Boolean Logic · 397
Bordering and shading · 207
Borders · 181
Borders and Shading · 181
Browser History · 548
BTW · 596
Bullets · 184
Byte *see also* Bit, Kilobyte, Megabyte · 24

C

C/C++ · 32
CAD · 36
CAD - computer aided design · 36
Calculator · 80
CAM · 36

Cameras · 9
CC · 585
CDR file format · 90
Cell Alignment · 285
Cell orientation · 286
Character Map *see also symbols* · 79, 81
Charles Babbage · 2
Chart scale · 332
Charts · 321
Charts and slides · 461
Circular References · 300
Clipart · 455
Clipboard · 167
Clock · 82
Closing windows · 72
Column Chart · 322
Computer Storage
    BIOS · 20
    CD/DVD-ROM · 23
    CD-ROM · 3, 7, 8, 21, 23, 25, 27, 56
    DVD-ROM · 3, 23
    Floppy Disks · 22, 85
    Hard Disks · 21, 85
    RAM · 6, 18, 19, 20, 21, 25, 115
    ROM · 3, 8, 20, 23, 25, 56
    Zip Disks · 22, 23
Computers in manufacturing · 36
Computers in shops · 35
Computers in the home · 38
Connectors · 13
Control Panel · 223
Copying · 96, 167, 168, 169
Copyright · 52, 56
Count() · 298
CPU - Central Processing Unit · 18
CPU – Central Processing Unit · 18
CPU Central Processing Unit
    Pentium · 18
Cray Supercomputer · 5
Creating a Folder · 91
Currency format in Excel · 367
Cursor keys · 163
Cutting · 167

D

Dan Bricklin · 268
Data Protection Act · 58
Database *see also Access* · 24, 37, 90, 351, 364
Databases · 348
Date
    and Viruses · 55, 142
    setting or changing · 106
Date and Time
    changing · 115
Date Field
    inserting · 180
Decimal places · 287
Default home page · 545
Delete key · 164
Deleting Files
    In Explorer · 97
    Recovering files · 98
Desktop · 3, 23
Digital · 42

Justification · 177

V

Valid e-mail Addresses · 585
Validation rule · 374
Vertical Text Alignment · 484
Video · 13
View modes · 221, 441
Virtual Reality · 10
Virus
   disinfect · 144
Viruses · *See* Security
VisiCalc · 268
Visual BASIC · 32

W

Wafer · 19
WAIS · 535
WAN · 39
wildcard · 107
WIMP · 28
Windows · 64
Windows Configuration · 114
Windows Explorer · 87

WinZip · 90
WinZip · 138
Wizards and Templates · 151, 228, 230, 232, 322,
   433, 434, 435
Word · 25, 148
WordArt · 498
Wordperfect · 148
Worksheets · 280, 308, 447
WRT · 596

X

XLS file format · 90

Y

Yahoo · 571

Z

Zip disks · 23
Zip File · 140
ZIP file format · 90
Zoom Tool · 450
Z-order · 512